Torture and Modernity

Institutional Structures of Feeling

George Marcus, Sharon Traweek,
Richard Handler, and Vera Zolberg, *Series Editors*

**Torture and Modernity: Self, Society, and State
in Modern Iran** *Darius M. Rejali*

**Dreaming Identities: Class, Gender, and Generation
in 1980s Hollywood Movies** *Elizabeth G. Traube*

Vinyl Leaves: Walt Disney World and America
Stephen M. Fjellman

**Lives in Trust: The Fortunes of Dynastic Families in Late
Twentieth-Century America** *George E. Marcus with Peter Dobkin Hall*

FORTHCOMING

Surrogate Motherhood in America *Helena Ragoné*

On the Margins of Art Worlds *edited by Larry Gross*

**Captive Self, Captivating Other: The Practice and Representation
of Captivity Across the British-Amerindian Frontier**
Pauline Turner Strong

**The Political Economy of Passion: Tango, Exoticism,
and Decolonization** *Marta Savigliano*

**The Talented One-Hundredth: Issues in
Ethnicity and Education** *Erylene Piper Mandy*

**The Semiotics of Exclusion: Puerto Rican Experiences of
the Race/Class Language Intersection** *Bonnie Urciuoli*

The Chicago Art Institute as a Cultural Institution
Vera Zolberg

The Inner Life of Medicine *Byron J. Good and Mary-Jo DelVecchio Good*

**Ot-Jumulo: Heads of Dogs/Puffing, Smoking Sea Monsters/
Andaman Islanders** *David Tomas*

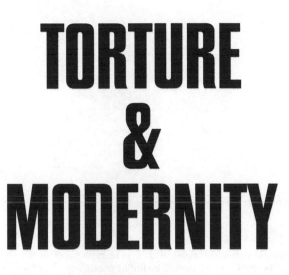

TORTURE & MODERNITY

. . . .

Self, Society, and State
in Modern Iran

DARIUS M. REJALI

WESTVIEW PRESS

Boulder • San Francisco • Oxford

Institutional Structures of Feeling

Copyright © 1994 by **Westview Press, Inc.**

Published in 1994 in the United States of America by Westview Press, Inc., 5500 Central Avenue, Boulder, Colorado 80301-2877, and in the United Kingdom by Westview Press, 36 Lonsdale Road, Summertown, Oxford OX2 7EW

Library of Congress Cataloging-in-Publication Data
Rejali, Darius M.
   Torture and modernity : self, society, and state in modern Iran /
Darius M. Rejali.
      p.   cm. — (Institutional structures of feeling)
   Includes bibliographical references and index.
   ISBN 0-8133-1660-X — ISBN 0-8133-1879-3 (pbk.)
      1. Torture—Iran.   2. Punishment—Iran.   3. Iran—Politics and
government—1979–   4. Power (Social sciences).   I. Title.
HV8599.I7R45   1994
365′.645—dc20   93-8524
                                                                                          CIP

Printed and bound in the United States of America

The paper used in this publication meets the requirements
of the American National Standard for Permanence of Paper
for Printed Library Materials Z39.48-1984.

10   9   8   7   6   5   4   3   2   1

Dedicated to the City of Montréal
and its people, who live by a cold, mighty river
and who took me as one of their own for a while

Analytic Table of Contents

Part Two: Tutelage and Torture   83

Part Three: Orienting Modernity 133

What is real power? The rise of the Iranian state.

Expectations at the outset of this study. Why they proved to be mistaken. What does this reveal about the nature of power in Iranian society? The changing nature of political struggles in the past century. The problem of exercising effective power: Qajar and modern solutions. Why the latter explains the anti-Western character of the Islamic Revolution. The problem of power as it is expressed in three classic works from the Pahlavi period: Al-e Ahmad's *Gharbzadegi*, Saedi's *Honeymoon*, and Baraheni's *The Crowned Cannibals*. The changing nature of violence forced them to ask the question: How did we Iranians become like *that?*

Punishment illustrates some ways the state exercises violence. It also illustrates some ways Iranians became themselves. How an account that brings these two themes together is a historical ontology.

Historical Ontologies. How Iranians were rationalized: disciplinary rationality, tutelary rationality, and carceral rationality. The role of each in Iranian politics. Contrasted with capitalist rationality.   **149**

State Capacity. Strategies of rationalization. Advantages of this approach to state capacity. Four constraints on state capacity. Functional and human trust.   **156**

11   *How Not to Talk About Torture*   160

Four possible explanations of torture examined: the humanist approach, the developmentalist approach, the state terrorist approach, and the revisionist-Nietzschean approach. Their weaknesses. Their strengths and how we can use them.

Tables and Illustrations

Tables

Illustrations

Preface

This book is not another monotonous effort to explain the Islamic Revolution. It is, rather, my antidote to the too comforting ideals of the past, a past that is shared by Iranians and non-Iranians alike. I hope I have spared no one a critical evaluation, one with as little cynicism as possible. Certainly I have not spared myself. Punishment is perhaps an inappropriate introduction to a people who love grace and beauty in so many things. Yet I found I could no longer love my past without keeping a steady eye on its darker side. This may not excuse the uncompromising tone of this work, but it may render this tone more understandable.

Brian Walker taught me to pay attention to the world, and I hope he will not begrudge me if I imitate his thoughtfulness. I want to thank my mother, who taught me to read English, and my father, who taught me to read the Farsi *alephba*. Dr. B—pour visited our house for seven years every week without fail to teach me Farsi when I was a teenager; he helped me appreciate Persian poetry and prose, and without his help, part of my past would be even more alien than it now is.

Life companions are rare, and I have been blessed with some precious old friends who cared about me more than the book: Jim Tully, Martha Huggins, Malcolm Willison, Stewart Thomas, Bethany Bechtel, Chris Udry, Susan and Beau Weston, Mohammad Rahimian, Ron Afzal, and Lisa Strauss. While writing this book, I also received great encouragement from many kind friends: Charles Taylor, Michael Fischer, Ervand Abrahamian, Sam Noumoff, Uner Turgay, John Dunn, Greg Ostrander, Guy Laforest, Jeff Diamond, Remi Roy, Levent Hekimoglu, Eric Worby, Gulrukh Selim, Eric Darrier, and Maya Berberi. I am especially indebted to Michael Fischer and Charles Taylor; the former for showing me that the hermeneutics of everyday life has an enduring contribution to make to the study of Middle Eastern politics and the latter for teaching me how a great philosopher can also be an acute political scientist. L. Black reproduced many of the photographs with painstaking care. Mila Birnbaum and Marc Hedlund, who are mature beyond their years, helped me when I was at my wit's end.

In an age when teaching is undervalued and research is undersupported, I was lucky to have many good colleagues and students at McGill University, Union College, and Reed College. Thanks to grants from the American Council of Learned Societies and Reed College, I also benefited from Latin American, Australian, and European colleagues I met during a session on the abuse of police power at the International Sociological Association in Madrid in 1990; it was a wondrous event to speak so frankly of such things on that very ridge where republicans had fought so fiercely against Franco's troops during the civil war. I have also tried in this work to fulfill the promise of a unique institution that no longer exists, the Community School of Tehran. Thank you all.

Darius M. Rejali
Portland, Oregon

Torture and Modernity

CHAPTER 1

Introduction

The man who cries out with pain, or says he has pain,
doesn't choose the mouth which says it.

—Ludwig Wittgenstein
The Blue Book

This book is about torturers and the world they live in. Most people who have bothered to write about torturers tend to give one of three accounts of their world. Some maintain that torturers do what they do because of necessity: Torture is a nasty business, but it also pays the bills and sends the children to school.[1] Others say that torturers do what they do because they lack a proper understanding of what they are doing: Torturers are held by some ideology that keeps them from recognizing torture for what it is.[2] Still others say that torturers inflict pain out of the desire to do evil: They do what they do voluntarily and with full knowledge of their situation, and they enjoy a feeling of excess power when they destroy another human being.[3]

I am not sure how one would go about proving this last claim without making exceedingly mysterious claims about the nature of power. I think the second claim is plausible, but often applied evasively. I agree with the first claim that the evil modern torturers do is banal, arising out of the types of rationality that are pervasive in contemporary institutions. That is the only account of evil the reader is likely to encounter in this book. I try to locate only what torturers do out of necessity or out of training. Perhaps Orwellian torturers exist, but I am not sure one can gain access to their minds through the study of the social institutions of a torturer's world. I imagine an analysis of the institutions of Hell would not get us any closer to understanding how an Angel of Light could run it.

One can, however, show how social institutions constrain the behavior of human beings and lead them to behave in different ways. In describing how torture operates, I also lay bare what torturers presuppose about human beings and society, politics and the good life. Accounts of how people are punished necessarily invoke conceptions of what humans are and what they might become. Another way of saying this is that I intend to place a question from the sociology of crime in developing countries into the larger contexts of social theory and political ethics. My aim is to make explicit these conceptions and situate torture as an integral feature of the modern age. I have chosen Iranian society as a focus for this investigation, but the questions raised here could be extended to all societies that partake in these modern preoccupations.

Two questions are particularly important in this regard. Do the accounts of political violence that we have developed over the past century have any real capacity to direct us in a world in which one out of every three governments tortures its citizens? Do these accounts have any real explanatory or even moral significance in such a world, or are they just consolations in the face of events we cannot fully understand? In the final chapter, I consider these questions in relation to four principal explanations of modern torture: the humanist account, the account given by theorists of modernization, the state terrorist account advanced by Noam Chomsky, and the Nietzschean account as advanced by Michel Foucault. I suspect none of these approaches is entirely satisfactory, but by recovering what is presupposed by modern torture, I hope to consider the strengths and weaknesses of each as guides to a world without torture.

How to Study Torture

Recently in Europe, there was an exhibition of medieval torture technology. What struck me about this exhibition was that no medieval peasant would have ever seen such instruments. However lively that peasant's conception of Hell, he or she would have remained blithely ignorant of the physical shape violence took up at the castle. And what would a modern museum exhibit of contemporary torture technology look like? I have never seen a German weightcuff, an electric bed, a modified cattleprod or field telephone, a parrot's perch, a magnifying helmet, an amputation machine, or the hundreds of different kinds of wire, rope, and leather thong used to flog prisoners, not to mention the rooms that house these devices. And yet torture is so exceedingly common today. Is my situation any different from that of the medieval peasant?

Working on torture is a methodologist's nightmare. Countries that torture are black boxes to the outside world. Sources are often biased in favor of the government or against it. One cannot independently verify such information with field studies or polling. One cannot always count on honest answers, even from those who have the greatest interest in being honest.

What counts as torture is disputed, which makes it difficult, for example, to build statistics on different kinds of violence. One can turn to the experts to guide one in understanding the nature of repression. Experts, however, disagree among themselves. Their varied access may lead to partial or exaggerated comparisons, and we do not have a method for weighing their different perceptions. One is left with the accounts, sifting, comparing, coordinating.

All this shows how much I depend on language to give shape to the violence of the world I live in. I depend on language to see what I cannot see, to conjure up for me the physical site on which torture takes place and the devices that are used. I also depend on language to make sense of these phantom devices and, in doing so, to guide others in how to deal with torture today. The question for me is whether the ways we have for talking about violence are equal to the task.

I have tried to employ six cautionary principles so that I may not stray off toward research orientations that have exhausted themselves. First, do not confuse the historical origin of a thing with its purpose, which may now be different.[4] For example, just because a giraffe uses its long neck to eat leaves in trees does not mean that historically it stretched its neck to eat leaves. This example confuses purpose with historical origins and suggests an unbelievable evolutionary history. It is a silly example, but confusions of this sort are exceedingly common in the case of torture. For example, just because the state's function is to ensure internal security does not mean that a particular torture was originally used because it made the situation more secure. There is no reason to assume this, although the temptation to do so is overwhelming.

To take a reverse example, one that confuses historical origins with purposes, consider the belief that because the sexual organs were made for reproduction, that is the sole purpose for which they are used. This example focuses our attention on one use of sexual organs but omits the bulk of contemporary sexuality as a result. An analogous mistake is often made when discussing torture. For example, just because torture was historically associated with confessions does not mean that this is the sole or even the main purpose of torture today.

Second, just because something is called *x* does not mean it is the same thing in every instance.[5] For example, that I call backgammon a game does not mean that it *must* have something in common with canasta just because it, too, is called a game. Yet too often we think that just because all sorts of practices are called punishment means that they all amount to the same thing and have the same purposes. The point is to stop thinking and look.

Third, compare a phenomenon with that which is familiar.[6] We do not get closer to an inexplicable phenomenon by hammering home its unfamiliarity. In the case of torture, and more generally punishment, this means refusing to limit this investigation solely to the study of legal and political institutions. Perhaps we can gain a better understanding of state punishment by comparing it with what goes on in homes, hospitals, schools, or factories.

(4)   Fourth, treat punishment as a complex political practice.[7] Think about each instrument separately and about how it is supposed to work. What is the point of inflicting pain in this way? What is the point of speaking about inflicting pain in this way? Try, in this way, to grasp the agent's point of view in applying this particular form of pain.[8]

(5)   Fifth, an interpretation is sound if it can explain everything other interpretations can and explain as well how they go wrong.[9] Comprehensiveness is, of course, not the sole criterion for a good interpretation. It can be objected that even though the interpretation is comprehensive, it is inferior qualitatively. It tries to explain aspects that are irrelevant or trivial to the issue at hand. Nevertheless, this principle can serve as an initial touchstone and encourage further dialogue.

(6)   Sixth, assume that self-interest tends to drive human behavior.[10]

In What Way Is Torture Modern?

Shortly after the Islamic Revolution of 1979, I was a dinner guest at the home of an old imperial general. I was introduced as a young scholar working on Iranian torture. A polite silence settled on the company, until the old general leaned over to me and said in a friendly voice, "Dear son, there wasn't ever any torture in Iran, and there isn't any now after the Revolution." And with that, he winked! Torture, it would seem, had become such a routine part of the Iranian experience that it did not raise eyebrows anymore. Iranians winked at it, acknowledged its inevitability, and felt no less modern for all that.

On another occasion not too long after the first, I met a man who came from a famous left-wing family but who had worked for the police under the Pahlavis. He was sophisticated, graceful, and well educated, in fact, one of the very few older Iranians who seemed to read avidly. The security police, after all, had "a higher number of Ph.D.'s than any other government organization in Iran."[11] When he learned I was writing a book on torture, he insisted on seeing the pictographic essay that now concludes this book. Looking over the Qajar and Pahlavi era photographs, he commented, "Remarkable! See what the Pahlavis delivered us from! Now it all comes back." What astounded me, and still does, was that this urbane man felt no incompatibility between his civility and the practices of the Pahlavi police.

I have talked to political prisoners, too, but these two stories stick in my mind because they show how deeply enmeshed torture is in modern life. A Western observer would be inclined to say that the general and the policeman suffer from false consciousness. Yet to argue that these individuals are deceived by a political ideology is to suggest, in less evasive terms, that they are stupid, and there is no evidence for this. To suggest that they deceive themselves is a desperate argument. Each argument saves our Western sensibilities in a different way: one by rendering Iranians into savage clods and the other by making their lives obscure. What does that matter, however, if our moral sensibilities survive?

I prefer to take seriously, as a hypothesis, that maybe these men have recognized an interesting aspect of modern life, namely, that torture is an integral part of it. Why not treat torture in this way? In the course of this book, I try to redeem this claim by considering torture in the context of "nice" practices and to suggest how torture stems from a similar way of acting and speaking.

Surely, it could be suggested, the argument would be stronger if I had chosen a thoroughly modern country—say, Nazi Germany—to make this point. Aside from my own personal interest in Iran, I suggest that there are good reasons to consider a country like Iran. One is that, as Karl Marx observed in *Capital*, the colonies mirror what the metropole refuses to see. In Marx's case, private property, which was taken to be natural, was revealed to be quite artificial when it came into contact with a culture with different understandings of property relations. It often became necessary to destroy such a culture through violence to ensure that private property became second nature. In Europe, this was simply harder to see because private property had emerged gradually and because the culture that opposed it had been so carefully obliterated.[12]

Something similar could be said about modern punishments. They may seem more humane because they have emerged gradually. When disciplinary and tutelary punishments are transferred to the Third World, one can see that these ways of punishing do not take hold naturally. On the contrary, violence and torture, drawing on the celebrated advancements of modern times, often accompany such transformations, so much so that in certain corners of the globe, torture becomes a routine part of life. What is interesting here is that routinized torture seems to be less extreme in some European countries. Rather than seeing torture as out of place in modern life, perhaps we can profitably reverse the question and ask why the rule of law survives in some countries rather than in others.

I am rather intransigent on how deeply torture today is linked to modern politics. However, even if we cannot agree on exactly how to interpret this link, at least we can agree that specific tortures are deeply indebted to the common practices of modern life. We can debate whether this connection is simply a perversion, rather than a constitutive element of modern practices, but we can all agree, I hope, on how important it is that the specific linkage be interrupted. For example, medical practices may not be as integral to modern torture as I argue, but we can agree that something needs to be done about the role doctors play in assisting torturers.

Finally, there is the issue of defining torture. Edward Peters suggests that one can distinguish among legal, moral, and sentimental uses of the word *torture*, and I agree with him that the legal definition is the most useful for analytic purposes. Torture, in the legal sense, involves the violence that public authority does or condones.[13] This definition has some shortcomings, however. Torture would be indistinguishable from other public acts of violence such as the death penalty, war, or mass genocide. Suppose, however, one qualified the definition further by saying that torture is sanguinary violence that does not end in death. Although this would distinguish torture from executions or genocide, it would limit investigation to what might be called *judicial* torture, that is, torture that precedes a court trial. It would exclude by definition any consideration of sanguinary violence that prepares the captive for execution, that is, *penal* torture. Yet penal torture is the main part of torture in many societies. Defining torture as sanguinary violence has the further shortcoming of limiting investigation to the study of violence that is bloody. It would exclude several punitive practices that are integral to modern torture but that do not produce blood, for example, electroshocks, momentary suffocation, sexual assault, solitary confinement, sensory deprivation, and mock executions.

These considerations bring out the danger of positing an ahistorical notion of torture by fiat. Just because practices are called torture does not mean that they are the same thing and that somehow one can talk about them all if one got the definition right. One might be better advised to stop theorizing and look at different punitive practices and compare their similarities and differences. Otherwise, one might lose sight of salient features of modern torture or classical torture.

Defining torture as sanguinary violence condoned by public authorities serves to identify tentatively a range of practices for investigation. In this sense, the ambiguity of this definition is not without its merits since perhaps we can learn something about different tortures by comparing them to things they appear to resemble. Our use of the word *torture* has been shaped by precisely these sorts of political debates, and it would be hubris to think that our age has finally got it right. Comparisons might make clear what it is that characterizes modern torture and how to watch for it around us.

Another strength of this view is that it distinguishes between public torture and torture in other contexts, such as families. Nevertheless, we need to be cautious about this distinction. Torture may have other functions besides that of supporting the state or the law, and keeping an eye only on torture's public dimension can obscure how deeply entrenched it is in other social structures. Rather than fixate on the distinction between illegal and legal violence, I often ask another question: How do the agents who practice torture distinguish between torture and nontorture? This may correspond to the distinction between legal and illegal violence, but it may not. For example, in nineteenth-century Iran, torture was illegal when it did not conform to specific rituals and legal when it did. Discipline in this sense was abusive torture. Or to take a modern example, electroshock treatment is legal treatment in asylums but counts as torture in prisons. Indeed, a key feature of modern torture involves the imperative to keep the tortured alive for as long as possible. If this is so, we may begin to see that torture is less related to the death penalty, which often tries to eliminate the duration of pain. Torture may have more in common with, say, the practices of intensive care units, and this, I think, leads us to ask some rather hard questions about other modern practices that aim at sustaining life at all costs and whether they would be legal if we were consistent in our definitions.

How to Read This Book

My friend O., a former Trotskyist, was once asked to sign a petition protesting atrocities committed in Iran. As O. signed, he said to the affable young man, "There! I hope that when you guys take power from them, you don't go running around torturing people." "Ahhh," the youth replied disarmingly, "once you have been tortured, you can't torture other people." As O. walked away, he remarked, "That guy believes that pain is the proof of the truth of your cause and the mark of your righteousness after you win. But history is a record of all the exceptions." Any cause can make a torturer out of a torture survivor. Deeply held convictions can become prisons for others.

I hope readers keep this story in mind as they read this book. I believe readers will get the most out of this book if they do not focus on their favorite political causes and figures. In this book, I focus more on *how* vicious practices change rather than on who performs them and for what cause. Modern torture has accommodated so many different political causes that to present them as causally salient is extremely misleading. My decision means that readers do not have to be Iranian specialists to follow the main argument. Those interested in detailed historical points can pursue them in the footnotes. I have also provided several aids to readers to guide them in their interests, including an old-fashioned analytic table of contents, a pictographic appendix illustrating a history of Iranian punishments, a brief chronological history of Iran, and a glossary of Farsi and Arabic words used in the text.

Some readers will prefer to get an overview of the book by reading Part 3 first. I have written the last three chapters with different readers in mind. A reader with an Iranian background will find Chapter 9 the most accessible introduction to the material. A reader with a theoretical orientation may wish to begin with Chapter 10. A reader with social scientific training may wish to turn to Chapter 11 first.

The main research emerges in the first two parts of the book. Part 1 covers Iranian politics from 1850 to 1979. I take as my point of departure a puzzle left by the late Michel Foucault, namely, that if societies, for whatever reasons, are becoming more disciplined, what then is the explanation for the emergence of modern torture? Part 2 takes a different cut of Iranian politics, roughly from 1950 to 1990. I required this new focus because it became clear that discipline and torture do not fully explain the nature of punishment in Iran; an understanding of penal change needs to include a study of tutelage.

This brings me to transliteration. As there is no standard system for transliteration from Farsi to English, I have followed the transliteration system for the Arabic alphabet provided by Farhat J. Ziadeh and R. Bayly Winder in their book, *An Introduction to Modern Arabic*. I have modified this system, however; the changes are as follows:

1. The letters *p*, *ch*, *zh*, and *g* represent the four Persian letters not in the Arabic alphabet.
2. The letter *v* is used instead of *w* to represent the consonant *vav*.
3. The letter *s* is used for both the letters *tha'* and *sad*.
4. The letter *z* represents both the letters *dhal* and *dad*.
5. The vowels *i* and *e* are used as pronunciation requires to represent the *kasrah* short vowel sound.
6. The vowels *u* and *o* are used as pronunciation requires to represent the *damma* short vowel sound.
7. The sign ' represents both the *'ayn* and the *hamzah* preceding the appropriate vowel.
8. A hyphen is used to separate prepositional suffixes such as *yi*.
9. Occasionally, a vowel is doubled for the sake of proper emphasis. For example, *T'aminat* is written *T'aminaat*.
10. The Arabic definite article *al* is elided when it is used in the genetive case (Dar *ul*-Fonun) or is followed by a Sun letter ('Itizad *as*-Saltanih).

All quotations referring to Farsi sources are my own translations except (1) in the case of the transcripts of Mirza Reza Kirmani's torture interrogation, where for the most part I have followed E.G. Browne's English translation, and (2) in the case of Jalal Al-e Ahmad's *Gharbzadegi*, where I have utilized Paul Sprachman's excellent translation. I have also translated the titles of Farsi texts into English following the original title. All dates are given in the Gregorian calendar. The only exception to this rule occurs in the bibliography and notes, where the date of publication of Farsi books is listed first according to the Iranian solar calendar and then according to the Gregorian calendar (in brackets).

Finally, the perceptive reader will observe that all torturers are referred to in the male gender. This usage is meant descriptively, not prospectively, but as I would not wish this prospect on anyone, I have not used gender-inclusive language in this instance. I have used gender-inclusive language otherwise, either by indicating the presence of both genders or, where this was not easily possible, by alternating between male and female pronouns. I have avoided, wherever possible, using gender-inclusive language as a substitute for real historical research. I urge others to look further into these matters if they find themselves wondering; there is still much to be done.

PART ONE

· ·

DISCIPLINES & TORTURES

A Klee painting named "Angelus Novus" shows an angel looking as though he is about to move away from something he is fixedly contemplating. His eyes are staring, his mouth open, his wings spread. This is how one pictures the angel of history. His face is turned toward the past. Where we perceive a chain of events, he sees one single catastrophe which keeps piling wreckage upon wreckage and hurls it in front of his feet. The angel would like to stay, awaken the dead, make whole what has been smashed. But a storm is blowing in from paradise; it has got caught in his wings with such violence that the angel can no longer close them. The storm irresistibly propels him into the future to which his back is turned, while the debris before him grows skyward. This storm is what we call progress.

—Walter Benjamin
Theses on the Philosophy of History

Foucault's Iran

I want to begin in the manner of Foucault, by comparing two examples of torture.

On 15 August 1852, thirty members of the outlawed Babi religion were found guilty of attempted regicide and apostasy. "By the orders of the most Exalted [the shah] and the *fetva* of the distinguished 'ulema (May Allah multiply their number!), death sentences were issued for Mullah Shaykh 'Ali and his followers."[1] Haji Sulayman Khan and Haji Qasim Nayrizi, the two leaders of the Babi plot, were immediately taken to the city and 'made into candlesticks.' Holes were dug in their flesh, into which lighted candles were inserted. "Accompanied by drums, musical instruments and a large crowd, they were led through the alleys and the bazaars. They were stoned by the people of the city until they reached the gateway of the Shrine of Shah 'Abd ul-'Azim where the court executioners divided their bodies into four parts and hung the pieces over the four gates of the city."[2]

"During these horrible tortures," reported Lady Sheil, "he [Sulayman Khan] is said to have preserved his fortitude to the last and to have danced to his place of execution in defiance of his tormentors and the agony of the burning candles."[3] The 'Itizad as-Saltanih wrote that "when they were leading Haji Mirza Sulayman Khan, after he had been made into a candlestick, he danced and sang this poem: Would that the curtain fall from that pleasant view / So that people could see [the corruption of] Negaristan. When they desired to execute him, he said 'Let Haji Qasim Nayrizi be the first to be delivered to this pleasant state, for he is my greater.' "[4]

Shortly thereafter, Mullah Fathullah, the would-be assassin of the shah, was brought before the throne. "In the midst of the royal camp, candles were placed into his body (by making incisions) and lighted." The steward of the royal household, as the shah's representative, shot the mullah "in the very place that he had injured the Shah."[5] The mullah was then stoned to death by royal attendants, and his body was "either cut to pieces or shot or blown from a mortar."[6]

"Then each of the Babis was surrendered to a group of nobles, to different classes of servants and craftsmen of the bazaar, and they executed them." Mullah Shaykh 'Ali, the chief religious leader of the Babis, "was handed over to the scholars and students of the religious sciences and they put him to death."[7] The Qajar princes, the minister of the "home office," and the relations of the grand vizier each slew a Babi leader. The minister of "foreign affairs" "with averted face made the first sword cut" on his captive,[8] and "the secretaries of his department finished him and cut him into pieces." The master of the horse and the servants of the stables horseshod their captive before slaying him. The artillerymen "dug out the eye of Mahommad Ali ... and then blew him away from a mortar." The remaining conspirators were distributed among the infantry, the cavalry, the students of the University of Sciences, "the chief servants of the court, the people of the town, merchants, tradesmen, artizans, who bestowed on them their deserts."[9] These individuals were led through the streets of their neighborhoods, tied together by ropes, and whipped as they marched. They, too, were made into living candlesticks, and many died by burning alive. When the moment came for their execution, "they danced and chanted in chorus the following words, 'In truth, we come from Allah and we return to him.' "[10]

"When these executions were over," wrote Lady Sheil, "it was said that the Shah's *meerghazabs* [executioners] had presented *sheereenee* [sweetmeats] to all the ministers of state, as a mark of their admission into the brotherhood." "In Tehran, when any one is installed in office, it is usual for his friends and those under his authority to send him *sheereenee* ... as a token of congratulations."[11]

A century later, Shokrollah Paknezhad was arrested and detained at the SAVAK station in Khorramshahr, a southwestern Iranian port. After being severely beaten, he was transferred to the regional police prison. He was placed in solitary confinement for one week. He was then transferred by a SAVAK vehicle to the notorious Evin prison in Tehran. Interrogations began as soon as he arrived. His two torturers, who addressed each other as "Doctor" and "Engineer," tortured him for one week. During the course of his interrogation, he was beaten and flogged and had his nails pulled out. He was forced to wear weightcuffs, a pressure device that can break the shoulders in less than two hours of agonizing torture. On the fifteenth day after his detention, Paknezhad was taken from solitary confinement and placed before a firing squad. He was reminded that "since I had been caught on the Iraqi border and nobody knew anything about my arrest, and since everybody thought I had gone to Iraq, hardly anyone would know that I had been executed." When Paknezhad still refused to write a recantation "according to their wishes," he was taken back to solitary confinement.[12] Paknezhad was released after eighteen days of detention but was arrested again within the year. After nine more months of imprisonment and torture, the Third Normal Court of the Military Tribunal found Paknezhad guilty of endangering state security and sentenced him to life imprisonment. He was released during the Islamic Revolution (1978–1979) but was subsequently arrested again in 1981. He was detained without formal charges or trial for several months and executed at Evin prison in December 1981.

These examples illustrate some of the main ways in which torture has changed in the past century. A century ago, torture was characterized by ceremonial processions, ritualized ways of speaking, and public executions. This sort of torture, which I call classical torture to distinguish it from the medieval torture of the Mongols and Timurids, had its origins under the late Safavid shahs of the seventeenth century. Classical torture took place not only in execution squares but also along the streets, in the bazaars, and in palaces. It was a public confrontation of society as a whole with the tortured. Torturers took their cues from custom and religion in the application of pain.

Today, classical torture no longer exists, although torture has returned. Modern torture is private, not public. It takes place in the basements of prisons and detention centers. Even the Islamic Revolution has not changed this practice substantively. Modern torture is clinical, not ritual, torture. The torturer operates on his patient. His methods and instruments are drawn from medicine, engineering, psychology, and physiology.

Modern torture is guided by a new punitive principle: Do not seek to punish the criminal act of the body; punish instead the delinquent life of your prisoner. This was an important development in Iranian penal history. All the subsequent violations of the body, the fury with which torturers attack their prisoners' flesh, may be traced to this elementary change in objectives. The body, the principal target of classical Iranian torture, lost its favored status. Now punishments were directed at a point slightly beyond the body. Their target was a finer, more diffuse object, a human life.

To strike a target so diffuse as a delinquent life, a new quality of pain was necessary, a pain that gripped the "consciousness," rather than the body of the prisoner. Under the gaze of the torturer, human life emerged as an object for research. The prisoner was grasped from within, through electric shocks, injections, internal pressure, and sensory deprivation. The marks of punishment were seen not merely on the body but also in the "eyes, [which] become frenzied out of fear, morbid dread and insomnia."[13] This was not, as Muhammad Reza Shah put it, "torture in the old sense of torturing people, twisting their arms and doing this and that."[14] This was a more "intelligent"[15] punishment, one designed to persist long after the moment of its application. The objective was not to scar the flesh with marks of infamy, but to locate, isolate, and cripple the prisoner's "soul."

Modern torture involves a specific way of acting on bodies. Torture is articulated onto the prisoner's body through a noncorporal reality referent, the "consciousness." Its application responds to the principles attributed to this concept: norms and pathologies. The history of the normal and the abnormal selves; the specific modalities through which they are envisaged, characterized, and treated; in short, the entire history of reforming individuals compose the correlative history of modern torture.

How might one understand torture today? One can say that there is nothing modern about torture. Modern torture is simply a survivor from a less progressive and humane stage of politics. It is a persisting "malignant growth on the body politic."[16] This amounts to a condemnation perhaps, but not to an explanation. Anyone who adopts this view would sense that people had become less humane and progressive, although one would be hard-pressed to explain why this has happened and why the excesses of force today are so often justified with reference to humanity and progress.

If this is so, one might wish to turn to the opposite end of the spectrum, to a theorist such as Foucault who seems to be much more cynical about progress, reason, and humanity. In *Discipline and Punish,* Foucault describes the shift from torture to imprisonment in the West. Far from being the humanitarian change others called it, imprisonment, Foucault argues, indicated a new way of exercising power.[17] Power could be exercised through discipline, rather than torture, and the prison was the most austere example of this new age. Insofar as European societies became disciplinary societies, torture became unnecessary as a means of government. Furthermore, the shift toward discipline facilitated economic development: "If the economic take-off of the West began with the techniques that made possible the accumulation of capital, it might perhaps be said that the methods for administering the accumulation of men made possible a political take-off in relation to the traditional, ritual, costly, violent forms of power, which soon fell into disuse and were superseded by a subtle, calculated technology of subjection. In fact, the two processes—the accumulation of men and the accumulation of capital—cannot be separated."[18] Humanists believed that penal reform was a moral improvement over what had preceded it. Foucault criticizes this view, arguing that penal reform simply made possible a more effective way of governing others.

I, too, have a criticism: Foucault's position is far too close to the humanist position he criticizes. Like the humanists but for different reasons, Foucault believes that, over the past few centuries, there has been a process at work that has rendered torture superfluous to the general exercise of power. If, as Foucault says, the world is becoming a more disciplinary place, then why did so many disciplinary governments, including Western ones, torture their citizens? Foucault's argument leads one to conclude that the world has become distinctly less disciplinary and normalized, although Foucault would find it difficult to explain why this transformation is so often justified with reference to discipline and order.

Neither Foucault nor the humanists can advance a satisfactory explanation for the return to torture, much less the features that characterize it. They are not alone in this regard. All major accounts of punishment subscribe to the view that as societies modernize, torture will become superfluous to the exercise of power. For humanists, this modernizing force is progress. For Foucault, it is discipline. For Marxists, it is the mode of production, although socialism shows no less a propensity for torture than capitalism. For Weberians, it is rationalization, which will render us more conscientious, specialized, and nonideological. Strangely enough, torturers seem to be rather conscientious, specialized, and nonideological fellows.

All these accounts treat modern torture too unproblematically. Does the practice of modern torture today indicate a return to the past? One might be tempted to believe this because modern torture is so severely corporal. But it would be a mistake to let corporal violence be the sole basis for one's judgment. Modern torture is not a mere atavism. It belongs to the present moment and arises out of the same notions of rationality, government, and conduct that characterize modernity as such. Modern ways of talking about violence lose sight of this fact and as such become hapless guides to the world of torture. These guides to modern life are good for visiting tourists perhaps, but I would not count on them much for shelter if one lives in a country where torture is a part of everyday life.

Some may object that modern tortures are characteristic of non-Western, or nondisciplinary, societies. Yet in a seminal work on the history of torture, Edward Peters has traced the assembly of modern torture as a distinct practice "to the watershed of 1917–1945."[19] It was during this period, Peters argues, that certain procedures characteristic of European and American police forces were systematized into the recognizable form of modern torture.[20] Peters's account suggests that the practice of modern torture is associated with modern European, that is, disciplinary, societies.

In any case, Foucault in particular is not in a position to make this qualification. In a series of occasional articles on Iran, Foucault acknowledges how torture took place in the context of a police system and prison system.[21] He protests that we Europeans could not generalize from this situation because Iranians "don't have the same regime of truth as ours."[22] Yet at the very least, Foucault must be able to account for torture under the Pahlavi dynasty, a regime that slavishly emulated the Western regime of truth. There are grounds to think that here a Foucaultian approach might be more useful than others. As Edward Said remarks, "Much of what he [Foucault] has studied in his work makes greatest sense not as an ethnocentric model of how power is exercised in modern society, but as part of a much larger picture that involves, for example, the relationship between Europe and the rest of the world."[23] In this part, I take Said's exhortation seriously.

We know that in the nineteenth century, many societies abandoned ceremonial torture. Indeed, for colonialists, this was a sign of progress. Yet after a worldwide decline, torture returned in the early twentieth century and continues to be practiced throughout the world today.[24] This revival is not a return to the ceremonial forms of torture that were once practiced in Europe and elsewhere. Modern tortures take place in the context of policing operations and prison discipline. They are apparently integral to the government of many societies. However, there is no distinct institution that fulfills the multiple tasks assigned to torture as the public spectacle once did. The manner in which modern torture assists in the government of societies remains obscure. Accordingly, one may ask three questions about modern torture: What is modern torture? What is the relation of torture to discipline? Can one specify how torture supports the operation of government? These are the questions that this part seeks to answer.

Iranian penal history is particularly suited for an investigation of such questions because it conforms well to the changes I have just outlined. In the nineteenth century, Iranians practiced classical torture. In Chapter 2, I describe how classical torture was practiced and the place it occupied in Qajar society. Toward the end of Qajar rule, between 1880 and 1900 to be precise, classical tortures disappeared as a result of the impact of disciplinary training. In Chapter 3, I discuss what discipline is and how it was perceived and adapted by Iranians in the late nineteenth century. In Chapter 4, I discuss the factors that led to the spread of new disciplinary practices and the construction of disciplinary institutions such as workhouses, asylums, reformatories, and prisons. Fifty years later, corporal punishments can be found in several types of carceral detention, especially in prisons, and in an entirely new form, modern torture. In Chapter 5, I discuss what modern torture is, the relation it bears to discipline, and how it facilitates government control.

CHAPTER 2

Qajar Punishments

Since the order of the world from the Artist stems,
Any order that exists in artistry begins.

—Ohadi

In the nineteenth century, there was nothing remotely resembling a state in Iran, not in the conventional sense of the word at any rate. The Qajars were despots, but they had at their disposal neither standing armies nor bureaucracies, and they possessed little ideological legitimation. Qajar rule involved not the art of government, but the art of equilibrium. Its general strategy, divide and rule, was supported by three techniques: "the collection of ordinary taxes, the infliction of extraordinary punishments and the disposition of periodic rewards."[1]

Unfortunately, little has been said about these political techniques, particularly the infliction of extraordinary punishments. In the absence of a distinct legal framework, it is often assumed that punishment depended on "the law-giver, his interest, his mood, and his pleasure."[2] Power was personal, and so punishment was arbitrary.

Now this understanding of Qajar rule comes down to us from the regime's opponents, and they had rather obvious reasons for emphasizing the capricious nature of power in Qajar society.[3] Yet the story they tell is very misleading. Extraordinary punishments lacked the predictability associated with a general legal code, but they were not entirely arbitrary either. Although each magistrate exercised punishment in his own interests, he did so through a common set of techniques.

In this chapter, I examine the practice of extraordinary punishments as a technique of power in Qajar society. I argue that the element through which power was exercised (and through which it was constrained to be exercised) was the sign as it was manifested on bodies. Through comportment, gesture, and inflection, individuals indicated familiarity or distance, subservience or authority, repentance or spirituality.

Because such signs were so important to politics, one can better understand the major place occupied by public spectacles of punishment, ceremonies of status, and demonstrations of tribute. This aesthetic style of conduct still exists in Iranian society, but it no longer occupies a central place in the general exercise of power. Indeed, I argue that the signification of individuals facilitated only the most superficial control of public life.

I begin, then, by looking at punishment as a ritual of religious law, then as an ethical ritual, and finally as a political ritual. In each case, I try to bring out the place of signs. Then I consider opposition to the Qajars. I look first at popular responses to Qajar justice and then assess clerical opposition to Qajar courts. I consider the impact each group had on the practice of punishment.

The Offense of Bodies

Like most Muslim societies, nineteenth-century Qajar Iran had inherited a criminal procedure that was centered on the act of the accused. Among classical jurists, verifying the deed was the main task of a judicial inquiry. Judicial verification was ipso facto an admission of guilt. It carried the same force as a full confession by the accused. Proof of the deed, however, had to be unquestionable. To prevent an abuse of justice, Islamic legal theory made proof of an offense very difficult.

This was especially true of crimes that carried mandatory punishments prescribed by the Shari'a, or religious law. The physical act alone constituted the crime. No other evidence was pertinent to the case. For example, in cases of liquor consumption, Shi'a Imamiyya jurisprudence ruled that "the smell of the breath, being patently drunk, or vomiting is not sufficient evidence in itself."[4] Proof of this offense required either the confession of the accused or the testimony of two reliable male witnesses who could verify the act. Similarly, an unexpressed denunciation of Islam did not constitute apostasy. Such an unexpressed belief had to "be accompanied by action or declaration."[5] If the accused confessed, the accused could withdraw the confession at any time during the course of the inquiry. It was even recommended that the "judge suggest this course of action to defendants who have already confessed."[6] There were also stringent prerequisites for the production of witnesses. For example, fornication or adultery required the testimony of four reliable male witnesses, who, according to classical jurists, "must have been present at the sexual act itself."[7] Finally, classical jurists maintained that if the physical act resembled a similar legal act, it could be presumed that the accused was behaving in accordance with the Shari'a.

This judicial importance of the act extended to penal procedures. Punishment was exclusively a punishment of the deed. It was, in the strictest sense, "the penalty for the offence of the body."[8] Punishment annulled the criminal act by reinscribing the offense on the body that committed it; the marks of the punishment were always decipherable. Often there was the use of symbolic torture where the type of punishment referred to the nature of the crime: Thieves lost their right hands, highway robbers lost the opposite hands and feet, and apostates were purged through fires. In some cases, the actual crime was duplicated on the offender. For example, would-be regicide Mullah Fathullah was wounded "in the very place that he had injured the Shah" with the very same weapon, a pistol.[9] Or to take another example, a baker who overcharged the price of bread was baked alive in his oven at the governor's order.[10] If marks were not inscribed onto the body, the body itself was used as a signpost: As late as 1884, one finds cases where brigands were thrust alive, head first, into pits along the road, leaving their legs exposed as a sign to others.

Careful attention was paid to the way wounds were cut into bodies. One can gain a keener understanding of this by consulting a slightly older text. In *Zakhira-yi Kamila* (The Perfect Treasury), the Safavid Hakim (Doctor) Muhammad expounds on major surgery and its techniques. He notes the therapeutic and judicial uses of surgery, especially in the case of amputation of organs and limbs. He discusses techniques specific to penal torture, weighing different methods of applying the same punishment according to their painfulness. Exoculation, for instance, may be achieved through piercing or gouging out the eyes, but the pain caused by the former is fierce. "What destruction will be wrought. ... Death is preferable."[11] In his discussion of treatment, the hakim distinguishes between two kinds of burns: accidental burns and burns "inflicted by the orders of someone in authority."[12] Here the treatment seems the same, but in the case of castration, the hakim prescribes different treatments depending on whether "it is desired that the patient live."[13] Penal cuts, then, were not left to the executioner's creative whims; they were part of an explicit body of knowledge that was simultaneously juridical and medical.

It was not sufficient, however, that the magistrate cut into the body "marks of the stigmatism of his justice."[14] It was also important that the offense be punished openly. The condemned man was ceremoniously paraded through the streets and bazaars. He was slowly flogged in the square, bastinadoed before an audience, or dismembered in the religious shrine. From the legal perspective, punishment had to publish the results of the judicial inquiry. Through the writing of the offense on the body, it now announced the criminal's own offense. In this way, punishment reinforced the judicial system.

The central element of extraordinary punishments was the body of the condemned. The body proclaimed the offense, confirmed the judicial process, and annulled the crime. It was invested with its own judicial life. No doubt this explains why the body of the dead criminal would be preserved, in some cases for ten days, so that it could be executed with his living accomplices. This also explains the tortures that continued after the death of the offender: the dismembering of the corpse, the blowing of the corpse from mortars, the dragging of the body through the streets, and its humiliating exhibition above the city gates.

This torture of the body did not conclude with the destruction of the corpse. Torture was also applied to the offender's divine soul. Evidently, the offender's soul was not an immaterial entity, but a subtle material body.[15] The punishment of the corpse therefore simply initiated the eternal tortures of the material soul in Hell.

The Conduct of Bodies

Qajar punishments, however, are not to be understood simply as enforcements of moral laws. They are also to be numbered among the rituals of ethical life. Ethical subjects ask, "What is proper at this moment, in this place, with this person, and in this situation?" Their comportment varies with social circumstances. Paying attention to the world around them is a natural, expected, and self-expected feature of their lives. Ethics contrasts with morals precisely because circumstances do not matter to moral subjects. Moral subjects simply know what their duty is in all circumstances according to some universal prohibitions such as the law.

I want to use the example of judicial torture to illustrate the place of ethics in penal rituals. The Qajars made a distinction between judicial and penal torture. In 1852, the British consul urged that the execution of the Babis "ought to be done without torture."[16] The grand vizier responded that "this was not the time for trifling. ... The punishment, however severe, of criminals who sought to spread massacre and spoilation throughout the length and breadth of Persia, was not to be deprecated, or to be included under the designation of torture, which had been defined to be the infliction of pain to extort a confession of guilt."[17] The British consul was conflating two distinct activities. Torture referred to the judicial production of the truth. Public punishment referred to the judicial production of order. Each possessed a different objective and responded to specific demands.

Among Qajar punishments, judicial torture occupied a strictly regulated place. The accused was punished only after partial proof of an offense had been established. This proof included documentary evidence written by the accused and witnesses to the criminal act. Judicial torture was, in this sense, *t'azir*, or discretionary punishment.[18] Judicial torture was also an investigative technique at the disposal of judges, and in this sense it was not *t'azir*. Although not prescribed by the Shari'a, judicial torture clearly conformed to the main requirements of Islamic legal procedures.

Like most Islamic jurisprudence, judicial torture investigated "the truth of the deed."[19] A written letter from the shah in turn directed public officials to proceed until the truth was known "more fully."[20] Investigators began with the display of "the instruments of branding and torture" during the preliminary investigation and slowly intensified the torment.[21] This investigation culminated in the final declaration of the accused. The offender declared his crime spontaneously and voluntarily before an audience of magistrates. This act confirmed that the charges were true and legitimated the earlier discretionary punishments inflicted on the offender. In this manner, the accused participated in the process of judicial torture.

Curiously enough, however, judicial torture was supposedly conducted within certain ethical limits. In a submitted report, the magistrate would attest that the examination had been "carried out with gentleness and politeness."[22] It was even expected that if this injunction to right conduct was violated, the aggrieved would claim *bast*, or sanctuary, and petition the shah "to send a third unprejudiced examiner to investigate the truth between [himself] and them."[23] For in administering *t'azir* in the course of an inquiry, the magistrate was now, in the view of classical jurists, legally liable for any unnecessary suffering.[24] And in fomenting unnecessary conflict among his subjects, the magistrate had to answer to the shah. Hence, even the corrupt magistrate would not resort to torture unless he could invent partial proof of a criminal offense and thereby justify his actions. Judicial torture was a torture of the truth, but it required the truth to be produced— at least apparently—within the limits of right conduct, not demanded at all costs.

The surest guarantee that this situation had obtained was the conduct of the accused. If the accused was indeed guilty of the crime, then he would embrace his suffering voluntarily. He would treat his torture as more than a mere effort to resist pain. He would welcome his suffering as an opportunity to transform himself. He would use it to achieve a *safa-yi batin*, an inward piety and an external detachment.[25] Following his torture, the regicide Mirza Reza Kirmani concluded his statement in this serene spirit: "Now that I have done this deed, I have no further hope of life, since it needs a magnanimity like that of God or but one degree short of this to pardon me."[26]

And this is why magistrates urged prisoners to bear themselves well: For in the prisoner's right conduct was also the surest proof that the magistrate had behaved properly. Torture was ideally a semivoluntary activity. Suffering was, at least in part, a choice the prisoner made independently of earthly rewards or punishments. In this respect, torture was linked to older rites of redemptive suffering,[27] albeit for prudential as well as religious reasons. As higher authorities expected magistrates to conduct themselves justly and properly, magistrates in turn solicited proper behavior from their prisoners and then offered this behavior as proof that they had met the requirements.

In penal torture, codes of etiquette were considerably more complex. To be sure, one finds the same encouragement to the prisoner to behave well. The prisoner was invited to bear himself, insofar as he could, with "complete serenity and calmness."[28] He honored the necessary ritual obligations, as in the case of the Babi Sulayman Khan, who deferred the honor of death upward to his elder, Shaykh Nayrizi. Prisoners also marked their deaths with delicate poems:

The world is that which sometimes graces, sometimes pains,
Its playful wheel has many childish games like these.[29]

If we were burdensome, we are gone.
If we were unkind, we are gone.[30]

For his part, the executioner honored the condemned and fulfilled his requests. Here is a tribal khan's self-description of part of his exoculation. After the khan criticized his executioner for poor technique, another executioner was called. "In the mean time, I got up with my one eye out, called for a calleoon [a hookah pipe] and smoked it, and then held up my left eye to the new fellow, begging him to give me as little pain as possible."[31] And here is how the Hujjat ul-Islam Shafti, who was given the honorary nickname Sufikush or the killer of mystics, would execute punishments: "[He] would lead the condemned with insistence, complete gentleness, and encouragement, [saying] that 'upon my ancestors, I myself will be an intercessor on your behalf on the Day of Judgment,' with openness, sincerity, and hopefulness. After that, usually in a state of tears, he would sever their heads, pray over their corpses, and, occasionally in the course of prayer, [he] would faint."[32]

Nevertheless, the opportunity for ethical conduct was not provided indiscriminately. The opportunity was signaled by physical or verbal cues. For example, in 1828, the Asif id-Dowleh, "a noblemen of the highest rank and a cousin of the Shah[,] suffered his punishment in the public square of Tehran, for having sustained a defeat by the Muscovites. As a homage to his rank, a [silk] carpet was spread on which he was placed, and the first blow was struck by the Shah's son, 'Abbas Meerza, the heir to the throne."[33] By contrast, in 1810, a slave who had poisoned the family he had served was "hung by the heels in the common market-place, and cut up in the same manner as a butcher does the carcass of a sheep: but he was denied the mercy shown that animal, of having his throat cut before he was quartered."[34]

These forms of penal torture do not correspond precisely to a division between the hereditary aristocracy and commoners. The grand vizier, Amir Kabir, was the son of a cook, yet he was permitted to name the manner of his execution.[35] However, penal tortures do reveal another division, the division between those capable of right conduct (noblemen, religious leaders, merchants, and male commoners) and those deemed incapable (slaves and women). These groupings do admit of relative distinctions. A peasant, for example, was not expected to carry himself like a nobleman given his lack of cultivation, but even he was aware of the punishments appropriate to his dignity.[36]

Similarly, women had a higher status than slaves in one way: They were not physically exposed in the course of punishment. The expectation of modesty, demanded or assumed, accounts for the tortures that characterized female executions: stoning, strangulation, and the casting of women off high towers and minarets. But the status of women, even of extremely cultivated women, was never secure. Women often shared in the misfortunes of their male family members. "When a nobleman or minister is put to death, it is not unusual to give away his wives and daughters as slaves; and sometimes (though rarely) they are bestowed on the lowest classes in the community."[37]

Thus, at the heart of Qajar punishments, one finds not a total coercion of the body, but the encouragement to bear one's body properly. Punishment was to be a teacher of the pious. It delivered the condemned from a condition of affliction to a state of detachment and inward piety. It is not surprising, then, that the condemned furnished not only examples of justice but also ethical models for emulation. How else might one understand the detailed descriptions of behavior and the careful notation of poetry?

Although the highest virtues were expressed only by those who, either through birth or achievement, belonged to the highest social ranks, all punitive participants practiced a complex style of etiquette called *t'aarof*. *T'aarof* comprised distinct styles of speech and behavior that were appropriate to each person's social status in an interaction. These linguistic and behavioral styles varied considerably depending on whether the person was an intimate or a stranger. They affected all the actions and exchanges that took place in an interaction. For example, providing a cup of water could be a *favor* if the torturer was a status superior or a *tribute* if he was a status inferior. In asking for a cup of water, the prisoner would use Arabic forms with Farsi auxiliary verbs if the torturer was a status unequal, whereas the prisoner would use Farsi if the torturer was a status equal. *T'aarof* was and still is a ritual practice that "underscores and preserves the integrity of culturally defined status roles."[38]

By participating in *t'aarof*, torturers and prisoners assumed the obligations imposed on them by their status. However, they could also manipulate these obligations using *t'aarof*. Consider the earlier example of the tribal khan who had his eyes removed. He was superior in rank to his torturer. This is why the khan could summarily dismiss the first torturer for poor technique and ask for a new one. However, when the new torturer arrived, the khan treated the torturer as an intimate and an equal, begging to be given as little pain as possible. Between status-equal intimates, no request could be easily denied, and the khan knew this very well. A torturer could thus be status inferior to a prisoner by rank as well as a total stranger but also be treated as a status-equal intimate because he was involved in so intimate a task as exoculation. In *t'aarof*, a person's status was relative to more than one standard, and one could try to manipulate the torturer by invoking a different standard through the language one used.

T'aarof, however, could also impose painful obligations. Consider, for example, the execution of Sulayman Khan. When it came time for his execution, Sulayman Khan deferred *the honor of death* to his elder, Shaykh Nayrizi. Beneath this simple description is a rather complex social process. Sulayman Khan treated the executioner as a status-superior nonintimate, *petitioning* him to execute Nayrizi first. The executioner performed this action as a *favor* to a status-inferior nonintimate, knowing that in return for this favor, Sulayman Khan was willing to suffer much longer. To do this, however, the executioner was obliged to recognize Shaykh Nayrizi as a status-superior nonintimate. In this way, Sulayman Khan also performed a *service* for the elder Shaykh Nayrizi, who was his status-superior intimate. Shaykh Nayrizi acknowledged this service as a *reward* for Sulayman Khan's devotion, for indeed there was probably no other way the shaykh would have been willing to die first. In this instance, executioners and the condemned linked the gravity of the moment with the virtues constitutive of *t'aarof*. Sulayman Khan in particular preferred to fulfill the obligations imposed on him by his status even though he had dozens of burning candles inserted in his flesh. In doing so, he affirmed the relatively hierarchical social order implicit in *t'aarof*.

In this way, penal torture reinforced the activity of the 'Urf. The 'Urf comprised judicial proceedings based on custom rather than on abstract legal rules. The justice of the 'Urf was, no doubt, a justice of the rich and the powerful. Yet it would be too extreme to argue that the verdicts of the 'Urf were sustained by sheer repression or, alternatively, "derived from some abstract notion of 'moral justice.'"[39] The authenticity of the rulings depended on how well they conformed to a common understanding of social obligations. Penal tortures also recognized these social obligations, dramatizing the tributes and services due to superiors as well as the virtuous favors and rewards granted inferiors, were they that fortunate.

Qajar punishments thus become more comprehensible once one refers to their rules and social effects. Looking at the judicial rules, one can see the central place occupied by the body and the signs written on it. Looking at the social effects it produced, one can see how individuals were provided an opportunity to express a specific range of ethical virtues. They were asked to behave according to their status. This behavior, in turn, served as a model for emulation by the pious and reinforced social distinctions. Now I want to turn to the political signs.

The Power to Take Life

There was, of course, a much older punitive demand, the law of revenge. When an injured party could not force the courts to observe this demand, he assumed that the power of punishment had reverted to him. In the case of murder, "assassination [was] applauded and through it, almost always occasion more murders, and interminable blood feuds."[40] In this fashion, blood feuds erupted among families, city wards, tribes, and villages.[41] The demand for qisas, or legal retaliation, could preempt official extraordinary punishments. In 1888, "a number of male collaterals of the royal family forced their way into the compound of the War Office, where a prisoner was confined who had murdered one of their relatives, hacked him to pieces with their weapons and burned his body with petroleum."[42] Fear of qisas also shaped the character of extraordinary punishments. For example, in 1852, even though the attempted assassination of the shah required severe punishment, the grand vizier "was fearful of drawing upon himself and his family the vengeance of the followers of the Bab."[43] Consequently, courtiers pressed the shah "to deliver each [offender] into the hands of a class of the people so that they may be executed ... and that this crowd [the Babis] may know that all the Iranian people are partners in their blood."[44]

Since the blood feud could destroy social order, many attempts were made to domesticate the law of retaliation. Villagers would seize the offender, deliver him to the injured party, and let his ill-will be the measure of the offender's punishment. Similarly, tribal and Islamic law acknowledged qisas but sought to temper the demand through arbitration. Appeals were made for forgiveness, and the offender would be required to pay compensation in money, goods, horses, or women. If he was unable to raise the amount, he was "obliged to wear a large iron collar round his neck and to beg till he collected enough to discharge the fine."[45]

Finally, tremendous efforts were made to wrest the power to take life from individuals and vest it in the shah. The Qajars assiduously cultivated their exclusive prerogative to punish using every symbolic device they could find. Whenever the shah traveled, courtiers displayed instruments of torture as part of the regal procession.[46] In the course of royal t'aziyas, or passion plays, vivid executions were performed during the appropriate scenes; with the shah as a witness of divine justice, the deaths of Yazid and his henchmen were used to illustrate a full range of penal tortures.[47] A portrait of the shah was "unveiled when the verdicts of the ['Urf] court were announced (see Figure 2.1)."[48] The shah "was not only the judge of criminals, but the witness of the execution of capital punishments."[49] Because the shahs presented themselves as neutral authorities, they never personally executed criminals even when entitled to *qisas* under the law.[50] When the shah could not personally observe an execution, this function was delegated to his representative, usually his governor, court executioner, or *farrashbashi* (steward).[51] Only the shah's officials punished regardless of whether the punishment was ordered by the 'Urf or the Shari'a courts.[52] The shahs possessed a torture that was exclusively theirs to apply at their pleasure, namely, exoculation.[53] Although only a *mujtahid* could issue a death sentence, only the shah could request a death sentence.[54] No execution took place without the display of the royal death sentence of the offender. However, the shah could reprieve the offender through a royal pardon if he was moved by last-minute petitions of mercy or if political expediency suddenly demanded it. Until the last moment, no one except the shah knew the outcome of the ceremony. He alone controlled the balance of life and death. As John Malcolm so shrewdly observed, "It is not only in attention to persons, deputed by the Kings and Princes in Persia, that respect for royalty is shown; it extends to the reception of letters, dresses, and presents, and every inanimate thing with which their name is associated. The object is to import to all ranks a reverence and awe for the sovereign and those to whom he delegates power. In short, no means are neglected that can keep alive, or impress more deeply, the duty of implicit obedience."[55]

Consequently, Qajar punishments were political as well as ethical and legal rituals. Punishment, regardless of the nature of the offense, manifested the absolute power of the shah. The shah possessed the "power of life and death over his subjects"[56] and exercised it on local communities. Fath 'Ali Shah Qajar threatened to have the province of Fars "ravaged by fire and sword. Crops were to be destroyed, villages burned, cattle plundered and survivors, whether villagers or tribesmen, were to be carried captive to Tehran."[57] Muhammad Khan Qajar carried out this ultimate form of communal punishment in Kirman City: He ordered his soldiers to decapitate 600 rebels, hang two heads on each of 300 other captives, march these exemplary figures 120 miles in front of the horses, execute the second group, and then build minarets out of the bodies of the 900 men. He then ordered the city notables to appear and pay homage to his person. After this, he had their ears cut off, their eyes removed, and their bodies cast from the top of the castle. He then took 8,000 children as concubines and pages for his

Figure 2.1   "The day they took the picture of Muhammad 'Ali Shah instead of the shah himself to the Blessed Parliament"

Source: Ahmad Tafrishi-Husayni, *Ruznameh-yi Akhbar-i Mashrutiyat va Inqilab-i Iran* (A Diary of Documents Concerning Constitutionalism and the Revolution of Iran), ed. Iraj Afshar (Tehran: Amir Kabir, 1351 [1972]), from the appendix of photographs following p. 302.

army. Finally, he "ordered his executioners to present to him seven thousand pairs of eyes of the despicable [and rebellious Kirmani] inhabitants."[58]

The shah exercised punishment over his subjects as the *Zil-Allah*, the "Shadow of God on Earth."[59] His punishment revealed the justice of Allah and established the place of execution as an extension of Hell. The shah also exercised punishment as the chief protector and patron of a social order. He was the "Supreme Arbitrator," keeping the peace among all his lesser communities. As Qajar chroniclers often reminded their society, only the shah "stood between communal tensions and total social anarchy."[60]

Nineteenth-century jurists reinforced royal authority in turn with the important doctrine of the *Na'ib-i Khass*. In 1809, with the threat of war with Russia imminent, the well-known *mujtahid*, Kashif al-Ghita', buttressed the shah's authority by declaring him special deputy of the hidden imam. The *mujtahid* permitted the shah to take whatever actions were necessary to repel "infidels, rebels, and those who have abjured the faith."[61] Since Kashif al-Ghita' took fighting Russians to be the same as punishing them, he reinforced the shah's authority to punish. This action provided the shah with "temporary, partial and derived legitimacy."[62] The *mujtahid*s retained the right to pronounce the law, but the execution of punishment was left to the shah.[63]

Criminal offenses therefore not only precipitated social chaos but also violated the justice of Allah. Royal punishment in turn restored true justice and the proper order of social life:

> According to royal command, their limbs and members were severed by the sword and dagger; and their souls bound in fiery chains were dragged to the lowest abyss of Hell where they quaffed from the hands of torturing Angels, the punishment of swallowing molten metal and putrefying gore. Then in the midst of the army a herald proclaimed:

> *Such is the reward of him who slays his lord!*
> *Even the most Merciful Creator never pardons*
> *The servant who smites his master!*[64]

For the court chronicler here, the royal punishment above ground could not be distinguished from the strange religious drama that took place below.

Carnival of Signs

Political violence may have lacked systematicity because jurisdictions conflicted, but it retained an overall coherence through its techniques. These techniques involved the inscription of signs, and it is therefore not surprising that the violence about penal rituals involved the misrepresentation of signs. In these struggles, participants engaged in a violent, farcical play, a *maskharih bazi*, of the accepted personifications of piety, justice, and political virtue.

One can find penal satire of this sort among groups that were dispossessed and consequently openly contemptuous of the status system. Country brigands and *luti*s, urban gangs, in particular, adopted this style.[65] There was, for instance, the case of a judge who fell into the hands of brigands whom he had once punished. The brigand leader decided to horseshoe the magistrate, thereby branding him as an ass.[66]

The brigand in this instance used punishment as a technique of representation. He did not obliterate the system of representations; he merely playfully changed what the signs meant. Crowd justice was more overtly antiauthoritarian. One finds the crowd striving to obliterate expressed distinctions of status. Yet in the popular imagination, rioting was closely associated with the satirical activity of the *luti*s as illustrated by the institution of the *luti bazaar*, or market of the *luti*s. This institution seems to have been "a right of insurrection to which the people of Qazwin resorted in cases of violence and oppression" and became synonymous with rioting and pillaging.[67]

Crowd justice usually involved the looting of property and the public execution or humiliation of officials. In 1870, for example, the *kalantar*, or sheriff, of Kirman was asked for cheaper bread. When he told the townspeople to eat the testicles of his horse, "the outraged population killed him on the spot."[68] Such events followed local grievances, famines, or spiritual ceremonies on holy days. For example, during the height of the Muharram holy days, crowds frequently attacked town stocks and jails to release convicted offenders.[69] Offenders could seek refuge from the authorities by taking *bast* at shrines, embassies, and public edifices. As long as they were in the shadow of these edifices, they could not be punished, and this led to strange scenes. For example, in the square of the Pearl Cannon, "a miserable group of offenders is usually to be found camped about the steps of the brick platform on which the cannon rests, while the officers of the law or relatives of the injured party wait patiently near until hunger shall drive them from the sacred precincts."[70]

Qajars tolerated crowd justice simply because they could not easily repress it. They also learned to manipulate crowds well, as Fath 'Ali Shah's handling of a major revolt in 1814 illustrated:

> One of his sons, while governor of the strategic fortress of Astarabad, allied with the rebellious Turkman tribes and claimed the crown. The *Shah*, instead of directly confronting the rebel, dispatched three *firmans* (royal letters): one to the prince pledging pardon if he laid down his arms; another to the religious leaders of the community, promising rewards and reminding them that the governor had unjustly imprisoned some of them; and the third to the city populace, denouncing the governor for levying unlawful taxes and warning them that the dangerous alliance with the nomads could result in a mass plunder of Astarabad. The last two letters produced "their desired effects." A large crowd, led by the religious authorities, seized the rebel, and promptly delivered him to the government before the Turkmans had a chance to rally. Astarabad was handsomely rewarded, the prince had his eyes taken out, and the tribesmen were persuaded to disperse home.[71]

Politicians also used the disaffection of brigands and *luti*s. For example, during the Constitutional Revolution (1905–1909), the Qajars utilized *luti*s to assassinate pro-Constitutionalist 'ulema[72] and employed brigands to crush Constitutionalist forces, as in the case of the notorious Rahim Khan, who led the siege on Tabriz. Similarly, the 'ulema frequently patronized *luti*s in return for their services in fighting royal authorities and, later, Constitutionalist forces.[73]

The classical power to punish was not coherent and monolithic. No single authority could impose its system on the country as a whole. Signs could secure external obedience only for a time, but just how reliable such obedience could be in the long run was always unclear.

Shahs and Clerics

In the past, nineteenth-century politics has sometimes been presented as a struggle between two mutually exclusive judicial systems: the 'Urf and the Shar'. On one side, there was the Qajar shah who constantly sought to curb the activities of the Shari'a courts. On the other side, there were the 'ulema who attempted to enforce orthodox Shi'ism and consequently persistently questioned the legitimacy of the monarchy and its 'Urf courts. I want to argue, however, that there was far greater collusion between the court and clergy than is often acknowledged.

To be sure, 'Urf and Shari'a courts often clashed, but an account that stresses these clashes alone ignores some interesting points. The Qajar period was actually "a period of the popularisation of Shi'i theology" and not simply because theologians wrote treatises.[74] Orthodox Shi'ism in Iran was also presented through a painful procedure that publicized punishable deeds and ethical conduct. In this respect, religious courts punished in the same way as secular courts did.

Moreover, this account does not mention that the Shi'i 'ulema did not want to execute punishments because spilling human blood polluted their purity. When a *mujtahid* executed punishment, it was a rare and disturbing incident.[75] Thus, even though Shi'i *mujtahids* may have contested the Qajars' claim to pronounce the law, they were more than happy to relegate the act of punishment to the shah and his officials, thereby enshrining the sovereign power to punish in judicial practices. In fact, *mujtahids* paid royal officials an execution fee for performing the punishment.[76] In this manner, *mujtahids* implicitly accommodated the de facto power of the Qajars.[77]

Finally, such an account overlooks the fact that the Qajars needed to punish so as to maintain their claim to sovereignty. Sovereign power, if it was to be recognizable, had to embody the power over life and death. Fath 'Ali Shah put it this way to the British ambassador:

> "I understand all you have said," he [Fath 'Ali Shah] observed; and after some reflection, he added—"Your king is, I see, only the first magistrate of the country." "Your majesty has exactly defined his situation." "Such a condition of power," said he, smiling, "has permanence, but it has no enjoyment: mine is enjoyment. There you see Suliman Khan Kajir, and several other of the first chiefs of the Kingdom—I can cut all their heads off: can I not?" said he, addressing them. "Assuredly, 'Point of adoration of the world,' if it is your pleasure."
>
> "That is real power," said the king; "but then it has no permanence."[78]

Here, the shah contrasts the bureaucratic power of the English king with his own. For the shah, bureaucratic power is permanent, but it is not real power. Without the power to punish, invested through divine authority, the Qajars had no tangible sign of their power or justification for its use. This is why Qajar shahs, immediately after their coronations, gladly executed the first brigands that fell into their hands. The Qajars' ability to inflict extraordinary punishments constituted a major pillar of an otherwise invisible dynasty.

Whatever disagreements existed in the nineteenth century about the right to judge cases, the 'ulema and the Qajar shahs never fundamentally questioned this right to exercise punishment. The two great systems of 'Urf and Shar' were interlocked through a judicial understanding of who exercised punishment and through a cultural understanding of what punishment represented.

Conclusion

By all accounts, Qajar politics was complex and confusing. Many loosely associated judges sat with uncertain jurisdictions and a marginal capacity to exercise systematic violence. They had different purposes in punishing others, but these purposes were secured through a common set of representational techniques in which signs were carefully inscribed onto bodies and codes were manifested in action and speech. If punishment helped a judge dominate a jurisdiction, then this penal alphabet helped indicate the nature of the political authority that exercised violence. In penal rituals, this alphabet spelled out royal presence, revealed religious prohibitions, and instructed others in the natural hierarchy of society. Punishment was, in the broadest sense, a political signature.

CHAPTER 3

Disciplinary Practices

In 1852, Nasser id-Din Shah narrowly escaped assassination. His assailant died an extraordinary death. Burning candles were inserted into holes of his flesh. He was shot in the same place he wounded the shah. He was stoned to death, and his body was ripped to shreds and blown from a mortar. All this occurred in the midst of a huge penal ceremony in which all classes of society executed Babis throughout the capital.

In 1896, Nasser id-Din Shah died at the hands of another assassin. The assassin's execution illustrated how much punishment had changed in fifty years. Mirza Reza Kirmani was sentenced to death and confined to the Cossack Barracks for the night. Early in the morning, he was conducted to the gallows by members of the royal family. A huge crowd gathered to watch the execution. At the last moment, he tried to speak to the crowd, but he was drowned out by the military band playing nearby. He died on the gallows in the military drill square. His body hung there for three days, and that is the last we hear of it.[1]

What had remained the same? Execution was still public. It was also clearly political, giving a prominent role to the royal family and the military that supported it. However, note the differences. The religious and social aspects of punishment had been marginalized. Kirmani was not allowed to speak. His body was not mangled. The crime was not reenacted. The procession was brief, and the people were not asked to participate. Here, there was neither Heaven nor Hell nor the great chain of being that linked the monarchy to its many constituencies. Rather, the monarchy stood firmly on the shoulders of its Cossack army before a docile crowd, a picture of the new order to come.

Regicide is an extraordinary crime in a monarchy, but this execution is almost democratic. Kirmani is treated as an ordinary individual who has committed a serious crime but not an extraordinary one. This crime disrupted the government but not the order of existence. His voice drowned out by the marching band, Kirmani dies an almost anonymous death. Furthermore, his body is not punished. It is not alive in itself. It is simply the means to kill the individual called Kirmani. Finally, the punishment is brief by comparison to classical punishments. Kirmani is imprisoned for a while and then executed on the gallows. He was lucky not to have received "a more horrible death."[2]

Kirmani, however, was not alone. By 1895, public executioners merely strangled, decapitated, or slit the throats of the worst offenders. In some areas, Iranians abandoned the penal spectacle completely. By 1880, the public stocks in Tehran were no longer public; they were hidden behind high walls. Travelers in villages and small towns still reported penal torture into the early twentieth century. In the cities, however, the old penal processions vanished. They were replaced by two new institutions, the public gallows and the town prison. These changes did not occur at the same time in every city, nor did they occur necessarily for the same reason. The transitional period seems to be roughly between 1885 and 1900.

Why did the old ways vanish at this time? This problem will not admit of simple answers. George Curzon cites the milder, more civilized character of Nasser id-Din Shah, saying that "fortunately, the visits of the Shah to Europe, and the increasing influence of civilized opinion, have had a wonderful effect in mitigating the barbarity of this truly merciless and Oriental code, and cases of unnecessary torture are now rarely heard of."[3] The shah did issue edicts, but their effects were negligible; the Qajars did not possess the army or bureaucracy required to enforce such dramatic changes in penal practice.[4] The Constitutionalists reformed penal law during the 1905 revolution, but these "drastic" legal reforms occurred *after* penal practices had changed.[5] If the timing of these changes coincided with a major shift in economic organization, we might speculate how such changes affected punishment. None of the economic histories, however, indicates that the last two decades of the nineteenth century brought about significant changes in the mode of production, at least in comparison with the preceding decades.[6]

So what was happening? Let us consider the nature of this new penal style. Kirmani's execution illustrated two aspects of this new style. First, punishment aimed at something beyond the body, seeking to deprive it of liberty, expression, and life. The consequences of this change included the brevity of punishment, the anonymity of death, and the irrelevance of the physical body to punishment. Second, punishment involved attaching bodies to machines that were designed to inflict pain on offenders in a precise, regulated manner. Consider the hanging of offenders on the gallows. Offenders used to be hung, but only by the feet and mainly to allow the executioner to cut into the body. In Kirmani's case, the exact moment and manner of death were left to the rope on the gallows, not to the executioner. In other words, instead of people acting directly on others, machines and institutions intervened between society and the criminal. Amir Kabir, Nasser id-Din Shah's greatest prime minister, envisioned a society much like a giant machine, one in which each demand would be perfectly implemented on the undisciplined and the irregular.[7] Such a society remained elusive in the late nineteenth century, but hopes for its imminent arrival were fostered everywhere, even among jailers.

These two aspects of punishment are related. Machines focus on predetermined units, not on individuals with assorted peculiarities. Docile individuals, in turn, can be linked to a variety of different machines, including punitive ones.

I want to call this manner of punishment a disciplinary punishment. Kirmani's execution showed how disciplinary punishments had displaced classical tortures. When torture returned to Iranian society, it arose not out of a society that lacked discipline, but out of one that had already made the transition to a disciplinary society. In this chapter, I want to discuss in more detail what discipline does and how it is expressed in Iranian society. In the following chapter, I trace the many ways through which discipline found its way into Iranian society.

Disciplinary Matrices

Discipline has three features. It subdivides coercive structures so that each body can be worked over individually rather than as part of a crowd. It brings to bear on a body techniques that break down gestures, regulate movements, and shape activities over time. It requires new coercive techniques based on constant management and supervision.[8] Disciplinary punishments are not less corporal than classical punishments, although they are less sanguinary.

In Iran, discipline arrived as part of the great renewal of the monarchy. A year before the spectacular execution of the Babis in 1852, there was another spectacular event. This was the opening of the Dar ul-Fonun (House of Sciences) in Tehran. The shah himself attended the opening of this institution in which "all the sciences were to be taught."[9] The House of Sciences was composed primarily of "disciplines" such as artillery, infantry, cavalry, military engineering, mineralogy, chemistry, physics, cartography, medicine, pharmacy, and surgery. In addition, it taught "some subjects representing the arts," including geography, history, and foreign languages, especially French.[10]

In 1863, an official paper ran a photograph of the Dar ul-Fonun (see Figure 3.1). The photograph depicts the northern wing of the institution. In the center is a line of weapons. At either end of this line, two disciplined men stand at attention. Shoulders are held straight, arms fixed at the sides, and feet slightly parted. The line between the two men extends in an ordered

Figure 3.1 The north porch of the *Dar ul-Fonun* (House of Sciences)

Source: Qodratullah Rowshani Z'afaranlu, ed. *Amir Kabir va Dar ul-Fonun (Amir Kabir and the Dar ul-Fonun)* (Tehran: Tehran University, 1354 [1975]), p. 302.

pattern: two tripods of rifles, an artillery piece, two further tripods. Slightly behind this line and at right angles to the mortar stands a third disciplined cadet. The row of pillars continues the pattern set by the disciplined bodies. Surrounding these figures is a traditional arrangement of signs: lions and suns for the shah and graceful Achaemenid designs representing ancient grandeur. By contrast, the rows of instruments, bodies, and pillars represent a military arrangement. The symbols of monarchy thus stand on the solid structure of discipline. Discipline organizes not only space but also time into discrete units. The Dar ul-Fonun has a clock tower, not a typical feature of Iranian building. The clock tower stands over the courtyard coordinating time and movement.

What this photograph communicates is a new model for learning. According to this model, education occurs only through discipline. Indeed, discipline is the measure of education: "Even now a good school is considered to be one in which discipline is rigid, and the one in which no voice is heard save that of the teacher, the one in which pupils do not run or jump or cry during the recess period, but walk silently and gravely with dignity into the courtyards of the school."[11] At the Dar ul-Fonun, for example, the disciplines were organized into seven branches. Students from each branch had their own distinctive uniforms. Each regiment pursued a course of study involving three annual exams over a cycle of six to seven years.[12] As one visitor to the academy remarked, "The extent of the curriculum, the drill, and the evident success of the instruction in the shah's college were a great surprise to us."[13]

Institutions such as the Dar ul-Fonun came and went in the nineteenth century. I call the Dar ul-Fonun and similar ensembles "disciplinary matrices."[14] A disciplinary matrix relies on at least three practices, each of which expresses a feature of discipline itself:

1. *A means of coercion.* A disciplinary matrix turns on a means by which bodies can be worked over in detail. In Iran, and more generally throughout the colonial world, the drill provided this disciplinary vehicle.

2. *An order of performance.* Discipline cannot be constructed on isolated drills. In addition to drills, the sequence of routines needs to be coordinated and regulated through training programs. Disciplinary matrices rely on programs, for example, educational curricula, military precepts, hospital regulations, and municipal ordinances. Programs rank priorities. They provide the means to coordinate and order drills in the most efficient manner.

3. *A modality for correction.* Programs need to be administered and evaluated. Teachers may need to intervene either to correct defects or to increase efficiency. A disciplinary matrix then needs a modality for correction. This feature in turn requires an apparatus for observation and a means of judgment.

For these three features to work effectively, disciplinary matrices require a highly flexible and adaptable space. This space should allow for detailed training of each individual, adapt well to different training programs, and facilitate observation and correction of each trainee.

In Iran, this kind of disciplinary space was inscribed into two architectural novelties of Qajar life: the drill square and the classroom. It might be helpful to briefly sketch what drilling looked like in the context of these disciplinary formations. It will come as no surprise that these formations were, and still are, deeply related for Iranians. After all, *mashq* (drills) are linked to the Qajar *maydan-i mashq,* "drill square," on the one hand, and to *mashq,* the schoolwork Iranian children lucky enough to get an education take home each day, on the other.

"It is to the military genius of the French," wrote Sheil, "that we are indebted for the formation of the Indian army. Our warlike neighbors were the first to introduce into India the system of drilling native troops and converting them into a regularly disciplined force."[15] The French were also the first to drill Iranian forces (in 1807), although they were not the last. They were followed by British, Russian, Austrian, American, and Swedish advisers, prompting one observer to remark that the Persian army had "been 're-

organized' oftener than any similar body of troops in the world."[16] Yet if Iranian military training was clearly eclectic, the drill provided the element of
continuity. All European advisers regarded the drill as an essential element
of military efficiency. "As the need also arose for military training at the
secondary level," schools and local military units cooperated in staffing
and maintaining a new series of military academies.[17] Prevailing methods
of military drill were often introduced into the physical education programs of schools. "Drill and regular movements of the body" were certainly
requisite parts of any proper education.[18] Mission hospitals, private
schools, and military academies also employed drills. Here drills entered
into programs in more subtle ways. Homework, for example, was a drill, a
process characterized by constant exercise of the mind and the memory.
Similarly, training in personal hygiene, hospital procedures, and laboratory
techniques all involved drills.

What did drills do to people?[19] They regularized each body's posture and
elementary movements, eliminating physically distinctive or expressive
gestures. They standardized the way bodies used objects such as desks, rifles, pens, and soap by breaking apart such actions into smaller units. All
actions were performed according to a timetable that was designed to
make exhaustive use of each moment, not merely prevent idleness. Drills
could be combined for different tasks. Accordingly, people became inter-
changeable in any operation, none being more skilled than others. Finally,
drills rendered people docile. Insofar as drills required an artificial order to
be imposed, a precise system of commands was required. Subjects were
not to try understanding commands; it was enough to perceive a "clear di-
rective"[20] and to react promptly by performing the proper code.

Drilling did not rest well with Iranians at first. For example, in military
life, the ideal warrior fought for his reputation as a brave man. This required distinctive heroic qualities including bold initiative and fearsome
gestures as well as swiftness and skill. To the drill instructor, such behavior
was pathetic. In 1878, the shah retained Lieutenant Colonel Aleksei
Ivanovich Domantovich, a Russian officer, to create a Cossack brigade.
When Colonel Domantovich reviewed the royal cavalry for the first time,
he was horrified by the "sorry sight," which was "full of disorderly gallop-
ing and shouting."[21] What Domantovich admired was the docile and regulated behavior of soldiers, but to the Iranians such docility was unmanly in
the extreme. When 'Abbas Mirza, the crown prince, first started drilling his
troops, the population of Tabriz ridiculed the tame and docile soldiers so
much so that drilling soldiers publicly became impossible.

Drilling required a specific architectural form in Iran not only because it
was requisite for disciplinary training but also because the social forces
that might undermine it had to be kept out. This, at any rate, is the history
of the drill square. The biggest open space in any Iranian city is the

maydan, or "square," and this quickly became the place where soldiers were drilled. However, the idea of a *maydan* exclusively for drills was a nineteenth-century innovation. In 1807, Gore Ouseley reported that 'Abbas Mirza caused his troops "to be drilled in a separate court by themselves in order that they might not be exposed to the ridicule of the populace."[22] A new *maydan* was laid out "for the troops he [was] organizing according to European tactics" and was "surrounded with barracks."[23] During Amir Kabir's reforms, military exercises were also conducted in a separate "parade square."[24] In the mid-1880s, Nasser id-Din Shah ordered the construction of a *maydan-i mashq* at Tehran. This *maydan* was "one of the largest enclosed grounds for maneuvering that there [was] in the world," surpassed only by a similar one in Peking.[25] With the use of the drill system in schools, the open drill square became a requirement of educational architecture. As one subsequent educational reformer complained, "A great many schools have their rooms built around a court in which it is impossible to carry out those physical exercises prescribed by the course of study."[26]

This brings me to the emergence of the modern school building. In Qajar Iran, most education took place in *maktabs*. *Maktabs* were held at any location, including mosques, shops, and private residences. The education they provided was rudimentary, but as Europeans conceded, it was cheap, generally available, and useful.[27] Nevertheless, Europeans maintained, *maktab* education was disorderly and unregulated: "The Moollahs, or candidates for that profession, sit in the school-room, writing lessons or copying books, upon the knee, while the scholars are scattered promiscuously on the rush-mat over the room, all reading aloud—each a different lesson—at the same time; learners constantly swinging the body back and forth as they sit upon the knees and feet, to keep from weariness, and the whole presenting a scene of singular confusion."[28] Given this kind of education, argued Curzon, it was no wonder that the Persian character was "obstinate," "retrograde," and "perfidious."[29] If Persians were to become familiar with "the ways and standards of civilization," it would be necessary to "open the youth of Persia to the benefits of a European education."[30]

Consequently, from the 1850s onward, one finds a new kind of educational structure, the modern school building. It was to be the instrument through which the "receptive, but lazy" Persian character might be corrected.[31] In these new buildings, space was carefully regulated. Classrooms were built around central courtyards for physical drills. Inside, each classroom was organized on a grid pattern and was reasonably well lit. Desks were distributed at regular intervals across the room. Through observation and training, the "dirty, slouchy looking" Persian was transformed into a "trim," regulated, and useful body.[32]

In the new educational regimes, punishment occupied an important place. Punishments were designed to be "derogatory to self-respect" (one would expect this in a status-conscious society). However, punishment struck the "idle" as well as the "insubordinate."[33] Cheaters were punished severely, a novel notion in Iranian education,[34] as was bad posture: "Jordan [the headmaster of Alborz High School] was a strict disciplinarian. He said people must stand straight, they must think straight, they must speak straight. ... And when new students would come in, if he would see anybody slouching over here he would take care of that immediately. ... Ali Akbar was a tall boy and he was all slouched over like this and suddenly something hit him on the back and he looked around and Dr. Jordan said, '*Injah jah barayeh shotor na-darim.*' We don't have any place for camels in here!"[35] Nonconformity became as serious an offense as breaking the rules. At the Dar ul-Fonun, students were punished if they spoke Farsi by eliding their *R*s in the French style rather than by rolling them, as in normal pronunciation.[36]

Punishments included corrective drills such as "standing sentry with a shoulder gun."[37] If a student loaded a cannon in a way that jeopardized the lives of others, that student was placed in the same dangerous position and the drill was repeated.[38] Corporal punishments were administered when disciplinary punishments had failed to achieve a corrective effect and included the bastinado and the cat-o'-nine-tails.[39] At Alborz High School, one of the oldest private secondary schools, a similar "Christian discipline"[40] was administered:

> If a boy became very naughty and needed personal attention, Jordan would take him outside and say, "Now, let your pants down. You are sick. You've done this because you are sick. And you know when you are sick you go to the drug store and get medicine, don't you?" "Yes, sir." "Now I'm going to give you some medicine. This is some black medicine and it will be very helpful to you." And he would take his belt off and would administer what the boy needed. And then he would say to the boy when the medicine had been received, "When you get medicine, do they give it to you or do you pay for it?" "We pay for it, sir." "Now you can pay me two rials for this medicine that I've given you." And he would charge the boy for his punishment which he had given.[41]

Punishments were part of an explicitly stated body of rules. "When they are punished the teacher must make them understand that the punishment is not by caprice but by the community's will formulated in some regulation."[42] School monitors who punished without reason were themselves subjected to punishment.[43] Punishments were always juxtaposed against rewards. Whereas infractions and laziness were punished, "outstanding performances" were distinguished with prizes and gratuities.[44] There was "a policy for eliminating rather than salvaging students who [did] not meet the arbitrary and rather artificial standards of academic excellence."[45] Grading ensured social conformity while at the same time identifying individuals who required disciplinary punishment.[46] Within Iranian disciplinary institutions, fitting the institution's idea of normalcy came to supplement and, in some cases, undermine whatever status or rank an individual might occupy in society.

Imitating Discipline

Perhaps the oddest part of this history of the drill is its profound emptiness. This is a history of exercises without meaning or purpose, soldiers who never fought marching in drill squares and classrooms in which nothing was learned but obedience to authority. What was distinctly lacking from Iranian disciplinary matrices were coherent and sensible programs for linking drills with constant supervision.

This was not because programs were not introduced. In Iran, most disciplinary institutions utilized programs already outlined in European texts. French and Austrian models tended to predominate. Between 1851 and 1914, teachers and students at the Dar ul-Fonun translated books such as *Military Treatise on the Science of Artillery, Austrian Centimetry, Natural Philosophy and Mechanics, Surgery, Elementary and Secondary Geometry, The Science of Artillery and Fortification, Principles of Chemistry, Anatomy, General Regulations and Duties of the Barracks, Infantry Formations: Austrian Method,* and *The Soldier's Whole Duty.*[47] These texts provided the foundations for the programs implemented at the new disciplinary institutions. The subject matters conformed closely to the disciplines being taught at the new schools. Moreover, the texts were published in limited numbers and were rarely distributed to the public. Indeed, "it does not appear ... that the writings of Iranian authors were generally intended for wide distribution. Rather the aim was more generally directed toward utilization by students and teachers at the Dar ul-Fonun."[48]

Programs then did exist. What was missing was any interest in modifying these programs to local conditions or in developing a body of knowledge that would facilitate local efforts in the future. In Europe, such systematic accumulation of knowledge made it possible to measure social phenomena, characterize social trends, analyze gaps between individuals, and judge their distribution within a given population. The social sciences (social work, criminology, social hygiene, military science, statistics, and business administration), in the first instance, were situated near particular institutions (prisons, hospitals, military academies, schools, and factories). These new scholarly disciplines were facilitated by disciplinary matrices and in turn reinforced the practice of discipline through policy formulation and institutional reform.[49]

In Iran, imitation replaced the actual mastery of a program of training. Actual efforts to introduce coherent programs appeared fairly late. The social sciences were introduced initially within a military and political context, but it eventually became clear that "military strength is derived from a varied and interrelated complex of technological and administrative skills, so the government revealed a greater interest in the educational system."[50] The major social scientific disciplines taught at the Dar ul-Fonun and other schools were sciences concerning military administration, strategy, and tactics. In 1901, the School of Political Science was opened by the Ministry of Foreign Affairs and eventually became one of the original colleges of the University of Tehran. In the 1920s, the activities of social scientists were increasingly tied to state efforts to modernize society. The emergence of the state was coextensive with the accumulation of statistical knowledge and the formation of bureaucratic planning. Teams of foreign social scientists, such as the Millspaugh missions, were employed to facilitate economic planning.

Such limited disciplinary coordination, however, fell far short of the perceived needs of the modernization process. In the early 1960s, one Iranian social scientist observed, "The government will have to realize that research in social sciences ... constitutes a most important and indispensable aspect of the dynamic and multi-faceted process of modernization."[51] It was in this context that enrollment in the social sciences was encouraged and expanded throughout the 1960s.[52] In 1968, the shah remarked that just as the natural sciences had ameliorated physical diseases in Iran, the social sciences could play an equally important role in dealing with "social diseases."[53] The range of the social sciences consequently would have to be extended beyond the military, political, and economic contexts. The social sciences were to play an equally important role in new areas such as health, education, family planning, and social work.

Despite the importance of Iranian social science, it was bounded by uncritical emulation and stereotypical education based on Western models. If one attributes this emulation simply to a sense of cultural inferiority, then one fails to recognize that uncritical emulation was understood as part of the positive goal of engendering a disciplinary society. Western disciplines, it was believed, would restore Iran to its rightful place in the world. If Iranians assumed that social progress in Iran would recapitulate European history and would be facilitated by European disciplines, then they were no different from their equally uncritical North Atlantic contemporaries who promoted a disciplinary society. Even when Westerners disagreed about whether progress was unilinear, they never doubted that, as Samuel Huntington remarked, "discipline and development go hand in hand."[54]

CHAPTER 4

Disciplinary Society

Throughout the nineteenth century, many Iranians promoted discipline as a major condition for national power. No less a figure than Malkum Khan, the "Father of the Constitutional Revolution," observed that European nations would not have progressed so far without discipline. The Europeans had progressed, he said, because they had made two kinds of factories: "They have constructed one type of factory out of bodies and metals and the other type, out of individuals, [through which] they have ordered mankind. For example, they have made a factory from wood and iron in which they pour raw wool in one end and collect woolen fabric from the other end, and in the same manner, they have constructed a factory out of mankind in which they put in ignorant babes from one end and bring out engineers and complete administrators from the other."[1] He added that the products of the first kind of factory "are more or less well known in Iran, for example, clocks, guns, telegraphs, and steamships; of this kind of factory we are, in short, well-informed."[2] However, if Iran was to progress, then "currently what is needed in Iran are factories for human beings: such as factories of taxation, factories of armies, factories of justice, factories of knowledge, factories of security, factories of order, and the like."[3]

I employ the term in use at that time, *Nizam-i Jadid*, to describe these changes. This phrase is sometimes translated as New Order or New Army, but it might be better described as New Discipline. Today, one might believe that disciplinary modernization was "inevitable."[4] But the advocates of the New Discipline knew that there was nothing inevitable about it. They were keenly aware of how often disciplinary reforms were opposed and how much violence was needed to keep discipline in place.

In this chapter, I do not intend to look at the spread of the New Discipline as manifesting an immanent historical process. To keep from falling into this way of storytelling, I focus wherever possible on the effects of discipline in local contexts. This focus can reveal interesting historical struggles and the violence sometimes needed to create discipline. I am especially interested in why and when this violence comes to be viewed less as an act of hostility and more as a disciplinary punishment.

I argue that the disciplinary society arises out of diverse self-interested motives. It might be tempting to argue nonetheless that the New Discipline particularly served the needs of capitalist interests. No doubt this was true, but historically capitalists were only one of many groups that introduced disciplinary projects into Iran, and they were among the last. Jalal Al-e Ahmad, one of Iran's most intriguing sociologists, has argued that the process by which discipline was introduced into Iran differed in at least one crucial way from the Western history. "In the West," he writes, "they arrived at regimentation, political parties, militarization via technology and the machine, however, we were just the opposite." Iranians started "from the bottom. That is, starting with the military ... we grow used to lining up, being regimented and uniform, so that as soon as the machine arrives, our progress (i.e., the machine's progress) will not be slowed down. That is the most charitable way I can describe our present-day reality."[5]

Al-e Ahmad is right to distinguish discipline from capital and emphasize the former, as the record shows. The accumulation of disciplined individuals is related but is by no means subservient to the accumulation of capital in the Iranian case. There were periods where discipline was more closely related to capitalism, notably during the Pahlavi period, but one would do well to avoid making an elementary mistake in social scientific explanation. To say that discipline serves the needs of capitalists is not to say that discipline is in the service of capitalists. It may not be possible to have capitalist societies without discipline, but disciplinary societies abound today that are not capitalist. This thought should caution us against assuming that the purpose of discipline today may also axiomatically explain its origin.

How, then, was the New Discipline introduced into Iran? One can specify at least seven different processes of reform: military, political, medical and moral, progressive, penal, police, and tribal and rural.

Military Reforms

One early way in which discipline was introduced into Iran was through military reform. The French military mission in 1807 was the first of several efforts to create armies in the European style for the Qajar shahs. By the early twentieth century, three major subsidiary and quasimilitary units had been trained: the Persian Cossack Brigade (1879), the Gendarmerie (1911), and the South Persia Rifles (1916). They were also initiated for diverse purposes: to challenge foreign enemies, to delight the shah's fancies, to collect revenue, to centralize authority, or to appease imperialist powers,

These facts are well known, but what is less well known is that "military reform weakened Iran from a tactical military point of view, at least in the wars against the Russians in the Caucasus."[6] How could this have happened if discipline is supposed to improve military performance?

Historically, the Qajars counted on several factors in fighting invaders. Weak communication routes, isolated cities, autonomous and potentially hostile tribes, and the difficult terrain of the Iranian plateau all presented sizable obstacles to an invading force. European forces required specific logistical support, and "the lack of compatible organizational capabilities in Iranian society made it extremely difficult for Russian (or British) armies to operate on Iranian soil."[7] Like the modern Afghan *mujahidin*, the troops of the irregular Qajar cavalry were skilled, tough fighters. "They never fought set piece battles and never engaged the enemy except on their own terms."[8] If they were defeated, they could live off the land indefinitely. Thus, "they might be defeated but never conquered. Therein lay their strengths when fighting against Western-styled armed forces."[9] "Persia," as one Russian officer observed, "can be conquered with a single company without firing a shot; with a battalion it would be more difficult; with a whole regiment it would be impossible, for the entire force would perish of hunger."[10]

The early Qajars knew this well, as the following story illustrates. While campaigning against the Russians, Agha Muhammad Khan Qajar urged his chieftains to charge the cannon batteries and cut the soldiers to pieces. Once the enthusiastic chieftains had departed, Agha Muhammad Khan asked his minister if he believed the speech. When the minister said he did, Agha Muhammad Khan retorted; "Are you also a fool? Can a man of your wisdom believe I will ever run my head against their walls of steel, or expose my irregular army to be destroyed by their cannon, and disciplined troops? I know better. Their shots shall never reach me: but they shall possess no country beyond its range. They shall not know sleep; let them march where they choose, I will surround them with a desert."[11]

Such knowledge was lost on the khan's successors. When 'Abbas Mirza decided that "it was in vain to fight the Russians without soldiers like theirs" and reformed his "undisciplined rabble" with the aid of British and French advisers, he unknowingly undermined his military assets.[12] As he destroyed his irregular armies, he was gradually forced into "playing the game by Russian rules and, it might be added, to Russian strength."[13] These reforms delighted the Russians: When "General Yermeloff, the Russian Commander-in-Chief in Georgia, heard that 'Abbas Mirza had begun to form a regular army, he exclaimed, 'God be praised! I shall be able to get at them now, which I never could do before.'"[14]

By engaging in set-piece battles with Russian forces, the Qajar suffered two devastating defeats in 1812 and 1827. As Henry Rawlinson concluded,

"It can be proved that whatever benefits Persia may have derived, as far as regards centralization of the power of her monarch, from the introduction into her armies of European discipline, she has been, as a substantive power, progressively weakened by the change, and rendered less capable of sustaining pressure from without; and it follows therefore that if she had been in danger of absorption under the old system, she must long ere this have ceased to exist under the new."[15]

Qajar military reform, then, is a remarkable example of the "paradox of discipline engendering weakness."[16] But this was not the only way more disciplinary training undermined Qajar rule. Discipline transformed the ways Qajars exercised power domestically, with devastating consequences for public relations. This becomes clear if we look again at the execution of Mirza Reza Kirmani on the gallows in 1896:

> [Mirza Reza Kirmani] was publicly hanged early on the morning of Thursday, the 2nd of *Rabi'i* [August 11, 1896] in the *Maydan-i Mashq*, or "Drill Square," at Tehran, in the presence of a great concourse of people. He was confined the previous night in the Cossack Barracks (*Qazzaq-khana*), and was accompanied to the place of execution by the *Shuja'u's-Saltana*, son of the *Sardar-i Kull*, and sundry kinsmen of the *Aminu's-Sultan*. It was said that Mirza Reza hoped until the last that the *Aminu's-Sultan* would deliver him from death, and that when he saw the gallows and realized he was to die, he tried to speak to the people, but his voice was drowned by the music of a military band.[17]

This was a distinctly political execution with no references made to the ethical and religious aspects of punishment. The ritual at the gallows underlined both how much power the monarchy now had through discipline and at the same time how poorly grounded it was in society. Disciplinary punishments might have illustrated the unregulated power of a despot, but they did not communicate the spectacular violence exercised by a divinely ordained shah. Such violence could not be viewed as legitimate, only as hostile. Discipline had found a place in the selfish aims of the monarchy, but other processes were required before such violence could be viewed as legitimate.

If the new military power did not render Qajar authority more legitimate, did it render that authority more secure? Here is a third way in which discipline engendered weakness. The primary loyalty of disciplined soldiers was to their officers (discipline works, after all, through a chain of organized commands). The officers, however, were foreigners contracted to train troops and possessed only nominal loyalty toward the throne. Consequently, even when disciplined troops were effective, this new security extended, not to the throne, but to the chief officers.

Yet even if discipline had a steadily corrosive effect on political life in the nineteenth century, that development was remarkably accidental. For example, the feared Cossack Brigade began as a ceremonial guard with a marching band. No one suspected that this royal toy had any political abilities since the Russian officers "never had an occasion to demonstrate its qualities except on the parade grounds."[18] All this changed with the sudden death of Nasser id-Din Shah at the hands of an assassin. This event "threatened to loose mobs" throughout Tehran as well as spark a struggle for the throne. The police force was "impotent to control such mobs and the army could not be relied upon."[19] At this moment, the Cossacks stepped into the breach. The royal toy suddenly assumed police and military functions, such as executing punishments, arresting offenders, and disrupting political protests. By 1900, the Cossacks had become the real power brokers in Tehran. One can only speculate about what would have happened to the Cossack Brigade if the shah had died in bed.

Political Reforms

Whereas Qajar shahs turned to discipline to secure their throne, political reformers turned to discipline to show just how vast and arbitrary the power of the shah had become. These reformers were educated in the new disciplinary schools. Although the new schools were established to perpetuate the aristocracy, "glorify the monarchy,"[20] or "train officers,"[21] they had the inadvertent effect of "contributing to the growing intellectual enlightenment."[22] The new schools introduced, among other things, "new concepts, new aspirations, new occupations," and, most important, a new class of intellectuals.[23] These intellectuals, who characterized themselves alternately as *rowshanfekr* and *munavir ul-fekr*, enlightened thinkers, were often the leaders of anti-Qajar protests during the Constitutional Revolution.

By describing themselves as enlightened thinkers, these intellectuals revealed a great deal about themselves. They were claiming not so much that they knew more facts than the traditional literati but that they had a certain superior understanding, an intuitive grasp of the modern state of affairs, and a "qualitative savoir faire to construct a modern society."[24] There was in this assertion the consciousness of a rare freedom: the capacity to act according to one's conscience instead of tradition. There was also an extraordinary sense of responsibility: the duty to reform society. Above all, there was a certainty that "progress was not only possible and desirable, but also easily attainable."[25] Their conscience would drive them to fulfill their duty, carry out their projects, and reform their society; for their conscience had made them regular, orderly, and calculable, even in their own self-image. For these self-disciplining men, a Western education involved not only knowledge but also responsibility and order. "Education, in short, is a social factory that produces not material goods, but responsible citizens and fully developed human beings."[26] Indeed, it was precisely because these intellectuals had become predictable and regularized that they could stand not only for their future but also for the future of others.[27]

These enlightened thinkers saw themselves as better politicians precisely for this reason. In contrast to themselves, the shah behaved capriciously. His politics lacked order and discipline. Malkum Khan, for instance, constantly emphasized the arbitrary nature of royal autocracy, contrasting it with the regularity and predictability of law-abiding citizens like himself:

> Everyone in India, Paris, Tiflis, Egypt, Istanbul, and even among the Turkoman tribes, knows his rights and duties. But no one in Iran knows his rights and duties.
>
> By what law was this mujtahed deported?
> By what law was that officer cut into pieces?
> By what law was this minister dismissed?
> By what law was that idiot given a robe of honor?
>
> The servants of foreign diplomats have more security than the noble princes of Iran.[28]

So subject was the shah to his passions that even if he wanted to, he could not rule effectively:

> *I drink for wine the blood of the people; I eat for*
> *roast meat the flesh of the people;*
> *I have no fear of torment and retribution; do not put*
> *me off with threats of tomorrow's Resurrection!*[29]

One might say that what was being criticized in the shah was not so much a taste for cruelty or a desire to violate "rights" but a poor economy of punishment. The excessive arbitrary power of the shah violated all limits and naturally encouraged protest and disorder.

How might order and security be restored in politics? Malkum Khan proposed "two simple remedies to save Iran: law and more law."[30] Who was to enforce this law? The Constitutionalists resorted to disciplined troops in defense of parliamentary sovereignty and not just to any troops but to the notorious Cossack Brigade. If before the revolution the Cossacks were "the tool of the Shahs in their struggle against the people,"[31] on 16 July 1909, the morning the Royalists were routed from Tehran, the Cossacks became an instrument of the Constitutionalists. After a token submission, the brigade returned to its usual task of "policing the town (to which, naturally, most of the Nationalist warriors were strangers), and in checking looting and disorder."[32] Since "security and order" were the "first conditions of any progress and reform,"[33] the Constitutionalists had no difficulty in treating the Cossacks as the defenders of the Constitution.

Perhaps the Constitutionalists had little choice. Even though they viewed themselves as perfectly decent and self-controlled politicians, they knew that most Iranians did not easily understand what it meant to be a subject under the law. However, if Constitutionalist thinkers did not in fact trust the populace they claimed to represent, then to what exactly did the Constitutionalist reforms amount? "Law and more law" sound intriguing, but what were these laws supposed to do? Laws redescribed political life in terms of the rights and duties of each subject; no exceptions were provided for rulers. Once individuals had responsibilities under the law, it was necessary to find a means by which to make sure individuals were performing their duties responsibly. Supervision became essential in locating responsibility and in holding individuals accountable for their actions. Thus, surveillance would focus not only on immorality but also on corruption, inefficiency, and "delinquencies."[34] The aim of punishment would be to correct these breaches of the law by disciplining individuals. Discipline, in turn, would work by denying or rewarding individuals of their rights under the law.

Law, in short, was a means of enforcing discipline in politics. This was why Malkum Khan differentiated "both religious canons (shari'a) and the old state regulations ('urf)" from the concept of *qanun*, law.[35] Neither of these older forms of law could describe political life with adequate precision to enforce the New Discipline. However, *qanun*s replaced the excessive, arbitrary power of the shah with the sovereignty of the people. They redistributed his power among the people's representatives, who administered the country for the public good. *Qanun*s were enforced through administrative principles, *usul-i idara*.[36] These principles were mapped onto the grid of juridical subjects. They disciplined by depriving delinquent citizens of their rights and by rewarding good citizens and directing them toward public improvement. It was precisely for this reason that, unlike other sorts of law, *qanun*s were "laws that would establish security and thus stimulate progress."[37] More to the point, such laws could be established with precision only by politicians who themselves were disciplined and self-controlled.

The Constitutionalists' great achievement was to redescribe politics in terms of rights and locate the source of these rights in the people. The Constitutionalists justified this change by emphasizing how true laws would bring about order in politics and progress in social life. Discipline was now introduced in the name of the people and their progress. But it would take more than this rhetoric to change how disciplined politicians actually behaved.

Medical and Moral Reforms

Among the dangers posed to Europeans living abroad, disease was among the most constant. The nineteenth century was the century of great epidemics. There were four global cholera pandemics, not to mention general outbreaks of plague, typhus, yellow fever, and smallpox. Aside from these dangers, Europeans stationed overseas had to deal with diseases specific to particular localities, such as malaria and sleeping sickness.

It is not surprising that Europeans should take an interest in transforming the environment in which they lived. Foreign legations began to patrol and monitor their localities for their own sake. Mission hospitals no longer simply cared for the sick. They also directed their efforts in six new directions: "to the preventing and further spread of ... disease," "to visitation of homes," to "patrolling the town for the removal of afflicted persons dying in the streets," to dispensing drugs for the poor, to circulating and collecting information, and to informing and utilizing the offices of local administrators.[38] Dispensaries were added to foreign legations, companies, and communication offices. From 1876 onward, a sanitary council was established at Tehran to handle public health concerns, especially epidemics. The council was composed of European medical officers; although its powers were technically advisory, its decisions were frequently enforced in areas of British and Russian influence. Municipal officers were encouraged to broaden streets and keep them clean. Unofficial quarantine measures were introduced in southern Iranian ports, and sanitary cordons were established along Iran's northern frontier. In 1896, the royal court formally charged British officers with enforcing international quarantine regulations in southern Iran. The quarantine services controlled naval movements and regulated the shipment of corpses to the holy cities of Najaf and Karbella.

Not all this effort can be put down to either charity or fear of disease. Networks of open streets facilitated the rapid deployment of a disciplined military force. Screening procedures helped identify slave traffickers and foreign agents. Control of shipping enabled British officers to "maintain their control of the Gulf," while Russian quarantine services were used "to strangle British trade from Northwest India."[39] Legation doctors served as "medium[s] of confidential intercourse between the Mission and the Shah"[40] and as means of access "to many leading Tehran families who trusted their medical skills."[41] Medical inspectors served as spies.[42] Finally, medical services were utilized "in the interests of trade promotion."[43] For example, the Anglo-Persian Oil Company employed a "Political and Medical Officer" to help secure the goodwill of local tribal khans.[44] As a doctor of the British legation remarked, "The objective of both Russians and British was the security and supremacy of their own trade. In passing judgement upon the high-handed action of the Persians 20 years later when they ejected both Russian and British medical officers with small thanks, the political motives underlying the foreign sanitary intrusion into their country should not be forgotten."[45]

In fact, medical surveillance frequently met with local opposition. In 1899, British attempts to take measures against an epidemic of the plague were met with "unconcealed" hostility by villagers and sparked riots in Bushehr.[46] In 1906, the Tehran Sanitary Council established a sanitary cordon in Khurasan against another plague epidemic and met with similar resistance: "So effective and so unpleasant was their method of isolation and disinfection that at the end of March, the people of Nasratabad could stand it no longer, rose in a body and destroyed the isolation huts. At the same time, they vented their wrath on the foreigner by destroying the British Consulate Dispensary and by a half-hearted attack on the Consulate itself."[47]

Occasionally, opposition took more subtle forms. For example, in 1813, in the midst of a smallpox epidemic, British doctors in Tehran began inoculating children against the disease. The Qajar court quickly dispatched agents to the consulate. While ostensibly acting as assistants to the legation, "their true purpose was to prevent any woman who brought he• child for inoculation" from gaining access to the embassy.[48]

As Iranians came to perceive foreign aid more suspiciously, they formed their own self-help societies. The Society of Muhammad sought to enforce public morality and check the spread of heathen ideas.[49] The *Shirkat-i Islami* (Islamic Corporation) sought to "preserve the country's independence by fostering such modern industries as textiles and by protecting the traditional handicrafts, particularly the miniature arts."[50] The Society of Learning sought to encourage parents to send their children to modern schools and collected "taxes" from merchants and shopkeepers to this end.[51] Finally, many societies had direct political intentions: to keep abreast of the Qajar court's activities, collect and publish political information, and organize social protests against state corruption.[52]

One can see the impact of such societies in the Great Tobacco Rebellion of 1891. In March 1890, the shah granted to a British subject a monopoly on the production, sale, and export of tobacco. Religious leaders and political opponents of the regime argued that the tobacco concession was against Shi'i law as well as free trade principles asserted by the West. Furthermore, many Iranians grew, sold, and used tobacco, and the notion that an infidel would be handling an item used daily by Iranians raised issues of religious purity.

Such circumstances would have triggered mass protests in any case. What was peculiar about the Tobacco Rebellion was that the protests were well coordinated and local enforcement was remarkably efficient. When British agents arrived in April 1891 in Shiraz, the center of tobacco cultivation in Iran, the central bazaar shut down. News of the strike was telegraphed to other cities, where merchants enforced similar strikes. Furthermore, the movement organized a strict national boycott on the sale and use of tobacco that lasted several months. The boycott involved supporting those poor merchants adversely affected by the strike so that they would not open their stores and as zealously discouraging those who continued to peddle or use tobacco. The boycott was so well enforced that even non-Muslims and the shah's wives stopped using tobacco! In the end, the tobacco concession was repealed, and the Great Tobacco Rebellion went down in Iranian history as the "first successful mass protest in modern Iran, combining ulama, modernists, merchants and ordinary townspeople in a co-ordinated move against government policy."[53]

What emerged toward the end of the nineteenth century, then, was a society in which movement, space, and behavior were more strictly controlled. This change occurred despite, and usually in response to, the decay of the Qajar state, such as it was. This situation was partly the result of Europeans' desire to control the environment and partly the result of Iranians' equally fervent desire to keep foreigners out. This change is important because discipline requires the ability to survey and correct the behavior of others within as well as beyond institutions. Policing is a classic example of how many individuals are brought under observation. Long before the advent of state policing, policing was already being carried out by many private and foreign organizations.

Progressive Reforms

So far I have been concerned with how specific groups seized on discipline as a way of governing situations they believed to be dangerous and uncertain. Qajars hoped discipline would defeat foreign armies and control mobs. Reforming elites hoped it would restrain the arbitrary rule of kings. Foreigners hoped it would minimize disease and economic competition. Local societies hoped it would keep the foreigners' influence in check.

Yet the New Discipline was appealing as well because it could make Iran strong again. When on a winter day in February 1921, Colonel Reza Khan Pahlavi marched on Tehran with his Cossack Brigade, he made it his task to fortify Iranian society, not merely protect it. He declared that "he was tired of weak governments and was determined to establish a strong one that would be ready to oppose the Bolshevik advance."[54] Military discipline would produce stronger soldiers and therefore a more efficient military machine. Educational discipline would create useful citizens.

The turn to productive use of discipline brought about a fundamental change in the ways Iranians saw themselves. Henceforth, to be modern meant that one was sane, healthy, orderly, educated, disciplined, and useful, whereas to remain traditional meant that one was insane, diseased, disorderly, undisciplined, ignorant, and useless. To be found wanting in this respect was almost to be asking for correction of the way one lived one's life. In the rhetoric of the New Discipline, modernity functioned as a norm, and this norm could be, and often was, invoked as a justification for repression and further discipline.

A brief survey of different political platforms over the past century will confirm just how closely modernity was associated with discipline. Constitutionalists were probably the first to appeal to the norm of modernity when they described the Qajars as lunatics with "disordered dream[s]"[55] or as "microbes in the belly of the Commonwealth."[56] The Constitutionalists, by contrast, were healthy and sane politicians.

Moderate socialist parties located Iranian backwardness in the undisciplined masses or, even worse, in corrupt popular traditions that kept Iran from the arrival of the modern Parousia: "If we desire to remedy the ills of Iran like true statesmen, we must focus our attention on the source of the malady—on the masses. We must save the people from corrupting superstitions, instill in them a love for their country, arouse in them the instinct for social progress, teach them to make personal sacrifices, and, most important of all, unite them into a nationally conscious people."[57] Nationalists identified ethnic difference with lack of modernity and demanded nationalist discipline: "The problem of communalism is so serious that whenever an Iranian travelling abroad is asked his nationality, he will give his locality—not the proud name of his country. We must eliminate local sects, local dialects, local clothes, local customs, and local sentiments."[58] Conservatives were even more forthright in advocating enforced disciplinization: "Our only hope is a Mussolini who can break the influence of traditional authorities and thus create a modern outlook, a modern people, and a modern nation."[59]

On the Left, the Tudeh, or Masses Party, hoped to create "a modern society, a socially conscious public, and an economically useful citizenry"[60] through the formation of a disciplined mass party organization. On the Right, advocates of the new monarchy maintained that the shah could effect a modern society precisely because he recognized that Iran needed disciplined experts, not amateur democrats: "The whole trouble with this country is that amateurs like you are sticking their noses in politics. Electrical and civil engineers should spend their time building houses and bridges, instead of sitting here and shooting off their mouths on state issues and other matters they know nothing about. If everyone did what they were trained to do, the country would not presently be in such a sorry condition."[61] Thus, discipline was identified with normality; normality, with modernity; and modernity, with the right to rule.

What does it mean to say that modernity functions as the regulative norm in Iranian politics? It means, in part, that modernness (to use an awkward word for lack of a better one) serves as a principle of coercion. Norms are powerful because they make it possible to compare, measure, or rank individuals, families, and communities. They also serve to indicate precisely what must change in the relationship individuals bear to themselves and to each other. They justify institutional intervention to homogenize populations. As Muhammad Reza Shah put it so succinctly, "We must straighten out Iranians' ranks. To do so, we must divide them."[62] And this is precisely what occurred in Iran in the early twentieth century. In hospitals, the sick were divided from the healthy. In mental asylums, the mad were distinguished from the sane. In "normal schools,"[63] the undisciplined and maladjusted were separated from the disciplined. In "Normal Court[s],"[64] the delinquent and the criminal were isolated from the obedient. Finally, it became possible to distinguish all these groups not only within institutions but also in society at large. This brings me to the prison and the police.

Penal Reforms

There have always been prisons in Iran. To understand when the Iranian prison became a disciplinary institution, one needs to inquire when the prison became a place where individuals were reformed. Discipline and torture, after all, were both highly corporal ways of exercising power. The difference, in part, lies in the way these were exercised on individuals. Traditional Qajar torture was not concerned with reforming the individual; discipline was. Disciplinarians took apart and reassembled individual habits, minds, and lives. This is why they required such intense forms of supervision, judgment, and correction.

In the late nineteenth century, most cities had public stocks "where vulgar criminals may be seen with iron collars around their necks, sometimes their feet in stocks, and attached to each other by iron chains."[65] Women and "male criminals of high rank" were detained in the houses of the 'ulema, this detention reflecting higher status and milder punishment.[66] Some offenders might be incarcerated in the shah's dungeons, but, as Curzon remarked, "there is no such thing as penal servitude for life, or even a term of years; hard labour is unknown as a sentence, and confinement for any period is rare." Persian punishment was in "no sense a reformation of the culprit."[67] Eventually, the old Qajar dungeons were destroyed in the interests of modern city planning, and the public stocks were walled off from the public. In the early twentieth century, a new prison was constructed in Tehran, but there is no evidence that it was anything more than a holding cell.

Under the reign of Reza Pahlavi, one does find reformatories, most notably Qasr prison. Was the prison-reformatory the invention of the Pahlavi dynasty? No, for there were several institutions during the late Qajar period in which corrective detention was practiced. Although these institutions were not directly connected with the penal apparatus, they provided the models for the new disciplinary prison.

Shortly after the Constitutional period, the Tehran municipality established several charitable projects to assist the poor. The new projects included a workhouse, an orphanage, a lunatic asylum, an arts and crafts school, and "employment schemes for the unemployed."[68] These municipal programs were designed to reform Iranians and put them to productive tasks:

If you look at the deeds of Despotism and Constitutionalism
The differences between Despotism and Constitutionalism are countless.
In the days of Despotism they sought dogs for the chase:
In the days of Constitutionalism they seek men for work![69]

The Constitutionalists were the first Iranians to try reforming individuals through corrective detention. They focused on beggars, women, unemployed workers, and abandoned children. Philanthropic activities, both private and municipal, were directed at teaching individuals a skill that might assist them in earning a living. The Constitutionalists also fostered discipline by engaging workers and training them to inspect themselves. As fear of superiors led each worker to anticipate their external gaze, she would begin to inspect herself, to supervise her own actions through an inner eye, which one might call a conscience.

During the Pahlavi period, prisons assumed this reformatory principle. Like the workhouse, the orphanage, and the crafts school, the prison introduced order, training, or "forced labour."[70] It intensified subjection and docility while at the same time increasing utility. Although prison labor was not economically profitable and often failed to transmit useful skills, it did create a useful human body, one that could be inserted into educational, military, or industrial machines.

By the early Pahlavi period, classical Iranian torture had disappeared. One cannot credit the Pahlavis easily with its disappearance. However, the Pahlavis did build many prisons. Through their efforts, the small network of town prisons gave rise to a vast penal archipelago. In 1925, Qasr prison, the first long-term penitentiary-workhouse in Iran, was established at Tehran. By the 1930s, Iran had created a penal system composed of short-term prisons, court prisons, penitentiaries, and labor camps. In 1975, exactly fifty years after Qasr prison was founded, the deputy director of the General Prison Department estimated that there were six thousand prisons spread throughout Iran.[71]

In this program, the Pahlavis received support from all Iranian parties because the reformatory prison fit into plans for modernizing individuals and supported the new legal regime advocated by reformers. This program had significant implications for punishment in Iranian society. Torture in the early Qajar period was distinguished from discipline precisely because it did not reform individuals. Reformatory violence, in turn, was viewed as legitimate, progressive, and humane. But this left the prison door open for a form of violence that, while not disciplinary, did seem to change individuals into useful social instruments. This was modern torture, and the reformatory prison was not just accidentally the place where a "takeoff" in new techniques of torture occurred.

Police Reforms

Police officers watch. This is not the only thing they do, but surveillance brings out what is special about modern police officers. Police surveillance is specialized, coordinated, proactive, and hidden in the everyday. One might contrast this with the typical person entrusted with community security in a traditional Iranian community, the *darugha*.

The *darugha* "paraded through the streets and bazaars in the daytime and at night," settling disputes according to informal rules of propriety.[72] His *ferrashes* (attendants) and *mir asas* (nightwatchmen) would patrol the streets singing loudly and pounding the walls with heavy clubs. Contrast this with the inobtrusive police officer who blends in with the crowd. This officer is a coordinated part of a disciplined corps. He is entrusted with more than catching the visible disturbance; he confirms suspicions and registers possible future dangers. The police force is not the only group capable of this sort of surveillance, as I have observed. What is distinctive about the police is that it coordinates its surveillance for bureaucracies, ensuring that decisions at the center are performed at the local level. That is why "one of the characteristics that mark a nation is, clearly, the possession of a national police system."[73]

Police forces, then, do not simply protect, punish, and enforce the law. They also survey, control, examine, and fortify society. Their activity extends to all areas of state concern, including health, education, economics, politics, and social custom. "The purpose of policing is to ensure the good fortune of the state through the wisdom of its regulations and augment its forces and its power to the limits of its capability. The science of policing consists therefore in regulating everything that relates to the present condition of society, strengthening and improving it, in seeing that all things contribute to the welfare of the members that compose it. The aim of policing is to make everything that composes the state serve to strengthen and increase its power, and likewise serve the public welfare."[74] This is the original European sense of policing, not the model that came to predominate in the United States, which gives a much more limited role to the police. And the role given to police surveillance in Iranian society was modeled on the European approach.[75]

In the 1890s, the Qajar court recruited Italian advisers to establish a security force. The new Tehran police introduced street patrols in upper-class neighborhoods and assumed control of the enclosed stocks and prisons. The Cossack Brigade ran security in other areas, boasting of the discipline it had brought to urban life since 1896. "At the time of the accession of the late Nasser id-Din," remarked Colonel Kosagovskij of the Cossack Brigade, "10,000 people had been killed throughout Persia; at the accession of this Shah—not one."[76] British and Russian troops enforced order in southern and northern Iranian cities, respectively. The Constitutionalists, aided by American advisers, established a treasury gendarmerie in 1909 to collect taxes and eventually organized a national gendarmerie with the aid of Swedish military advisers. The Swedes founded a college for police officers in 1915, established a police hospital, and organized Iran's first secret police, the T'aminaat, or "Securities."

In 1921, the Ministries of War and Interior assumed control of all these organizations. With the assistance of French and, subsequently, German officers, the Gendarmerie-Police complex, the Cossack Brigade, and the various provincial forces were integrated into a single arrangement. Moreover, police forces became increasingly specialized and tailored to the needs of specific bureaucracies. The new paramilitary complex soon included a national police; a rural gendarmerie; a railroad police; a customs police; the Amniyya, or "Road Guard"; and the Red Lion and Sun Society, a mobile medical service attached to the Ministry of War. The T'aminaat also persisted and was transformed into the Kar Agahi (Intelligence Agency).

Since police forces appear to increase the power of specific bureaucrats, it is not surprising that state officials rarely opposed new policing forces and often wholeheartedly encouraged them. The new police officers were posted at crossroads, registering legal infractions, examining circumstances surrounding accidents, and enforcing modern dress codes. They moved in mobile units, investigating crimes, drafting tribesmen into military service, enforcing health and sanitary regulations, destroying squatter settlements, and inspecting schools, baths, and brothels. They screened how travelers moved, how diseases spread, how goods were registered, and where suspicious characters went. In short, they composed an active, uninterrupted gaze.

However, police forces are not simply a means the bureaucrat and the politician can use to their own ends. The bureaucrat and the politician can be the objects of police surveillance as much as anyone else can; they are not autonomous and separate from the way police power may be organized. Furthermore, police forces instigate their own procedures and act on supposedly higher institutions. Police surveillance brings its own disciplinary norms to bear on the everyday, focusing on the "filth and irregular" lives that cause "foreigners to think that Iran was a backward country."[77]

Because police are proactive, they try to locate and give shape to new criminals: delinquents, drug addicts, vagrants, squatters, fanatics, subversives, and nomads. These identifications become the terms in which judges and bureaucrats pass laws. And who would know more about such figures than the policemen who work so closely with such criminals? For police work is not only proactive, normalizing, and coordinated; it is also specialized, and this provides a certain degree of expertise.

The main point to be made is this: Although the state reorganized the police in such a way that it became contiguous with society, the state did not control disciplinary power. Discipline is a modality of power that can also be exercised in independent, enclosed institutions, such as schools, prisons, and hospitals. It may circulate within families, embedding itself in the old patriarchal structures regulating family life, particularly the relationship between parents and children. It can be used by traditional organizations, such as religious foundations, to ensure the proper functioning of their authority. Even the police, closely associated with the state, can function and act on the state in ways that are autonomous. In short, the state cannot on its own create discipline; rather, it thrives on discipline and can even at times be overwhelmed by the disciplinary organizations that make the state possible.

Tribal and Rural Reforms

The rise of a disciplinary state made possible a control over rural life that had not been possible before in Iranian politics. Biological pressures had exerted themselves for generations on Iranians in rural areas, but now the state came to replace Allah and fortune as the source of beneficence and poverty. State concern for life could be felt both in relation to individuals and to populations as a whole. At the local level, disciplinary efforts sought to ensure good health, foster strong bodies, fortify diets, and produce intelligent minds. At the level of populations, policing operations gathered a huge statistical text on biological life. Administrative procedures were developed to manage populations, natural resources, livestock, diseases, and ecological disasters. Life itself was examined, probed, and manipulated, sometimes severely so.

The new capacity to master life could be used for good or ill. On the one hand, it could be used to fortify life processes: "One is amazed at the high level of centralization achieved within the last decade. The government now interferes in practically all aspects of daily life. Land is contracted for cash by the government, fruits get sprayed, crops fertilized, animals fed, beehives set up, carpets woven, goods sold, babies born, populations controlled, women organized, religion taught, and diseases cured—all by the intervention of the government."[78] On the other hand, it could be employed to abandon living beings until they eliminated themselves. For example, during the 1930s Reza Shah initiated several campaigns against autonomous tribes. Rather than employ the army to eliminate the tribes, the Iranian military cut off the migration routes of tribes and starved them into submission. For state bureaucrats, the ability to control agricultural resources and manipulate populations "was social engineering on a grand scale."[79] Yet on the tribal reservations, one found no happy peasants, only starving pastoralists. And in villages that bureaucrats considered marginal, "the overall effect of the government's agricultural policies was to increase the difficulties most peasants experienced in trying to make a livelihood from their landholdings."[80]

Regardless of how one uses such power, this way of exercising power imposes its own internal norms. Power does not function here in terms of the old Qajar power of taking life or letting live. This new way of exercising power serves to "foster life or disallow it to the point of death."[81]

It is tempting to locate the rise of bio-power in relation to capitalism. Development programs required a calculus for administering human beings that ensured capital accumulation for financing economic growth. Western technologies required "increasing efficiency," "changes in scale," and precise, regular laborers.[82] New means of training were necessary to handle increasingly more complex weapons, economic machinery, medical procedures, and academic knowledge. Bio-power provided administrative procedures necessary for capital accumulation. It introduced "mechanisms of integration and social control" compatible with social and economic development.[83] It promoted a "system of norms and social sanctions appropriate to higher levels of development."[84]

All this, however, lay very much in the future. Historically, bio-power emerged in another sort of context. It was connected with a growing fear of the large, disorderly populations that controlled the cities and the countryside. From 1900 to 1920, Iran was "a hotbed of misrule, enemy intrigue, financial chaos, and political disorder."[85] Country bandits and tribal wars rendered the transport of goods and supplies extremely difficult. Huge urban protests made propertied families fear that "Bolshevik poison was rapidly working among the populace." Subsidiary military organizations grew disgusted with weak central governments and a Qajar shah who was "so nervous for his own safety that he was no longer accessible to reason."[86] A specifically antinomadic political technique was needed, and discipline provided it. Disciplined forces controlled tribal and urban populations in new ways, forcing them into smaller, tighter spaces. As General Edmund Ironside realized in 1921, "A military dictatorship would solve our troubles and let us out of the country without any trouble at all."[87] Similarly, in 1922, two hundred merchants addressed a letter to Reza Khan praising him for his introduction of order: "Before our beloved commander saved us, the Islamic Empire of Iran was fast disintegrating. The army had collapsed, the tribes were looting, the country was the laughing stock of the world. Thanks to the army commander, we now travel without fear, admire our country, and enjoy the fruits of law and order."[88] Disciplinary society had arrived.

Disciplinary Society

Think for a moment of the tremendous transformation that occurred in the course of a century. A hundred years ago shopkeepers made fun of soldiers drilling, religious leaders dismissed self-disciplined reformers, families treated doctors with suspicion, villages reacted with anger at quarantine regulations, and populations reacted with horror and hostility to the violence a disciplined force could effect. It would be hard to capture the world in which such attitudes characterized daily life, one in which discipline was always viewed as something alien. Nor does returning to such a world strike me as something desirable.

We are inclined at any rate to say that such a world vanished for reasons having to do with the superiority of the New Discipline to the old ways in bringing about all the ends desired by Iranians. There is room, nonetheless, for considerable doubt. Military discipline did not strengthen the Iranian state but weakened it. Prisons controlled criminals but did not necessarily improve them. Education made for more obedient students but not necessarily for more accomplished ones with greater depth and learning. Quarantines were effective at controlling trade but not necessarily at eliminating disease. Modern doctors did force out traditional practitioners but not without the help of a state enforcing educational requirements and controlling licensing. Disciplined politicians did not turn out to be better than the corrupt Qajar court at running politics. Economic discipline may have enriched some factory managers but did not bring about the degree of material progress that was expected; oil money was required for that. Police power may have helped extend the power of state bureaucracy, but it worked as well to disempower each specific bureaucrat and render him a hapless toady.

To put it another way: Iranians who turned to the New Discipline believed that it would help them *know* more about the world in which they lived, *control* the processes that affected their lives, and allow them to *judge* the appropriate means to attain their ends in this context. However, to say that Iranians today understand, control, and judge the context of their lives cannot be endorsed without great qualifications.

Do Iranians know more about the modern world through discipline? Discipline no doubt allows for a greater accumulation of information, but it also requires intense specialization for each individual. A person in a large disciplinary organization knows less than a craftsperson or the traditional religious scholar about the processes that affect his or her life. Just how ignorant Iranians have become of the processes that affect their lives can be recognized by how quickly one can get lost in the maze of bureaucratic offices in downtown Tehran when one has the least problem to settle.

Do Iranians have better control of the processes that now affect their lives? Disciplinary organizations have certainly made it possible to control many distinct social and economic processes, but efforts to manage them can bring about unintended consequences. The size that such planning efforts require raises new problems and requires greater efforts at coordination. Coordination, however, can be fragile and unpredictable, requiring new inventions by disciplinary organizations. The cycle seems endless.

Can Iranians determine the ends to which disciplinary organizations will be used? Disciplinary organizations have their own internal norms, which resist guidance by outsiders. The people who work within these organizations are either too detached from daily operations to care or too specialized to notice what is happening to the organizations as a whole. Not surprisingly, disciplinary organizations do not necessarily perform precisely what they were designed to do and can often fail to transfer even the basic skills with which they were entrusted. Iranian education is a paradigmatic case in point. Furthermore, precisely because disciplinary organizations operate on their own internal norms, they are not neutral with respect to the ends for which they are used. The Qajar kings would no doubt have a great deal to say about the disciplined military in this respect.

The transfer of discipline, like that of technology, has not delivered on its promise, but this situation is nothing new. What is interesting is that each failure brought about a new push for more discipline; the failure itself was attributed to the backwardness of Iranians. Why were Iranians backward? They were not modern, surely. It is hard to gain a critical distance on this point, to reflect on how discipline itself was never the panacea it was claimed to be and to recognize how much self-deception and violence were required to keep the issue from coming up.

Iranians have such a stake in the New Discipline that it would be hard to imagine Iranians without it. Iranians are dependent on what disciplinary institutions have to offer, for example, health, security, and education. They earn their livelihoods principally by working in disciplinary institutions, submitting to the training and correction that are required. Discipline has become second nature. Furthermore, Iranians define the ends they pursue in terms of the means provided by disciplinary institutions. Whatever alternative institutions Iranians imagine, these political utopias are shot through with discipline. As Al-e Ahmad remarks, "Attendance at party meetings and unions which require uniformity in dress, gesture, greeting and thought is also a 'third nature' conforming to the machine."[89]

CHAPTER 5

Carceral Society

If Iranian society was in the process of becoming a disciplinary society, then how did torture become a normal part of the way the new state governed its population? The opposite conclusion—namely, that torture would disappear as the state became more modern, disciplined, and rationalized—would have seemed the expected result. The task of this chapter is to locate torture in relation to disciplinary society, and to do that I compare the disciplinary institutions with the political system in which torture occurred. Perhaps one may get a better grasp of torture in this period by considering what these institutions shared.

Approaching torture in this way is not typical. When analysts look at torture in modern Iran, they distinguish sharply between civil crimes and political crimes. They posit the existence of a civilian legal and prison system that was adequate, although inefficient, on the one hand, and the presence of a political prison system with its own rules and modes of operation, on the other. Such an approach seems to me to be premature since the Iranian government itself did not consider the distinction between the two systems to be nearly as sharp. Political prisoners were often incarcerated alongside common criminals. SAVAK (The National Information and Security Organization) was not the civilian police, but its duties carried over into diverse aspects of civilian affairs, including control of the narcotics trade and the welfare system for factories. A worker guilty of theft was treated differently from a wildcat striker, but this distinction was part of a general scheme of illegalities that included prostitutes, students, drug traffickers, murderers, and the mentally ill.

If one is to grasp the place of torture in a disciplinary society, one needs to consider the agent's point of view at least as a preliminary step. One can debate later whether the agent's point of view—here the perspective of those who disciplined and tortured—is the best point of view for understanding torture. In any case, to posit a sharp distinction between civil and political systems creates some serious difficulties in analyzing torture. For one thing, torture is said to belong to a political prison system about which little is known, except through prejudiced sources. Since one can compare it with nothing else other than equally obscure systems elsewhere, torture becomes unanalyzable. One can get no farther than emphasizing the mysterious and horrifying side of what is already mysterious enough. Furthermore, analysts may miss features that are shared between the civilian and the political prison systems. To the extent that analysts do register such common elements, the scheme under which they operate leads them to treat any use of a civilian technique in political prisons as a perverse accident. In short, by distinguishing sharply between civil and political prison systems, analysts ignore and apologize for the place torture occupies within a disciplinary society.

Such effort would be better placed at capturing what the systems have in common. My goal in this chapter is to map, through a series of examples, some of the essential techniques that most easily spread from one policing activity to another. These techniques are minute, detailed, and everyday. They show how people were constrained or learned to constrain themselves in relation to these techniques. To this extent, these techniques illustrate a way of thinking and behaving, a rationality, if you will, constitutive of modern torture.

How might this rationality be distinguished? It can be characterized in terms of the element on which procedures were applied and from which knowledge was gathered: the psyche. It can be identified in the terms of the practices employed to open the private concerns of bodies to public controls: the psychological and medical disciplines. It can be characterized in the terms of the social data that are produced: human profiles or life histories of individuals. Finally, it can be distinguished in the terms of a minute circuit, the "case file," which constitutes a form of knowledge and a means of transformation.

The Model of Delinquency

Between 1920 and 1975, the government introduced broad measures to clean up milieus of delinquency in Iranian society. Prostitutes were confined in police-supervised brothels. Beggars and criminal gangs were relegated to leper colonies, labor camps, prisons, and hospital barracks for the retarded. Abandoned and retarded children were gathered in orphanages and nurseries to prevent them from leading wayward lives. Addicts and mentally abnormal individuals were quarantined for therapeutic rehabilitation in asylums.

Yet as early as the 1940s, it was evident that these measures neither reformed individuals nor diminished the crime rate. In fact, if carceral institutions were contributing to any process at all, it was to maintain, augment, and produce delinquencies. Critics pointed to a number of problems with incarceration.

Carceral institutions constituted in themselves milieus of delinquency. They bred promiscuity (homosexuality, prostitution, abuse of retarded children), immorality (pregnant or addicted children, married women leading lives of prostitution), and crimes (theft, murder, and the creation of juvenile gangs) and spread diseases (typhus and syphilis).[1] "Who is it that has not inspected our prisons, asylums, and hospitals, and has not felt the enormous and horrifying danger posed by these improprieties and diseases which unfit habitats and people's neglect of the societal and municipal environment have fostered?"[2]

Carceral regimes often failed to reform individual behavior. Within forced labor programs, individuals occupied the place of "slaves," a place that invariably bred resentment and resistance.[3] These individuals rarely received skills that would enable them to earn a living on release. Personnel were unqualified, poor, or addicted to opium. They failed to care for the destitute in their charge (nurseries, leper colonies, orphanages, and barracks) or made profits out of human misery (brothels, addict barracks, pauper asylums, and prisons). "We should not praise ourselves by saying that once upon a time Cyrus the Great conquered the whole world. In what other country can you find so many traitors, adulterers, and embezzlers all immune from punishment?"[4]

Carceral institutions professionalized delinquents. Children born into brothels and pauper asylums were likely to pursue the same activities as their parents.[5] In turn, "antisocial" children "gathered by the police in courthouses and prisons are being exposed to an enormous danger since as a result of their association with other delinquents, they will commit repeated and more serious offenses."[6] Similarly, arrested political dissidents used prison to study and make contacts with other dissidents. "It was in prison where everything started," remarked one famous old dissident. "Or rather, it was the authorities who claimed that our group was a party. In fact, there never was a party at all."[7] Some organizations even had communes in every major prison, recruiting newcomers and providing pamphlets on what to expect in prison.[8]

Incarceration created recidivists, especially in the case of addicts and ex-convicts. Lacking employment and unable to move to other areas to earn a living, individuals were likely to engage in the same criminal activities and circulate among institutions during the course of their lives. In this manner, the state was paying the high costs of arresting, detaining, and supporting recidivists.[9] Incarceration also impoverished families by removing the breadwinner, forcing the families of prisoners to lead lives of crime and delinquency.[10] Sometimes poor families deliberately had dependents incarcerated to avoid paying for their sustenance.[11]

These criticisms of disciplinary institutions should be seen in the context of even graver protests against the government. Iranian modernization had been characterized by unrelenting discipline under Reza Shah. Factory workers had been subjected to inflexible disciplinary training that had transformed them from undisciplined peasants into a productive work force. However, disciplinization created not only solidarity among workers but also greater mechanical coordination. In fact, the industrial strike was the predicate of disciplinary training. The organization of demonstrations, the enforcement of picket lines, and the policing of strike discipline would not have been possible without the creation of a disciplined work force. In efforts to avoid communist insurrection and encourage modernization, Iranian politicians had managed to create what they feared most, Marx's reserve army of the unemployed.

Universities, too, became places where dissidents met and protested against the state. Universities sought to create specialists for the modernizing effort, but like the factory and the prison, the university also professionalized student activism. When the students were violently repressed, the professional activists resorted to armed struggle. Here was another unexpected result of disciplinary institutions, guerrilla warfare.

Another new illegality arose out of the government's success in breaking down tribal resistance to the centralized state. Tribes, unable to resist the state's new disciplinary powers and yet unwilling to change their way of life, turned to smuggling. Many, of course, were forced to settle in tribal encampments, but others smuggled slaves, guns, and, increasingly, drugs. Drug smuggling operations had two major effects on modernization programs. First, drug addiction impeded modernization efforts by lowering economic productivity.[12] In 1945, the Society Against Opium and Alcohol estimated that there was a daily loss of 500,000 work hours that could be directly traced to addiction.[13] Second, drug smuggling cut into the state revenues collected from opium cultivation, revenues that financed modernization. Police efforts to crush drug smuggling contributed indirectly to the expansion of the black market in narcotics. This market not only exploited the needs of addicts but, by the 1950s, was also beginning "to have a definite impact on Iran's balance of payments in that large amounts of gold were leaving the country to pay for smuggled drugs."[14] The tribes, even in their weakened condition, had found a new way of undermining the power of the disciplined state.

Carceral institutions shared an important feature with factories, universities, and tribal settlements. In these institutions, discipline was viewed not as a just punishment, but as an act of hostility. Unexpectedly, disciplinary institutions professionalized resistance to the state. What distinguished students, tribespeople and workers from delinquents, however, was that they questioned the law in a more thoroughgoing manner; they questioned not only the legal claim to punish the specific crime but also the very legal claim to punish. By contrast, delinquents had few political objectives. They were an economic burden but not a serious obstacle to government programs. They were unable or unlikely to organize themselves into a political movement. The conditions imposed on their liberty enabled the police to locate, arrest, isolate, and coerce them. In contrast to students, smugglers, and strikers, delinquents constituted an asocial, apolitical, and dependent illegality.

Is this a significant difference? Yes, because delinquency presents us with a model for treatment of other opponents to the government. If opponents could not be reformed by being placed in institutions, they could be rendered ineffective and unable to hamper government objectives. When it was impossible to change someone, he or she could at any rate be rendered neutral.

Three changes signal this shift from improving an individual's character through discipline to rendering that person impotent and harmless. One is a greater emphasis on the technology of rehabilitation, and a good example of this was Iran's drug maintenance and rehabilitation system. In less than twenty years, the Iranian government moved from a laissez-faire policy with regard to drugs to a complete prohibition and finally to a massive drug maintenance and rehabilitation program. This latter policy included the use of a methadone maintenance program as well as specialized training for Iranian narcotics officers through U.N. technical assistance programs. In less than twenty years, the Iranian addict population was reduced from, conservatively speaking, 1.5 million (in 1955) to 400,000 (in 1974).[15] Medical technology thus came in to fill the gap that discipline had left behind.

Another indication of this change was the new emphasis on reducing the costs of incarceration by ensuring a degree of self-monitoring on the part of delinquents. Between 1959 and 1975, the Iranian prison system underwent four major reforms. One result of these reforms was an extensive system of "open prisons." The model of the open prison had been developed initially during the 1960s by American critics of closed prison systems. In open prisons, prisoners were neither systematically supervised nor forced to wear prison garb. Quite frequently, they were not expected to return to their prisons for the evening and were permitted to spend "the night in hutments provided for this purpose." Although prisoners were expected to find work on the outside, they often could not except in state programs, a feature that led one European jurist to characterize the system as one of "semiliberty" rather than one of "external work."[16] Disciplinary work within the prison was not replaced with productive external work; rather, the convicts were left dependent on the system but not necessarily monitored by it. The government also persistently rejected proposals to suspend sentences of prisoners when they had an exemplary record of good behavior. The model of the open prison, in these respects, signaled a change in the notion of how much policing was required as well as a growing skepticism about the effectiveness of prison labor in reforming individuals.

A third indication of this change was that policing itself became more proactive than reactive. Its function was increasingly less to hem in people in than to anticipate and neutralize them before they became problems. In 1957, the old internal security system was abandoned, and a new police organization, SAVAK, was established.[17] Simultaneously, the National Police, which had been for a long time a military organization, was gradually "demilitarized." This demilitarization was "accompanied by the upgrading of the quality of the personnel, the modernization of virtually all aspects of their operations, and the doubling of the size of the force between the mid-1950s and the mid-1970s."[18]

These changes did not go by unnoticed. As one criminologist observed of the civilian prison system, "It is obvious that, in the formulation of these rules, the aim of rendering criminals harmless (*neutralisation*) is more the subject of attention and supervision than the aim of reforming the behavior and manners (*re-adaptation*) of criminals."[19] The shah made the same point about the political system. "Today, every free country needs a political security agency which, in cooperation with other Government departments, can detect and neutralize attempts [to topple the government]."[20] The shift from readaptation to neutralization did not involve any lesser commitment to the notion of transforming individuals into something else. It did involve, however, new techniques. I have more to say on how medical technology, proactive policing, and open prisons contributed to the neutralizing of individuals. In tracing this history, I intend to show that such changes did not occur all at once in all areas of the prison system but built up gradually. Often these changes came about as prison officials and police officers found themselves caught between recalcitrant prisoners and the equally serious system imperative that the individual be transformed.

Case Files

To transform someone, something has to be known about that person. I want to consider the detention of the petty abuser of opium because it illustrates a particularly common way in which knowledge was gathered in the prison system. By understanding what happens to a petty abuser of opium, we may also be able to clarify aspects of a torture interrogation as well.

So what does happen to a petty abuser of opium when he is detained? The suspect is arrested on the grounds that he possesses a small amount of opium. The police question him and attempt to identify the source through which he purchased the drug.[21] The offender is then delivered to the public prosecutor, who constructs a dossier on the circumstances of the arrest.[22] This dossier is presented to the court. If the accused has been arrested previously, the dossier is accompanied with legal and, if possible, medical records of recidivism.[23]

On the basis of these documents, the court delivers a verdict sentencing the offender to prison for a period of one to three years. He is then delivered to penal authorities for detoxification and rehabilitation. The possibility of rehabilitation is evaluated. The type, severity, and duration of the addiction are assessed. The extent of physical and psychological deterioration is determined.[24] If the prisoner is capable of rehabilitation, he is detoxified, set to work, and, where possible, encouraged to undergo therapeutic counseling.[25] Release is determined on the basis of an evaluation of the prisoner's behavior during the course of incarceration.[26] If the prisoner is incapable of rehabilitation, an official drug regimen is prescribed. A card is provided that permits the addict to purchase opium at a specific dispensary.[27]

In either case, when the prisoner is released, his prison file is not closed. Conditional liberty is granted on the ground that he remains in constant contact with the police and prison authorities. No probation is granted even on demonstration of good behavior.[28]

Thus, the offender moves through many minute proceedings. In the course of these proceedings, data are gathered: police records, legal dossiers, medical files, therapeutic casework, and prison evaluations. These items do not simply constitute a record of a misdemeanor; they comprise the knowledge of a whole life. The offense of the petty abuser has been transformed into a psychological profile of a criminal. A whole account has become available of the factors that constitute a specific criminological pathology.

Here, then, is a monotonous procedure, one that was endlessly repeated for beggars, prostitutes, and criminals. It presupposed seven rules for interpreting the behavior of a suspect.

1.   Distinguish different categories of prisoners. Let separation reduce medical dangers, prevent moral improprieties, and facilitate treatment and questioning. Separate first offenders from recidivists; the sane from the criminally insane, the retarded, the diseased, and the malformed; the passive from those "prone to violence";[29] juveniles from professional vagrants and prostitutes; petty abusers of opium from pushers, traffickers, drug magnates, and other kinds of addicts; and murderers from thieves, troublemakers, and foreign agents. "Students are treated differently from dope smugglers, communists from general dissidents such as writers and poets and

others whose activities are confined to the dissemination of ideas; as distinguished from political dissidents who rob banks or kidnap officials for political purposes."[30]

2. Isolate the criminal behavior. Do not question the subject about his or her good deeds since these are incidental. Examine only the factors that caused the crime.

3. Postulate a general source of causation. Consequently, demand a complete account of the criminal behavior. If the subject is a delinquent beggar, solicit a history of her "problems and needs."[31] If the subject is a juvenile, "prepare a social study of the child and his family."[32] If the subject is a political criminal, extract a full history of his or her illegal activities. "Politically! What were you doing *politically*, you jackass?"[33]

4. Identify common environmental factors that induced an unhealthy disposition and consequently manifested themselves in "social maladjustment."[34] This common environmental factor might include a profession (mendicity, prostitution), an association (drug addicts, communists), or a condition (a neighborhood, a childhood, a university).

5. Give these factors a central role in explaining pathologization or normalization of behavior. Trace the mutations of a single factor into various pathological behaviors. "Orphan abandonment, before it is an individual misfortune, is a major social problem in which the origin of many delinquencies, social failures, retardations, murders, suicides, prostitution, and psychological diseases must be sought."[35] Subsume all other aspects of the individual's life to this factor. Render his good behavior contingent to an explanation of his life.

6. Detain the person once it has been determined that he has pathological characteristics. Here is a remarkable example of how this can play out. During the Islamic Revolution, police officers were dispatched to arrest a group of demonstrators. When the officers arrived, the demonstrators had disbanded. Still determined to make arrests, the police asked all the people on the street what their profession was. Eventually, police arrested nineteen people who had answered that they were students; this answer in itself showed that they were really demonstrators. That this was the sole criterion for arrest was "supported by the fact that the the police immediately released three of the nineteen who were able to prove they were *not* students."[36]

7. Give the offender's pathological disposition a place in judicial proceedings. For example, in 1960, the General Criminal Law of the civil courts introduced measures to deal with delinquents considered dangerous by reason of their antecedents and their

personality. The law of 1960 authorized the detention of the insane in asylums, of repeated recidivists in deportation camps, of vagabonds in work camps or in agricultural colonies, of alcoholics or drug addicts in medical treatment centers, and of young delinquents in education centers.[37] Similarly, in 1965, members of the League of the National Movement of Iran were arrested and brought before a military court. Although "the court could not recognize the four guilty of any specific crime," it "wanted despite this to 'punish' their 'antimonarchial ideas.'"[38] In all these cases, a minute mechanism was at work, one that found "a state of danger (a serious probability of a future offence)" in the criminal's life profile.[39]

Thus, the criminal becomes intrinsically dangerous. This danger is determined not only by examining his or her deeds but also by identifying factors that reveal a pathological disposition for criminality. In this manner, the objective of carceral procedures shifts. Police officers, jurists, analysts, and prison officials are no longer simply concerned with the juridical crime (violation, felony, capital offense) or with the disciplinary nonconformity of behavior (misdemeanor, contravention), but also with the danger imbedded in the pathological personality. "We just proved you were a criminal. We don't have to go to a court to prove the already proven thing. You are a criminal. We start from there. The rest is mere ceremony."[40] Where the individual cannot be readapted to normal society, he or she may at least be neutralized through treatment.

It is tempting to call this linguistic process through which individuals are constituted as another sort of confession. In one sense, there is something to this assertion because by speaking, the subject has become the object of truth. Yet if one wants to talk about this process as a confession, then one must carefully distinguish between two types of confession. The first is the traditional sort of confession, whereby individuals are encouraged to speak the truth about a particular deed that has been done. The second is this modern sort of confession, whereby individuals are encouraged to speak about themselves and where the probing does not concern information anterior to them. In this sort of confession, individuals become subjects of disciplinary knowledge and objects of medical techniques. It is misleading to call modern torture confessional without making this distinction clearly.[41]

The Carceral Clinic

The use of medical technology in carceral regimes is not a development peculiar to Iranian society. In Europe and North America, medical technology has always occupied an important place in the treatment of the incarcerated. Doctors maintain the health of individuals during prison epidemics. Medical techniques are used to detoxify addicts and neutralize abnormal behavior. Between 1935 and 1955, for example, more than seventy thousand lobotomies were performed in the United States and England.[42] Finally, medical techniques are employed to execute criminals. The American electric chair, for example, brings together two medical practices: electric shock, which was initially used in the treatment of the insane, and inoculation of drugs to deaden the nervous system of the condemned. Surgery and psychology join in the practice of death.

What is interesting in the Iranian case was how quickly the use of medical techniques moved from the civilian to the political prison system. This occurred very early in the twentieth century. The first Tehran prison contained, among other services, a hospital to maintain the health of prisoners. Mental asylums commonly employed electric shocks to treat patients and neutralize violent behavior. Just how common was revealed by a 1960 study of an Isfahan mental hospital, which found that electric shocks were used a total of 1,163 times in the course of a year for a population of 170 patients.[43] The police rented 'Alim id-Dowleh hospital in Tehran to execute criminals. The technique commonly used was "the fatal injection of an air bubble by Physician Ahmadi."[44] Medical technology acquired a further utility: to assist in the interrogation and punishment of suspects. Most of these procedures, such as shock treatment, came directly from local asylums and hospitals. The weightcuff is the only torture device that can be traced convincingly to a foreign source, probably Germany.[45]

Through these medical techniques, a new knowledge of pain was extracted from human beings. This knowledge contributed to a new punitive technology. By the 1970s, the new penal technology included methods such as dipping a truncheon in acid before beating the prisoner[46] or using "the gallows," where "they hang you upside down, and then someone beats you with a club on your legs or uses the electric prod on your chest or your genitals."[47] It also included new punitive machinery such as the "hot table" and "the pressure device which imposes pressure on the skull to the extent that you tell them what they want or let your bones break into pieces."[48] Some devices were made specifically for the torturers' sake, for example, helmets that refracted and magnified the prisoner's screams but spared the torturer.[49] Finally, the new technology included the organization of space as a form of pain. For example, the cells of Evin prison, Tehran's most modern prison facility, were constructed according to physiological requirements. Many of the Evin cells were built to be just short of the average height of the human body. Regardless of whether the prisoner stood up or lay down, he could never completely extend himself. The cell itself constituted a punitive device. A whole science of minor pains ran along its walls.

Or to take another example, adjacent to the torture chamber was the *Otaq-i Tamshiyaat*, or walking room. Prisoners were forced to walk in this room after torture "to help their blood circulate."[50]

Like all medical procedures, the new penal technology controlled biological processes. It enabled technicians to empower bodies or emaciate them until the suspects were on the verge of death. "You recant and you stay alive; you don't recant and you rot or die in prison."[51] But this technology could also eliminate the possibility of death: "He was kept awake for 50 hours during his interrogation, then given a beating that led to his admission to an army hospital, where the interrogation proceeded as he lay in bed."[52]

In this manner, the penal technician gained a new hold on his victim's body. He could inflict pain continuously. However, the converse was also true. Death marked the failure of a medical technology designed to manipulate life. No doubt this explains why the prisoner was taken to the *Otaq-i Tamshiyaat* after the torture interrogation and why, throughout his detention, he received medical advice from his guards as to how to maintain his wounds.[53] It also explains why bodies of dead torture victims were so rarely found;[54] such a physical testimony could be embarrassing and detract from the terror of the new punitive technology.

Thus, beneath the unrestrained, blustering violence, one finds in modern punishments the regulative principle of the operation: the imperative to maintain life at all costs. Since this principle underlies modern medicine as well, an Iranian doctor is "in a painful dilemma, not wanting to serve the regime in such a capacity yet professionally bound to help those who needed his services."[55] The torturer and the doctor both want the prisoner to live and bring to bear the same technology, however much their ends may differ.

It might be useful in this respect to contrast modern torture with torture in the early Qajar period. These tortures are articulated onto the prisoner through a bio-medical representation of the body, not through the ceremonial requirements of justice. They are clinical, rather than ritual, tortures. The instruments impose their own norms (to foster or disallow life) onto the process of torture and so make possible new ways of interrogating individuals. As Muhammad Reza Shah put it so succinctly, modern punishments were "not the torture in the old sense of torturing people, twisting their arms, and doing this and that. But there are intelligent ways of questioning now."[56] The key element, however, is the use of knowledge and technique to transform individuals. It is this aspect that modern torture shares with discipline and that leads people practicing it not to see modern torture in the same light as they would see classical atrocities. This is the subject I consider next.

Open Prisons

In Europe, torture was historically associated with the confession. As the confession came to occupy a pivotal place with the legal framework of the Latin church, torture was increasingly valued for a specific effect, the production of a confession. Torture, it was believed, should not be employed to force an admission of guilt but rather to gather the specific details of a crime that could be known only to its perpetrator. It would be misleading to say, however, that torture was linked in every case to the production of confessions, even if one broadens the sense of confession considerably.[57] In modern Iran, such confessions of the truth were rarely solicited from suspects. This is not to say that modern torture did not have specific results, only that the supposed utility of torture should not be sought solely in the practice of the confession.

In fact, the effects for which torture was valued were numerous. Torture was employed to neutralize opposition to authority. For example, prominent leaders and intellectuals were constrained to recant their views on the national media. Unlike confessions, it did not matter particularly whether the recantation was true. As a consequence of this recantation, these regime opponents were "isolated from the mainstream of the opposition and considered traitors."[58] Their public appearance was also believed to influence the activities of their audience. Their recantation incited their audience to be more self-vigilant, unobtrusive, and innocuous: "The idea of arresting and jailing persons who act against the higher interests of the State is to punish the condemned person and to make an example of him for others. If a prisoner realises his mistake, and if authorities become aware of it, he will not be kept in prison much longer."[59]

Recantations can be contrasted with another verbal effect of torture, condemnations. Condemnations differed in that one did not renounce one's beliefs; one merely spoke against a rival political movement. For example, SAVAK would release mullahs after they had publicly condemned Marxism, a tactic calculated to drive a wedge between religious leaders and radical student organizations.[60]

Torture was also used to deprive prisoners of protection under the law. Often a condition for release from torture was pleading guilty to a lesser charge. The charge to which one admitted may have had little to do with the reasons for detention, may not have been committed by the suspect, and may not have even occurred. Usually, the prisoner purchased his freedom on signing the proper forms. Yet this procedure opened new avenues of action for policing agencies. The admission of guilt made it possible to harass, blackmail, torture, discredit, detain, prosecute, or imprison the prisoner at some later date. It could be used to justify subsequent detention of the prisoner before domestic and international audiences. It also reinforced the legitimacy of the security agencies. Without the production of crimes, it would have been difficult to justify the existence of a group of well-armed men with the exclusive right to bear arms, watch one's home and one's public activities, and torture one's relatives and acquaintances.

Torture also served to recruit individuals for police agencies. Some prisoners, for example, became informants rather than suffer further maltreatment.[61] Similarly, on the same grounds, certain intellectuals assisted SAVAK in disseminating "confusionist 'opposition' thinking" and thereby inciting factionalism among opposition groups.[62] As Fred Halliday remarked, "Such is the suspicion of Iranians about SAVAK and so multifarious are its forms of activity that almost anyone who does voice protest against the government runs the risk of being suspected as a SAVAK agent. Conversely, at home and abroad, the regime encourages a climate of hostility among dissidents in which each and every one is suspicious of the other working for SAVAK. It is a very effective and insidious way of demoralizing any opposition."[63]

Psychological effects were among the most serious and valued effects of torture. There was the distortion of the prisoner's felt image of his body. A particularly good account of this was given by a South African detainee:

> There are weird symptoms which, when taken in conjunction, present a picture of incipient mental disintegration. Often when I lie on my bed I feel as if my soul is separating from my body. ... My limbs, my trunk and my soul floats gently to the ceiling, where it coalesces and embodies itself into a shape which lodges in the corner and which stares at me, calmly, patiently and without emotion. It is my own owl, my own I. It is I staring at myself. What's more I am aware of the whole process as though there is yet another self, which watches the I staring at myself. I am a mirror bent on itself, a unity, and yet infinite multiplicity of internal reflections.[64]

There was the process through which the prisoner's life was raised above the threshold of description and constituted as a separate body of knowledge. Through questioning, the details of the prisoner's life were solicited and gathered into a body of knowledge. If the prisoner distorted his past in interrogation, this was at the cost of losing the sense of who he was:

> I know that I am dealing with a crisis of conscience. I am also dealing with a crisis of consciousness and the subconsciousness, be it individual or collective, familial or social. I am dealing with the distortion of faces, names, memories, languages, patterns and colors. I distort them first, then I transport them through the invisible channels of my mind into the pockets of my subconscious. I have a huge fist, a clenched fist in which everything is hidden. It has grown like an enormous tumor in my spirit, and no "doctor," including this Dr. Rezvan, will be able to descend far enough to extract it or perform an autopsy.[65]

In short, the prisoner came to view his body, his recollections, and his self-characterizations as foreign and external to his condition. Throughout the interrogation, the prisoner struggled with his alienated life. Of course, the prisoner's condition was not a battle between an alien "tumor" and himself. One might say rather that the problem was one of a badly beaten, poorly integrated body.

It is in this context that one may understand many of the symptoms that characterize survivors of torture on release: inabilities to govern basic life functions, impaired memory, communication disabilities, deterioration of self-image, unsociability, introversion, anxiety, and vigilance. It is now possible to understand the pastoral character of the torture interrogation. No longer at home in his being, the prisoner lived in a condition of dread, self-mortification, and helplessness. In this context, the interrogator sought to assume a position of confidence and trust. He presented himself as a mediator between the victim and his or her condition: "Dr. Sabeti suddenly gets up. He unbuttons his jacket and tries to reach out from across the table in the middle of the room to attack me. The General jumps up and puts both arms around him pleading: 'Forgive him, he is foolish, he doesn't know what he is talking about! If he were not a fool, he wouldn't be in prison in the first place!'"[66]

In essence, the interrogator said, "I am not torturing you; you are torturing yourself. I can, however, intervene on your behalf and liberate you from this unfortunate condition. But our success depends on your cooperation." This procedure was shaped by psychological and medical practice. Its therapeutic character has continued to pose enormous difficulties in the subsequent medical treatment of survivors of torture:

> One of the most striking difficulties recorded by therapists who have treated victims of torture is the extraordinary degree of tact that must be used in therapeutic situations that bear even a slight surface resemblance to the original circumstances of torture. Questioning of victims must not be intensive; methods of physical therapy and medical examination must not be used if these (e.g., swimming or traction therapy, or EKG analysis) too strongly resemble the original methods of torture used. The temporary confinement in hospital quarters sometimes reminds patients involuntarily of their original confinement. Since the torture victim's only previous contact with medical personnel may have been in the place of torture itself, the medical personnel involved in rehabilitation work under this further strain and a further irregular aspect of their normal professional treatment of patients.[67]

The torture interrogation is pastoral because torturers attempt to incline the prisoner toward a certain course of action and to fix a habitual mental and/or physical disposition one could call normality. The prisoner was conducted (in the double sense of being led or learning to lead oneself) according to a requested norm. She was invited to recant, to condemn, to inform, to admit guilt, or to cooperate.

Such dispositional effects were, in part, voluntary. They depended on the prisoner's acceptance of "professional" advice and her willingness to follow the suggested course of action. A certain freedom was essential to the torture interrogation and its "follow-up" procedures.

This essential freedom posed an intractable difficulty for torturers. Prisoners could reject the advice either through force of argument or physical resistance. "They threw us into a tub full of scalding water, so that we were thrashing around with our arms and legs. Do you follow? This thrashing around of the arms and legs was, in itself, a political act."[68] To execute the prisoner in such circumstances would only confirm a successful resistance. Here, then, was an ironic inversion. During the Qajar period, death confirmed the judicial process. During the Pahlavi period, death undermined the penal apparatus and attested to the deceased's fortitude: "'I thought you said you would kill me.' 'We don't need another stupid martyr in our history. But we can kill you at any time we want. You are always in our clutches.'"[69] The essential freedom required by torture always made possible an implicit, accessible ground for resistance. This characteristic explains why the death of torture victims was so often trivialized: "fell out of the window,"[70] was shot "resisting arrest,"[71] or was caught in a "confrontation with officers while escaping prison."[72]

Modern torture works by transforming individuals into asocial, apolitical, and dependent individuals if it does not deliver a personality in shreds. The results here closely match those of the delinquents described earlier in this chapter, individuals who were neutralized through disciplinary incarceration. Delinquents, one might add, were used in specific ways by the police, and this police usage was similar to the way tortured individuals were used.

Delinquents were sometimes employed as political agents. They served as demonstrators for various politicians throughout the 1940s and 1950s. They disrupted crowds of protesters in the streets.[73] They were introduced into prisons to beat political prisoners and into factories to intimidate workers.[74]

Delinquents were also utilized to infiltrate more dangerous illegal activities. For example, by 1974 the police had utilized delinquent addicts so successfully that they had driven drug manufacturing into the countryside.[75] Similarly, between 1963 and 1970 SAVAK employed student informers successfully to dismantle most radical student groups in Iranian universities.[76]

Finally, delinquents were employed to run drugs on behalf of the police and government officials. In fact, Teymour Bakhtiar, the first head of SAVAK, built a fourteen-story apartment in Tehran "which Tehranis dubbed the 'Heroin Palace,' since rumors had it that it was financed by his profits from narcotics."[77] Moreover, delinquents ran specific police-supervised brothels enabling policemen to extract indirect profits through the exploitation of sexual pleasures. It was no accident that during the Islamic Revolution, the aggrieved prostitutes of Tehran marched in groups chanting, "Muhammad Reza, Shah-i Ma; Khahar-i Shah, Khahar-i Ma" (Muhammad Reza is our shah; the shah's sister is our sister).

Numerous objectives were achieved by incarcerating offenders, neutralizing them, and permitting delinquents to circulate in society. Indeed, it is in this context that one should understand the continued existence of the government-sponsored "gray market" in drugs,[78] the provision of open prisons, and the release of torture detainees.

Proactive Policing

In the early twentieth century, internal war was waged by armies. The history of Iranian wars was primarily a history of military campaigns, maneuvers, and security operations. Increasingly, however, the responsibility for internal order shifted from the military to the police. This shift toward a more proactive police system served to bring together the different elements that I have been describing into a torture complex.

In the 1920s and 1930s, the Iranian army assumed the responsibility of maintaining domestic order. The army intervened to crush provincial uprisings in Azerbaijan and Gilan as well as suppress clerical opposition in urban areas. Most important, it conducted a series of campaigns against various tribes: the Kurds of western Azerbaijan (1919–1920), the Shahsevan (1922), the Kuhgiluyeh (1923), the Sanjabi Kurds of Kurdistan (1923), the Baluch (1924), the Lurs (1924), the Turkmans (1925), the Kurds of Khurasan (1925), the Arab tribes of Khuzistan (1925), the Kurds of western Azerbaijan (1926), the Lurs (1927–1928), the Haft Lang Bakhtiari (1929), the Qashqa'i (1934), and the Boir Ahmadi (1934). In 1946, the Iranian army moved to crush provincial uprisings in Azerbaijan and Kurdistan. In 1953, the Iranian military, assisted by the CIA, intervened to reinstall Muhammad Reza Shah on the throne. Between 1953 and 1957, Iran was ruled through military governors as troops arrested members of the Tudeh party and crushed labor activism wherever it appeared.

At this juncture, military intervention almost completely disappears for two decades. The last major military operations occurred in the early 1960s when Iranian forces disbanded protesters led by Shi'ite religious leaders and conducted a campaign against the Qashqa'i tribe. This interlude marked, not the dissolution of armed conflicts, but the new predominance of paramilitary organizations in Iran. As one U.S. officer remarked, "After 1963, when the Shah used the army to put down street demonstrations in opposition to his 'white' revolution, internal security was relegated to a secondary role for the armed forces. ... Responsibility for internal security, including intelligence operations, was relegated to the Imperial Iranian Gendarmerie and SAVAK."[79]

What accounts for this sudden change? The explanation lies, at least in part, in the impact of U.S. strategic thought on Iranian security strategies. In the 1950s and 1960s, U.S. strategic thought focused on how to combat communist insurgency.[80] The U.S. government created the Office of Public Safety (OPS) Program, which helped upgrade policing agencies in developing countries. The rationale for this program was laid out succinctly by the U.S. Agency for International Development (USAID):

> [The OPS Program] is based on the premise that, to maintain internal order, local governments depend primarily on their police and gendarmerie supported, as necessary, by the army. Police constitute the first line of defense against subversion and terrorism. The earlier the police can meet such threats, the less it will cost in money and manpower and the less interruption will occur in the vital process of development. Moreover, the police are a sensitive point of contact between government and people, close to the focal points of unrest, and more acceptable than the army as keepers of order over long periods of time. The police are frequently better trained and equipped than the military to deal with minor forms of violence, conspiracy and subversion.[81]

Through improved policing and paramilitary capabilities, state security strategies did not have to be predominantly reactive. States could shift toward more proactive strategies, modifying potential violence and inhibiting its accumulated effects.

In 1953, U.S. officers arrived in Iran to advise the Imperial Iranian Gendarmerie. Iran was also among the first countries to receive aid through the OPS Program in the late 1950s; with the dissolution of the program in the early 1970s, U.S. aid was rerouted through the International Narcotics Control Program of the USAID.[82] In 1959, U.S. and Israeli advisers assisted in the reorganization of the Iranian secret police and in the subsequent training of SAVAK agents.[83] Consequently, by the early 1960s, internal security had become overwhelmingly proactive and designed to anticipate, isolate, and neutralize opposition.

In this context, the United States provided extensive moral and technical support once the Iranian government adopted torture. Jesse Leaf, the chief CIA analyst on Iran from 1968 to 1973, spoke frankly on this score after the Islamic Revolution: "Mr. Leaf also said in the interview that he and his colleagues knew of the torture of Iranian dissenters by Savak. ... Furthermore, 'a senior CIA official was involved in instructing officials in the Savak on torture techniques,' although Mr. Leaf said that to his knowledge, no American did any of the torturing. ... 'I do remember seeing and being told of torture. And I know that the torture rooms were toured and it was all paid for by the U.S.A.' "[84]

But why did Iranians adopt torture? Historically, modern tortures have proven to be adaptable to too many different regimes (including radically different Iranian regimes) for them to be attributed to a single source, such as the United States or Germany.[85] At any rate, one does not have to posit hypothetical torture schools in the United States to explain torture in Iran.[86] A successful proactive strategy depends on "the seeking, at any cost, at every moment, always with the greatest urgency, of intelligence from which resulted the creation of special services and special methods of interrogations."[87] Torture responded to this demand not because it was particularly utile or rational, but because the elements constitutive of it were immediately available and well known to correctional and police agencies. And that is why Iranians adopted it.

What is remarkable about Iranian torture is that it cannot be fully explained exclusively by this priority. It is a mark of the complexity of Iranian torture that it was not governed solely by the imperative for intelligence or by a conscious entity that directed it toward this goal.

Intelligence may have been an initial reason for resorting to torture. In the long run, however, torture became a complex social system in which forms of subjection were constituted. One can distinguish three features of this complex. There were the discourses that characterized communication between actors, that is, the kinds of questions and answers, the marks that assigned different values to beings, and the signs of obedience and understanding. These discourses included psychiatric and medical reports, judicial instructions, penological programs, rehabilitation schedules, and military regulations. There were the actions that worked on the conduct of persons, including those who tortured: hierarchies, rewards and punishments, and panoptic surveillance. There were the particular dispositional effects achieved: cooptation, neutralization, or depoliticization.

Describing how these elements relate also accounts for what people do and why they do it when they torture or are tortured. One describes a practical rationality that characterizes a torture complex. A torture complex is also a practice, a way of acting on oneself or others. More specifically, it is a way of fixing norm-governed behavior and normalizing forms of subjectivity. Resistances to torture, then, were not merely struggles against the state but also rebellions against forms of rationalization.

What Is Torture?

Torture complexes become less mysterious when they are compared with aspects of the civilian penal system, and it may be well worth stating some of the main similarities. Through elaborate ways of questioning, both systems tend to focus more on the person than on the act that served to incarcerate him or her. The incarcerated become subject to a hermeneutics of suspicion in which their lives are constantly examined and judged in light of what counts as a normal human being. Medicine increasingly occupies a more central place in both systems. Medical techniques are used in the maintenance of health and in the treatment of the incarcerated. Less emphasis is placed on internalizing the disciplinary gaze, and more is placed on grasping the incarcerated from within through medical techniques. Civilian and political administrators work to produce socialized and dependent individuals. Individuals of this sort are coopted into other activities by police and politicians. Both systems tend toward a preventive, proactive way of surveilling individuals. Both systems have an unpredictable result: They serve the incarcerated by bringing them into contact with individuals similar to them and thereby inducing further resistance.

These processes did not occur to the same extent and at the same time in all civilian and penal institutions. Furthermore, what passed as torture in one did not always pass as torture in another, even if the techniques were similar. No doubt, those more committed to the notion of discipline had grave reservations about such techniques for they seemed to depart in some ways from the notion of discipline. The key difference seemed to be the extensive reliance on medical and psychological knowledge as a means of coercion. In other respects, torture complexes were quite similar to disciplinary ones. Although the means of coercion were different, these techniques were performed in specific orders on different individuals in accordance with institutional regulations. Further knowledge was gathered that served as a modality for work on others. Proactive policing served as a means of observation and of judgment. Modern torture appeared in disciplinary institutions and, not surprisingly, had many similar characteristics.

It is not simply that political and civilian prisons systems underwent similar transformations. It is also the case that torture complexes shared many of the same features associated with disciplinary institutions. Surprisingly, government officials did not draw a sharp distinction between modern torture and what passed as punishment in the civilian penal system. In this they were mistaken since modern torture differs from discipline in at least one crucial respect, namely, the greater role of the medical and psychiatric disciplines. Critics of modern torture, however, mistakenly equate modern torture with classical torture. To be sure, modern torture is intensely corporal, but disciplinary exercises can be as well. Modern torture shares more with discipline in the way it is applied to bodies than with the ceremonial tortures of the Qajar period.

Any adequate account must be able to distinguish among the different ways in which violence can be exercised. This is precisely what both the critics and practitioners of torture lack. The former lump modern torture with all atrocities in the history of humankind, while the latter locate modern torture in the context of all other modern forms of violence that work to transform individuals. In both cases, normative rhetoric has replaced an effort to speak discriminately about violence.

PART TWO

. . . .

TUTELAGE & TORTURE

It is a self-deception on the part of philosophers and moralists to imagine that by making war on decadence they therewith elude decadence themselves. This is beyond their powers: what they select as an expedient, as a deliverance is itself only another expression of decadence—they alter its expression, they do not abolish the thing itself.

—Friedrich Nietzsche
Twilight of the Idols

I begin here with a text that captures the main elements of the argument thus far. In 1964, a book was published in Tehran entitled *The Defense of Society Against Crime and the Criminal,* by Hafez Iyman. The defense of society, Iyman asserted, turned on three "apparatuses":[1] reforming and cultivating persons through religious and secular rules of conduct, disciplining criminals through punishment and preventive security measures, and transforming the material life of the population through economic development. "The defense of society," Iyman summed up, "is complete and rendered effective only when all these apparatuses of government including religious, judicial, cultural, economic and the like, completely and with the utmost synchronicity, perform their duties with meticulousness and zeal."[2]

Notice that Iyman's discussion of government is a very broad one that includes activities not directly under the control of the state. The art of governing society here is to fix a power relation that induces habitual subjection; where such habits exist, state direction is unnecessary. Various apparatuses, that is, various constellations of actions, work on other actions to secure a desired behavior. One is led or learns to conduct oneself with a certain disposition and, ideally, finds this conduct fulfilling.

For Iyman, government reforms, and he distinguishes three areas where different reformatory techniques are required. Public life is reformed by using punishment and policing. Economic life is reformed by managing life more carefully. Private life is reformed by exhorting others to good conduct. These categories correspond roughly with discipline, biotechnology, and tutelage, and Iyman is in fact enumerating the three apparatuses through which government was pursued in the past century. First, there were the disciplines of public life: the drills that functioned as punishment but also as training, work, education, policing, and fighting. Second, there were the technologies of life: the techniques characteristic of labor management, medical treatment, and modern torture. Third, there were the tutelary techniques of private life: the discrete exhortations that reformed corrupt behavior and effected good habits.

Tutelary practices are the main focus of the next few chapters. Tutelage describes the forms of supervision that are concerned with child care, welfare, and, in general, the moral care of bodies. Practices of this sort were not unknown in Iranian society, but Pahlavi society brought with it a host of more specialized tutelary practices. Families learned about tutelage through therapeutic counseling, pediatric manuals, and hygienic instruction on a broader scale than before. Tutelary institutions were created, such as welfare bureaucracies, social service centers, community welfare networks, and charitable activities associated with religious institutions. Tutelage emerged as a subject of general social conversation as Iranians became more concerned with drug addiction, alcoholism, child neglect, delinquency, mendicity, and excessive population growth.

Tutelage can be contrasted with discipline. Tutelage differs from discipline in that custodians do not achieve normalizing effects through drilling individuals but through engaging in dialogue. Individuals are treated not as objects that require training, but as subjects of questioning and guidance. Tutelage alters self-understanding and so behavior. In this respect, it assumes that individuals possess within them a deeper self that is realized through speech. In practicing tutelary techniques, individuals realize themselves as normal members of a moral speech community.

In contrast with discipline and biotechnology, tutelage may appear to be an innocuous activity. Nevertheless, tutelage has played three significant roles in modern Iranian politics. First, it helped create the modern Iranian working class. This is the argument of Chapter 6, as it lays out the place tutelage occupied in Pahlavi society. Second, tutelage provided the vehicle through which revolution against the imperial government was successfully organized. This is the argument of Chapter 7. Third, tutelary supervision supported the cultivation of new moral habits after the Islamic Revolution, and nowhere is this more clearly evident than in the domain of carceral detention. Here, tutelage accompanies and supports the practice of torture. This is the argument of Chapter 8.

To trace the lineage of tutelary practices, I begin with their humble appearance in the field of family welfare. More specifically, I examine the manner in which tutelage responded to a major social crisis in mid-twentieth-century Iran: massive, uncontrolled urbanization, with its concomitant effect of social "corruption."

CHAPTER 6

Protecting Children

In the early 1930s, Asghar Qatel was hung. For months, he had terrorized Tehran, raping and murdering young boys. His arrest and public execution seized the public imagination such that decades later, young boys would be urged to "behave properly or else Asghar Qatel will get you." One day, a more complete account should be written of how the figure of the sexual delinquent shaped the policing of urban life. Political analysts will write on the communist threat in this period,[1] but Asghar Qatel's death was more portentous than the trial of the "Fifty-Three" leftists in 1937. In this section, I trace the history of the marginal figure in shaping urban life.

We may never know who Asghar Qatel was; the name simply means Asghar the Murderer. Every town, however, had its Asghar Qatel, and the danger he posed to children was magnified with rapid urbanization. Even foreign residents cautioned that "child rape murder was common. Young children, both boys and girls, were continually disappearing, and the fact that many of them were American and European was kept quiet by the press."[2] By the 1960s, "the defense of children"[3] had become a prominent theme in the advice literature. Children needed to be protected not only because there were so many of them but also because there were serious moral dangers that threatened the welfare and stability of Iranian society. Writers, notably Nasser id-Din Saheb oz-Zamani, made national reputations for themselves on weekly radio broadcasts to the nation on the state of youth and the great need for mental hygiene.

The state of youth, according to those writers, was critical. Children were endangered by numerous perverse desires spawned by urbanization. Migration had increased the number of young men in large cities and had created an imbalance in the ratio of young men to young women.[4] "[This ratio] during the most critical years of adolescence, for a city of 2 million, [and] from the perspective of the '*accumulation of frustrated sexual energy*,' must be understood as a behavioral and medical danger. Under such conditions, the prostitute market will flourish quickly, due to numerous sexual solicitations. Behavioral foundations in areas dealing with sexual and matrimonial problems will become subject to abnormalities and laxities."[5]

Among these laxities and abnormalities, writers counted the sudden emergence of groups of youths intent on carousing and delinquent behavior; the increase of sexual promiscuity among urban youths, "especially in the higher segments of society"; the rise of perversions among lower class youths, which were "manifested in sexual crimes" such as homosexuality, rape, and prostitution; and the increased incidence of children born outside of marriage to the younger generation, which "endangered the ancient customs of the family."[6] These sociological problems rendered neighborhoods unsafe for children. Unsupervised children passing through city streets were now more than ever before in potential danger of delinquency, rape, or perversion.

That was not all; there was also the problem of uncontrolled Westernization. Children were being stimulated into excessive sexual frenzy. Modern society was hastening the sexual maturity of children. Radio, films, and books were inducing greater sexual awareness among young children. The "physical and sexual growth" of young children was no longer on a par with their "rational and emotional maturity."[7] Consequently, children were now more prone to engage in improper sexual activities. The increase of juvenile delinquency, remarked one criminologist, could be linked to "the appearance of modern civilization through films, theatre, evil magazines and television programs ... each of which constitutes an academy for corruption and a school of criminality for innocent children."[8] One child psychologist went so far as to recommend that children not see any romantic material that "stimulates the emotions and enters into their thought" and suggested that children be permitted to see only those films that concerned nationalism, science, and hygiene.[9]

This delicate situation was being aggravated by lower-class mothers who failed to socialize their children properly. In a pediatric manual aimed particularly at "the second and third class,"[10] mothers were warned that the sexual perversions of puberty could be directly linked with improper maternal care in earlier periods of childhood: "Experience has proven that one must not pamper children too often and touch their bodily parts. This accurate observation is not well attended, and out of love, [mothers] hold, kiss, caress, and pamper their children. This extremely simple and superficial activity has a profound and bad influence on the psyche and body of the child, stimulates the movement of personality traits and emotions, and brings the final force to a frenzy."[11] Note the oblique message to upper-class families here: Since many lower-class women served as nannies and servants in upper-class families, the danger could be transferred. Consciously or unconsciously, such women perverted children by offering improper maternal care or by introducing their charges to playmates, including their own children, who might corrupt them.

In addition, the educational system was corrupting children, creating social maladjustments, and producing delinquents. Children were caught between two forms of "despotism."[12] On the one hand, parents were making excessive demands of their children. On the other hand, teachers and school officials were treating children arbitrarily based on "uncritical whims."[13] Caught between high expectations and poor academic performances, children were resorting to acts of self-destructive aggression. "It is sufficient for a youth to receive a poor mark in high school or university for him to decide that his future is ruined and to turn to suicide."[14] Other children were turning to alcohol, narcotics, gambling, and delinquency. "Many of these delinquent youths," said one alarmed analyst, "are not from poor families, and even youths from middle-class backgrounds and higher-than-middle-class backgrounds form robber bands and similar organizations."[15] These problems, as a team of American analysts suggested in 1949, did not constitute a "technical failure of the schools." The school system was in fact accomplishing "with relative success the aims which consciously or unconsciously motivated its founders ... that of producing a distinguished intellectual elite." Part of this educational process simply involved eliminating students who failed to conform to the requirements of the "stereotyped" curriculum and the "authoritarian methodology."[16]

In short, children were in peril because of uncontrolled Westernization, urbanization, bad mothers, and improper education. Notice that these are themes that received great prominence after the Islamic Revolution, but here they were being articulated by secular pediatricians, doctors, and state health experts. These agents spoke in martial terms of cleansing the nation of moral corruption: "The prevention of delinquency is not an easy matter and is possibly the most difficult one that mankind has confronted. Consequently, its prevention cannot be the responsibility of a single organization. The war against delinquency is the responsibility of every person animated with a new spirit of humanitarianism, with this meaning that each person, whether man, woman, son or daughter, must struggle with delinquency and the corruption of habits."[17] At stake was not merely the happiness of the family or the well-being of children but the fate of the nation itself. The protection of children "concerns everyone. ... The life of the young generation is [the life of] this nation and if it is lost, it cannot be recovered."[18] It became the duty of psychologists, criminologists, and sociologists to "attend to this fundamental matter more than any other."[19]

Such then was the beginning of a diffuse social campaign against juvenile promiscuity and delinquency. It was led by politicians, doctors, families, feminists, and religious leaders. To reform social life, many people would turn to tutelary procedures of surveillance and examination. Their pedagogical campaigns brought to bear new techniques for liberating children from moral hazards and bringing into existence guarded zones in which they might live out their innocence. Innocent, carefree childhood was the ideal goal, but in a society with sharp inequalities in wealth and status, only certain children could live this ideal. Social campaigns of this sort were fraught with contradictions they could not overcome without tackling the question of social inequality. This is precisely what differentiated the religious clerics from the secular hygienists in the end.

In any case, I want to look more closely now at two elements of these campaigns. I want to examine the steps families took on their own to protect their children in a rapidly urbanizing society. Then I want to show the impact of state authorities in directing and guiding family concerns. In particular, I want to draw attention to the use of certain coercive techniques that are not easily characterized as discipline or torture. Tutelary punishments were used principally to reform children or those who were deemed to be like children.

The Moral Freedom of Rich Families

I begin with upper-class families since the earliest contact between the state and the extended family was made here.

Family Surveillance. What disposed families to pay attention to what the experts told them? To be sure, families loved their children, but there was more. Children played a double role within the Iranian extended family. On the one hand, they were invested with a certain genealogical value. They were repositories of a name, a heritage, or a line of prestige. On the other hand, children had a particular tactical value. Since Islamic inheritance procedures did not recognize a system of primogeniture, children were the only means by which families could preserve their possessions. Without family alliances forged by children, the wealth and position of families could fragment within a few generations.

Although these two roles did not necessarily complement each other, they showed the place children occupied within a system of family alliances.[20] Nothing terrified families more than the possible corruption of their children. Corruption simultaneously threatened the child, shamed the family, and eroded the system of alliances. Consequently, the extended family met the moral hazards of urban life with increased vigilance. A study of lower- and middle-class families highlighted some salient features of this transformation. "Many mothers were fearful of having their small children of either sex play outside the compound because of bad influences and dirt." Several mothers "spoke of the need to keep them [their daughters] from playing with neighbor boys even inside the compound." Fathers who desired more children were afraid to have them because of the difficulties of surveilling them and the hazards to which the children were constantly exposed.[21]

Even more severe precautions were taken among upper-class families. Families policed all forces prejudicial to their status, prestige, and standing. Playmates were screened.[22] The activities of servants and their families were discreetly observed.[23] The movement of adolescents was confined. Advisers wrote that "after sunset, the children should not leave the perimeters of the house for cruising, partying, or games."[24] Furthermore, "suspicious of what a child may do when away, parents require constant reporting of his whereabouts, even if the son is in his twenties."[25] Rich families migrated to safer neighborhoods and demanded that the police evict squatters, beggars, and other undesirables who threatened their families.

The protection of children was also entrenched in the law. It is no accident that the Special Criminal Law of the Iranian Penal Code placed "offenses against children and offenses against the respect due to the dead" immediately after offenses against the state and attacks against the physical person.[26] Children and the dead stood at opposite ends of a vast system of family allegiances. Asghar the Murderer, whoever he was, loomed large in the Iranian imagination precisely because he threatened this system.

There was, however, a closer danger, one that stemmed from the very values that families placed on their daughters and sons. On the one hand, since the daughter was instrumental in forging family alliances, her chastity and virginity were highly prized. On the other hand, while the son was expected to protect his sister's honor, he was also expected to prove his virility and assertiveness. Consequently, the son "is designated to be the protector of his sister but at the same time he is not at all restrained towards other girls. He is thus a real threat to them."[27] This double standard of the Iranian family set in motion a conflict that could not be neutralized by family policing. Its solution was predicated on a revaluation of the system of family alliances in Iran, which no one was ready to question. The problem of moral corruption thus persisted, and families did not become less anxious about their children.

Given the place of children within Iranian families, it is easier to understand why families responded to the "hygienic and sociological psychology"[28] promulgated by journalists, doctors, psychologists, criminologists, and sociologists. Hygienic psychology was closely associated with the protection of children, an association that greatly facilitated the prevalence of "psychohygienic" explanations, techniques, and procedures among the leisured classes.

Public Advice Literature. Radio commentators and journalists often warned of the psychological dangers facing children and were important agents in shaping child care. They complained that the general public did not understand such important medical themes and tended to confuse psychology with philosophy, mysticism, theology, and physiognomy.[29] I want to look now at some of the main themes of this public advice literature.

According to these writers, the body was not a mechanical system; rather, it was a delicate balance of physical and psychical processes. Ill-health and social maladjustment were consequently two facets of the same disease. Social and environmental stresses were responsible for physical disorders, and physical disorders were manifested in social diseases.

Social and physical disorder required a careful probing of the psychosoma. The more carefully one conducted this examination, the more likely one was to provide a new formulation of the patient's condition, one that facilitated health. Whatever the particular patterns of self-invigilation prescribed, the new formulation had to be such that "the person seeking counsel willingly follows."[30] The patient had to be exhorted to recover his or her place within a healthy community. Good health was a product of good "mental hygiene."[31]

Not surprisingly, this literature focused on childhood since here human beings were more sensitive to damage. Childhood became a general source that in the long run determined the health of the individual in adolescence and adulthood. "One cannot fail to see reflected in the behavior of adult humans traces of the influence of the family, the school, and the natural and social environment. Today it is now more or less, in the most evident manner, confirmed: Joyfulness, preservation of the body and spirit, zest for life, and delight in one's work during the period of youth and maturity are dependent to a great extent on the character of one's childhood."[32] Insofar as childhood was identified as the basic factor in hygienic psychology, the family emerged as the crucible of societal health and degeneration. The family became the subject of political evaluation.

The main political theme here was the place of freedom in society. Different sorts of families allowed different sorts of freedoms, which was why there were so many problems. The modern family provided too much freedom to children and neglected proper socialization. "Even in the formative years of their child's cultivation," remarked one sociologist, "some parents will not sacrifice their desired entertainments such as night life, gambling, and the like."[33] In this neglect lay the source of juvenile promiscuity and delinquency in better families. As one criminologist remarked, "That is, for women who are engaged in work exterior to the home and whose children are cared for and raised by others, it is not possible to cultivate those habits and humanity in the child, and as a result [the child] is deprived of public-minded habits and internal harmony. Consequently, the crimes of juveniles in adolescence are coming into existence, and whereas once they did not exist at all, currently they have emerged, and while they are quite small, they are unfortunately on the rise."[34] There was no discussion here of the economic realities that forced mothers to work away from home; the problem here was with the mother, who would not stay home to take care of the children.

The traditional family, by contrast, provided too little freedom. This "family organized along the lines of a disciplined military group" under the surveillance of a patriarch might once have served a function but was now wholly anachronistic.[35] Such a family placed enormous demands on children and, moreover, enforced their ignorance concerning their own sexual growth. In this unmitigated despotism, one could find the source of rebellion and social maladjustment. Psychologists, doctors, and journalists cited incidents where such patterns of discipline led to mental and physical harm to children.[36] They called on the police to protect and liberate children from the despotism of such parents.

If the family was the microcosm of political society, then here is a badly disguised parable about Iranian political society itself. The state wanted neither too much freedom for its citizens nor too little. It wanted enough to ensure responsible behavior without having to use force. Gentle tutelage at the earliest stage of childhood was the answer. "*Discipline* and fundamental principles fortify the child and prevent children from the plague of bad habits."[37]

The tutelage of families began with the self-invigilation of parents. Mothers were urged to inspect their own psychological and physical states, especially during pregnancy, since these states could have detrimental effects on the child: "If the mother comes under the influence of harmful environmental factors, those factors will be imprinted into the body, in the spirit, of the baby, since the child in the fetus, like a collecting apparatus, records the influences on the spirit of the mother, and the circumstances of the mother's being induce psychological traces in the fetus."[38] Parents had to be aware of the effects of their care, such as "the effects of clothes on the child's psyche."[39] They had to recognize certain behavioral codes that would lead to promiscuity and delinquency: masturbation, inferiority complexes, sibling rivalry, adolescent anger, and spoiled behavior.[40] They had to habituate the child through a discrete and loving care. Parents and teachers should not "behave in such a manner that the child in kindergarten should decide that he is in a prison and revolt against the imposition of a heavy program."[41] They had to gently exhort him to proper behavior as a good member of the community. Finally, it was not sufficient for parents to stand guard over their child's health and sex. Tutelage had to ensure self-invigilation. "The spirit of the child is a mirror in which every kind of beautiful and ugly behavior, angelic and heavenly traits, base and unclean behaviors, are reflected; [it] has the ability for every kind of correct and incorrect training, and [consequently] the supervision and education by the father and the mother are, in themselves, not enough. Children and children alone must be good learners and prefer the path of education over following [the path of] the inclinations and deviation from wisdom."[42] The child had to internalize the policing of the family.

One can see that far from existing in a state of leisured freedom, the Iranian upper class was in a state of persistent anxiety over its children. It was intensely concerned with preserving its moral significance from the threats of uncontrolled modernization and Westernization. Such anxiety led upper-class families to subject themselves to a dense web of tutelary techniques. Regardless of whether such techniques were in fact adequate, upper-class families took proper tutelage as an affirmation of their moral superiority in relation to other sorts of families. Other families, notably the traditional-authoritarian family and the modern-immoral family, needed to be held in check and, if possible, improved.

Socializing the Modern Working Class

The living conditions of the Iranian proletariat in the early twentieth century demonstrated anything but a concern for the health, sexuality, or bodies of its members. The working class was subject to "low wages, long hours, high consumer taxes, forced transfer of workers to the malaria-infested regions of Mazandaran, and labor conditions that, in the words of a European visitor, 'practically resembled slavery.'"[43] The health and reproduction of the working class were taken to be unproblematic since more young migrants were always available.

Politicians had to become concerned with several political emergencies before they became concerned with the welfare of the working class. These emergencies included the need for a healthy, competent work force to carry out the state's industrialization programs;[44] a growing concern about the effects of alcoholism, drug addiction, and other social diseases on economic productivity;[45] and a demand, especially after the 1955 census, to regulate population growth.[46] Between 1934 and 1965, the Iranian population doubled, increasing from 13.32 million to 26.40 million.[47] From 1934 onward, rural-urban migration proceeded at an annual rate of 6–7 percent.[48] Urban migration constituted 61 percent of all internal population movements. Of the 100 cities extant in 1900, 13 had "dropped out of the urban category by losing population" by 1956.[49] As workers migrated to industrial cities, they created not only a vast squatter problem but also a major medical hazard. The spread of infectious diseases, especially venereal diseases, cholera, and smallpox, precipitated a series of new health measures.

The state, based on its own concerns, then extended welfare to the working class. No doubt the state hoped as well to regulate potential political conflict by providing better services in key industries. One cannot be wholly satisfied with this as an explanation of social welfare programs,

however. It explains why politicians provided welfare to the modern proletariat, but it does not explain why working-class parents voluntarily spent
so much time rationalizing their own families. To attribute this cooperation
to false consciousness is a rather forced argument. I want to draw on the
previous analysis to provide another explanation—that working-class parents shared the same anxieties about raising their children in the new cities
as upper-class parents did. They adopted tutelary procedures in imitation
of the upper class and with the understanding that this served to distinguish them as more moral and modern within a well-established political
code.

The rich family, however, enjoyed an independence that left it less reli-
ant on the state. Working-class families depended on the state, and the process by which this exchange of services occurred had a distinctly political
tone. The services to which they turned opened their private concerns to
public scrutiny, and families did resist efforts to police their activities. Yet a
social welfare system works precisely by opening private concerns to public scrutiny and by bringing public programs to bear on private life.[50] In this
section, I want to trace three areas in which this process of tutelary scrutiny went on: in clinics, social service agencies, and housing projects.

Clinics. If the man was supposed to work and the woman was supposed
to care for the children, who better to turn to than the woman to learn
about and transform families? Let us look first at the odd process by which
women became agents of the medical system.

In the early twentieth century, medical professionals did not see it either
necessary or desirable that women play a major role in matters of health
and hygiene. Traditional hakims were concerned with the pleasures wom-
en's health afforded men. In the area of gynecology, hakims wrote books
such as *The Exhilaration of Princes in the Cure of Diseases of Women* and
Women's Rags in the Science of Medicine. These books were clearly addressed to men, and even though they treated female disorders, their popularity was based "on their erotic contents."[51] Modern doctors, for their part,
were preoccupied with the dangers women posed to men through sexual
contact. Although the responsibility for the spread of venereal diseases
could have been attributed to either sex, women were subjected to health
and premarital examinations by law. Doctors presented women as passive
transmitters of disease rather than as active promoters of their own health.

Women's health, then, was entrusted to men and defined by what men
needed from women. The Iranian feminist movement made the first efforts
to change this understanding. In the period following World War I, feminists were particularly concerned with the deaths of mothers and children
as a result of poor medical care, unsanitary conditions, and superstitious
medical practices. Syphilis was "the most often discussed disease," and
"men were consistently blamed for transferring syphilis to their wives." A

letter published in a women's magazine went so far as to suggest that "the only way a woman could stay healthy was by not getting married." Although early feminists were members of upper-class families, their position on hygienic issues was "classless." There were, for example, "a great sensitivity to and an acute understanding of, the prostitutes' condition, especially child prostitutes. They were viewed as victims of male trickery and intrigue."[52]

Even though the changes advocated by feminists applied "not only to the upper middle class but also to the lower classes," the feminist movement was too weak to bring them about. Feminists turned to the state for it was "a relief to be part of a government that possessed enforcement power."[53] The state, for its part, was concerned with the health of women, but only to the extent that it ensured the birth of healthy children and resilient male soldiers.[54] As Muhammad Reza Shah remarked about his father, "Reza Shah never advocated a complete break with the past, for always he assumed that our girls could find their best fulfillment in marriage and in the nurture of superior children."[55] In health campaigns, state agents persistently warned women of the dangers posed by excessive childbearing to their teeth, breasts, figure, strength, and health.[56] They urged women to pay closer attention to their health by emphasizing proper child care.

In short, even though state bureaucrats encouraged women to play a new active role in promoting their health, women's health was still defined in terms of men's needs. Of course, bureaucrats defined women's health not in terms of what *adult* men wanted, but in terms of what *children*, especially boys, needed. Insofar as the state privileged the care of children, women could rely on other authorities to enforce their will against that of their husbands and fathers in certain areas of family life. What was once evidence of a woman's secondary status—her procreative and maternal functions—now became, at least potentially, a point of resistance against traditional patriarchy.

This strategy had a hidden cost for women. Women could challenge traditional patriarchy only by submitting to another group of men—state bureaucrats and health professionals. Who, after all, defined what children needed? Modern doctors, not women, were charged with the "protection, observation, and preservation of children from the period of pregnancy to adolescence."[57] Politicians, in turn, helped Western-trained doctors squeeze out traditional hakims "on a competitive basis that [had] little to do with treatment."[58] State regulations "made the treatment of venereal diseases compulsory; made free medication available to needy patients; made willful, knowing, or negligent transfer of such diseases, as well as fraudulent promises of a cure, subject to punishment; and provided for periodic inspection and certification of brothels."[59] State radio and television also produced a flood of public advice literature on the doctors' behalf. In effect, women were rendered into medical agents of a patriarchal health system.

Is it fair to say that doctors came to dominate in child care less on the basis of their expertise than on their association with the state? To be sure, infant mortality declined dramatically between 1949 and 1960. Infant mortality rates dropped from more than 50 percent in 1949, to 20 percent in 1961, to less than 12 percent in 1975.[60] Were doctors really responsible for this decline? Doctors became important with the invention of vaccines for child-killing diseases,[61] but one needs to consider this claim a bit more closely in Iran. As late as 1957, less than one-third of the country had access to modern medical facilities,[62] and even twenty years later the situation was still worse than in other Middle Eastern countries.[63] This makes it difficult to believe that doctors were responsible for the change in infant mortality. Infant mortality declined in part because of better sanitary conditions, regular health inspections of institutions, and the availability of pasteurized milk, developments for which the state, not doctors, was responsible. Vaccinations, too, played a role. "Vaccination certificates were required of all children yearly at the time of entering school and of all job applicants,"[64] but doctors were not specially qualified to vaccinate. This task could be and was handled by other medical personnel, such as nurses and medical assistants. Briefly, doctors became important in child care because of factors not intrinsic to their training, particularly state legislation, advances in consumer packaging, and the patriarchal nature of Iranian society.[65]

This suggests that some of what doctors actually did was ritualistic and designed to invoke confidence by playing on uncertainty. In particular, it puts the doctor's examination of the patient in an entirely new light. Medical examinations were at best a peripheral element of Galenic medicine as it was practiced in Iran. European-trained doctors, however, examined routinely. Indeed, this medical ritual became the emblem of their superiority. It distinguished real doctors from quacks.[66] Before the doctor was a healer, he was an inspector.

The difficulty was that doctors could not "inspect" women, and this created a major impediment in transforming women into medical agents. Many women were hesitant to submit their bodies for direct physical examination by a man.[67] They were vulnerable and sensitive to charges of immorality by their male relatives. This attitude was reinforced by religious rulings of the 'ulema:

> There was the Islamic law on the impropriety of looking upon a woman, above all on looking at her genitalia. Theologians had divided up the organs of the human body into Organs of Honour and Organs of Shame. The second of these two classes was known by the general title of "*aurat*," a word which by an obvious change has come to mean "woman" in modern Urdu. The word "aurat"

in theology means those parts of the body which must not be seen by another. In a man, this area extends from the navel to the thigh, in a woman from the neck to the knee, though rigorists say to the ankle. So unreasonable was this theological prohibition that both doctors and patients were perpetually at war with it.[68]

Doctors found that the emblem of their medical superiority put them at odds with traditional patriarchy. The state had helped them gain a monopoly in the field of pediatrics, but it could not help them overcome social resistance.

The solution was to emphasize the illocutionary aspect of the medical examination. Doctors urged women to speak about their symptoms, habits, family life, and diets. Insofar as women could expose their concerns and their problems within the family *by speaking*, doctors could prescribe treatment or enlist the help of authorities to support women's actions within the family. This brings me to another way in which private concerns were opened to public scrutiny.

Social Services. Between 1955 and 1965, social workers and hygienic psychologists posed the following problem: Given that modern society "has caused a horrifying increase in psychological diseases" among the lower classes,[69] how can we encourage families to bring forward their problems and histories? How can we "discover and understand their mental needs, difficulties, and most intimate concerns, which [are] suppressed especially by the traditional '*kitman*' or secretiveness?"[70] In short, how can we generalize confessional procedures among groups where this practice is "practically unknown"?[71]

The solution, as it gradually emerged during this period, was to rework the medical examination into a general advocatory procedure. Through this "two-way" procedure, social workers "learned about community problems and how to deal with them and neighborhood residents were made aware of the services available to them."[72] This relationship, however, was more helpful to social workers than to families. Even though families were made aware of social services, they could not make use of these services unless they were interviewed and approved. Approved families had to make themselves available to regular visits and questioning by social workers to preserve their access to food, medical assistance, and social programs. In this manner, the advocatory procedure served as both a means of policing households and a device for gathering a knowledge of families.

By the 1960s, worker-advocates had appeared in several areas. Social workers came to have a direct utility for the state primarily in the field of collecting case files on workers' families and assessing the feasibility of providing emergency loans. Local security officers acted as advocates in factories, encouraging profit-sharing programs and workers' insurance programs. A host of societies were created with the purpose of assisting the incarcerated, modifying the civilian prison system, and reforming marital law: the Society for the Protection of Prisoners, the National Association for the Protection of Lepers, the Association for the Guidance and Support of Defective Persons, the Association for the Support of Invalids, the Qaleh Prostitution Welfare Center, and the Society for the Protection of Children.

Within this broad network of moral tutelage, advocates rendered families of the incarcerated into policing units. This effect was achieved through bail, fiscal assistance, and provision of social services, all of which were contingent on families monitoring their relatives. The channel could also be reversed. If delinquent individuals failed to meet the expectation of authorities, families were subjected to fiscal and moral reprimand: "If families of delinquent youths do not pay greater attention with respect to the behavior of their children, in the event of repeated offenses by them, the name of the youths and their family names will be generally distributed for the information of the public."[73]

Moreover, officials used their knowledge of families to create a typology of abnormal families. For example, consider the discovery of the delinquent mother. This figure was gradually constituted in the early 1960s through the identification of physical signs (a degenerate body from excessive childbearing) and pathological behavior ("never leave their homes," "are not only ignorant of the skills and crafts of urban women, but also have as a result of urbanization forgotten their rural skills").[74] This prototype gained a wide circulation within academic circles as a causal source of delinquency.[75] It was also employed to normalize other families. For instance, during population control drives, instructors would single out women in the group who fit this typology for the instruction of other women in the audience.[76]

In this manner, a certain kind of pastoral power[77] was generalized among the lower classes. It was concerned with the welfare of the whole community as well as the care of each individual during the course of his or her life. It was linked to the production of a certain knowledge of families. It solicited views, explored thoughts, gathered personal histories, and produced case files. Finally, it was connected with the self-invigilation of behavior. It interpreted behavioral codes, proffered counsels, and directed activities.

Housing Projects. Housing projects were a third way in which private concerns were opened to public scrutiny and management. If the working-class family was to play a disciplinary role, its living space should serve to break down traditionalism, exclude inappropriate behavior, and facilitate health and productivity. This was the view that lay behind the politics of housing.

Housing projects emerged during the late 1950s. State architects had two stated goals: to construct healthy intermediate housing located between the "luxurious palaces" of the rich and the "base homes" of the poor and to "reconcile class conflicts between these poles."[78] To achieve this goal, architects had to preserve the medical health of the family, "respond to the needs of the human psyche,"[79] ensure economic productivity and encourage savings and investment, and discipline the habits of the working-class family. Housing was to be directly linked to the transformation of behavior. It had "to take into consideration changes in science and industry, and in particular, imitate today's life and style of thought and, through this vehicle, expose the Iranian to the world."[80]

Conventional housing was unsuited for this task because it possessed private secluded areas, the *anderun*,[81] or interiors, that were not readily open to surveillance and that reinforced the ostracization of women from modern society. Moreover, the rooms were multifunctional, a characteristic that posed dangers to health and hygiene. "There are no special dining-rooms, or bed-rooms, or drawing rooms in a Persian house. The meals are partaken of in any room, according to the momentary whim of the master of the house, and the night is often passed on the same spot which had just served as an apology for a dining room."[82]

By contrast, in planned housing, rooms responded "to their real functions." They were arranged to suit specific tasks and redirect those who lived in the home: "Three important and central sections of residence, that is, sites of consumption, sleep and service, must be thoroughly arranged and articulated such that they are distinct and separate from each other, within reach of each other, and interrelated."[83] Moreover, housing arrangements were designed to be "logical," employing an economical use of space and a proper distribution of light. The residence was made available to a mother's surveillance, which could be employed to enhance child care and satisfy "the complete requirements of hygiene."[84]

Housing projects thus made it easier for families to become socialized and to recover the proper way to live. Through a distribution of spaces, the state advocated a "new architecture, from the perspective of behavior and function, which is directly linked to the customs, habits and spirit of our people."[85] Working-class women, once again, were its agents.

Tehran's Moral Geography

What I am describing in this chapter is a partial history of the moral life of late Pahlavi society. Central to this life was the persistent fear of corruption. Around this anxiety, many groups sought to protect themselves by resorting to tutelary practices that preserved their groups' integrity. These practices gave a distinct shape to Iranian cities.

Tehran, the capital city, had a distinct pattern of spatial segregation that most visitors noticed at once. According to two Iranian sociologists, Tehran was intriguing because it had "brought into existence about itself a number of smaller satellite cities such as Narmak and Qulhak," each of which was "more or less specifiable as the residence of a class or classes."[86] This arrangement was only the most visible manifestation of a moral geography, for it expressed differences not only in income but also in moral worth. The city brought together people, but their interrelationship was sketched out according to different tutelary codes.

The wealthy voted with their money and their feet, moving to secure guarded neighborhoods. They lived schizophrenically, benefiting from the economic system, yet suffering at the hands of a social and political system that constantly put their families in jeopardy.

The modern working class lived in a regime of supervised freedoms and proudly distinguished itself from others. "The industrial working class identifies himself [sic] as a worker, and makes a sharp distinction between his class and the traditional working class [artisans] and lumpenproletariat. To make this distinction clear, instead of the three-class terminology used by the upper classes, they usually use a four-class terminology, and thus identify themselves with the members of the *third class*, while identifying, the *lumpenproletariat* with the fourth class."[87] The industrial working class zealously guarded its new social status. Owners of small firms "recruited virtually all of their unskilled and semi-skilled workers from among applicants appearing at the factory gates, most of whom had been informed by friends and relatives working in the factory that new workers were being hired."[88] Even the more religiously minded would distinguish between "two kinds of people: those who were really needy, often not even pressing their legitimate claims, were good people; then there were those, like this man, who ran their troubles as a kind of business and even would use children as a way to extract money."[89]

The poorest of the poor lived in squatter settlements in chronic need and were persistently excluded from good society. "Our total life is a problem. From the moment we recognized ourselves, we had nothing but problems. Look at the present situation. Now they say that the old regime is gone and the hands of the exploiters and oppressors are cut off. But my problem, and that of thousands of other squatter families, is lack of jobs and living quarters. I have had no income for the past year. I have eaten whatever I had. There is no food for tomorrow. Believe me, I don't know how I am going to live tomorrow."[90] Even during the Islamic Revolution, the poor did not protest since, as one squatter put it so well, "to demonstrate, you have to have a full stomach."[91] Nevertheless, poor people were numerous and threatening, and this was enough to remind others of what might happen if social order was corrupted.

CHAPTER 7

Creating a Moral Public

In this chapter, I want to emphasize the continuities between the ancien régime and the new revolutionary regime. I show the ways in which the Pahlavi state sought to exercise a moral power over its subjects and not merely a materialistic one. Conversely, I show how the 'ulema's concern with moral corruption led to a greater appreciation of material inequalities. Then I discuss the interplay between the war on corruption and the provision of social services in the new Islamic regime.

Pastoral Politics

So much has been written about the Pahlavi state's efforts to marginalize religious institutions that it is difficult to think of such a government as exercising a moral and pastoral power over its subjects.[1] Traditionally, religious leaders instructed and advised on physical health, sexual relations, family affairs, economic well-being, protection against accidents of all sorts, and spiritual salvation. To marginalize the clergy's role in this respect meant that other groups had to take up these tasks and exercise what used to be the clergy's moral power.

From the 1920s onward, numerous social groups assumed the task of teaching and policing families. Leftist women's groups, such as the Socialist Patriotic Women's Society (circa 1920) and the Tudeh's Society of Democratic Women (1949), launched campaigns to mobilize and educate women. Wealthy women founded philanthropic associations such as the Family Aid Society, the Family Planning Association, the Community Welfare Clinics, and the Women's Organization of Iran. In the late 1930s, the Foundation for the Protection of Mothers and Children was created. In 1959, the Mental Health Section of the Ministry of Health was established to monitor public mental health, disseminate information on mental hygiene, and take measures encouraging a healthier society. The government also urged young adults to pursue careers in social work, social insurance, nursing, and teaching. "Government ministries, private charitable organizations, philanthropic individuals, and concerned citizens began to see some advantages in preparation of better educated social workers to man the social agencies in the country."[2] Such careers particularly attracted women from modern working-class and propertied middle-class families.[3]

In this way, the clergy was replaced by a new group of moral professionals. These individuals were not concerned with the minutiae of ritual purity and how they might affect the soul. They were more interested in changing attitudes concerning the self. They wanted to illustrate the real importance of self-care as the basis of personal happiness and in this manner reform how individuals conducted themselves in private and public. Nevertheless, it would be hard not to call this sort of activity anything but exercising a moral power over subjects.

One by one, public and private professionals assumed the functions of the clergy. The Pahlavis contested the right of the 'ulema to advise on anything except spiritual matters. Even this last function was disputed when, just before the Islamic Revolution, Pahlavi bureaucrats proposed a religious corps, on the same model as the older Literacy Corps, whose function it would be to instruct Iranians in spiritual affairs. By 1976, the state-sponsored Resurgence party was describing the shah as essentially exercising a pastoral power over his subjects: "The Shah-in-Shah of Iran is not just the political leader of Iran. He is also in the first instance teacher and spiritual leader, an individual who not only builds his nation roads, bridges, dams and qanats, but also guides the spirit and thought and hearts of the people."[4] Aside from illustrating the apparently boundless enthusiasm of Pahlavi officials for the shah, this statement also describes a style of leadership reminiscent of similar enthusiastic descriptions of Ayatollah Ruhollah Khomayni's authority: They are political leaders not so much because they manage capital well or promote discipline efficiently, but because they exercise a moral power.

Was this merely rhetoric? I want to consider two examples of Pahlavi tutelage. The first is the role SAVAK played in securing the welfare of working-class families. The second is the role of the Hujjatiyeh, an anti-Baha'i society cultivated by the government. Each shows in a different way how the Pahlavis tried to promote a moral public.

SAVAK Cares. SAVAK's tutelary role should not be surprising given the long history of Iranian policing, but it might serve to show how exercising such moral power served to ensure stability in key sectors of the Iranian economy. SAVAK advocated demands on behalf of workers; it did not simply repress strikes. SAVAK situated its agents between workers and owners, usually in the state-organized trade unions. These agents mediated labor disputes and, if necessary, created "difficulties for management." "It would not be inconsistent if some of the wage rises in the mid-1970s had been urged on employers by SAVAK representatives in the trade union structure, aware of discontent within factories where they were stationed."[5]

SAVAK representatives also secured and administered welfare programs on behalf of workers. They would "incorporate workers into a number of welfare schemes related to insurance, housing, pensions, and the like. These are both a means of increasing the workers' sense of security (especially in the difficult housing market) and of encouraging saving."[6] Representatives were quite militant on this issue since agitation served to "shift the locus of workers' demands away from wage demands as such onto the the form of benefit scheme set up by the state."[7]

From SAVAK's perspective, such schemes gave workers a stake in the state, something that mere increases in wages would not achieve. Welfare schemes also fortified workers' skills and health, provided information on workers' families, and rendered them more dependent on the state apparatus. In promoting these programs, representatives would remind workers of their moral debt to the state, the state's sacrifices on their behalf, and "the question of increasing output."[8] They would urge workers to "work harder, improve their skills, and raise productivity in an effort to repay their debts to the Shahanshah."[9]

In the figure of the secret police officer, amazingly, we find the social worker. Such an observation points to the spread of a pastoral power to the state prior to the Islamic Revolution. It was therefore not surprising that the effort to reform society under an Islamic tutelage found such ready supports in the ruins of the old regime. Indeed, one need only look at the Hujjatiyeh.

The Hujjatiyeh. If SAVAK's tutelary work ensured stability in key areas of the economy, the activity of the Hujjatiyeh served to ensure the loyalty of the Religious Right to the Pahlavi state. The Hujjatiyeh emerged to combat heresy. In the early 1950s, several theology students engaged in the study of heresiology abandoned Shi'ism for Bahaism.[10] This incident "humiliated the whole clerical establishment" and raised the fear that "Bahaism might not only influence uneducated lay people, but even infiltrate the theological schools."[11] Under the leadership of Shaykh Mahmud Tavalla'i (Hallabi), the society was created to police the theological seminaries. It established "a program of study aimed at opposing Bahaism"[12] and worked hard at "surveying the people and watching the seminary students."[13]

In the cold war era, the Hujjatiyeh flourished. It was not only violently anti-Baha'i but also anticommunist. In the 1950s, it became an instant success and gained enormously popularity. Since it was one of the few tolerated and activist reform societies, it drew a large following. Its membership included, among others, mullahs, seminarians, civil servants, and elementary school teachers. It gained the approval of prominent religious leaders, notably the preacher Shaykh Muhammad Taqi Falsafi. It also received financial donations from pious foundations.[14] In the 1960s, the Hujjatiyeh "was able to set up branches in various cities and towns, each under the sponsorship of a local mullah."[15] It developed a national program that included "publishing abusive literature, disrupting Bahai meetings and religious services, and attempting to identify Bahais in public employment to pressure officials to enforce various discriminatory measures."[16] It also developed educational programs, built clinics, and encouraged sports activities for youth. By 1977, the Hujjatiyeh was boasting of twelve thousand members nationwide.[17]

Throughout this period, the Hujjatiyeh enjoyed the support of the shah's officials. Since it was dogmatically anticommunist, the government tolerated its activities. The Hujjatiyeh diverted attention from the regime's problems and channeled protest toward minorities. In times of crisis, the Hujjatiyeh frequently collaborated with SAVAK in anti-Baha'i campaigns.[18] Furthermore, in the early stages of the Islamic Revolution, the Hujjatiyeh remained neutral with respect to the government. In fact, in 1981 a government newspaper chastised the Hujjatiyeh for its early ambivalence: "Before the Revolution, you were either against the revolution or indifferent towards it. Have you now changed your policy?"[19]

In the wake of the Revolution, however, the Hujjatiyeh was wholly embraced by the Shi'i 'ulema. Apart from leftist groups, the Hujjatiyeh possessed the largest nationwide organization and in addition was properly fundamentalist. Consequently, "overnight, individuals whom one might have expected to see join their SAVAK patrons before the revolutionary firing squads emerged instead as members of the komitehs [Revolutionary Committees]."[20] Between 1979 and 1981, the Hujjatiyeh emerged not only as a major force within the Islamic Republican party but also as the party's mobile militia. For Hujjatiyeh members, opposition groups such as the Baha'is were hypocrites because they dissimulated their true intentions, pretending to be good Muslims when they were not. And as Hujjatiyeh members were apt to chant, "Hypocrites are more dangerous than infidels."[21]

Today, the Revolutionary Guards have displaced the Hujjatiyeh and similar Hizbollahi (Party of God) societies as the military wing of the Islamic Republican party.[22] As a political organization, the Hujjatiyeh was demolished in the course of doctrinal disputes with the religious leadership.[23] Even so, the Hujjatiyeh has assumed a familiar place within the social service network of the new society. The Hujjatiyeh's revised internal constitution defines the goals of the society as follows:

(1) holding scientific and religious conferences and seminars in different parts of the country in accordance with the law; (2) publishing scientific and reli-

gious booklets and periodicals in accordance with the press law; (3) setting up classes teaching Islamic culture and ethics; (4) opening libraries and sports centers; (5) engaging in public charity affairs and giving cultural aid to Islamic institutions (at home as well as abroad); (6) holding training sessions to train people for scientific, literary, and religious debates in Islamic circles; (7) establishing cultural institutions (schools, etc.); and (8) creating therapeutical centers (clinics, etc.).[24]

This strange history shows how easily the pious social worker could become a zealous police officer of public life.

The New Clergy

Like many secular reformers, religious reformers believed that the social problems spawned by urbanization were a threat to public morals and social decency. Some argued that "the only way to solve these problems was to strictly enforce religious laws."[25] In the 1940s, Ayatollah Khomayni was the most fervent exponent of this position: "These schools mixing young girls and young passion-ridden boys kill female honour, the root of life and the power of manly valour, are materially and spiritually damaging to the country and are forbidden by God's commandment. ... Music arouses the spirit of love-making, of unlawful sexuality and of giving free rein to passion while it removes audacity, courage, and manly valour. It is forbidden by the Shari'a and should not be included in the school programmes."[26] Khomayni went on to argue that if Islamic punishments were enforced for one year, "the seed of injustice, theft and unchastity will be eliminated from the country."[27]

Not all religious leaders, however, defined the notion of strict enforcement of religion so narrowly. For example, in his lectures on child care, Shaykh Muhammad Taqi Falsafi, a popular conservative preacher, argued that the use of psychiatric procedures was in full conformity with the rational foundations of Islam and that by familiarizing oneself with these procedures, one could achieve a deeper and more complete piety.[28] At the same time, health professionals sought to enlist religious leaders in an effort to instruct families concerning proper care, diet, and hygiene. Health professionals maintained among themselves that intervention in families would be most effectively accomplished if the approach suited and built on the religious beliefs of parents.[29]

Pietist organizations such as the Hujjatiyeh were not above borrowing and adapting techniques from secular organizations. Religious leaders funded hospitals, schools, libraries, construction projects, and "rationalized welfare programs" centered on religious foundations such as the Daftar-i Khayrat-i Islami (Office of Islamic Charity).[30] It became possible to form new tactical alliances with secular agents also fighting moral corruption. At the local level, social workers and mullahs often facilitated each other's welfare activities.[31] At the political level, various groups would occasionally merge to form highly vocal organizations, such as the important prohibitionist organization of the 1940s, the Society Against Opium and Alcohol.[32]

However, by the 1970s, many mullahs had decided that the imperial government, either consciously or unconsciously, was unable to adequately address major social problems typical of urban areas, such as disease, hunger, unemployment, alcoholism, drug addiction, and sexual promiscuity. This evaluation convinced many of the mullahs that the government had to change. Young men drawn to the Hujjatiyeh, for example, gradually turned its youth wings, such as the Mahdiyun and the Askariyun, into anti-Pahlavi political organizations.[33] Radicals such as Ayatollah Khomayni's son, Ahmad, admitted later that many of the 'ulema did not support the revolution at first but "eventually joined the revolutionary movement because the regime had failed to attack moral decadence and clean the streets."[34]

The Iranian mullahs, as we now know, were in a particularly good position to initiate political opposition to the regime. They were traditionally independent of the state and had their own sources of funding. Although they were besieged by Reza Shah in the early twentieth century and stripped of many of their social functions, this isolation served to reinforce their identity as a social group. Reza Shah banned the wearing of religious garb by anyone other than registered religious students and preachers and exempted them from military service. Such factors served to identify the mullahs as a group with its own uniform and privileges and also encouraged internal reform. In the 1950s, Ayatollah Mohammad Hussayn Borujerdi reorganized the religious seminaries throughout Iran and centralized the financial system of the seminaries. During the boom of the 1960s, pious merchants and industrialists gave more charitable donations to the seminaries. The clergy thus benefited from Pahlavi modernization programs and was able to expand its size. By the mid-1970s, there were 100,000 preachers and 15,000 students.[35] "By the mid-1970s, the religious establishment was big enough to send preachers regularly into shantytowns and distant villages, probably for the first time in Iranian history."[36] There was also something of a religious revival during this period in informal religious groups, perhaps as many as 12,300 by 1974.[37] When the mullahs threw their weight behind Khomayni, they put at his disposal a formidable institutional network.

At any rate, religious leaders turned to politics not because they wanted to, but because they perceived no other choice as good ministers.[38] For religious reformers, moral reform could no longer be accomplished without reforming the government that often seemed to encourage corruption. As Ayatollah Morteza Motaheri explained, "Any reformer ... who is able to direct the attention of the minds toward the true Islam; who is able to banish corrupt practices and superficialities from the lives of the people; who can satisfactorily bring order in the civic life by providing, among other things, the basic necessities of food, shelter, medical aid and education; … and who can give society a truly Islamic cadre of administrators to lay down rules and regulations for conduct of puritanic administration shall have, in fact, achieved the maximum success as a reformer."[39] Religious ministry thus focused on material as well as moral issues. Preachers emphasized inequalities in wealth distribution and the dangers of uncontrolled consumerism. Their moral concerns forced them to take the problem of social inequality seriously. They sought to create, as Ayatollah Akbar Hashemi Rafsanjani put it, a "new atmosphere that is conducive to [the] remaking of human beings, to the cleansing of society."[40]

The War Against Corruption

In the last years of his life, Ayatollah Khomayni was adamant about the need to uproot every last trace of corruption. "The fight for victory," he said, "shall be realized only when the rotten roots of the former regime and its supporters are uprooted."[41] Ayatollah Khomayni's emphasis on corruption was not novel. Psychologists, criminologists, social workers, women's societies, and politicians had always been preoccupied with the "vast corruption and turmoil of cities like Tehran."[42] In the war against the nascent guerrilla movement, the Pahlavi regime "argued incessantly that they were 'juvenile delinquents' and that their parents had the patriotic duty to turn them in to the authorities." The regime used the theological term *monafiqin,* or "hypocrites," to characterize them, a term used later by revolutionary authorities as well. Repentant guerrillas publicly charged their colleagues with "sexual promiscuity."[43] The shah's government also waged its own war against what it called economic corruption. The Resurgence party sent gangs of students into the bazaars to wage "a merciless crusade against profiteers, cheaters, hoarders, and unscrupulous capitalists."[44]

And it is often forgotten that the arrest of members of the ancien régime for corruption began under the last imperial officials. In 1976, the regime arrested rich businessmen such as Habib Elqanian and Rasul Vahabzadeh. In September 1978, the shah ordered General N'ematollah Nassiri, the former head of SAVAK, to return from safety in Pakistan to Tehran to stand trial.[45] Premier J'afar Sharif-Emami began a well-advertised campaign against prominent figures who were alleged to be Baha'is. He dismissed major bureaucrats and officers and had Hojabr Yazdani, a wealthy entrepreneur, charged with grand larceny. In November, General Ghulam Reza Azhari ordered the release of political prisoners and simultaneously arrested 132 former government leaders, including former Premier Amir

Abbas Hoveyda. Azhari made these arrests under Article 5 of the Martial Law Code, which covered "corruption and misuses of power."[46] On 7 November, the shah delivered a speech on the war on corruption, while elsewhere in Tehran "Lt. General Khademi, a Baha'i, commit[ed] suicide under strange circumstances."[47] In January 1979, Premier Shahpour Bakhtiar released more prisoners and ordered the arrest of more former ministers, promising to hang "those convicted of the most flagrant violations."[48] On 10 February, Mehdi Bazargan referred to "several hundreds of civil servants and senior officials" already under arrest or banned from leaving the country.[49]

Following the collapse of the government, these prisoners and many others were charged with *mufsid fil-ard*, "corruption on earth." Charges such as corruption on earth were so vague as to permit severe punishment by revolutionary tribunals for any action.[50] However, the fact that there were charges at all helped exclude, rather than grant license, to the populace. For Ayatollah Khomayni, if the corrupt went unnamed and unprosecuted, then spontaneous justice would ensue. This was a "danger which is worse than the danger of the previous regime." This elementary discursive act, the naming of a criminal, in turn served as "a bridle" on popular justice.[51] As Ayatollah Khomayni frankly observed on 26 April; "If the Revolutionary Courts did not prosecute them, the people would have gone on a rampage and killed them all."[52] It is for this reason that very early on, conflicts arose between the local populace and the revolutionary tribunals.[53] It is also in this context that one can understand why the populace turned to the most trivial of offenders: SAVAK informers, prostitutes, homosexuals, adulterers, alcoholics, conscripted soldiers, and local policemen.[54] The real targets of popular justice were already beyond its reach.

Once the tribunals had disposed of the prominent figures, identifying corruption became a complex problem. The issue was not a judicial one of identifying prominent members of the imperial government—these officials were well known. Nor was it a political one of deciding which revolutionary was a good Muslim and which one practiced a corrupted Islam— this was or would be determined by Ayatollah Khomayni. The problem was the identification of corruption at the level of the everyday. As former Prime Minister Muhammad 'Ali Raja'i explained, "I know Tudeh [socialist party] people who pray. My brothers and sisters, I have myself an experience with a member of Paykar [a leftist guerrilla organization] being a chaplain and followed by a few Muslims."[55] The problem, in other words, was that the corrupt could dissimulate and appear to be righteous and upstanding citizens. Since many of the accused insisted that they were innocent, it must also be the case that they were *monafiqin*. For this reason, as Ayatollah Khomayni remarked, "the *monafiqin* are more dangerous than the infidels."[56] To identify a hypocrite, one needed to be an expert.

How could one distinguish the hypocrite from the pious person? What activities made corruption visible? One had to watch for how individuals omitted performing certain acts: "About three weeks ago, the Pasdaran [Revolutionary Guards] went into a high school in Tehran and arrested four teachers. The teachers had neglected to have their students sing the official national anthem, to observe the obligatory prayers—in short, they were suspected of counter-revolutionary activity."[57] "Nurses are arrested and charged with neglecting wounded Pasdars in the hospitals."[58] One watched as well for refusal to perform certain acts: "Any non-conformity—from the refusal of workers to pray in an Iranian factory to the refusal of women to wear a headscarf—was treated as 'un-Islamic,' and, therefore, suspect."[59] One watched as well for excessive demands that interrupted habitual routines. "The demand for a 40 hour work week is a political deviation. It means the imposition of a one day strike on the nation's economy."[60] One watched for peculiar behavior, such as "looking at the scene of a bomb blast"[61] or "sending money out of the country."[62]

In other words, one identified corruption against a background grid of routines and norms of performance. Identifying corruption meant identifying nonconformity and demanding normalcy. Since there are always minute lapses and breaches in norm-governed behavior, corruption is at once potentially present, ever pervasive, and almost invisible. Its identification requires persistent surveillance and evaluation of even the most minute activity. Precisely for this reason, "the regime has publicly urged teachers to inform on students, students on teachers, landlords on tenants, tenants on landlords, neighbor on neighbor—the list is endless."[63] Such hidden surveillance had to be uninterrupted and discrete if it was to catch evidence of corruption. As Ayatollah Muhammad Beheshti remarked to a group of schoolchildren, "It is not enough to be honest and simple; one must be honest and crafty."[64]

Tutelary Policing

The ideal citizen, according to a high school text, acts as "the eyes and ears of the state."[65] Indeed, such texts boast that whereas despotic states, like the old monarchy, required complex security and intelligence-gathering services, the Islamic Republic has a "thirty-six million member intelligence service."[66] This statement brings out precisely what is new about the postrevolutionary state: constant, proactive, tutelary policing. In the prerevolutionary period, people tried to protect particular enclaves from the broader corruption of society. Vast sectors of society, such as the slums and shantytowns, were wholly ignored. Other areas (for example, milieus of delinquency, brothels, and drug markets) were supervised, although this supervision aimed not so much at eliminating corruption as at employing "the corrupt" for intelligence, financial, and political purposes. Today, however, there are many societies and organizations dedicated to the moral tutelage and reform of society.[67] I want to briefly discuss three examples of tutelary policing: workers' councils, revolutionary committees, and welfare charities. Each of these policing agencies has its own political focus. The first ties industrial workers to the state, the second keeps an eye on the Westernized urban dweller, and the last ensures support for the regime among the traditional middle and lower classes.

Workers' Councils. In the wake of the Revolution, workers' councils eliminated "corrupt" members,[68] including irresponsible managers and former SAVAK informers. They also initiated moral edification campaigns. The leftist council of one factory, for example, supplied workers with "radical Islamic writings" and held general assemblies "to provide a lecture forum for council members."[69] In the Caterpillar tractor factory, to take another example, "a zealot who, when the council was first set up, objected to the presence of leftists on it, had been allowed to set up an 'Islamic society' in the factory for purposes of 'education' and was clearly having an influence on some of the members."[70]

It makes little difference to my argument whether the councils were leftist or Islamic. Leftists members rejected discussion of civil and democratic rights, considering them liberal bourgeois demands.[71] Like Islamic members, the leftists advanced a notion of moral guardianship that was hostile toward democratic norms. One can say that the workers' councils failed to institutionalize democratic procedures because "during the last thirty years, democratic institutions (whether state or nonstate) have been almost totally nonexistent in Iran."[72] The converse is also true. Precisely because the workers had operated under systems of tutelage for thirty years, they knew very well how to practice moral guardianship.

Workers' councils, of course, had many responsibilities, but maintaining discipline and tutelage were always among them. Councils hired workers, paid salaries, reached agreements with technicians, operated the factory, and maintained discipline on the shop floor. They "built libraries, instituted bus service to and from the plant, provided free work clothes, increased housing allowances for workers, and democratized and improved food services."[73] Since 1982, they have also mandated "compulsory collective prayer, dispatching *mullahs* into the production units on a permanent basis."[74]

Revolutionary Committees. Revolutionary committees also policed for immoral behavior. According to the Central Provisional Committee of Tehran, the tasks of committees included the creation of "classes for persons in authority to familiarize them with their religious and ethical duties" and the establishment of "public gatherings for the purpose of delivering talks to inform the people about the Islamic Revolution and to 'familiarize them with their religious duties at this delicate time.'"[75] Committees banned the sale of alcohol, records, and cassettes. They prohibited dancing, films, and other forms of entertainment. They punished public behavior that suggested sexual promiscuity and evaluated the clothing of citizens to ensure that public decency was not violated. They set and enforced prices for the sale of goods, supervised the collection of garbage, confiscated property, and arrested counterrevolutionaries. Today, operating from neighborhood mosques, they "pass regulations, run courts, collect taxes, write schoolbooks, oversee the army, dispense ideology, recruit volunteers, and funnel rationed goods to the deserving masses."[76]

In short, the revolutionary committees were police agencies, welfare services, and societies for moral guidance. In some cases, their impact extended far beyond their neighborhoods. Islamic societies in the universities, for instance, engaged in a reconstruction crusade in rural areas. They built public works (roads, public baths, health centers, schools, and unfinished industrial projects), transformed the rural credit program into a welfare system, and initiated educational programs designed to improve peasant literacy and "propagate Islamic culture."[77] Similarly, committee patrols formed the original corps of the Islamic Revolutionary Guards. The Revolutionary Guards, which numbered approximately thirty thousand prior to the Iran-Iraq war, maintained security but also established special labor groups in workplaces to provide "ideological, organisational, and military training"[78] and supervised the operation of regular army units.

Welfare Charities. Institutionalized charity also served as a vehicle for moral edification and material comfort. To this end, countless pietist institutions have been established since the Revolution. These include the Foundation of the Dispossessed (the successor to the Pahlavi Foundation), the Martyr's Foundation, the Foundation of Housing, the Urban Land Agency, the Center for Combating Sin, the Economic Mobilization Organization, the Foundation for the Affairs of the War Inflicted, the War Migrant Foundation, and the local Imam's Assistance Committees.

These institutions arose to meet the growing problems of housing, hunger, unemployment and disease. Caring for the dispossessed was a major problem after the Revolution. In 1980, between 2.5 and 4 million people were unemployed out of a total work force of about 10 million.[79] This situation was later compounded by the influx of 1.5 million Afghan refugees, 1.5 million refugees from the Iran-Iraq war, and 10,000 people expelled from Iraq.[80] Refugees "were first taken to camps but the refugees soon moved out in pursuit of better housing. There is no indication that they will return to the villages, even if the war ends."[81]

Today, these charities provide employment, construct housing, supervise rationing programs, subsidize food, organize relief work, and provide for the health and hygiene of neighborhoods. They serve to win the support of those social groups considered by the government to be critical for political stability, the lower classes. They also provide moral instruction on hygiene, child-rearing, family life, and public behavior.[82] Indeed, one can scarcely receive aid if one does not live a moral life. The concern for the well-being of the dispossessed is also a concern for their salvation.

Conclusion

Like the ancien régime, the revolutionary regime is obsessed with creating a normal society. Once modernists homogenized individuals in relation to Western norms, asserting that "we must eliminate local sects, local dialects, local clothes, local customs, and local sentiments."[83] Today traditionalists use disciplinary, tutelary, and carceral technology to enforce another set of norms: "Western patterns of life have to be eliminated in all areas: food habits, clothing fashions, architecture and city planning, education and manners."[84] Ironically, the Islamic Revolution has not eliminated Western forms of power; on the contrary, the Revolution has facilitated a greater totalization. It is therefore not the case that contemporary traditionalism and modernism are somehow diametrically opposed. Indeed, any analysis that proceeds by asserting this distinction ignores the fact that in contemporary Iran, both traditionalism and modernism operate through modern forms of power. They both insist on conformity to the norm. As Ayatollah Khomayni explained, "We have tried to refine their manners. If we don't succeed, then we imprison them. If this doesn't work, then we refine them for good."[85] This brings me to the place punishments occupy within such a state.

CHAPTER 8

Convictions into Prisons

In this chapter, I argue that revolutionary ideals have not shaped Iranian prison practices. I argue that punishment under the Islamic Republic bears almost no resemblance to classical punitive practices. I show how torture complexes shape the lives of those convicted by revolutionary courts in much the same ways as they did before the Revolution. I then discuss how tutelage has become an integral part of prison life and the social policing of society in general and show how contemporary punishments, even the supposedly Islamic ones, reveal features of disciplinary society. Finally, I consider the problems that the new government has in exercising such punishments and how it has become a prisoner of its own convictions.

Carceral Practices

It might be useful to recall some essential features of modern torture under the Pahlavis. An investigation of the civilian and political prison system revealed some interesting commonalities. Through elaborate ways of questioning, both systems tended to focus more on the person than on the act that led to incarceration. The incarcerated became the subjects of a hermeneutics of suspicion in which their lives were constantly examined and judged in light of what counted as a normal human being. Medicine increasingly occupied a more central place in both systems as a penal aid. Medical techniques were used in the maintenance of health and the treatment of the incarcerated. Less emphasis was placed on internalizing the disciplinary gaze and more on grasping the incarcerated from within through medical techniques. Civilian and political administrators worked to produce socialized and dependent individuals. Individuals of this sort were coopted into other activities by police and politicians. Both systems tended toward a preventive, proactive way of surveilling individuals, and both systems had unpredictable results. In particular, they served the incarcerated by bringing them into contact with individuals similar to them and thereby inducing further resistance.

How does this compare with torture after the Revolution? I argue here that postrevolutionary punishment follows this pattern closely. Let me review the way prisoners are questioned, punished, released, or executed.[1] When individuals are arrested, they are photographed and questioned. Questioning may be done by guards or even the governor of the prison as prisoners line up to be processed. Prisoners are also placed in cells, given paper and pens, and asked to write down their "problems," their political views, their life histories, or the names of all the political activists they know. This information is demanded regardless of whether it is already known to the authorities.[2]

Once prisoners write these life histories, they become a feature of later interrogations. Each interrogation begins with an accusation, sometimes even accusations inconsistent with previous ones. For example, in different interrogations, one prisoner "was accused of being a coordinator of the armed rebellion in Kurdistan, a member of the *Peykar* organization, head of a section of the People's *Mohahedine*, military leader of the People's *Fedai* Organization and the theoretician of the *Tudeh* party."[3] In this way, prisoners are "persuaded to confess to lesser misdeeds" as they deny the greater allegations.[4] The new information is then processed. Prisoners are told, at the discretion of the interrogator, to rewrite their stories. This process can be endless. Prisoners may even be told to write their wills in preparation for a mock execution.[5] This form of interrogation focuses less on specific acts and more on the prisoner's life as a whole. One prisoner was told by the judge that "the young people could smell that I was a counterrevolutionary, so I had to stay in prison."[6] Appearing in court is sufficient grounds to indicate guilt for the rest of the prisoner's life.

Questioning is accompanied by torture, but torture is not always related to questioning. As one prisoner put it, "The beating has nothing to do with interrogation—that's why Gohar Dasht is so frightening. It's just part of prison life. It's not done simply to extract information. If, for instance, they entered a cell and saw a mark or a line on the wall, even if it was there before, they would say, 'Why is that there? What did you do it for? You're fined 200 *tomans*'; then they'd beat you."[7] Prison torture does not differ substantively from torture under the Pahlavis. Revolutionary Guards beat, rape, flog, burn the flesh with cigarettes, and stage mock executions of the prisoners.[8] They also use technology developed by Pahlavi torturers. Prisoners are often hung from hooks with one arm manacled over the shoulder, following the fashion of the German weightcuff.[9] They are also placed in extremely small cells specially designed to constrict the body. Evin prison possessed such cells, but the new government has apparently built more at other prisons.[10] Even SAVAK's formidable reputation is used to ensure obedience: "We were told by a guard that we were being taken to a cell which had been equipped by SAVAK and was no ordinary cell because it was full of hidden cameras and microphones."[11]

The most common kind of punishment is flogging. In the case of men, flogging is usually administered to every part of the body, especially the testicles. Sustained whipping in this area induces an inability to urinate. As a result, prisoners are caught in a physical and moral dilemma. On the one hand, if they act cooperatively, "a guard will bring in some drugs" to induce urination.[12] On the other hand, the failure to cooperate will lead to further flogging, and "after days of trying unsuccessfully, their urea count rises. If they are not treated, they die."[13] More typically, prisoners lose sensation in part of their bodies or faint because of extensive flogging. Doctors are brought in to revive these prisoners, and they receive a "shot for extreme pain."[14] Once the prisoners regain sensation, the flogging is resumed.

Medicine still plays a prominent role in the prison, even in a practice as common as flogging. To be sure, preventive medicine is hardly heard of in Iranian prisons. Medical practitioners are rare in prison, and often guards or prisoners provide rudimentary health care. Prison doctors who do not actively participate in torture misdiagnose its effects on their patients and prescribe aspirin and ointments.[15] However, medicine plays a role in sustaining prisoners under torture. A woman imprisoned at Evin noted that the stairs going down led to the torture chamber, while the stairs going up led to a dispensary and surgery. "Prisoners," she added, "are usually taken there immediately after torture."[16]

What are some of the roles of carceral medicine? Medical probes are used to evaluate the moral decency of women. For example, women's genitalia are probed on arrest "to prove later to the prison authorities that they are not good girls" and thereby justify arrest.[17] Medicine is also administered to restore the health of prisoners wounded in street battles and prepare them for interrogation: "A Mojahed named Hamid Ghafouri, son of Habib, was taken from the hospital bed to the torture chambers."[18] Carceral medicine was also enlisted in the war with Iraq. In a memorandum issued to all Islamic Revolutionary Courts, the Chief Prosecutor's Office stated that the Revolutionary Guards wounded in the course of street warfare and at the battle front were dying as a result of the unavailability of blood plasma. Consequently, the following order was issued: "In order to solve this problem, you are requested to give the order that the blood of those persons who are sentenced to death and whose executions are to be carried immediately, should be transferred, by means of a syringe, and under supervision of trustworthy medical personnel, into suitable containers."[19]

Prisoners then are "morally purified," either by the neglect of their life processes or the cultivating of their bodies. The imperative is, not to take life, but to maintain it for as long as possible on the threshold of death. As in prior decades, death is treated as a failure to purify the soul, and the bodies of the tortured are frequently hidden: Bodies are buried inside the prison, large fees are posted for the collection of bodies, or announcements are made that the arrested person is dead "so that no questions will be asked if the victims later die in captivity."[20]

Torture still produces the same dispositional effects. Survivors of torture become disoriented and separated from their own lives. Losing control over one's own bodily functions seems to be related to losing trust in the world. "Until my period in solitary confinement I trusted everybody—all the prisoners," remarked one survivor. But following such confinement, "I suffered from this lack of trust—the unsettling feeling of not being able to trust anybody."[21] Others become self-destructive.[22] Once again, interrogators present themselves in the role of intercessors between the prisoners and their alienated lives. "The interrogator, with a kind look, said to me: 'Son, I hope you have come to your senses and are not going to torment yourself any more. Tell us everything and save yourself.'"[23] 'Somebody told me that I should take pity on my own youthfulness and confess all I knew and had heard."[24]

The loss of trust is also characteristic of torturers and interrogators. Because interrogators assume that individuals must be guilty, they do not trust professions of sincerity.[25] They come to distrust physical signs of exhaustion: "At one point I pretended to be unconscious, but they just beat me harder, accusing me of trying to fool them."[26] One prisoner reported how guards refused to treat a woman who persistently banged her head against the wall with violent force. The guards rejected the doctor's recommendation that she be removed to sanatorium. "They treat them as though they were normal and consider their strange behavior a sign of resistance."[27] The torturers oddly mirror the tortured in their distrust of other human beings.

Torturers still urge their victims to either confess, recant, renounce religious beliefs, or condemn others.[28] The trial at which individuals are released appears to be a mere formality.[29] Torture produces dependent and utile individuals. Public recantation neutralizes the prisoners, discredits a political cause, or serves to instruct the populace. Prisoners are still reminded that they can help themselves "by giving testimony the interrogators wanted to hear"[30] or by recanting their crimes publicly "using a prepared and rehersed [sic] script."[31] As in the past, torture is used not to crush prisoners, but to win "their souls."[32] As one prisoner remarked, "We have Tazir here [discretionary punishment through flogging]. I confessed to a crime, it is better to confess."[33] Some prisoners report having been comforted by another prisoner, "only to find that the latter was a repentant prisoner attempting to gather information on their political activities and contacts."[34]

Recantations also render other political figures suspect. For example, in May 1982 former Foreign Minister Sadeq Qotbzadeh recanted publicly stating that "he hoped to unseat the current government" and claimed that Ayatollah Kazem Shariat-Madari "was aware of his plan, provided financial assistance, and promised to bless the takeover of the government if it succeeded." Although Qotbzadeh was executed in September 1982, his allegations "were used to organize an intense campaign against Shariat-Madari."[35] Recantations are also used to retroactively justify the arrest of various revolutionary factions. In the summer of 1982, for instance, the entire leadership of the Tudeh party, led by party leader Nureddin Kianuri, appeared on national television and "abjectly confessed to a series of offenses ranging from espionage to treason and pleaded forgiveness."[36] Their public appearance enabled the government to justify the original purge of the Tudeh in May 1982 before national and international audiences.

Released prisoners are often still at the mercy of authorities. The Supreme Judicial Council has stated that anyone "having a record of committing crimes, whether or not they again commit crimes," may be arrested or exiled for two months to two years.[37] Released prisoners often sign documents promising to remain apolitical, and sometimes relatives pledge money, property, or themselves as guarantees for good behavior. Released prisoners are in this sense perpetually dependent and utile.

In securing recantations, torturers still have the same difficulties as their predecessors. The procedure for securing a recantation still relies on the willingness of the prisoners to recant, and this willingness frequently has not been forthcoming.[38] Torturers continue to sway uneasily between releasing or executing prisoners, recognizing that in either case it is the procedure itself that is discredited. In the closing days of the Iran-Iraq war, the government initiated retrials or "formalized interrogation sessions designed to discover the political views of the prisoner in order that prisoners who did not 'repent' should be executed."[39] Known as the Death Commission, the court traveled to different prisons and questioned prisoners. Judging by the bodies of the missing, more than two thousand individuals reported so far, torture had done little to change the views of many individuals.[40]

By gathering so many individuals into confined institutions, the prison actually helped these individuals resist torture. Iranian prisons suffer from chronic overcrowding. A large cell can include up to three hundred men or women and children and a small cell as many as twenty-two.[41] Prisoners care for each other.[42] They also share knowledge to evade playing into the hands of torturers. For example, Amnesty International explained the disproportionate deaths at Evin prison, a maximum security prison and torture center, in this way: "In Evin there was no way for prisoners to communicate with each other, so they were unable to prepare answers to questions put to them by the 'Death Commission' as prisoners in Gohardasht had done."[43] Prisoners use crude medical techniques to counteract the effects of torture. In some prisons, prisoners have "hidden medical instruments away in their cell block to help their fellow prisoners" and use these in particular to "induce urine" after a prisoner has been flogged.[44] Furthermore, relatives of the prisoners often gather outside of the prison gates seeking information, and this, too, leads to new support networks outside of the prison. Families of the executed gathered regularly at the cemeteries in defiance of government orders: "On Friday all the mothers along with family members got together and we went to the graveyard. What a day of mourning, it was like *Ashura* [A religious festival of particular importance to Shi'a Muslims, commemorating the martyrdom of the Prophet Muhammad's grandson Hossein.] Mothers came with pictures of their sons; one has lost five sons and daughters-in-law. Finally the Committee came and dispersed us."[45] Families also try to aid new prisoners being brought into the prison: "I was taken to Evin prison. I knew it was Evin because as the vehicle I was in went through the gates I heard women shouting "Evin prison, Evin prison." As a rule, prisoners' families are outside the prison gates and when they see a blindfolded prisoner being brought in they shout to enable the prisoner to be less disoriented."[46]

In such solidarity, one can find perhaps a keener understanding that modern torture arises out of the prison system, not out of the state in general. As a Tehran bus driver said after the Revolution, "This time when we take Evin prison, we'll destroy it."[47] In other countries, the families of the tortured are less interested in sending torturers to jail than they are in establishing the truth about what happened. Perhaps in Iran it is so as well.

Tutelary Practices

Immediately after the Revolution, Ayatollah Khomayni "made it an absolute to turn the prison into an educational institution, where Islam and the Revolution dominate."[48] Iranian prisons became novitiates where prisoners were taught the elements of good behavior and the pains that are the reward of evil conduct. From the government's perspective, prisoners are children. The problem is one of providing the right combination of freedom and moral tutelage. If prisoners are given too much freedom, they will never repent their evil deeds. If they are coerced too much, they will not truly repent; they will dissimulate. Torturers shift uneasily between the two extremes, unable to find the magic combination.

Today, prison life is characterized by a constant effort to persuade and teach, something that was not prominent during the Pahlavi regime. The rhetoric of prison life is quite diverse, and I want to list here some of the main techniques. Prisoners are educated through what they say, hear, see, and do not see. Each technique is meant to persuade or induce a change in how individuals see their situation.

Prisoners are often instructed through constant repetition of phrases. Prisoners are asked to recite short parts of the Quran, slogans such as "God is great; Khomeini is our leader," or phrases such as "This is not a prison it is a university. / We are happy to be here."[49] By reciting a part, the reciters become instilled with the meaning of the whole. In this sense, punishment presupposes anamnesis, that is, that prisoners will recollect what it is to be moral. This comes out clearly in retrials of prisoners when the judge inquires whether the prisoners came from religious families: People whose parents were not religious are given lighter sentences precisely because they cannot be expected to recollect proper morals.[50] Torturers also recite phrases. For example, during flogging, each blow is accompanied by the chant "God is great."[51] Repetition here serves to give a rhythm to the activity. It also aims at conveying to prisoners their errors. Punishment, to use more technical terms, becomes a mnemotechnics, an aid for strengthening the memory.

Repetitive recitation is one technique. Another is to guide the prisoners by what they hear, by auriculation. Prisoners are exhorted through loudspeakers or closed-circuit TVs throughout the prison to change and repent. Prisoners who have recanted are interviewed for the prison audience and sometimes make videos to be played elsewhere.[52] Reformed prisoners are still kept in prisons and provided privileges "as an incentive to the others."[53]

For prisoners who are unable to trust anybody, the broadcasting of prayers and religious speeches is deeply troubling.[54] Since prisoners are constantly trying to understand why they are imprisoned, they attribute meaning to the cacophony of the prison. Numerous accounts attest to the deep suspicion that almost all sounds are meant to intimidate and change the prisoner:

> On the stairs in Block 209 at Evin Prison, people were lying covered by blankets. They left me there for some time so that I could hear the shouts and moans of other people being beaten. I stayed in the corridor blindfold[ed] for eight days.[55]

> The sound of the firing squad from the courtyards of other areas of the prison were continual reminders of where we were and of what was happening beyond our walls.[56]

> There are four stories in the Komiteh building, each ringed by a circular balcony. The guards call the prison the "Hen House," probably because many of us have to squat for days on end on the balconies. ... You are left blindfolded

for days. ... Every night until the early morning hours, people were tortured either in the open courtyard or in the rooms off of it. The screams were terri-
ble.[57]

Another way in which prisoners are exhorted is through what they see.
Human beings, whether dead or alive, are used as symbolic devices for
other prisoners to think about. Corridors are lined with handcuffed prisoners hanging from bars over doors,[58] and executed prisoners are put on display for the other prisoners to witness. Consider the following example:

> I went into a large hallway where there were many people and a woman guard
> came and hit me on the chest and told me to speak and confess or else I would
> see incredible things. There was a lot of crying and wailing; then I was told:
> "we are going to take off your blindfold. You mustn't look to the side, just look
> straight ahead." I opened my eyes and saw a boy hanging from a tree. Both his
> arms were bandaged up to the elbows and both legs up to the knees. He was
> very thin and his name was written on a card round his neck. A guard stood
> next to the boy and poked the body with a stick making it turn around and
> around. Meanwhile other guards watched the prisoners to see their reactions.
> Then we were blindfolded again and taken for interrogation.[59]

Here the only thing the prisoner was allowed to see was the dead body. Her
reaction was evaluated, and then she was taken to interrogation. One can
assess the importance placed on this sort of instruction by the fact that a
while later, "a guard came again and asked who hadn't yet seen the corpse
and who wanted to see it again. ... Those who raised their hands actually
were taken to see the corpse again."[60] Witnessing executions is also common: "Mojahed supporter Habib Olah Eslami, was hung at Evin prison in
front of the entire prison population, who were forced to chant, 'Down
with Rajavi [the leader of the Mujahidin guerrillas],' while they watched
him die."[61]

Mock executions are other occasions in which prisoners are forced to
watch the death of others.

> They took me to a yard where there were four wooden posts in a semi-circle,
> and they tied each of us to a post. ... I asked them to remove my blindfold, so
> this time they didn't blindfold me. I saw the bullet hit the PMOI boy and the of-
> ficer was hit in the stomach. The *Peykar* man may already have been dead, his
> body didn't react to the bullet. The young boy was shaking violently with a bul-
> let in his body. His hands were tied and he was trying with all his might to free
> himself. He was bleeding profusely. I shouted "What are you waiting for? Why
> don't you shoot me?" They laughed, and I could do nothing. The young boy
> died, then the officer. I had just stood there and watched them suffering. ... I
> try very hard not to remember.[62]

The prisoner here tries hard not to remember, but the point of the mock execution is precisely that he should remember what he has seen in the

course of his interrogation. In short, no visible means is overlooked in impressing on witnesses the gravity of their situation.

Yet another technique is to gesture to things that cannot be seen entirely. For instance, "you could see bloodstains in the corridor which were deliberately not cleaned up in order to frighten the prisoners."[63] Violence is implied here but not seen. It is in this sense that one can understand other examples, such as interrogations carried out while the individual lies in a grave or the display of the torture equipment. It is as if the tutor is saying, "Let me make no mention of the instruments of torture here. I am sure you will handle yourself with distinction." One might call this sort of technique paralipsis.

What is interesting here is that all these rhetorical techniques take place within the confines of a closed institution, the prison. Penal tropes are aimed at the prison audience, not at the public at large. The prison has indeed emerged as an educational institution. Punishing the corrupt in this sense, declared Hujjat ul-Islam Lajevardi, "is not torture; in fact it purifies their soul."[64] There is something to this view. Tutelary tortures are distinguishable from carceral tortures precisely because they have such a strong rhetorical dimension.

Islam and Punishment

Among the legislative goals of the Islamic Republic, restoring Islamic law is a high priority. The Islamic Penal Code of Iran in particular appears to restore Islamic punishments, such as *Hudud* (punishments prescribed by the Quran), and includes *qisas*, *t'azir*, and *diyeh* (the paying of blood money). But there is such a difference between what is prescribed by the law and what is done in Iranian society that it might be worthwhile to look closely at the current record of punishment. Let me consider executions, mutilation, and flagellation in turn and then consider the general influence of Islamic legal concepts on punishment today.

Take executions. The Islamic Penal Code allows for *salb* (crucifixion), *rajm* (lapidation), strangulation on the gallows, and shooting by firing squad. Now consider some figures on executions in Iran. Sources on executions are sketchy, but one might begin with the executions of Mujahidin, the most prominent opposition organization and one that was virtually demolished in the 1980s. Ervand Abrahamian has compiled a list of how members of the Mujahidin died between 1979 and 1985 based on the organization's own records and supplemented with obituaries from other sources.[65] Of the approximately 6,800 members who died in prison, most were executed by firing squads (92 percent). Of the remainder, more members died by torture (4.5 percent) than by hanging (3 percent). Of the total 9,067 Mujahidin deaths, more members died in prison (75 percent) than

outside prison (15 percent); the remaining 10 percent died in unknown circumstances. Abrahamian recorded that 31 people (4 percent) were burned
or dragged to death, executions that might have been forms of classical penal torture, although he did not specify this exactly. It would be difficult in
any case to attribute these deaths to the influence of Islamic Penal Code
since the new code does not allow for death by dragging or burning. One
might keep in mind as well that being an opposition group, the Mujahidin
have the greatest interest in bringing out the most brutal aspects of the current government.

Consider now some other sources on executions in Iran. Table 8.1 lists
the figures for executions Amnesty International has documented from the
official press and supplements these figures with deaths Amnesty International has documented on its own, but Amnesty International believes that
these figures are still too low. Even so, it will do to show the relative significance of Islamic punishments. Among so many executions, there is not one
reported case of crucifixion.[66] There are a "few cases" of beheading or amputation before death.[67] As for lapidation, Amnesty International records
four cases of death by stoning in the first half of 1986 and dozens of cases
since 1987, especially for adultery, prostitution, pimping, and homosexuality.[68] Even if this figure were in the hundreds—say, 200—since 1987 this
would comprise only 10 percent of the officially acknowledged executions
and an even smaller percentage of the number of real deaths.

The vast majority of prisoners, in other words, are executed by a firing
squad and, less frequently, by hanging on the gallows.[69] Are these Islamic
punishments prescribed by the Quran? Clearly not. In fact, these punishments were introduced by the Qajars in the late nineteenth century as part
of Western penal reforms. When it became apparent, moreover, that public
hangings were "creating sympathy for the opposition, the regime returned
to the more modern method of implementing death sentences within the
confines of prison walls and making only brief announcements; sometimes
it did not even make an announcement."[70] Today, hangings and firing
squads occupy a place within a disciplinary prison and police system. The
Islamic Penal Code may lay equal weight on different styles of execution,
but the Western ones prevail in practice.

The code also does not provide for some traditional forms of execution—for example, *zendeh beh gur* (burying prisoners alive), *sham'i ajjin*
(burning individuals with candles in the flesh), blowing the convicted alive
from an artillery cannon, suffocating individuals in a Persian carpet, cut-
ting people's throats with a large knife, killing individuals in the same way
they had killed, drawing and quartering, throwing women off high towers
and minarets, strangulation, or beheading. This list should remind one precisely how modest this return to traditionalism is. To be sure, there have
been a few incidents that recall classical punishments. For example, Yusef

TABLE 8.1   Recorded and Reported Executions, 1980–1990

	1980	1981	1982	1983	1985	1986	1987	1988	7/88–12/89	1989	1990	1/90–6/90
Reported by Amnesty International	1,000	2,616	624	400	470	115	158		2,000			300
Reported by the government					337		158	142		1,500	300	

Sources. Amnesty International Report, 1980, 1982, 1983, 1984, 1986, 1987, 1988 (London: Amnesty International Publications, 1980, 1982, 1983, 1984, 1986, 1987, 1988), pp. 329, 323, 304, 333, 327, 340, 235, respectively; Amnesty International, *Iran: Violations of Human Rights* (London: Amnesty International Publications, 1987), pp. 42–43; and Amnesty International, *Iran: Violations of Human Rights, 1987–1990* (New York: Amnesty International U.S.A., 1991), p. 6.

Yusefi was executed on 10 September 1981; among the signs of torture on his body was a phrase branded onto his torso reading, "God is great, Khomeini is our leader."[71] Amnesty International reports for the first cases of beheading occurred in 1990, usually for homosexuality and male rape. One case in particular sounded like a true classical punishment. This was a provincial execution in which, according to this report, the victims' families had a role in exacting *qisas*: "In February 1990 two men were knifed, then flogged and finally beheaded as a retributive punishment for multiple murder and bank robbery in Hamadan. A third prisoner in this case was flogged and then hanged. The bodies of the three men were displayed around town and then burned by a mob."[72] This execution is interesting precisely because it is an exception to the routine way in which most individuals are executed. Indeed, Hujjat ul-Islam Rafsanjani has made the point that even death by stoning should be discontinued and that currently it is imposed only by "tasteless judges."[73] The record here bears him out.

Turning to mutilation, the Islamic Penal Code provides for amputation in cases of recidivism, particularly with respect to crimes such as theft or robbery. Spokespersons for the regime attest that amputation is a common practice. In 1984, Hujjat ul-Islam Moqtadaie, spokesperson of the Supreme Judicial Council, asserted that there had been "numerous cases of severing of hands in Tehran and other provincial cities."[74] In 1984, Amnesty International reported that only "a few instances of amputation of fingers or hands and of stoning to death as judicial punishment have been reported in the press outside Iran."[75] Iranian newspapers reported eleven cases during 1985 and 1986.[76] During 1989, Amnesty International recorded nine cases of amputation for theft.[77] Once again, one may assume that reports of amputation are underreported. This figure ought to be contrasted with the figures for theft and robbery in this period. Such figures are unavailable, but it is hard to believe that the figures for robbery were so low and therefore difficult to believe that amputation has replaced incarceration as the most routine punishment for theft.

In 1984, the Judicial Police announced a new innovation in amputation, namely, "a device that severs a hand in a tenth of a second." This electric guillotine was installed in Qasr prison in 1985. In May 1986, "such a machine was used in the courtyard of Mashad city police headquarters to sever four fingers from the right hand of a convicted thief in front of reporters, legal officials, and prisoners."[78] How often it is used is unclear. What is clear is that building it involved considerable coordination between medical and political authorities: "To facilitate the enactment of Islamic law on severance of thieves' hands, help has been sought from relevant competent authorities such as the Coroner's Office, the Ministry of Health, and the Medical Faculties of Tehran and Beheshti Universities."[79] Furthermore, amputation is carried in conjunction with medical authorities: "For example, in January 1990 a convicted thief had four fingers of his right hand amputated in Tehran, after being sentenced by a court in Shahroud. The amputation had to be postponed once because the convict was found to be suffering from high blood pressure."[80]

The machine is praised for two features, the speed with which it severs limbs and the fact that it is built on correct medical knowledge. These characteristics are features of modern punishments; modern gallows are praised in much the same way. They are not features of traditional punishments. Recall, for example, how the Safavid Hakim Muhammad weighed different methods of amputation according to their painfulness.[81] Mechanization was not valued because it intruded on the executioner's ability to modulate the pain to fit the punishment.

Turning to flagellation, the Islamic Penal Code enjoins flagellation for adultery, fornication, homosexuality, lesbianism, drinking, and malicious accusation. Flagellation is clearly the commonest form of public punishment.[82] There were 4,467 incidents of flogging between 1986 and 1987.[83] But flagellation was common practice in Iran under the Pahlavis. It was used extensively inside prisons in the course of torture. So what is new is, not that flagellation is practiced, but that it is now judicially sanctioned and occurs in public. What needs to be explained about flagellation is its publicity, not its existence.

It might be helpful to put the issue of public punishments into historical perspective. Classical punishments were not exercised merely for their deterrent or retributive role. They played a complex role in sustaining the legitimacy of judicial proceedings, ethical and status roles, and the political standing of local authorities. They did this through marking the body with signs that illustrated the moral order and the borders of its domain to others. Flagellation was no exception. It occurred in the context of a series of signs indicating the status of the prisoner in the eyes of society.

Contemporary flagellation, however, is remarkably egalitarian. The status of prisoners is not registered, except that provisions are made if the prisoner is a woman. Flagellation is not applied merely to acts condemned by the Quran, such as sodomy, drinking, adultery, lesbianism, pimping, and malicious accusation. It is also applied to delinquencies—that is, any deviation from a disciplinary norm, such as misuse of a military uniform, negligence that results in the escape of a convict, driving without a license, tampering with a speedometer, and misuse of an official seal. Flagellation is also applied in the case of misdemeanors—that is, deviations of demeanor from tutelary norms, such as an unmarried couple caught kissing, a woman not wearing a veil, medical personnel revealing a patient's secrets, failure to support a wife, or acceptance of a bribe. And this list does not cover the wide range of infractions for which flagellation is utilized in the course of carceral interrogation. In these cases, flagellation is applied, not because of what the person has done, but because of who he or she is, for example, a *monafiq* or a Baha'i.[84] In short, flogging has a place not only within the law but also within disciplinary, tutelary, and carceral regimens. The authorities believe that flagellation has a role in deterring further infractions from the norm. This, one might add, is precisely the way flagellation was used in the Qajar Dar ul-Fonun and other disciplinary academies: to reinforce conformity to the norm.

Another reason flagellation is public is to assert the government's revolutionary credentials. Official histories maintain that the Revolution was for Islam, and a key feature of Islam is the practice of Quranic punishments. As Amnesty International remarked, "Public executions, floggings and amputations are a relatively easy way [*sic*] for the government to demonstrate its uncompromising commitment to revolutionary Islamic values. Curtailing the use of such punishments could be interpreted as capitulation to pressure from the West, and could be exploited by the radical faction to advance its political cause at the expense of the moderates."[85] Since Islamic punishments have become a touchstone for legitimacy, it is unlikely that they will vanish soon.

Reviewing the practices of execution, mutilation, and flagellation, one can only conclude that Islamic punishments in Iran are notable not because they are representative of routine punishment, but because they are so exceptional. Those that do persist do so because they occupy a place within a disciplinary apparatus, such as flogging, or because they conform to modern notions of speed and efficiency, such as the amputation machine. This is not a significant change from the early days of the Revolution. Even at the height of revolutionary terror, most punishments conformed to prerevolutionary practice.[86] The Islamic Penal Code, then, is not a good guide to the actual practice of punishment in Iran. It does not give an accurate sense of the distribution of different sorts of punishment.

Perhaps, however, the code affects punishment in a different way. The code regards confessions as conclusive evidence of guilt as well as means by which to reduce the penal sentence. "This emphasis on confession," according to Amnesty International, "may provide an incentive for law enforcement officials to inflict torture."[87] Indeed, it does in judicial systems that do not accept circumstantial evidence or probable guilt.[88] This, however, is not a good description of the Iranian judicial system. In Iran, preventive detention exists for people who may pose a danger to the regime. Judges possess wide discretionary powers to decide on their own behalf whether the trial was impartial. Ayatollah Khomayni put it this way: "The judge is permitted to rule on the basis of his own knowledge without needing proof or confession or oath, be it concerning the 'rights of God' or 'the rights of the people.'"[89] Furthermore, those who are tortured are not asked to offer confessions at their trials. Consider the following description:

I was taken to a building called the court where there was a mullah behind a desk who must have been in his early twenties. There were four chairs on one side of the room and I sat down with three other women. None of us had anything in common politically. We gave our names one by one and were each asked which organization we had been arrested in connection with. ... The court convened for no more than five minutes. There was no one else in the room, but there were interruptions the whole time. The judge asked if he was free to do this or that, or when he could talk to this person or that—it was all very strange. After five minutes we were told to leave the room and there were no further questions.[90]

Given all this, it is hard to believe that Islamic law encourages torture to produce confessions, especially as modern torture was a feature of the previous regime, which did not place as high an emphasis on confession. Consequently, among the factors that cause the persistence of torture in Iran, the Islamic Penal Code must count as one of the least persuasive.

Reasons of State

If Islamic punishments are in fact such marginal features of punishment in Iran, then why does the regime tolerate this situation? I wish to draw attention to the role played by the doctrine of *zarurat,* or "necessity," in contemporary politics. This doctrine holds that "the primary rulings of Islam may be temporarily waived in emergencies or conditions of overriding necessity."[91] Judges originally invoked necessity in the case of individuals, for example, a person eating pork because he or she would otherwise starve. Ayatollah Khomayni, however, developed the doctrine of *zarurat* into something akin to the European doctrine of reason of state. Thus, he argued that one may ignore Islamic dictates if the state is threatened or if inaction leads to "wickedness and corruption."[92]

Early in the Revolution, the minister of justice invoked the doctrine of *zarurat* to justify revolutionary tribunals. These were trials, he said, held under extraordinary conditions, "like wartime trials acting under their own rules and regulations."[93] Under these emergency conditions, the tribunals adapted the procedures of normal military courts under the imperial government. Prosecutors were assigned to build up case files on individuals. These files did not provide evidence; they determined criminality. "We try these people according to documents, but our objection is that criminals should not be tried. They should be killed."[94] The objective of the trial was to set forth the truth about the criminal, not to determine the guilt of the accused: "You are being tried in this court as a criminal, not as an accused."[95] Even the prosecutor general, Ayatollah 'Ali Qoddusi, admitted that no revolutionary tribunal bore "the least resemblance" to Islamic courts.[96] Not surprising, many judges were reluctant to participate in them, and staffing the judicial system remained a serious problem.[97]

Authorities rejected Amnesty International's criticisms of the tribunals. As Ayatollah Khomayni put it, "There should be no objection to the trial of these people because they are criminals, and it is known that they are criminals. ... These are not people charged with crime, they are criminals."[98] From the regime's perspective, there is no reason to grant people who are clearly criminals an automatic right of self-defense. Authorities charge that human rights organizations would defend the corrupt and ignore the rights of innocent victims who suffer at their hands.[99] To make this point, authorities have held a few political trials in public in which the accused were surrounded by photographs of their victims.[100]

The doctrine of *zarurat*, in other words, allowed for the quick adoption of the procedures of the ancien régime. This doctrine makes it easy to waive any Islamic considerations in dealing with corrupt individuals: "They beat me up because I hadn't wanted to let them in, and burst into my wife's bedroom. She told them that if they were good Muslims they should wait till she was dressed, but they hurled insults at her, and then called me a homosexual. They threw my wife out of bed and dragged my son in by the hair and beat him. Afterward they took him straight to Evin prison."[101]

Narcotics trafficking, in particular, serves as a good ground for waiving Islamic considerations. Because narcotics trafficking is viewed as moral corruption in the West as well as in Iran, authorities often execute prisoners on such charges to make the punishment acceptable. Political prisoners, homosexuals, and adulterers are charged with narcotics trafficking as part of the punishment.[102] As Ayatollah Sadeq Khalkhali explained: "I haven't executed anyone for *zena* [adultery] or *lavaht* [homosexuality] unless they were [drug] addicts as well. ... But generally speaking, I agree with punishing sinners. After all, we've made an Islamic Revolution so we should act 'Islamically.'"[103]

As with SAVAK under the shah, the current regime is particularly concerned with prosecuting drug addiction. In various antinarcotics campaigns, authorities have allowed guards to whip offenders on the spot or to hang offenders on hooks on the back of pickup trucks that were then driven through the city streets. In one day alone, 16 January 1989, fifty-six offenders were hung throughout Iran.[104] Such campaigns seem to be entirely unrelated not only to judicial considerations but also to practical ones. As Hujjat ul-Islam Karrubi remarked, "It does not matter whether it [the execution] resolves the problem or not."[105]

To the extent that one may speak of Islamic doctrines affecting the general tenor of punishment in Iran, one must refer to the doctrine of *zarurat*. Of course, this doctrine can have narrow as well as broad interpretations. Khomayni himself provided a very broad definition, arguing that an Islamic state has such absolute powers that it can "unilaterally revoke any agreement with the people" and can even suspend the exercise of the five pillars of the faith, including fasting, prayer, and pilgrimage to Mecca.[106] Although Khomayni retreated from this rather extreme view, a doctrine that allows for suspending the five pillars of Islam would have no difficulty allowing for modern torture, disciplinary punishments, and tutelary exhortation. In the authorized commentary on Khomayni's judicial doctrines, the commentator makes this quite clear: "If the judge acquires knowledge of certainty concerning the facts of the case through the reliable modern means and instruments such as fingerprinting, medical examination, the infra-red camera which photographs the past and other instruments for detection of crime, this knowledge is more valid for him than ... proofs of the Sacred Law such as confession, witnesses, and oath which are of the next [i.e., lower] order."[107]

Guards may fast during the month of Ramazan while they torture.[108] They may marry prisoners, rape them, and execute them so as not to be accused of having killed virgins. Some guards have even approached families of such women with bride money.[109] Overriding necessity in the fight against corruption can excuse all these events. Yet clearly, adherence to the broad interpretation of *zarurat* will leave the Islamic Republic only Islamic in name.

Evidence that this has already occurred within torture complexes is abundant. Because modern torture is still a bureaucratic process of enormous proportions, it displays some of the features that characterize bureaucracies. Torture complexes produce a range of experts who take themselves to be better situated than judges to determine what is to be done to the prisoner. Although the Revolutionary Guards are formally related to the Prosecutor's Office, a former Islamic revolutionary judge made quite the opposite point: "The IRGC [Islamic Revolutionary Guard Corps] is an absolute power in Iran. Theoretically, on security and intelligence matters, they receive orders from the Prosecutor's office, but in fact the IRGC can even bring about the transfer or removal of the *hakem-e-shar'* [religious judge] or the Friday Imam [prayer leader]. They have created an atmosphere whereby even the *hukkam-e shar'* are cautious in their dealings with them. They consult the IRGC when issuing a verdict and even when passing sentence."[110]

Established judges have spoken openly about the failure of the IRGC to conform to legal considerations. Ayatollah Hussayn 'Ali Montazari in particular has been a strong and vocal critic: "I have repeatedly said that the revolutionary guards and all other officials should not just on mere suspicion of a plot against the revolution engage in any anti-*Shari'a* acts by entering homes or by arresting private individuals out of curiousity. The *Qur'an* says: 'Do not be suspicious or curious.'"[111] Similar statements have been issued by the revolutionary prosecutor general and the head of the judiciary.[112]

Although conflicts would normally exist between judges and guards, the fact that many judges are young and inexperienced tends to play into the hands of prison guards. "The judge asked if he was free to do this or that, or when he could talk to this person or that—it was all very strange."[113] All this points to the fact that the dictates of law, even Islamic law, are marginalized in the prison system. Prisoners report that when they announce that they are protected from torture by the constitution of the Republic, "prisoners [are] made fun of and beaten simply for mentioning their rights under these instruments."[114]

Judges regard legal violations as technical failures in discipline, not as the sociopolitical issue that torture persists in an institutionalized form under the Revolution. Judges think of torture complexes as disciplinary organizations that have temporarily failed to perform their function. However, torture complexes are not disciplinary organizations, and within them discipline tends to decay. Guards associated with torture complexes engage in robbery and excessive violence; personal interest comes to replace disciplinary training.[115] Even the Revolutionary Guards are apparently frustrated with the lack of discipline within torture complexes. They become impatient when execution orders are delayed, they are frustrated with excessive noise in the women's wards, and they execute the wrong prisoners by mistake in the confusion.[116] Indeed, if one frees oneself from the assumption that torture complexes are disciplinary and looks at them from the standpoint of carceral rationality, one can see that they are working much as they always have in Iranian politics. What Islamic judges perceive to be failures of discipline are in fact integral features of modern torture.

Revolution and Terror

Since the Revolution, torture complexes have worked much as they always had. The key difference is that the prisons have abandoned their disciplinary role more than they had done even under the Pahlavis. What has emerged is a prison system in which tutelage and torture occur side by side. Inside and outside the prison, public punishments are used symbolically to illustrate the regime's enduring commitments to revolutionary ideals and to reinforce discipline. Most of the new Islamic punishments constitute only a fraction of the cases of punishment in Iran.

This is surprising given how much opposition there was to torture in the postrevolutionary period. In spring 1979, leading 'ulema prohibited torture and arbitrary punishment, including Ayatollah Sharabyani (17 February), Ayatollah Khomayni (18 February), Ayatollah Shariat-Madari (24 February), Ayatollah Abdollah Shirazi (6 March), Ayatollah Muhammad Reza

Mahdavi-Kani (8 March), Ayatollah Mahmud Taleghani (24 May), and Ayatollah Khomayni again (24 June). On 3 July, the provisional government stated that "torture and cruel treatment were prohibited under Iranian law and any violation was punishable under Articles 131, 132, and 136 of the penal code."[117] In autumn 1979, torture "for the purpose of extracting confessions or gaining information" was prohibited under Article 38 of the new Iranian constitution.[118] Among the newly elected parliamentary representatives, there was also strong resistance "to legislation in Majlis [Parliament] to create an Intelligence Ministry" to replace SAVAK.[119] In April 1981, two venerable ayatollahs of the Mashad hierarchy proclaimed that "torture, arbitrary trials, confiscation of private property are all against Islam's precepts. Islamic courts are staffed by corrupt and cruel individuals."[120] In December 1982, Ayatollah Khomayni once again sharply criticized "the courts and komitehs [Revolutionary Committees] for their excesses in arrests, executions, and invasion of privacy."[121]

Yet torture continued throughout this period. On 21 May 1979, Ayatollah Tabataba'i Qomi complained that "unjust" and "unwarranted tortures" were being administered to prisoners "even after they had been found not guilty."[122] In May 1981, the official government Torture Probe Commission concluded that "certain exceptional cases of torture were observed in some of the prisons."[123] President Abol-Hassan Bani-Sadr's office went further, submitting five hundred individual claims of torture, while the Mujahidin reportedly submitted several hundred more allegations.[124] An American journalist detained in Evin prison also observed that torture was practiced there and elsewhere between July 1980 and February 1981.[125] One despondent prison guard bitterly complained, "They've ruined the revolution—they've arrested too many people, they've tortured and executed too many people."[126]

Why did torture persist despite so much opposition? One common account asserts that the factional warfare of 1981 triggered the reappearance of organized torture. This account assumes, mistakenly, that torture was *not* practiced before 1981. Since it was, factional warfare cannot account for torture's persistence. Another common account asserts that torture persisted because former SAVAK officials found a new home in the revolutionary SAVAMA, a new secret police.[127] SAVAMA continued practicing torture in the early years of the revolution. There is, however, little "hard evidence" that this organization exists[128] or that if it does, it is of any importance. When former President Bani-Sadr was asked whether SAVAMA existed and if General Hussayn Fardust, the former head of the Imperial Inspectorate, was directing it, he replied, "People have told me this. ... I do not know if Fardust is really running SAVAMA. It does exist but it is not so important: it is mainly staffed by old SAVAK officials concerned with external intelligence and counter-intelligence." It has, he added, no "internal functions."[129]

In the end, torture may be too shrouded in state secrecy to account adequately for its persistence. Be that as it may, torture is not an integral part of a revolution, for much depends on the social forms that preceded the revolution. In the Iranian case, torture seems extremely likely given the history of punishment there. Throughout this century, Iranian governments had administered populations through disciplinary regulations, judicial prohibitions, police surveillance, economic incentives, carceral training, and tutelary instructions. It was not particularly surprising that state functionaries continued in this fashion after the Revolution, although they placed greater emphasis on tutelage. The lesson is a cautionary one: Iranian revolutionaries can succeed in overthrowing governments only by maintaining and more deeply entrenching prior practices. In Iran, revolutionaries did so not because they were inherently evil, but because they utilized whatever they could find under constrained conditions. The challenge now, under less pressing situations, is for the Rafsanjani government to change penal practices in a way that precludes torture.

PART THREE

. . . .

ORIENTING MODERNITY

It is easy to imagine and work out in full detail events which, if they actually came about, would throw us about in all our judgements.

If I were sometime to see quite new surroundings from my window instead of the long familiar ones, if things, humans and animals were to behave as they never did before, then I should say something like "I have gone mad"; but that would merely be an expression of giving up the attempt to know my way about. And the same thing might befall me in mathematics. It might e.g. seem as if I kept on making mistakes in calculating, so that no answer seemed reliable to me.

But the important thing about this for me is that there isn't a sharp line between such a condition and a normal one.

—Ludwig Wittgenstein
Zettel, No. 393

Throughout the twentieth century, different groups have fought each other for control of the state. One can describe these situations as struggles to seize power and direct political structures to function in the interests of those who govern. This description is misleading, however, in that it fails to recognize that "the problem is not to seize power, but to make power."[1]

A century ago, Iranian society was powerless. Whoever tried to seize power lost it just as quickly as he or she gathered it. The Qajars described their own capacity to exercise political violence in precisely these terms. "'That is real power,' said the King; 'but then it has no permanence.'"[2]

Remarkably, in less than a century, such power *has* become a permanent element of Iranian society. How did this occur? Many Iranians learned to organize their actions according to a certain rationality, and what amounts to the same thing, others could predict their behaviors and could count on these habitual patterns of individual action to build new durable social structures.

The Iranian state was one such structure. When reformers assumed control at Tehran, they did not really seize power. Rather, they brought particular ways of conduct to political life. They reformed subjects according to particular political rationalities, some of which are illustrated by reformatory punishments. Once any particular rationality gained this kind of political salience, it was understandable as a general strategy for reform.

In the next three chapters, I intend to develop this argument in different ways. In Chapter 9, I discuss in a general way the interrelationship between state violence and what Iranians have become. I shall try to situate my argument in the terms of other Iranian theorists of violence, most notably Jalal Al-e Ahmad, Gholam Husayn Saedi, and Reza Baraheni.

In Chapter 10, I take up the theme of rationalization in Iranian society. I show how an analysis of punishment clarifies not only different ways in which violence can be exercised but also why subjects behave as they do. This gives us a more finely grained approach to the study of state capacity.

In Chapter 11, I use the conceptual distinctions developed in the previous chapter to evaluate contemporary social scientific explanations of torture. My aim is to show how all these explanations are misleading in crucial ways.

CHAPTER 9

Questioning the Subject

When I began this study, I expected that changes in punishment would mirror changes in the state, and in this I was disappointed. Instead, I found that changes in punishment often *preceded* changes in the state by a decade or two. More specifically, I identified three periods where I expected to find dramatic changes: the Constitutional Revolution (1905–1909), the regime of Reza Shah (1925–1941), and the Islamic Revolution (1979–1981). During the Constitutional Revolution, I postulated that punishments would become more humane in contrast to Qajar punishments. During the reign of Reza Shah, I expected punishment to become more disciplinary. Following the Islamic Revolution, I expected to see punishments, including torture, to conform more closely to Islamic law than to the arbitrary practices that preceded them.

None of these expectations proved to be correct in the end. Looking at the Constitutional Revolution, I noticed that the actual punishments practiced during this period did not differ significantly from punishments during the late Qajar period. Most of these practices had their origins in the late nineteenth century; the Constitutionalists simply justified them in new ways.

The regime of Reza Shah did not significantly alter the emphasis on disciplinary punishments. Punishment changed radically only after the reinstallation of Muhammad Reza Shah in 1953, where a veritable take-off in punitive techniques occurred, techniques I characterize as carceral and tutelary punishments.

After the Islamic Revolution, the actual practice of punishment turned out to have little in common with old nineteenth-century punishments and much more in common with the punitive practices of the previous regime, despite rhetoric emphasizing radical juridical changes, as in the Constitutional Revolution.

Why should changes in punishment precede changes in the state? When new politicians come to power, they look for administrative techniques, particularly punitive ones, to enforce their political agenda. Time and availability shape the exact techniques such leaders choose. So these techniques must have preceded the politicians to have been available at all. Change in punishments seems to occur in periods of political stability, not instability. It occurs when public officials are not preoccupied with political survival and when private citizens are relieved of the constraints of daily survival. Political actors at such times are more likely to respond to external influences, whether these be foreign states, military advisers, missionaries, or, thankfully, human rights organizations. That, at any rate, is the Iranian record.

Punishment, then, like labor and sexuality, possesses its own periodization and social history quite apart from the state. Iranian penal history casts a very different light on the development of state power in this respect. It suggests that one should pay less attention to who exercises power and more to how power is exercised. Revolutions may change who rules but not necessarily how one is ruled. Suppose one retold modern Iranian politics with this study in mind. What would it look like?

One might begin with the Qajars. The Qajars were despots, but they had at their disposal neither armies nor bureaucracies and possessed little ideological legitimation. How, then, did they exercise power? The element through which power was exercised in Qajar society (and through which it was constrained to be exercised) was the sign as it was manifested upon bodies. It is in this light that one can understand the central place occupied by public, illuminated rituals: spectacles of punishment, ceremonies of status, and demonstrations of tribute. This style of conduct still persists in Iranian society, but it no longer occupies a central place in the general exercise of power. For that matter, the signification of individuals was adequate for only the most superficial control of public life.

The problem of power, as the Qajars posed it, was one of reliability: To what extent was an individual dissimulating his or her intentions behind this sign? It was not so much a question of ascertaining whether signs were true or false (the social exterior, *zahir*, of each individual was always a mask and so always deceptive) but one of gaining access to the hidden flaws, weaknesses, passions, ambitions or, in short, the *batin*, or interior, of individuals. Each individual struggled to protect the purity of his or her *batin* from being violated by others and simultaneously tried to uncover and gain access to the *batin* of others through social dissimulation.[1]

Analysts characterize this kind of interaction in different ways. American political scientists describe it as "the politics of distrust," reducing it to psychological features of the Iranian personality.[2] Neo-Marxists characterize it as "the politics of social conflict," reducing it to the conflicting interests of classes and groups.[3] Both views are quite mistaken since such interaction is a cultural style with distinct rules, one that occurs in the absence of conflict and that persists *within* families and groups and not merely between them, as anthropologists have shown.[4] The problem is that anthropological studies fail to articulate such a cultural style as a problem of power. My claim is that these traditional practices of self-subjection were the main ways in which power was exercised, but they have been increasingly marginalized. Modern efforts to instill organizational discipline are not efforts to rationalize otherwise irrationally suspicious and distrustful Iranians but efforts to displace one stylized way of exercising power over others with another.

Qajar society differed crucially in this respect from those that followed it. In Qajar society, power was exercised principally through the process of representation. In later societies, it was exercised through modes of subjection. The problem of gaining access to the interior of individuals was replaced by the problem of fixing a particular type of subjectivity on individuals. I document this transition by describing the kinds of subjection associated with punishment in the Constitutionalist period, the Pahlavi modernization programs, and the Islamic Republic.

What was at issue in the Constitutional Revolution was how power could be exercised to promote economic prosperity and strengthen national sovereignty. The Constitutionalists agreed with past Qajar reformers that these goals could not be achieved through a form of power that was exercised through royal signs, spectacles, and ceremonies. They promoted the intensive use of European discipline, a form of power that had been exercised in several areas prior to the Constitutional Revolution. They tried to foster subjects who conformed to the law by the force of an inner necessity, their conscience. The Constitutionalists drew a close relation between juridical sovereignty and social discipline: A populace, in exercising its sovereign rights, could act to move the state toward sound national policies and at the same time induce in itself a more thorough discipline in political and economic affairs. This kind of republican government had its ideological locus in the Tobacco Rebellion of 1891–1892, "the first successful mass protest in modern Iran."[5]

The Pahlavi reformers were also concerned with political centralization, economic development, and social discipline. Pointing to the experience of the post-Constitutional period, they maintained that the exercise of positive rights was not crucial for promoting discipline. For them, Iranians used appeals to positive rights to interfere in sound disciplinary programs and mask their self-interest, as the experience of the post-Constitutionalist period showed. Furthermore, enforcing the law secured only superficial changes, always leaving open the possibility for social anarchy. The problem of power was to promote disciplined obedience even where the state police was absent. The Pahlavi reformers endeavored to create subjects who disengaged themselves from traditional values and conducted themselves according to objective economic norms. The problem was a matter of scope (for example, incorporating whole populations under a general state surveillance), intensity (for example, promoting severe but brief discipline at a particular time and place for a specific population), or duration (for example, supervising specific social groups or persons over the course of their lives).

After the Islamic Revolution, the problem of power was put differently. What kind of practices, revolutionaries asked, can we exercise on ourselves and others that will disrupt and undermine the forms of cultural domination that characterized Pahlavi society? The revolutionaries adapted a well-established technique for exercising power over subjects, tutelage. Through a tutelage at once personal and universal, the Pahlavi state had set out to preserve Iranians from the moral corruption generated by Western culture and modernization. Today the Islamic revolutionaries are engaged in shaping subjects who express authentic Islamic norms in their conduct. Through tutelage, Iranians were encouraged to alter Western habits (by wearing veils, refusing ties, growing beards) and to express a certain moral authenticity in their conduct (by praying or chanting).[6]

In each of the major political phases, then, a particular technique of power (law, discipline, or tutelage) is exercised on or through a particular kind of subjectivity (juridical, normalized, or authenticated). These techniques separate an individual from others, isolate him or her from specific communities, force self-reflection, and bind the person to his or her character in a constraining way. Once habituated, state officials can exercise power more effectively precisely because individuals have become more predictable.

We now have a general type of power that characterizes the state. It is exercised through subjects, not through signs, as it was in the Qajar period. The point here is not to replace a simplistic interpretation of Iranian politics with another but rather to think about how this alternative history can help clarify the nature of the Iranian state's capacity. From where does the modern state derive its strength?

The state derives its strength in part from political affiliation, economic revenues, and modes of subjection, but the precise combination has varied over time. One can get an idea of the changing combinations by examining patterns of political conflict. As the state changed the sources of its power, new political conflicts arose as well. In the early nineteenth century, the prevailing form of conflict was against the domination of particular tribal confederations (the Afghan, the Afshar, the Zand, and the Qajar), although other factors, especially economic exploitation, may have played a role.[7] In the late nineteenth century, protests against Western economic exploitation became more important, although rebellions against political domination or protests against Western modes of conduct were not absent.[8] More recently, the prevailing conflicts have been concerned with relations of subjection. Of course, there have been notable popular movements against political domination (the Constitutional Revolution) and economic exploitation (the Oil Nationalization Movement of 1951–1953).[9] However, the Islamic Revolution is particularly important in Iranian politics because so many Iranians contested the modes of conduct that characterized themselves. Iranians set out to disrupt the relations that held them to themselves, relations that placed them with reference to a kind of subjectivity and disposed them to submit to the actions of others.

One can argue, of course, that these struggles against subjection may be explained with reference to more fundamental relations. Some have derived the "religious" or "anti-Western" character of the Islamic Revolution from class conflict,[10] political xenophobia,[11] or social anomie.[12] However, there are good reasons to take the Islamic Revolution at face value. Its anti-Western character is not a epiphenomenon, but neither does it suggest a more fundamental explanation. The modern state now draws part of its strength from modes of subjection. To be sure, the state also exploits revenues and depends on political affiliation, but this is precisely the point: None of these relations is more or less fundamental than the others. In the course of the twentieth century, the subject has come to be situated at a major locus of power, and so, quite appropriately, it is a locus of political struggles more so than ever before.

Is it simply anachronistic to read themes central to postmodern theorists, especially Foucault, into Iranian politics? No, because the problem of subjection and violence has been central to Iranian analysts reflecting on the state for some time now. It might be well worth reflecting on earlier treatments of the subject.

One might begin with a famous diagnostic and polemical work of late Pahlavi society, Al-e Ahmad's *Gharbzadegi*.[13] Among its many remarkable features, this book might be noted for the manner in which it approaches Iranian politics. Here, the exercise of power is analyzed in the terms of the question of subjectivity.

Almost a century ago, Malkum Khan explained to Iranians that the progress of the West had been made possible by two kinds of factories: one that transformed inanimate objects into finished products and one that reformed animate beings into trained individuals.[14] In a similar vein, Al-e Ahmad explains the dominance of the West with reference to two processes: mechanization and regimentation. The West, he explains, comprises "all of the countries which, with the aid of machines, are capable of converting raw materials into something more complex and marketing it in the form of manufactured goods."[15] Through economic production, these societies produced not only finished products, but finished natures for human beings. "Conformity in the face of the machine, regimentation in the factories, going to and leaving work on time, and a lifetime of doing the same tedious job because [*sic:* becomes] second nature to all those who work with machines." Regimentation in turn disposes individuals to have a "third nature," one that is characterized by a desire for conformity. "Attendance at party meetings and unions which require uniformity in dress, gesture, greeting, and thought is also a 'third nature' conforming to the machine."[16] Western politics takes its general forms from "a liberal inheritance from the French revolution";[17] it draws its vitality from mechanization and regimentation. Occasionally and inevitably, the latter undermine the democratic process as such. He observes that "conformity in the workplace leads to conformity in the party and the union, and this itself leads to conformity in the barracks; that is, for the machines of war!"[18] Fascism and imperialism are merely different political forms that the process of regimentation takes.[19]

Al-e Ahmad draws attention to three relations of power that entrench Western regimentation throughout the globe: relations of exploitation, relations of investigation, and relations of discipline. Each carries with it a particular mode of subjection. Non-Westerners participate in regimentation by producing raw materials for export and consuming the finished products of Western societies, including machinery. However, the non-Westerner does not possess a machine but rather "is possessed by it because he must live in the shadow of its protection and find refuge in it."[20] This psychological dependence is in turn re-inforced by all the political maneuvers designed "to insure that this one-way relationship shall remain stable forever, and that the ties between buyer and seller will never be broken."[21] Consequently, non-Westerners mistakenly judge their economic roles to be natural and inevitable and for this reason do not resist the exploitation of their specific national economies. As he puts it, "Our sense of competition has been lost and a sense of powerlessness has taken its place, a sense of subservience"—for example, "they take the oil because they're entitled to it and because we lack [the necessary] capability."[22]

Al-e Ahmad also points to the ensemble of practices through which non-Westerners became subjects for knowledge. He notes that in the past Westerners collected this knowledge "to keep us impoverished."[23] Today, however, each national culture has become "an object suitable for investigation either in a museum or a laboratory."[24] It is a mistake, then, to think that the West only processes inanimate raw materials from non-Western areas. "These raw materials are not just iron ore or oil or gut or cotton or tagancanth. They are also myths, principles of belief, music, and transcendental realities."[25] The factories that process these materials are occidental universities, institutions in which specialists constitute an opposite against which to "see the other side of the coin of their own urbanization in the primitive areas of Africa."[26] The finished products are economic policies that are taken to suit particular nations or values that are said to be authentic expressions of particular cultures. Ironically, Al-e Ahmad points out, "we not only no longer feel ourselves worthy and justified ... but, when justifying something which has to do with our livelihoods or religion, we even rely on their standards and on the instruction of their advisers to evaluate it."[27]

Finally, Al-e Ahmad notes the ensembles of practices through which non-Westerners were made into subjects of discipline. In this context, he offers a general account of how Iranians came to be disciplined:

> But as for us, a people who know nothing about democracy and nothing about the machine and therefore no realistic perception of the regimentation necessitated by the machine, the funny thing is that we also have a tailor-made party system and democracy! With mechanization we become regimented and then we are induced to join parties and become a democratic society, then introduce that same regimentation into the military—it is as if we have started from the bottom. That is, starting with the military (which by the way is never used for military purposes, except in street fighting) we grow used to lining up, being regimented and uniform, so that as soon as the machine arrives, our progress (i.e., the machine's progress) will not be slowed down. And this is the most charitable way I can describe our present-day reality. In the West, they arrived at regimentation, political parties, militarization via technology and the machine, however, we were just the opposite, i.e., we went from the barracks and streetfighting drills to regimentation, then politicization, and then we became servants of the machine. Or rather we want to serve the machine. I will be discreet and stop right here.[28]

For Al-e Ahmad, Iranian regimentation was an autonomous process that preceded and supported the introduction of machinery into society. Al-e Ahmad also makes the point that regimentation, unlike exploitation and investigation, is a localized process. Exploitation and investigation involve the export of certain materials to complexes in the West. Regimentation, however, involves the import of disciplinary complexes to the rest of the world.

What intrigues Al-e Ahmad is that the spread of regimentation has given rise to a particular mode of conduct characteristic of Iranians. It is not that Iranians feel unworthy, unjustified, and helpless before Western corporations. Nor is it that they can justify, recognize, and define themselves only through the procedures and knowledge provided by the Western social sciences. "But what is really interesting is that we get married exactly the way westerners do; we mimic the cause of liberty as they do; we judge the world, dress, and write as they do; and we even rely on them to confirm whether it is day or night. One would think that all of our own standards are extinct."[29]

Al-e Ahmad calls this mode of conduct *gharbzadegi*, or Westitis, but this quasi-medical metaphor obscures Al-e Ahmad's focus on the manner in which Iranians imitate Western culture. Iranians may feel helpless and alienated, but these factors in themselves are not sufficient reasons for such blind and avid imitation. What is required is not a sense of subservience or a feeling of self-alienation, but a strong disposition for conformity.

Such a disposition, as Al-e Ahmad points out, arises through the practices of regimentation and becomes a "third nature" for regimented individuals. It is a relation of power that grasps individuals not from without, but "from within."[30] It is, in other words, a kind of subjectivity that accompanies and entrenches disciplinary habits. What are its symptoms? A West-stricken man is disengaged from life,[31] ethically unscrupulous,[32] instrumentally rational,[33] bureaucratically disposed,[34] infinitely malleable,[35] likely to blow with the political winds[36]—in short, "a nowhere man, not at home anywhere."[37] Such an individual lives according to disciplinary norms.

Over the last two decades, Al-e Ahmad's *Gharbzadegi* has come to mean different things to different people. It would be premature to reduce it to a single theme, nor is such an approach necessary. For the purpose at hand, it is sufficient to observe that the issue of the subject has been in the air for some time in Iran. If there is a question behind Al-e Ahmad's considerations, it might be articulated in the following terms: What are Iranians right now? As Al-e Ahmad put it, "Today the issue is not whether they want the oil of Khuzestan or that of Qatar, or whether the diamonds of Katanga are cut or the chromite ore of Kerman is processed. It is, rather, that I, the Asian and African, must even preserve my literature, my culture, my music, my religion, and everything else I possess exactly as if they were freshly unearthed antiques so that these civilized gentlemen can come, dig, take them away and place them in museums and say, 'Yes, here we have another primitive culture!' "[38] How did contemporary Iranians come to *be* themselves? Can one give an account of the specific practices that played a role in their formation?

Increasingly, these questions received their most potent formulations in the course of reflections on political violence in Iranian society. Al-e Ahmad wrote his analysis in the early 1960s just as efforts to liberalize Iranian politics were being undermined by the shah's military administration.[39] Regimentation and conformity were integral features of the political situation with which Al-e Ahmad was confronted. In the subsequent decade, Iranian writers became more concerned with the secret police rather than with the military.[40] They wrote about torture, not discipline. They focused on censorship, not merely as a political program, but as a particular form of artistic subjectivity in which the individual learned "to censor himself [or herself]."[41] They saw in the late Pahlavi state a form of power that did not aim merely at torturing intellectuals but also at promoting a particular type of responsible intellectual.

Among the writers who were tortured in this period, two were especially important in this respect, the playwright Gholam Husayn Saedi and the novelist Reza Baraheni. In *Honeymoon*, Saedi located torture in a complex scheme in which the state accumulates dependent individuals. A newly married woman and man are unable to get rid of an abrasive guest, an old woman who insists on teaching them how "to host" correctly with the aid of two state torturers. The human trust that made the marriage possible is undermined and is replaced by a functional trust, one in which the two are more married to the state than to each other. Celebrating their newly found relationship, the husband, wife, and old woman then set out to teach others the proper art of hosting.[42]

In *The Crowned Cannibals*, Reza Baraheni presented torture as the extension of sexual repression in Iranian society. Baraheni maintained that Iranian politics had been a "Masculine History" in which "the subject-victor emasculated the object-victim."[43] The emasculated victim, in turn, discharged his repression by emasculating men beneath him or by alienating women from their female characteristics and making them emasculated men. The torturer "represents the sexual extension of the Shah's rule. The Shah has turned all his political prisoners into meat and has included in this category even the guards themselves; this guard was taking his turn as the slave had taken his turn with his wife."[44] Baraheni saw the Iranian disposition to conformity as having indigenous roots. Iranians had been subjects of localized "cannibalism" long before they became subjects of Western exploitation. Indeed, "our indigenous Masculine History has finally turned into a pimp, a comprador pimp, and pandered us all to the West."[45]

In the Islamic Revolution, so many individuals protested against torture specifically that its persistence came as an enormous shock. In the soul-searching period that followed, people desperately tried to explain how the Revolution had betrayed its true spirit as they saw it, whether this was the spirit of Islam or nationalism or democracy. Some characterized the violence as a consequence of theoretical error. They explained the violence by pointing to how people misread revolutionary thinkers such as 'Ali Shari'ati or Taleghani. Others saw it as a historically necessary stage through which Iran had to pass. They pointed to the retarded political development of Iran, the peculiar role of religion in Iranian politics, or the specific economic difficulties and class alignments of postrevolutionary Iran that made the violence causally necessary. Still others disassociated Ayatollah Khomayni, and the violence of the Islamic Republic, from Islam "itself," and this made it possible for them to champion a convenient utopianism according to which all violence was condemned. Yet others dissolved the violence in an acid bath of historical terrors. They equated Khomayni with

Adolf Hitler, Pol Pot, and Genghis Khan and tried to arouse in others a spirit of universal moral condemnation.

Such explanations are evasive and uncritical. They are examples of how convictions can become prisons. I chose instead to question Iranian politics by looking at what Iranians are actually doing when they practice violence. Rather than seeking to point to errors, deviations, and misunderstandings in revolutionary theories, I prefer to ask what it was in modern Iranian society that made torture possible and that makes its presence palatable today and even tomorrow. I take it that was precisely the approach taken by Al-e Ahmad, Baraheni, and Saedi, despite their very different answers. Each was compelled to ask the question: How did we Iranians come to be like *that?* This book, too, tries to give an answer to that question.

For Iranians abroad, the Islamic Revolution was important precisely because it made possible critical reflection on the kinds of subjection with which modernization was associated. If the Islamic Revolution poses an overwhelming political issue for them, it is not whether this regime should be overthrown and another established. It is rather how Iranians can continue to be associated with forms of self-subjection that put them in so much danger. The violence that has followed the Islamic Revolution, however severe, in no way undermines the possibility of or the urgent need for such critical reflection on the present. In these respects, Iranians abroad are in much the same situation as the new people among whom they find themselves.

CHAPTER 10

The Rationalization of Iranians

Punishment serves to illustrate several techniques that facilitated the Iranian state's ability to exercise systematic violence on a grand scale. Punishment also serves to clarify some of the ways Iranians—survivors, observers, and practitioners—became who they are today. If this is so, then the analysis of the Iranian state should be related to the sorts of subjects Iranians have become through punishment. In this chapter, I want to pull together these two themes, illustrating their strong and often complicated relationship. I call such an account a historical ontology, emphasizing that what Iranians came to *be* is a product of historically specifiable practices.

A historical ontology pulls together an account of who Iranians are with an account of the state's abilities to exercise violence. Its main goal is to describe different ways of reasoning, each of which simultaneously explains what state violence is at that moment and why individuals act as they do. A historical ontology then captures ways in which societies are rationalized.

By way of introduction, I want to consider three questions. Has punishment always been tied to modes of subjection in Iran? If not, why was it taken up as a way of subjectifying individuals? Can we call this trend toward shaping individuals a rationalization of the means of coercion in Iranian society? Briefly, I argue that punishment has not always been related to subjection and that it became so only as part of a trend toward the reformation of Iranian society. Furthermore, this movement can be described as rationalization provided that one takes care to distinguish different ways in which the process of rationalization operates or, to put the matter another way, provided one can distinguish different types of rationality.

Punishment and Rationalization

Political violence seems to bear no relationship to the question of subjectivity in the nineteenth century. In this period, many loosely associated courts operated with uncertain jurisdictions and little capacity to exercise systematic violence. In this context, punishment lacked the predictability associated with a general legal code; yet it was not entirely arbitrary. In penal rituals, signs were used to illustrate royal presence, reveal religious prohibitions, or instruct others in the natural hierarchy of society. If punishment was a means of ensuring domination in one's jurisdiction, then common techniques of representation occupied a pivotal place by illustrating the nature of the political authority that exercised violence. Punishment was, in the broadest sense, a political signature everyone understood.

How is it then that the exercise of punishment came to be a mode of subjection? Classical punishments have this much in common with the punishments that followed: They were practices that inflicted pain on an offender. They differed, however, in the meaning ascribed to the infliction of pain. In the nineteenth century, the infliction of pain compensated for an offense, retaliated for an injury, or deterred future misbehavior. Increasingly, however, politicians and intellectuals maintained that pain reformed individuals into useful members of society. They drew attention away from the control of outward behavior and toward the shaping of internal states of character. If, they argued, the purpose of classical punishments was really to improve individuals, then clearly classical punishments either effected only temporary improvements in character or (what was more likely) altered these states for the worse. It became possible now to introduce and justify new punishments.

Can one treat this trend toward reformatory punishments as a movement of rationalization in coercion? One might observe that what is considered to be rational in penal practice seems to depend on the nature of a particular society. What an analyst counts as rationality exists in the context of specific impediments to and opportunities for action. Punitive rationality incorporates within it the demand for specific foresight and calculation in the face of this situation and consequently describes a form of conduct that fixes one's actions or the acts of others within a particular style.

Capitalist rationality, for example, arises out of the constraints and opportunities of a market situation. Individuals perform a particular quantifying form of foresight in managing money, and this conduct constrains affects and behavior for the sake of economic interest. To explain market behavior is to describe individual rationality. Capitalist rationality is only an example of a more comprehensive social phenomenon; Western "bourgeois-capitalist man" is not the only model of rationality.[1]

In the study of Qajar Iran, one encounters at least two types of noncapitalist rationality, each of which is an example of what Max Weber calls "ethical rationalization."[2] The rationality that characterizes *t'aarof* defines a kind of foresight found in a court society. It involves a sharp curbing of one's comportment, speech, and action to make people, honor, and prestige calculable as instruments for political advancement.[3] The rationality that concerns ritual purity is distinctly different from that of *t'aarof.* What is at stake is one's future salvation, not one's immediate prestige within a stratified arrangement. A particular circumspection is required to deal with the acts that might threaten one's salvation. One is highly self-conscious of bodies and the foods, liquids, objects, and beings with which they come into contact. One also learns to decide when, where, and how to apply purgative procedures so that bodies may be cleansed and souls prepared for salvation.[4]

Such ways of acting and thinking were forced into existence in princely courts and theological seminaries; yet one can see traces of them in the ways actors behaved in punitive ceremonies. Now one might consider the original question more clearly: Did the move away from classical punishments and the turn toward punishments that were said to reform individuals mark the birth of a new type of rationality? One can say that this shift marked a moment when the punitive context, perhaps for the first time, came to play a role in rationalizing subjects. However, it might be more accurate to say that this context made possible several rationalities. In this new effort at reformation, people used statutory, disciplinary, tutelary, and carceral punishments, each of which illustrates a way of rationalizing subjects.

Here it is important to caution against a misleading interpretation. There is no reason to think that because all these punitive styles can be characterized as reformatory, they *must* have some common rationality—say, capitalist rationality—that defines them. Even classical punishments can be characterized as reformatory from the reformist perspective, although they can scarcely be described as bourgeois-capitalist forms of punishment. Little insight can be gained by using the characterization of punishment as a guide here. It is necessary, not to think, but to look: The issue requires empirical comparison, not theoretical assumptions.

In considering the aforementioned four kinds of punishment, one finds various similarities and relationships, not a common element. Consider, for example, statutory punishments. In such examples, pain is inflicted indirectly through the deprivation of rights. Deprivation occurs according to certain universal principles specified in written statutes, the laws. The laws constrain, instruct, and so habituate individuals in the proper exercise of their rights.

Now look at disciplinary punishments. They are similar in practice to statutory punishments. In disciplinary actions, individuals are isolated and punished by deprivation. They are targets of general institutional rules that govern their detention. Through these rules, individuals perform exercises that habituate their behavior to certain routines. Yet there are important respects in which disciplinary punishments differ. Whereas statutes do not distinguish among persons who have committed the same offense, disciplinary regulations do involve such distinctions. Disciplinary regimes distinguish individuals according to their performance of routines. These judgments are based on variations from specified norms of behavior rather than on the earlier violation of the law. Individuals are treated as objects to be normalized by the exercise of discipline rather than as subjects of a freedom to be realized through the proper training in their rights.

Turning to tutelary punishments, one finds that punishment is effected once again through isolation. In this case, individuals are placed under custody. As with discipline, the tutelary exercise is a normalizing procedure. Custodians check the progress of individuals against certain norms of behavior and habituate them to perform correct actions. There is, however, an important difference. Custodians achieve normalizing effects not through disciplinary drills, but through dialogue. Individuals are not treated as objects that require training. They are treated as subjects of questioning, exhortation, and guidance. Tutelage emphasizes iteration, auriculation, and illocution as three ways of altering self-understanding and behavior. In this respect, tutelage draws closer to statutory punishments. Both kinds of punishment involve the expression of a deeper self within the individual. It is only that in the case of statutory punishments, individuals realize themselves as free members of a juridical community, whereas in the case of tutelary punishments, they realize themselves as normal members of a moral speech community.

Finally, consider carceral punishments—for example, electroshock therapy, traction devices, drug treatments, and lobotomies. They differ from the earlier examples in a general way: They involve the direct infliction of pain on an offender. However, a closer analysis points up several similarities in detail. Like statutory punishments, carceral punishments involve the isolation of an offender from society. As with discipline, their application is regulated by judgments of normalcy. In carceral regimes, individuals are characterized with reference to norms such as corrigible/incorrigible or curable/incurable. If disciplinary punishments work over the bodies of the corrigible and the curable, remedial punishments operate on the incorrigible and the incurable. In both cases, the life processes of individuals are objectified and made available to manipulation. Their bodies are treated as machines that direct pain to and alter the state of the psyche. There is also an illocutionary feature that corresponds to tutelage. The progress of individuals is followed by questioning after their personal states (How do you feel? What are you thinking of?) and their recollections (Where are you now? Where were you then? Whom do you recognize?). Individuals are enjoined on courses of action that render them more malleable and so more receptive to observing specified norms of behavior. In this manner, they recover and are recovered for society.

All these punishments can be distinguished by their target. Unlike classical punishments, they aim at something slightly beyond the body. They are said to reform internal states. Yet it is difficult to find a common means they all utilize or to argue that their effects are identical. To be sure, they do exhibit certain family resemblances that set them apart from classical punishments. The four kinds of punishment are related to one another through a complicated network of relations. Occasionally, there are overall similarities, and sometimes there are only similarities of detail.

Historical Ontologies

The four types of punishment exemplify four different rationalities. These ways of thinking exemplify both how violence is exercised and how people act. I now want to consider the history of three types of rationality in the Iranian context: disciplinary rationality, tutelary rationality, and carceral rationality. I do not discuss statutory rationality because, regrettably, the rule of law plays such a marginal role in Iranian politics. I then situate capitalist rationality with reference to tutelage, incarceration, and discipline.

Disciplinary Rationality. The turn to reformatory punishments is an instance of a more diffuse trend toward political reformation. Political reformation defines the state of modern Iranian politics; it is the direction toward which most political activity has tended, although it has been interpreted differently by contending factions. Iranians have supported one reformist faction against another but what they never question is the urgency of political reformation itself.

There was once a slogan that signaled the beginning of reformatory politics in the Middle East: *Nizam-i Jadid.* It was the phrase used to describe the measures enacted by Selim III and Mahmud II in the Ottoman Empire, Muhammad 'Ali in Egypt, and Prince 'Abbas Mirza in Iran.

It is true that the *Nizam-i Jadid* was a short-lived historical event in Iranian politics. These days, nobody would think of describing modern Iranian politics as a New Discipline. The phrase itself has an archaic sound, and all the political institutions with which it was associated no doubt disappeared a long time ago.

Yet it might be useful to distinguish carefully two aspects of the *Nizam-i Jadid:* the political institutionalization that was sought and rarely achieved in the nineteenth century and the disciplinary activity that has long since spread and proliferated outside political institutions. In the course of the nineteenth century, an important event was taking place within the body of Qajar society: Civil society was being modified by a new rationality, disciplinary rationality. This mode of thought and action was generated through the compulsion of disciplinary matrices. Within these matrices, individuals exercised a particular foresight on their conduct. They evaluated actions that maximized or impeded operational efficiency and economized their affects and behaviors accordingly. This self-corrective foresight regulated their conduct for the sake of functional interests and enabled them to manage multiple detailed tasks.

Some analysts have already pointed to the nascent appearance of capitalist rationality in Qajar Iran. National markets can be formed, after all, only because individuals conceive of themselves as beings who possess, sell, and buy labor. Analysts have identified numerous small and often unrelated economic activities that generated "possessive individualism" within Iranians.[5] Less attention has been drawn to the emergence of disciplinary matrices in the latter half of the nineteenth century. They were often small and fulfilled very limited aims. As with the emergence of capitalist enterprise, the degree of systematization was not as important as the historical effects of these reformatory initiatives. Disciplinary matrices inculcated corrective individualism within Iranians or, to put it another way, encouraged Iranians to practice a disciplinary ethic. Wherever such individuals came to dominate in society, they brought this form of rationality to their station.

Nowhere is this more clearly illustrated than in early modern Iranian politics when reformers, whether liberals or conservatives, gradually transformed political structures into disciplinary matrices. One can point to the new political parties that subjected individuals to party subordination, to the new government bureaucracies that policed and trained employees, and to the new military organizations that trained troops.

This new state structure is remarkably tenacious. Leadership, parties, and even whole classes may be violently ousted without altering in the slightest the character of Iranian society as a society in which practices and practitioners of discipline play major roles. It is not so much that the disciplinary aspects of the state are "stable in contrast to the political structures of traditional Iran, especially that of the previous dynasty."[6] Rather, the state is more stable than older political structures are in the present social context. This context is one in which many Iranians have learned to exercise disciplinary rationality on their conduct. Insofar as they can act according to a disciplinary ethic, they can be managed and organized into military squadrons, administrative departments, literacy corps, and other disciplined formations.

The Qajars depended on a very different way of exercising power. For them, the court, not the state, was the most durable political formation in Iranian society. Courtly life changed over the centuries and particular courts were destroyed, but these events would not alter Iran's character as a dynastic court society. Sooner or later, the court would be reinstituted by some leader, and individuals, calculating on political advancement and expending their prestige, would seek a place in the new court. However, by the early twentieth century, courtly rationality had become less crucial for the exercise of power, and so the tendency to regenerate courtly structures became increasingly uncertain. The princely court survived as an appendage to disciplinary institutions. Regularly, politicians tried to abolish it in favor of some other way of government: by Colonel Reza Pahlavi in 1924, by Premier Muhammad Mossadeq in 1951, and by Ayatollah Khomayni in 1979.

Today, the modern court might be the focus of affect, but not of government. It has been replaced by disciplinary state structures, and these structures endure for the same reasons that court societies once did: Since so many Iranians conduct themselves according to a disciplinary ethic, it is simply easier to organize political structures according to this rationality than any other. It has become customary.

Tutelary Rationality. Another way in which Iranians became governable was by interesting them in the care of their health, sex, personal security, and salvation. A key feature of this tutelage was that it required individuals to think of "their" capacities as products of "their" state. The state guarded one's health, welfare, and salvation and to this extent enhanced one's capacities. One cared best for oneself when one put oneself under its moral guidance. Precisely for this reason, individuals were also at the disposal of the state to expend in a variety of activities, such as warfare or economic development. Individuals simply became more or less calculable and manageable. Here, then, was another way in which the state entrenched itself in who Iranians became.

Tutelary rationality is a qualitative reflection on the actions that may foster or damage the constitutive elements of the self, such as health, soul, or sex. This type of rationality describes a circumspect conduct that regulates actions in the interests of protecting this fundament. One learns to exercise this kind of forethought in tutelary regimes. In these regimes, individuals are observed and instructed in the care of their selves. They are warned against neglecting instructions that may cause harm to themselves and admonished for the good of their selves. In this manner, they develop a habitual disposition to observe a power that furnishes guidance rather than one that issues commands or provides incentives. They recognize in this guidance the source of their potentials and abilities. They find it reasonable to

observe tutelary instructions because they have an analytical solicitude for
their inner selves.

The Islamic Revolution, it is often claimed, marked a profound break
with the old way of doing politics precisely because it emphasized moral
tutelage. Where politicians were once preoccupied with the material transformation of a backward society, they now became concerned with the
moral purification of a corrupt society after the Revolution. Where they
were once concerned with internal impediments to development, they
were now concerned with external sources of corruption.[7] This view, however, is overly simplistic. It masks the much more equivocal record of the
prerevolutionary period. In this period, when Iranians emphasized discipline, it was not only to develop economically but also to develop culturally and assimilate Western characteristics. When Iranians emphasized tutelage, it was because they had a hysterical concern with uncontrolled
urbanization, Westernization, bad mothers, homosexuals, and corrupt
sources of education.

Critics of the Islamic Republic cite the execution of drug smugglers and
addicts, the ill-treatment of prostitutes, and the restructuring of the educational system along moral and ideological criteria as examples of the new
concern with corruption, as if such activities had never been even heard of
under the shahs.[8] Yet the late Pahlavi government often governed individuals through tutelage. The shah was said to exercise a power of a pastoral
type over his subjects. He was "in the first instance a teacher and spiritual
leader."[9] He was, as Khomayni later claimed of himself, a leader not so
much because he managed capital well or promoted discipline efficiently
but because he provided moral governance. These observations point to
the spread of pastoral practices to the state prior to the Islamic Revolution,
practices in which the new revolutionary government found ready supports.

Carceral Rationality. What about the state's repressive apparatus? Does
not the Iranian state govern as much by torture as by discipline and tutelage? Now one point should be quite clear: Although a state can mutilate,
murder, or cause untold suffering by means of torture, it cannot govern by
torture. Rather, it governs by means of the rationality characteristic of
carceral institutions. Torture may play a role in supporting or even general-
izing this rationality, but it does not constitute its principle or basic nature.

Carceral rationality is not a general fear or terror, rather, it is a particular
kind of fear and terror. For every form of conduct that has been discussed
thus far is made possible by an uneasiness concerning an element constitutive of one's self (health, sex, labor, prestige, self-mastery, salvation) if certain actions are not undertaken. Thus, to say that the state governs by
means of torture in the sense that it governs by means of fear is to say very

little indeed. The rationality with which we are concerned here is not something as general as fear.

Out of the new disciplinary order, there emerged a new type of supervision for individuals who resisted disciplinary or tutelary normalization. The carceral was a government for the incorrigible: addicts, alcoholics, recidivists, vagabonds, mendicants, lunatics, the retarded, and the sexually perverted. Incarceration was a ceaseless effort to instate, work over, and supervise an element of danger in such individuals. It was not so much a way of reformation as a mode of insulation.

Individuals were first rendered more conspicuous and isolated from society. Isolation was a task not merely for carceral agents (policemen, social workers, and educators) but for the informed public or, rather, a public of informers. One can call this tactic *moralization*. Once isolated, individuals were then questioned, diagnosed, and treated with the right reformative technology (penal, medical, or psychiatric). One can call this tactic *remediation*. Then individuals were induced to report regularly to authorities. This was done by providing conditional liberties, exploiting these individuals' dependence on certain commodities (such as drugs), rewarding constant reporting, and suggesting the possibility of further treatment. This tactic presupposed the existence of a hierarchy of surveillance, one that was partly official (officers, welfare inspectors, and doctors) and partly private, if not secret (relatives, employers, informers, and undercover agents). One can call this tactic *parole*.

To the extent that individuals were made insular, dependent, and vulnerable through this kind of regimen, they were fairly easily coopted and used by carceral agencies. The delinquent was the most visible example of this kind of individual. By the 1940s, delinquents had become visible agents of social control. They were employed to crush factory unrest, to disrupt antigovernment demonstrations, and to control other kinds of illegalities, such as prostitution. They also played a role in restoring Muhammad Reza Shah to the throne in 1953. Their increasing prominence marked the disturbing moment when criminality was integrated into the procedures through which Iranians were governed. The delinquent had joined the soldier, the bureaucrat, and the social worker as a representative figure of the modern state apparatus.

Delinquents were only the first incarcerated individuals to play significant political roles. SAVAK ran torture complexes for political prisoners, a "politregime" to use Aleksandr Solzhenitsyn's expression.[10] Through this politregime, SAVAK isolated "workers, farmers, students, professors, teachers" as well as members of guilds, "political parties and other associations."[11] These individuals informed, condemned, recanted, or confessed to false crimes, and insofar as they did, they were easily governable. They developed a habitual disposition to observe a carceral power, a power that provided conditions and served warnings. They found it reasonable to observe police instructions because they had a stake in their insularity. Carceral rationality was a calculus of the actions that disclosed or disguised one's identity. It described a hypervigilant conduct that regulated actions in the interests of anonymity.

How important were these incarcerated individuals to the operation of the Iranian state? One can get an idea of their importance by considering the enigma of the Pahlavi secret police, SAVAK. Although SAVAK had a reputation for being a pervasive force in Iranian society, the actual organization was quite small. Estimates of its size vary from 3,120 to 60,000 members.[12] It would be difficult to explain the enormous power attributed to SAVAK without referring to its carceral networks. SAVAK may have been a small organization, but it governed a vast number of incarcerated individuals. In 1974, SAVAK employed approximately 3 million "part-time informers."[13] This participation accounts for the enormous capabilities attributed to SAVAK because it made possible a constant, pervasive surveillance of Iranian society. This system continues today, much as it always has. Ex-SAVAK officials can boast of 3 million informers. Today, high school texts boast that whereas the old monarchy required complex security and intelligence-gathering services, the Islamic Republic has a "thirty-six million member intelligence service."[14]

Capitalist Rationality. Capitalist rationality, as I observed earlier, arises out of the constraints and opportunities of a market situation. Individuals perform a particular quantifying form of foresight in managing their property, including their labor, and this conduct constrains affects and behavior for the sake of economic interest. To explain market behavior is to describe individual rationality. To describe how individuals buy, sell, or dispose of their labor in a market is to characterize individuals who have come to view themselves as sole proprietors of their own capacities and free only to the extent that they can exercise this capacity.

States promote possessive individualism not only because market behavior generates resources but also because it makes subjects that are politically calculable or reliable. Individuals subject to capitalist rationality become governable in the sense that they respond to economic incentives in predictable ways and as such can be relied upon to perform certain tasks on behalf of the state. In this sense, the Iranian state promoted possessive individualism by breaking down preexisting barriers to exchange, protecting private property, and distributing resources to favor entrepreneurial behavior.

Some analysts have tried to explain the Iranian state entirely in terms of capitalist rationality. For them, the capitalist class "provides the social basis of the state, the sector on whose cooperation it rests and without which it could not remain in existence."[15] Among the most acute of such analysts,

Fred Halliday has observed the limitations of this approach when it is dogmatically applied.[16] He observes that "the degree of state political control in Iran has gone far beyond that in other capitalist states in the third world which have superficially similar repressive regimes."[17] There have been periods when the state encountered extensive political opposition but it would be difficult to explain the degree of political control simply with reference to these political crises. As Halliday puts it, "In itself this is not an adequate answer since the repression continued long after 1953 and 1963, when it might have been thought to be most needed to crush opposition."[18]

Halliday, however, turns the limitations of his approach into a strength. Precisely because the state's behavior, particularly its tendency to violence, cannot be explained entirely in terms of capitalist rationality, the state must have fragile class foundations, and that is why it must resort to force more frequently.[19] Following Halliday, Abrahamian puts the matter in the same way: "But [the political structure built by Reza Shah] was unstable in comparison with the political structures of the modern world, particularly those of the West. For the new regime, despite impressive institutions, had no viable class bases, no sound social props and was thus without firm civilian foundations. The Pahlavi state, in short, was strong in as much as it had at its disposal powerful means of coercion. But it was weak in that it failed to cement its institutions of coercion into the class structure."[20] Insofar as the state was unable to enlist a class on its behalf, the state "increasingly resorted to violence to control class and ethnic opposition."[21]

I have several objections to trying to explain the Iranian state in these terms. Halliday and Abrahamian have not really told us anything about the sort of rationality that explains state violence. They have merely asserted that the state would be less violent if it had a class foundation. They assume that no state is *truly* strong unless it has popular support in a class. This is surely not empirically true since many states have lasted a long time without popular support, including the Iranian state. It is not clear what it means to say that the state is "weak" in Abrahamian's sense if a state endures as long as it did in Iran. One can say that this "weak" state endured because it used violence, but this is surely a circular argument. One cannot say that the state was violent because it was weak and then cite as proof of its weakness the fact that it was violent. Nor does this approach adequately explain why the state uses violence against the capitalist class on which it supposedly depends. In any case, even if it is true that class-based states are less violent, there is no account here of how a class basis enhances a state's capacity. Why would a class-based state not resort to violence, including torture?

In short, the Neo-Marxist approach to the state cannot explain state capacity well because it simply does not have the theoretical terms with

which to characterize different sorts of rationality besides capitalist rationality and in this sense is precluded by theoretical choice from illuminating
these problems. My analysis of these shortcomings is not meant to detract
from the stronger points of these pioneering studies. Neo-Marxist writers
have illuminated many aspects of state policy in terms of capitalist rationality, instead of referring to the rather vacuous concept of modernization
used by liberal political scientists. They correctly criticize others for stating behavioral features of the state's system of domination without examining the social context in which those features are located. Although the
state is no doubt best explained in terms of civil society and its institutions,
there is simply no justification for asserting that the essence of civil society
is conditioned principally by factories and banks rather than by patriarchal
families, hospitals, prisons, and churches. Modernity is characterized by
more types of rationality than the capitalist one.

State Capacity

In *The Nation-State and Violence*, Anthony Giddens argues that the administrative powers of the modern state have been misunderstood in at least
two ways. One way has been to overemphasize the state's powers to allo-
cate resources and to minimize its capacity to govern men and women. Another way has been to overemphasize the state's disciplinary powers and to
minimize the different ways in which it governs men and women.[22]

This study confirms Giddens' suspicion that the administrative powers
of a state are far more complex than is commonly allowed. The Iranian
state is not only a coercive social formation. It came into being gradually by
integrating individuals into particular social arrangements. People passing
into the orbit of the state were charged with a new savoir faire, whether it
was disciplinary, capitalist, tutelary, or carceral rationality. In this respect
the state was a matrix of subjection. Perhaps one is well advised to concen-
trate less on *the* state and more on the kinds of rationality that state officials exercise and count on to govern Iranians. By distinguishing different
rationalities that characterize individuals and institutions, one can understand more accurately the state's capacity to govern.

The Iranian state derives its enormous capabilities by structuring fields
of action in these ways and expecting disciplined, incarcerated, or possessive individuals to act in a predictable fashion to promote the state's goals.
Just as state officials guarantee the conditions for reproducing capitalist
economic structures, they also guarantee the conditions for reproducing
political structures. As has been suggested by events in numerous countries, it is entirely possible for the state to reproduce itself in the absence of
capitalist structures because capitalist rationality is not the sole rationality
that characterizes the state. Socialist states may not promote a possessive

ethic in their subjects, but they are no strangers to the task of promoting a disciplinary ethic.[23]

Possessive individualism, then, is not the sole form of imposed subjectivity fostered by the state. This is particularly important because different modes of subjectivity lead to different ways of acting and thinking about situations. For example, possessive individuals conceive of their bodies as belonging to them, whereas disciplined individuals conceive of their bodies and capacities as being at the disposal of the organization. Soldiers march to war, but capitalists have to be paid to become mercenaries. Similarly, individuals subjected to tutelary rationality regard their powers as coming through their masters. Authenticated individuals can be inspired to go to war, whereas soldiers are merely ordered. Or to take another example, incarcerated individuals regard their bodies as alien entities at the disposal of parole officers. Incarcerated individuals march to war, not because of financial incentives, orders, or guidance, but because they have compromised themselves and fear for their lives.

Once one recognizes that different modes of subjection lead to different ways of acting, one can also see how they can conflict. In this respect, it becomes easier to avoid the weaknesses of a purely economic approach to the state. For example, Halliday explained the state's repression of the capitalist class by characterizing it as a conflict between public-sector capitalists and private-sector capitalists.[24] This categorization barely serves to explain the conflict since the latter phrase is simply tautological and the former is simply a contradiction in terms. Rather than qualify capitalism by distinguishing between public and private capitalists, a misleading distinction at best, why not discuss the conflict as one produced when different types of rationalizing strategies meet one another? In this view, it is not surprising that disciplinarians and capitalists can conflict. A policy may be rational from a disciplinary perspective but wholly irrational from a capitalist perspective and vice versa. This is clearly not the only example. Security police and military officers can be at odds as to what policy best promotes order since what appears rational from a carceral perspective appears to be a lapse of discipline from a military perspective.

One can also clarify different kinds of violence against civilians rather than treat state violence as an undifferentiated terror. One can explain why individuals are acting violently in one way rather than in another. For example, when looking at carceral torture, one can see it not merely as a form of repression indistinguishable from all others but also as a distinct way in which the state tries to accumulate utile and manipulable individuals. One can recognize its place as part of a system of surveillance aimed at supporting various political initiatives. The richer characterization of the carceral apparatus helps explain as well why violence persisted in Iran despite the absence of formidable opposition to the state and why it was inflicted on those suspected of the most trivial offenses.

What is particularly striking about the Iranian state is not how fragile it is, but how durable it is. What needs to be explained is why the Iranian state structure is so durable *and* violent. In the last century, politicians might be overthrown, institutions might be purged, and even classes might be violently ousted. Despite these events, sooner or later the same state institutions were reinstituted by some group, and people calculating on political advancement and practicing discipline, tutelage, or torture seek to find a place within them. One might ask why this sort of institution, as opposed to some other, constantly comes into being. The answer is that the state is rooted firmly in the habits of Iranians. The new state emerges in a context where individuals have been trained to conform by habit to discipline, tutelage, policing, torture, economic incentives, or laws. It relies on such individuals and, through them, exercises tremendous powers. The state also sets up new opportunities and impediments, trying to create the sorts of individuals it requires.

If these forms of rationalization enhance state capabilities, they also impose constraints on the state in several ways. Dominant strategies for control cannot be changed quickly. If state bureaucrats rely on carceral strategies and proactive policing for maintaining domestic order, they cannot easily shift to military discipline once the former have proved ineffective. As William Hickman demonstrated in the Iranian case, the military might have been a disciplined tool for foreign adventures, but it lacked the capabilities and equipment to impose discipline in urban conditions. It was thus unable to maintain social order once SAVAK was overwhelmed.[25]

Particular state institutions can bring to bear their own norms on the state. The police, for example, can undermine the judicial apparatus by subtly undermining rights and replacing them with disciplinary norms. Local formations can insinuate themselves on the state apparatus. For example, analysts have pointed to the way in which court rationality insinuates itself upon the operation of bureaucratic politics in Iran.[26] This sort of ethical rationalization survives in Iranian families and brings to bear a competing set of opportunities and impediments for state officials. Of course, families cannot compete with the state well, and whatever claims can be made on the pervasiveness of the system of informal political circles, or *dowrehs*, this much is clear: Court rationality may advance the careers of particular individuals, but it cannot deliver food, weapons, supporters, or money with the speed that modern politics requires. Court rationality may impede the operation of the state, but it cannot challenge it or replace it.

Furthermore, the state is not the only institution that relies on disciplined, incarcerated, possessive, or inspired individuals. Other institutions may use these rationalizing strategies in new ways to compete with the state, as in the way religious foundations, guerrillas, and unions appropriated tutelary and disciplinary rationality to their own ends. The irony here is that each successive effort to resist or seize the state has involved a further habituation of different kinds of conduct. The revolutionaries are constrained by the modes of power that enabled them to seize the state in the first place. And in implementing the new revolutionary principles, they are constrained by the modes of power that the old state apparatus makes available to them. In this sense, the state is becoming increasingly more entrenched in the population with each successive revolutionary struggle.

Politics is founded on trust among people, but there is a vast difference between human trust and functional trust. Human trust is the stuff that binds communities together, yet it is also fleeting and fragile. Since this trust is so fragile, it is tempting to build politics around functional habits. In Iran, this was particularly tempting since the country had been through such wrenching dislocations in the nineteenth century. By training human beings according to discipline, tutelage, torture, economic incentives, or legal rules, one can indeed make possible new institutions with tremendous capabilities. These institutions can deliver food, weapons, and supporters to politicians from all points of view. This is the promise of modernity. Yet when politicians and reformers substitute functional trust for human trust, there is also the great danger that what is human in politics will be lost. Modern torture illustrates this point vividly by showing how human trust has to be disrupted to create dependent, utile individuals. Yet what is true of modern torture is also true of disciplines and markets. Modern torture in this sense is only the most vivid reminder of this feature of modern times. The problem is, as I argue in the next chapter, that we work hard to avoid seeing this.

CHAPTER 11

How Not to Talk About Torture

In this chapter I wish to examine some common approaches to modern torture and consider whether they are reliable guides for thinking about torture. More specifically, I set out to dislodge certain tempting misconceptions about political violence today by simply laying out what we now know about torture. Torture is a good example because such misconceptions are particularly enticing in its case.

I consider four approaches to torture in this chapter. These approaches are what I call the humanist approach, the developmentalist approach, the state terrorist approach, and the Foucaultian approach. What I do is briefly consider the weaknesses and then the strengths of these approaches. I wish to broadly consider how these approaches are inadequate as guides to torture and how, by considering their strengths, we can turn our thoughts in a more promising direction. In doing so, I draw not only on the example of Iranian torture but also on examples from other countries where torture is practiced.

The Humanist Approach

Humanism involves the very strong claim that human beings are inherently worthy of respect. For many humanists, this claim cannot be separated from the creation of a vital public sphere in which individuals treat and learn to treat one another with dignity. Briefly stated, the humanist approach is the view that as societies become civilized and establish vital public spheres, barbaric practices such as torture will eventually disappear.

In the nineteenth century, many humanists believed that such a public life was firmly established in Europe and that the prospects for the rest of the world looked good. Pointing to the disappearance of many ceremonial spectacles of penal torture in the colonies, humanists could assert optimistically that torture would shortly disappear throughout the world as a result of the impact of enlightened government.[1] Today, this version of events seems wildly implausible even as a description of the nineteenth century. European and American police practices were notoriously brutal, and these practices set the standard for colonial interrogations as well, notably in India and the Philippines.[2] Since then, many Western societies, including Germany, France, England, and the United States, have resorted to torture or, at the very least, to training others in the use of torture.

Humanists are hard-pressed to explain these events. One can say that torture persists because modernizing societies have failed to adopt civilized norms. But this explanation simply sidesteps the main issue, namely, that European societies themselves have practiced torture in the last century. A more interesting explanation was advanced by Hannah Arendt in *The Origins of Totalitarianism.*[3] Although Arendt affirmed the importance of a public sphere, she argued that this sphere is under considerable pressure from the bureaucratic tendencies of modern societies. For Arendt, torture appears whenever bureaucratic life overwhelms the public, democratic life of modern societies. I focus on Arendt's work, not because it is unique, but because it is so representative of radical humanist writers.[4]

Arendt's argument turns on a familiar thesis: that there is an inevitable tension between bureaucracy and democracy in modern states. On the one hand, democrats need capable bureaucrats to administer the law impartially and effectively. On the other hand, bureaucrats are specialists and are hostile to amateur politicians interfering with their work. Furthermore, because bureaucratic work can be quite technical, democrats have a hard time regulating bureaucracies or making sure that work is being done properly. As a result, bureaucracies can expand in unregulated and sometimes antidemocratic ways. If democrats cannot do without bureaucrats, it is equally clear that democrats empower "a bureaucratically articulated group which in its turn may occupy a quite autocratic position, both in fact and in form."[5]

Arendt explored the tension between bureaucracy and democracy further. What happens if, as in Nazi Germany and Stalinist Russia, the tension is resolved as a victory of bureaucratic life over public life? In such conditions, she observed, people no longer interact as equal subjects deliberating on a common good but rather as objects within a huge chain of command. To put it another way, men and women no longer act according to the rule of law (a substantive understanding of human dignity). Rather, they act according to administrative rules and quotas, what Arendt called instrumentalist rationality.[6] Arendt illustrated this point forcefully in the case of Adolf Eichmann. In the process of submitting to bureaucratic regulations, Eichmann learned to disregard any residual notions of dignity he possessed.[7] The disastrous results—repression, torture, and genocide—illustrated the workings of administrative terror. In the modern age, violence is no longer necessarily exercised by evil, cruel tyrants, as it has been in the past. Rather, it is exercised by bored, yet dutiful bureaucrats, thereby pointing up the fact that in the modern age evil is banal. And what is most troublesome is that evil of this sort is imbedded in beings who are indispensable for modern political systems, bureaucrats.

This sort of account, although gripping, is quite misleading as an account of modern torture. The difficulty is that writers in this genre often simply denounce terror rather than explain it.[8] They do this despite their desire to clarify how torture works today. In fact, they are driven to do so by the very way in which they talk about the world.

The humanist approach turns on a key distinction: that between the public realm and the realm of administration. Actually, this simple distinction hides a remarkable dissymmetry. In the humanist view, the ideal of public life is set forth, and everything that is not part of this life is labeled "administration." The notion of rule by bureaucracy is constructed on the basis, not of observations, but of a hypothetical opposite to rule of law. This fact is reflected in the problems that arise when we try to use the humanist distinction empirically.

Torture is obviously administered by bureaucracies, but it is exercised in remarkably different ways. The manner in which torturers act on captives can vary according to the type of rationality that characterizes an administrative system. However, in the humanist approach, all these modes of governing individuals are thrown together in the same category, although they share little more than a label. And to the extent that humanists ignore these differences, they have a harder time explaining what is going on in torture bureaucracies.

Let me illustrate this point by noting briefly the variety of different administrative rationalities and how these are related to torture. In some bureaucracies, human beings relate to one another solely as *objects* to be manipulated, that is, they act according to instrumentalist rationality. Yet there are also bureaucracies in which people are treated as *subjects* to be transformed, converted, or healed. Examples of such bureaucracies may be church or psychiatric bureaucracies, all of which have had historical roles in the development of torture. Indeed, in the 1950s, one of the key ways in which torture changed was the introduction of psychological warfare and, with it, the participation of a new group of specialists in torture. The purpose of these specialists was to treat their captives, not as objects of punishment, but as subjects whose perceptions had to be altered.[9] In

Iran, treating prisoners according to a tutelary rationality seemed highly compatible with torture.

Humanists, of course, are less concerned with these modes of administration than they are with modes of administration that treat people as objects. But it is a mistake to think that because some bureaucrats treat persons as objects, there must be *a single rationality* that characterizes all their actions. There are at least three different types of instrumentalist rationality, that is, three different ways in which people learn to treat other people as objects.[10] Each of these describes a particular type of administrative structure. One can, for instance, treat people as a means to an end, as is the case in a military organization or a post office. Or one can interact with them as part of a system, as in an information network. Or one can interact with people as opponents to be strategically defeated or won over, as in a policy institute.

Torture may be characterized by one or another or some combination of these instrumentalist rationalities, as in the Iranian case. One may torture people for confessions, that is, use them as a means to an end. Torturing people in this way seems to be particularly associated not so much with lax judicial systems, but with judicial systems with particularly rigid and severe standards of legal proof. This is because in such systems confessions are often the only sure way of obtaining a conviction.[11]

Or one may torture individuals simply to set an example to others. Thus, we have the spectacle in many countries today of tortured dissidents appearing on national television to praise the regime's policies. There is a semiotics of torture here that needs to be deciphered, one in which individuals and their torturers operate as part of a large media spectacle. This sort of media attention, as the Iranian case shows, can raise the climate of fear and suspicion, and sometimes governments that torture welcome independent coverage by journalists. Amnesty International reports that in Guatemala, newspapers are allowed to publish pictures of dead torture victims, although the accompanying articles are faithful to the government line.[12] The main point is that in such a system, torture does not cease when individuals confess because in most cases individuals have little or no information to give. They are of no use except as parts of a system of media representations. And that is why they are tortured.

Finally, torture may be characterized by strategic rationality, especially when it occurs in the context of counterinsurgency warfare. For example, during the Huk campaigns in the Philippines, torture was part of a carrot-and-stick approach to win the support of the peasantry and to strategically undermine the rural support of Huk insurgents.[13] What is worth emphasizing here is that torture was not used primarily to win confessions or to use individuals as part of a communications system, but rather to strategically outmaneuver an opponent. Individuals could be tortured even when torturing them served no intelligence or public relations purpose. The main point was simply to make the environment too hostile for political opposition to operate, and one way of doing this, it seemed, was to torture peasants.

So torture can be exercised by different sorts of administration characterized by specific forms of rationality. The torturer may act on the tortured as a priest seeking a conversion, a surgeon operating on a patient, a psychiatrist transforming a subject. He may explain what he does in the same terms as a detective, a publicist, or a counterinsurgency expert. Each of these ways of acting describes a distinctive mode of government and casts an entirely different light on how torture operates in a society.

Can humanists integrate these insights into their explanatory scheme? They can acknowledge that they conceived of administrative torture too unclearly, but in any case torture does occur when administrative rationality overwhelms public, democratic life. The test of this, of course, would be to show that torture decreases as democrats gain more control of public life. But the record on this score is more than a little mixed. Torture has been practiced by many Western democratic states, such as France, and continues today in others.[14] Perhaps humanists have in mind an ideal of public life rather than contemporary democracies; but in that case they should not give the impression that they are trying to *explain* torture.

But even if we accept the humanist approach on these terms, I fear the normative ideal of public life serves as a poor guide for how to struggle against torture. On the humanist approach, the key problem is to establish rule of law and basic democratic institutions; democrats will then solve the torture problem.[15] I am not persuaded that this argument is applicable to more than a handful of countries today, forgetting as it does so many states that torture and have little prospect of becoming democratic. More than that, this argument is misleading; it asks us to struggle against torture in the wrong places. If torture is shaped by administrative rationalities, then human rights groups must struggle directly with these rationalities of modern administration—as, in fact, they do.[16] Finally, even if democracy is reinstituted in repressive societies, this does not put politicians in a better position to confront the administrative groups responsible for torture. In 1989, the Uruguayans absolved military officers responsible for human rights violations by a 60 percent majority. They did so not because they forgave, but because more democracy has not put Uruguayans in a better position to confront torturers. At best, the struggle for democracy may be related to the struggle against torture; but one is not identical with the other, for democracy does not provide adequate tools for confronting modern administrative rationalities.

The Developmentalist Approach

The developmentalist approach is concerned with the dynamics of economic modernization. Briefly, it is animated by the belief that as societies modernize, there is a decrease in the corporal severity of punishments. This decrease does not necessarily occur because people become more enlightened. Rather, it is brought about by the rationalization of economic and political life. As individuals are introduced to civic and labor discipline, they learn to regulate themselves according to their consciences.[17] External sanctions, at least barbaric ones, are no longer necessary to maintain order.

This argument had a tremendous influence on social scientists studying the process of modernization in developing countries. Nonetheless, these scholars disagreed among themselves as to the kind of development that should be emphasized. Some believed that economic development itself allowed for a decrease in the severity and extent of violence over time.[18] Others—notably Samuel Huntington, Lucian Pye, and Mancur Olson—argued that economic development itself had a destabilizing effect on societies and promoted violence.[19] On the latter view, the real cause of violence was the lack of *political*, not economic, development. Developing states were simply unable to broaden the scope of political participation fast enough to meet the new demands placed on them. As a result, disaffected groups turned to violence, and governments resorted to harsh sanctions, including torture.

As the second view was the one that eventually became orthodoxy, I focus mainly on the way its adherents dealt with torture. For modernization theorists, the question was this: How could governments expand the scope of political participation while in a potentially violent and unstable situation? Huntington and Pye placed particular emphasis on counterinsurgency warfare.[20] Counterinsurgency warfare not only contained the extent of random civil strife but also facilitated the process of political development. This was because, by training police and military to work effectively, one created individuals who regulated themselves rather than individuals who acted in response to the threat of external sanction. Such self-regulating individuals were crucial for the development process: "The capacity for coordination and discipline are crucial to both war and politics, and historically societies which have been skilled at organizing the one have always been adept at organizing the other."[21] State warfare plays a role in the formation of disciplinary habits, which in turn facilitate political and economic development. "Discipline and development," as Huntington says, "go hand in hand."[22]

From this perspective, the violence of the state can be characterized as an unfortunate, necessary, and (in the long run) beneficial response to high levels of civil violence in developing countries.[23] To be sure, counterinsurgency warfare is violent, but it is far more preferable than government torture and civil strife. As Huntington puts it, "The civil violence which development produces is not the violence that produces development."[24] And if counterinsurgent troops did on occasion torture, this was clearly a technical problem of providing adequate resources and training to troops on the field: Good soldiers would simply know better.

Now it is reassuring to know that torture is a temporary aberration, a dysfunction produced by the lack of political development. The trouble is that, although economic modernization can lead to increased civil strife, there is no clear relationship between civil strife and the extent to which a government resorts to torture in Iran. Furthermore, in certain regions, notably Latin America, civil strife is strongly correlated with other factors. States that do torture are also mainly states that receive the highest per capita foreign aid prior to repression, or military regimes that receive counterinsurgency training, or regimes with weak organized labor and high levels of direct foreign investment.[25] One hopes that military training can reduce random violence in the long run, but this does seem to be a dim prospect indeed.

Furthermore, development theorists suggest that when governments resort to torture, this is primarily reactive. The trouble is that at least in Latin America and the Middle East, the proactive element is an important feature of government repression. The Iranian case suggests that the cause of such proactive violence was counterinsurgency training or narcotics control training. This has been true elsewhere. For example, in Brazil the military had always played a role in maintaining internal order. However, counterinsurgency training intensified the military's interest in internal, rather than external, warfare. Once the military was shaped in this way, soldiers set about performing this task in a professional, disciplined way. And this meant that rather than wait for a real incident of violence, paramilitary forces sought out social groups that they suspected might protest government actions.[26] Counterinsurgency training does entrench better organizational skills, but it will not necessarily reduce government violence against civilians.

And this leads to a third problem with the developmentalist approach. Development theorists suggest that torture occurs only in proportion to the extent of civil opposition, whereas in many cases torture continues long after there is no organized civil opposition to the state. In Argentina and Iran, for example, the intensity of government violence seems to bear no special relation to the extent of civil opposition. These states tortured systematically and intensely even when the opposition had been deci-mated.[27]

Why is the developmentalist approach so misleading about the world of torture? The reason has to do with the way in which development theorists think about the determinants of political stability. For them, political stabil-ity is based on the consensus of the political community. And this consen-sus grows to the extent that political systems allow for popular participa-tion and effectively meet social demands.

Now even though political community may enhance political stability, it is not the only factor that conditions political stability. Take the example of South Africa. The lack of political consensus in this country may explain the high levels of civil strife, but it does not account for the continued sta-bility of the South African regime. Its continued persistence raises an inter-esting theoretical point, namely, that the lack of political community can be offset by the efforts of a determined minority as long as it is willing and able to repress a population.[28]

Most states today do possess large and well-armed standing armies as well as efficient means of transport and communication. Many of these states, notably those in Africa, Asia, and Latin America, are led by rather determined elites that are quite willing to employ force to achieve their ends. The difficulty with the developmentalist approach is that one finds it hard to conceptualize such states within its framework. If such brutal states persist, it *must be* because they enjoy some measure of political community.[29] But of course this does not have to be the case at all. It is just that development theorists draw the conditions for political stability too narrowly. They assume that only the consent of the governed is sufficient to ensure persistence of a regime. In this way, development theorists turn a blind eye toward the commonest experience of the last century, namely, the creation of military-industrial states that have deliberately set about deporting, torturing, and exterminating their populations.

The State Terrorist Approach

Although death squads and terrorist groups may torture individuals, only states have the resources to torture systematically. States possess the fi-nancial and human resources to sustain a torture complex. Furthermore, they can rely on support from other sectors of society to provide technical support (hospitals and mental asylums) and information (universities, unions, and the criminal underground). If state officials are responsible for most tortures, then state terrorism, not civil strife, ought to be the focus of analysis.

Analysts who adopt this perspective work within what I call the state ter-rorist approach. Rather than survey this literature, I focus on the work of

Noam Chomsky and Edward Herman, analysts who have done more than many others to provide a coherent picture of state terror in the late twentieth century.[30] Of course, Chomsky and Herman do not attempt to explain state terrorism everywhere, only in states closely allied with the United States. But what is especially distinctive about their approach is that they put the focus firmly on the "economy of violence"[31] in these countries, not, as many others do, on the economy of exploitation.

Chomsky and Herman draw attention away from torture to what might be called a torture complex. Torture, they point out, is "a mode of governance"[32] characterized by "standard operating procedures in multiple detention centers, applicable to hundreds of detainees and used with the approval and intent of the highest authorities."[33] There is some dramatic evidence to support this claim. In 1978, the Vietnamese routed the Khmer Rouge from Kampuchea. The retreat was so sudden that the Khmer Rouge left behind an intact torture complex, the Tuol Sleng prison. Amnesty International researchers have uncovered remarkable material at Tuol Sleng, including torture manuals; biographies of torturers; very thorough prison records; detailed accounts of interrogations, confessions, and medical examinations; and elaborate diagnostic flow charts showing the interrelationship of enemy networks based on the forced confessions.[34] Similarly, in 1975, human rights investigators visited the Second Army Headquarters in Sao Paolo, a site of numerous human rights abuses. They found the headquarters to be "a huge torture complex which has at its disposal the most modern and sophisticated equipment, and which requires an increasing number of staff—jailers, drivers, executioners, typists, public relations officers, doctors and others—to run."[35]

Chomsky and Herman also point to the international side of torture, including the arms suppliers, the various foreign governments that provide training, and the way torture complexes interact on a global scale.[36] Again researchers have gathered evidence that gives qualified support to this thesis.[37]

Finally, Chomsky and Herman link torture complexes to the international economic system. On their account, torture appears due to the creation of national security states in developing countries. The task of these states is to crush class protests while maintaining economic growth on behalf of multinational interests.[38] In short, torture exists to maintain labor discipline and to keep the cost of labor within a range acceptable to capitalist interests. Thus, Chomsky and Herman have no difficulty explaining why government violence is proactive or, for that matter, why this violence is disproportionate to the incidents of civil opposition.

Nevertheless, Chomsky and Herman do describe the operation of torture complexes in the language of economics, and it is here where difficulties arise. No doubt repression may be useful in maintaining exploitative economic relationships, but this does not clarify the character of repression. Why, for example, is torture employed over a more intensive disciplinary system? And what accounts for changes and variations in a torture complex, for example, from prison-based torture to the psychoprison?

Moreover, even though economic rationality explains why capitalists support regimes that torture, it does not explain the behavior of those who torture. A torture complex is in fact a very costly and inefficient system by economic standards. It is costly because it involves large expenditures of money, equipment, and training for torturers as well as for the maintenance of extensive detention facilities. Yet despite these expenditures, torture complexes are remarkably inefficient. Within them, discipline becomes lax, as the Iranian case shows. Bureaucrats and guards stop performing their duties and become more involved in the pursuit of personal profit and pleasure. These activities may range from forms of sadism and blackmail to large-scale prostitution or drug-smuggling operations.

The Tuol Sleng "Interrogator's Manual" illustrates some of the problems that administrators confront in running a torture complex. At one point, the instructor tries to explain the ethics of torture to his students: "The purpose of torturing is to get their responses. It's not something we do for fun. We must hurt them so that they respond quickly. Another purpose is to break them and make them lose their will. It's not something that's done out of individual anger, or for self-satisfaction. So we beat them to make them afraid, but absolutely not to kill them. When torturing it is necessary to examine their state of health first, and then whip. Don't be so bloodthirsty that you cause their death quickly. You won't get the needed information."[39] Here the instructor lays out a basic paradox of torture. Torture involves the destruction of human beings, but torturers fail if they allow captives to die. Torturers must have a particular discipline to keep their captives in pain and useful for political purposes. Yet torture just encourages the loss of this self-control. As the instructor explains, "Our experience in the past has been that our interrogators for the most part tend to fall on the torture side. They emphasized torture over propaganda. This is the wrong way of doing it. We must teach interrogators how to do it."[40]

So torture complexes encourage indiscipline, and this can pose tremendous difficulties for governments that torture. The Brazilian military government, for example, phased out torture in part because it needed to bring "those undisciplined military and police personnel under at least a degree of central government control even though there was little effort to punish them for their crimes."[41] But this is not all. It is not entirely clear whether torture produces any documents that are particularly useful. Torturers do not seem to be more successful than regular police officers in securing confessions or reliable logistical information and have greater difficulty than police in keeping their prisoners alive long enough to provide such information. If Tuol Sleng is any indication, torturers use the confessions they gather simply to invent fanciful antigovernment plots, which helps them justify torturers' continued operation.

Finally, it is not clear how torture induces economic productivity. There are two separate issues here. First, does torture induce greater productivity in labor? Well, if an economy relies primarily on unskilled manual labor, then one might agree with Marx that torture is rather directly related to economic productivity: Human beings might work harder to avoid torture and so produce more.[42] But torture seems out of place in an economy that relies on skilled labor and industrial discipline.[43] The problems associated with low labor productivity in Third World countries (lack of any real skill training and long work hours) do not seem to be problems that torture can address. In Iran, torture was so unhelpful that SAVAK not only tortured workers less but also lobbied to improve salaries and managed welfare programs so that workers would produce more.[44]

But perhaps states employ torture to destroy labor unions and thus keep wages in a range acceptable to industrialists, multinational corporations, or the International Monetary Fund.[45] There is a great deal to be said for this account of why states repress labor unions; but it does not explain why states resort to torture. It is worth recalling that the most famous repression of labor agitation, the repression of the French Revolution of 1848, was conducted *without torture* by an extremely vengeful and powerful police force and that this was certainly not because torture was unknown to French police and military officers.[46]

States may perceive the need to repress the labor unions, but this in itself is insufficient to explain why states resort to torture. Torture is not essential to such repression; more intensive discipline could be just as effective. Indeed, disciplinary punishments would seem to conform well with the demands of an industrial system, more so at any rate than torture.

In short, torture is difficult to explain solely in economic terms, although the temptation to do so has been simply overwhelming since Marx. We can use economic motives to explain why capitalists and state officials support torture, but we are at a loss to use economic rationality to explain what goes on in torture complexes. To claim an economic rationality for all this is not simply misleading; it also provides a rationale for the behavior of torturers, which makes their behavior a little more acceptable. No doubt, many torturers also prefer to claim that they are fulfilling an essential function in the process of economic and political modernization.

Nietzsche's Children

In *On the Genealogy of Morals*, Friedrich Nietzsche argued that punitive retribution had functioned as a mnemonic device in human history, that is, as an aid in strengthening the human memory. Through punishment, people learned to regulate their actions. They were punished so severely that the very thought of punishment served to regulate most human behavior. This capacity for self-regulation through memory was what Europeans came to designate as a moral conscience. To become conscientious meant to learn how to punish one's self through one's memory rather than through others.[47]

Nietzsche's argument exemplifies a thesis that still exercises a tremendous influence, namely, that the abolition of torture from Europe can be linked to sociological processes through which Europeans became self-punishing and so self-regulating individuals. The disappearance of sanguinary tortures has been linked in this way to Protestant ascetic practices,[48] a new organization of labor discipline in industrial economies,[49] electoral discipline in liberal-democratic states,[50] a perceived need for a specifically antinomadic technique to control the urban poor,[51] a major change in doctrines of judicial proof in early modern Europe,[52] the spread of neostoic doctrines of social discipline,[53] the pivotal place of systems of surveillance,[54] and the spread of new disciplinary techniques of punishment.[55]

There would be no reason, on these accounts, for a disciplinary regime to resort to torture and genocide, certainly not a European regime that has labor discipline, police surveillance, prisons, judges that exercise probabilistic reasoning, and two centuries of ideological socialization. Yet fascism and Stalinism did occur, and they cast long shadows over these theories. It may be that analysts have accurately cited some factors that led to the abolition of torture in the past, but this has to be weighed against their awkward silence about the political experience of the present.

Among the many distinguished analysts, only Foucault seems dimly aware of the challenge modern torture poses to these theories. He notes that fascist and Stalinist states were paradoxically *disciplinary* regimes that employed extremely wasteful and violent forms of power, including torture and genocide.[56] Nazism, for example, combined "the fantasies of blood and the paroxysms of a disciplinary power."[57] Stalinism and fascism involved a "relationship between rationalization and the excesses of political power." Foucault adds that "we should not need to wait for bureaucracy or concentration camps to recognize the existence of such relations."[58]

What precisely is the relationship between political rationalization and political excess? Following Georges Bataille,[59] Foucault believes human economies cannot be understood simply as systems of production. Human needs are much more diverse than this restricted notion of economy allows. Bataille had recognized the need not only to preserve life but also to release its vital forces in moments of anguish, nausea, or orgiastic excess. There is a general economy of waste beyond the instrumental realm of the restricted economy, one that never disappears and that competes with the purely instrumental economy.

Foucault appears to identify discipline with the restricted economy. Discipline is efficient and allowed for an economic and political takeoff in early modern Europe. Modern tortures, in contrast, belong to the general economy of waste. Foucault describes the shah's regime as a disciplinary regime with a police that "was certainly not very effective but made use of violence and cruelty as a replacement for finesse."[60] Modern tortures are even more excessive than classical torture. He contrasts the regulated practice of inquisitional torture with the "savage" and "unrestrained torture of modern interrogations."[61] In an increasingly technological world, our moments of waste take highly technological forms.[62] To understand torture in this fashion is to see it as part of a vast destructive arsenal whose sole purpose is to destroy life and waste money: biological warfare, chemical warfare, nuclear warfare, and genocide. Torture belongs to this arsenal that, in its construction and ultimate results, can belong only to a general economy of waste.

Is this a good explanation for what modern torture is and how it fits into the operation of government? No, because one cannot clearly distinguish between economies of waste and utility. What may have been a paroxysm of disciplinary power in modern Europe seems to have occurred with some frequency in European colonies, for example, in General Thomas-Robert Bugeaud's administration of Algeria.[63] Nor has this situation changed appreciably in the twentieth century. In modern Iran, paroxysms of disciplinary power are rather hard to distinguish from the normal course of events. Regrettably, Foucault's account of modern political violence is based on an essentially "European vision of Europe,"[64] where periods of discipline and torture supposedly alternate. However, as Amnesty International observes, "European domination of the world reached its apogee before World War I and the five centuries of European expansion have been accompanied by many crimes including torture and genocide."[65]

Utility, furthermore, is a matter of interpretation.[66] One judges utility with respect to some predetermined agreement as to what counts as utile. In the case of torture, utility signifies a ratio between the amount of work performed and the total amount of energy expended. For this judgment to make sense, we need standards in terms of which work and energy can be identified and measured. Only then can we decide whether torture is wasteful or utile. But to choose standards involves an interpretation of what is important in political situations of a certain type—useful, one might ask, in terms of what factors: money, labor, suffering, time, consumption of precious fuels? In short, there can be no judgment of utility without an interpretation of what counts as useful or wasteful, and consequently, there can be no inherently utile or wasteful economies of violence.

We are not always sensitive to the notion that utility itself is a matter of interpretation, especially in the case of torture. We tend to assume its utility or disutility, but this can get us into all sorts of analytical trouble. If we assume that torture is inherently useful, then we often rationalize strange behavior. Chomsky and Herman, for example, insist on torture's inherent utility in supporting capitalist exploitation. From this perspective, aspects of carceral government that are wasteful become either excusable or incomprehensible. Foucault, to take another point of view, insists on torture's inherent wastefulness, but then he is apt to overlook how carceral government works. The Iranian case suggests that carceral government plays a role in supporting the domination of specific political groups and classes. In other words, carceral government is useful *for some people.* Foucault also assumes that discipline is inherently useful, but again this is clearly not the case. In the Iranian case, the introduction of discipline often had the paradoxical effect of undermining the abilities of its practitioners. In other words, disciplinary government is wasteful *for some people.*

The Road from Here

None of these criticisms is meant to detract from the stronger features of these four approaches to modern torture. In fact, I think researchers have grasped key features of torture despite their constant urge to misunderstand violence today. For none of the problems we encountered using these approaches was empirical; rather, these problems were solved by looking to the workings of language and showing how the vocabulary of each approach tugged our attention away from the world in which we live. And I think that if we consider the strengths of these approaches from the right perspective, we can gain a tentative way of understanding modern torture.

The strength of Nietzsche's approach and those who followed him is that they point to the sociological processes that shape punishment. They help us gain a critical distance from complacent, self-congratulatory accounts of our moral progress. Among these many historical accounts, Foucault's approach is particularly important. Its strength is that it articulates discipline as a theoretical concept, and this allows us to assemble the earlier works more coherently. Foucault also acknowledges the existence of modern torture and points to its excessive and wasteful character. He is hampered, however, by too absolute a notion of what does and does not count as waste, and this prevents him from thinking about how modern torture works in detail.

The strength of the state terrorist approach is that it is concerned with torture as a mode of government. It draws attention away from incidents of torture and toward the systematic and international nature of torture today. But its chief difficulty remains moving beyond statistics and personal narratives of detainees to descriptions of this mode of government. And this difficulty arises because it is hampered by an unduly narrow conception of torture as a form of economically rational behavior.

In this regard, the developmentalist approach is much stronger. It focuses on counterinsurgency practices. These practices describe some of the military, police, and bureaucratic conventions employed by those involved in torture. However, because developmentalist theorists regard torture as a premodern or accidental feature of politics, they remain peculiarly blind to the relationship between counterinsurgency practices and torture. All they can see is a technical failure in discipline, not the sociopolitical problem of the emergence of torture.

This sociopolitical problem is not lost on the humanists or the state terrorist theorists. Although they have a hard time explicating what goes on in torture complexes in detail, they do make the point that torture complexes are part and parcel of modern political systems, that they are constituted out of the same sorts of rationality that also characterize bureaucratic systems. They do not arise accidentally in the twentieth century. They are not aberrations of the modernization process or remnants of traditional society.

To put these insights more constructively, torture is a part of modern life in the sense that torture complexes can be best elucidated by means of ordinary features of modern life. Torture complexes are closely related to bureaucracies, prisons, hospitals, and, to a certain extent, factories. And sometimes we can understand what people are doing when they torture by comparing their activities to these related institutions.

Indeed, sometimes the similarity between other practices and torture is so close that it poses tremendous difficulty for action against torture. Medicine, for example, has a particularly close relation to torture because interrogators use medical practices, hospital facilities, and doctors in this work.[67] Consequently, other doctors have to overcome major obstacles to help survivors recover from the trauma of torture. Doctors use too many techniques that are similar to the kinds of tortures experienced by survivors. This applies not only to actual physical techniques but also to the ways in which doctors examine and interrogate their patients. Doctors have to exercise tremendous care in the way they speak and treat their patients for the patients themselves can no longer effectively distinguish between what is torture and what is medicine.[68]

Of course, we can evade the deep interrelations between torture and modernity by invoking the term *developing societies* (logically, something belonging to the past of the "developed" world and consequently saying little to the present of the developed world), but we should be aware that in this brave new language, "becoming modern" no longer functions as an empirical category but rather as a moral one. The humanists never tire of insisting on this point. But this means that we are left with a vocabulary through which we can reaffirm our confidence in the celebrated aspects of modernity, but only at the price of being unable to talk about torture except in the vaguest way.

If there is one difficulty that runs through all these approaches, it is that none of the approaches provides satisfactory *explanations* for modern torture. The causes they identify are too general to account for the details of torture complexes. Nevertheless, they have a tremendous hold on our imagination for they articulate visions of the kind of political community in which we aspire to live. And it is the power of these approaches to grasp our moral imagination that accounts for their persistence today, not their supposed ability to provide a detailed explanation of what is going on in the world of violence or how we got here. Our concern with the ideal turns our attention away from the present and so defers a pressing question: In what ways and at what cost can we get from the world of torture to the ideal of political community? In particular, we should pay less attention to the question "Why is there torture today?"—a tale that may be too tangled and deeply enshrouded in state secrecy—and much more attention to "How does torture work today?" For it is by increasing our scrutiny of how torture works that we can understand how we do (or do not) benefit from torture as well as to what extent we can (and cannot) challenge this practice.

Of course, I am arguing that torture does not work in any of the conventional ways theorists suppose. Torture does not increase labor productivity, does not produce any better intelligence results than ordinary police work, and has a detrimental effect on social and bureaucratic discipline. And I want to take a moment to spell out the implications of this thesis.

One implication is that if torture does not work in these ways, then there is little justification for the use of torture. Torture's apologists always assume that torture works in these ways; their task was merely to provide moral justifications for torture.[69] Now it appears that even this assumption can be questioned. Torture's apologists must explain if it works at all, and this is a much heavier burden of proof to shoulder. However, if torture does not work in these ways, then what needs to be explained is why the practice of torture persists today. Perhaps it is because torturers are just protecting their jobs.[70] Or perhaps intense social fear mobilizes social elites to engage in "permanent counterrevolution"[71] in which torture may play a part. But I think a more promising explanation is to consider how modern torture is related to the different ways in which human beings are habituated to act and made available to others. In the Iranian case, modern torture seems to be part of a process in which individuals—torturers, guards, politicians, and prisoners alike—are transformed into dependent, apolitical, and asocial individuals. They come to practice a certain style of reasoning that characterizes the operation of a torture complex.

If this is a credible explanation of why torture persists, then we need to pay more attention to the relationship between torture and the process of rationalization. In part, this involves examining the relationship between torture and other social institutions. In his book on torture, Edward Peters argued that historically torture was not a primitive practice that survived into the medieval period. Rather, torture was introduced in Europe in opposition to tribal punishments, and its practice served to rationalize state power.[72] My study suggests a similar point, namely, that carceral rationality is one way in which functional trust displaces human trust and not a particularly good way at that. Max Weber once described the process of rationalization as "an iron cage"; he had no idea that the cage could be real.[73]

We also need to pay careful attention to the process of linguistic rationalization. This means that we need to be careful about how the use of increasingly specialized ways of talking can serve to mislead us about what is actually happening when torture occurs. Torture seems to thrive not so much on this or that ideology but rather on gossip, rumor, media sensationalism, and bureaucratic, social scientific, and legal jargon.[74]

Torture needs all the publicity it can get, but we have to be more careful about *how* we speak about torture. This does not mean that we should abandon the traditional ways we discuss torture, only that we should critically evaluate them at every opportunity.

Appendix A
A Study of Political Visibility

The photographs included here were taken for specific purposes. The camera's eye was not neutral. It belonged to the Orientalist, the tourist, the political journalist, and the religious fundamentalist, each with his own audience in mind. Yet what the photographer hoped to record was constrained by what the society opened up to him. His line of sight was shaped by the lines of buildings and by the way bodies habitually grouped or separated from one another. I am less interested here in what the photographer intended and more in what society revealed and in what the camera inadvertently recorded.

Classical Punishments

Figures A.1–7 depict some common kinds of classical penal torture. These include decapitation, burying captives alive, hanging carcasses like animals, impalement, flogging, punishment on the bastinado, and blowing the body into bits with a cannon. By the age of the camera, some famous penal tortures were no longer practiced, notably the torture of *sham' ajjin*, in which burning candles were inserted into the flesh and the captive was made into a candlestick. Nor should one regard everything these photographs illustrate as being "traditional" Iranian punishments. Blowing individuals apart with a cannon was a British-Indian invention, or at least it is reported to be. Figure A.1 includes an "execution pole" from which bodies were hung. This appears to be a nineteenth-century invention, or at least earlier histories make no mention of this device. When the British ambassador hired masons to build the flagpole for the embassy, he noticed it had an uncanny resemblance to the execution pole in the main square of Tehran. Indeed, it was designed by one and the same person. The flagpole was immediately chopped down.

In the past century, these ways of exercising punishment disappeared because power was organized in new ways. The exercise of sovereign power, which depended on spectacular signs, gave way to the exercise of disciplinary power. The camera records a gradual shift from ceremonial visibility, where a central space is highlighted for an undifferentiated audience, to panoptic visibility, where space is organized for the surveillance and correction of those who use it. In Figures A.1–7, the camera focuses on the bodies of the victims. These are living examples to the audience. The observers are barely differentiated. They are lost in a crowd (A.1, A.2, A.4, A.5, A.6), have their backs to the camera (A.6), or are ignored altogether (A.3, A.6, A.7).

Disciplinary organizations make possible new kinds of photographs, notably Figures A.9, A.12, A.15–18. The camera focuses not on a spectacle, but on a careful, meticulous individuation of space, the space for surveillance, examination, and disciplinary correction. These photographs also point up the many places where panoptic visibility was deployed: in schools and academies (A.11, A.12), in military and police units (A.9, A.15–18), in dormitories and barracks (A.13), and in prisons (A.22).

Contrasting Disciplinary and Sovereign Power

In Figures A.7–18, one can contrast panoptic and ceremonial visibility more thematically. Take, for instance, two photographs of "education": Figure A.7 (punishment at the writing school) and Figure A.12 (the School of Arts and Crafts). In the writing school, a variety of tasks are going on at the same time: Pupils are writing, punishing, or reading aloud to themselves. The tutor (at the rear and to the left) cannot see much less supervise his pupils from his position. The right-hand side of the room is obscured in shadows. The pupils are sitting in a random arrangement. Many are not even facing him or are hidden from him by other pupils. The only arrangement that is distinctive is the execution of punishment at the bastinado in the center of the room. By contrast, at the School of Arts and Crafts, students are doing exactly the same thing. They are situated at regular intervals and available to regular inspection.

Take the photographs of "policing": Figures A.8 (the Qajar constabulary) and A.9 (Tehran police officers). In Figure A.8, the new police officers stand at attention in a disciplined formation. Each policeman has the same comportment as the others and holds his rifle according to a standard procedure. In Figure A.9, by contrast, the older watchmen stand in no particular order, have no specific style of comportment, and observe no particular rule as to the handling of their weapons. Their effect derives from the particular fear they invoke as signs of sovereign power rather than as hidden surveyors of behavior.

Take the photographs of "fighting": Figures A.14–18. There are, on the one hand, the seeming chaos and nationalist passion of irregular troops (A.14), and, on the other, the seeming order and self-control of the Cossacks, the Road Guard, the nationalist forces, and the Assyrian peasants (A.15–18). These photographs illustrate as well the many different sources through which disciplinary practices took root in Iran.

Finally, consider the photographs concerning *salaams* (royal receptions): Figures A.10 and A.11. These are the most telling photographs since they represent the fount of power itself, the shah. In Figure A.10, Qajar nobles pay their respects to the portrait of Nasser id-Din Shah. They stand casually in a loose line before the portrait. Figure A.11 illustrates another royal reception, this one at the military academy. Here the cadets are at attention in solid lines, waiting to be inspected by Nasser id-Din Shah. Nasser id-Din Shah is not so much a king as a general. Figure A.13 completes the transformation. Reza Shah, the old Cossack general, is now king, but the king has become a barracks inspector.

Incarceration

Figures A.19–24 depict the transformation of the prison. Figures A.19 and A.20 cover two ends of the old economy of incarceration. Each city possessed an *arg*, or citadel, in which prisoners could be condemned to the dungeons. Each city also possessed many sites of *bast* from judges or vengeful citizens. If the dungeons of the citadel marked the complete authority of the sovereign's law, then the sites of sanctuary marked the limits to sovereign power. Here subjects stood beyond the law.

In Figures A.21–24, the spectacle of punishment gradually disappears behind the prison walls. The chain gangs at Tahur give way to the silent stocks of the old Tehran prison. Here, there is a spectacle, but it is an empty gesture. There is no audience, only the guards watching from the corners and the guard atop the tower. And then this odd scene, too, is gone; punishment becomes inaccessible to the camera and to the public eye. We can look only at the bricks of Qasr prison; there is now a place beyond the law once again, and it becomes the site of modern torture.

New Punishments

Classical punishments did not disappear everywhere at the same time. Well before the Constitutional Revolution, executioners commonly turned to hanging or shooting the condemned (Figures A.25–28). Consider the fate of Muhammad Ali Shah's general. In an earlier time, he might have suffered a far worse fate than being executed before a firing squad wearing what must have been an indignity, the clothes of a common convict (A.26). The shah's other allies, the Turkmen chiefs, suffered a more traditional fate, decapitation (A.25) Why this contrast? We cannot say, but we know that in the case of the jungle Mujahidin, Reza Shah ordered that the leader's head be displayed publicly so all would know that he was dead. And in this case, the guerrilla leader had already died in the mountain snows; the soldiers merely severed the head. The shah had his soldiers hang the rest (A.28). Disciplinary power reduced the moment of death to a brief instant.

Eventually these public exhibitions also disappeared behind the prison walls. Here, a new technology of punishment developed, modern torture (A.29–32). The camera cannot see it; one can only sketch it furtively in the midst of a trial (A.29) or reconstruct it from the accounts of prisoners (A.30). Torturers made use of new technology, including electricity and weightcuffs. What photos exist come to us from the torture bureaucracy (A.31), more precisely in the context of coroners' reports (A.32). Here the doctor and the torturer work together. They present the picture of an accidental death as the victim was confronted by counterinsurgency officers. We see what the bureaucracy wishes us to see.

The Islamic Revolution

If the Islamic Revolution of 1979 constituted a return to "old" punishments, then this was a return principally to the punishments of the Constitutional period, not to classical punishments. General Nassiri, the head of the secret police, suffered no worse a fate than Muhammad 'Ali Shah's general, execution before a firing squad (A.33). In general, most people who were executed died before firing squads (A.34) or on gallows (A.36). Many are still flogged (A.35), but this is not really a revival. Flogging was common in prerevolutionary torture. What is different is its public nature. Today, flogging serves as a simple way of confirming the regime's religious credentials, as does the occasional lapidation (A.37).

In the prisons, discipline has given way to exhortation and tutelage. In Evin's prison workshop, the prisoners chant slogans while they work and change shifts (A.38). Posters exhort prisoners to change their ways (A.38–39). And, most interestingly, the organization of space has changed. In the large communal cells, guards are not interested in isolating and disciplining each prisoner (A.39). Moral exhortation seems to have a higher priority than panoptic visibility.

In the Qajar period, a portrait of the shah was revealed when sentence was passed on the prisoner. Today, the accused are surrounded by portraits of their victims (A.40). The dead now stand in judgment over the living; their eyes are everywhere, whereas the shah had only two. Photographs have become a link in the vast chain of punishment and accusation, a chain that binds the living to the dead (A.41).

Figure A.1 "Execution of a Persian criminal"

Source: Clive Bigham, *A Ride Through Western Asia* (London: Macmillan, 1897), opposite p. 102.

Figure A.2   Bodies hung over city gates

Source: Ghasem Safi, *Historical Photographs of Iran: Dignitaries, Spectacles, Architecture and Social Environment*, 2d ed. (Tehran, Tehran University Press, 1370 [1991], p. 280.

Figure A.3   "Burying brigands alive"

Source: David Fraser, *Persia and Turkey in Revolt* (Edinburgh: William Blackwood, 1910), opposite p. 198. Reprinted by permission of Pillans and Wilson, Edinburgh.

Figure A.4 "A criminal about to be blown from the mouth of a fieldpiece"

Source: Francis A.C. Forbes-Leith, *Checkmate: Fighting Tradition in Central Persia* (New York: Robert M. McBride, 1927), opposite p. 207.

Figure A.5 "Death of a Baha'i"

Source: Geoffrey Nash, *Iran's Secret Pogrom* (Suffolk: Neville Spearman, 1982), p. 57. Reprinted by permission of C.W. Daniel Co. Ltd., Saffron Walden, England.

Figure A.6 "The capital punishments of Fereydun Parsi"

Source: Ahmad Tafrishi-Husayni, *Ruznameh-yi Akhbar-i Mashrutiyat va Inqilab-i Iran* (A Diary of Documents Concerning Constitutionalism and the Revolution of Iran), ed. Iraj Afshar (Tehran: Amir Kabir, 1351 [1972]), from the appendix of photographs following p. 302.

Figure A.7 Punishment at the *maktab* (writing school)

Source: Muhammad Hejazi, *Mihan-i Ma* (Our Country) (Tehran: Ministry of Culture Publications, 1338 [1959]), p. 442.

Figure A.8 Some of the Persian constabulary

Source: John H. Wishard, *Twenty Years in Persia* (New York: Fleming H. Revel, 1908), opposite p. 274. Reprinted by permission of Fleming H. Revel Co.

Appendix A

Figure A.9 Members of the Tehran police

Source: Ahmad Tafrishi-Husayni, *Ruznameh-yi Akhbar-i Mashrutiyat va Inqilab-i Iran* (A Diary of Documents Concerning Constitutionalism and the Revolution of Iran), ed. Iraj Afshar (Tehran: Amir Kabir, 1351 [1972]), from the appendix of photographs following p. 302.

Figure A.10 A *salaam* (royal reception) before the portrait of Nasser id-Din Shah

Source: Iranshahr (Tehran: Tehran University Press, 1963), vol. 1, p. 909.

Figure A.11 The Dar ul-Fonun during a *salaam* (royal reception)

Source: Qodratullah Rowshani Z'afaranlu, ed., *Amir Kabir va Dar ul-Fonun* (Amir Kabir and the Dar ul-Fonun) (Tehran: Tehran University, 1354 [1975]), p. 304.

Figure A.12   School of Arts and Crafts for Young Women

Source: Muhammad Hejazi, *Mihan-i Ma* (Our Country) (Tehran: Ministry of Culture Publications, 1338 [1959]), p. 331.

Figure A.13   Reza Shah as inspector

Source: Muhammad Hejazi, *Mihan-i Ma* (Our Country) (Tehran: Ministry of Culture Publications, 1338 [1959]), p. 327.

Figure A.14   Irregular troops during the Constitutional Revolution

Source: W. Morgan Schuster, *The Strangling of Persia* (New York: Century, 1912), p. 144. Reprinted by permission of Mage Publishers, New York.

Figure A.15   The Persian Cossack Brigade in a drill square

Source: Ahmad Tafrishi-Husayni, *Ruznameh-yi Akhbar-i Mashrutiyat va Inqilab-i Iran* (A Diary of Documents Concerning Constitutionalism and the Revolution of Iran), ed. Iraj Afshar (Tehran: Amir Kabir, 1351 [1972]), from the appendix of photographs following p. 302.

Figure A.16 The Amniyya (Road Guard)

Source: W. Morgan Schuster, *The Strangling of Persia* (New York: Century, 1912), p. 144. Reprinted by permission of Mage Publishers, New York.

Figure A.17 Constitutionalist forces in Tabriz

Source: W. Morgan Schuster, *The Strangling of Persia* (New York: Century, 1912), p. 211. Reprinted by permission of Mage Publishers, New York.

Figure A.18   British officer drilling Assyrian Levies near Hamadan

Source: Denis Wright, *The English Amongst the Persians During the Qajar Period, 1787–1921* (London: Morrison and Gibb, 1977), opposite p. 157. Reprinted by permission of the Imperial War Museum, London.

Figure A.19   The Pearl Cannon, a site of *bast* (sanctuary) from the law

Source: William P. Cresson, *Persia: The Awakening East.* (Philadelphia: Lippincott, 1908), p. 64.

Figure A.20 The *arg* (citadel) of Tabriz, in which prisoners were jailed

Source: W. Morgan Schuster, *The Strangling of Persia* (New York: Century, 1912), p. 218. Reprinted by permission of Mage Publishers, New York.

Figure A.21 The prison at Tahur

Source: Clive Bigham, *A Ride Through Western Asia* (London: Macmillan, 1897), opposite p. 136. Reprinted by permission of Macmillan Publishers, Ltd., London.

Figure A.22 The Tehran prison

Source: George N. Curzon, *Persia and the Persian Question* (New York: Barnes and Noble, 1966), vol. 1, p. 458. Reprinted by permission of Frank Cass & Co. Ltd., London.

Figure A.23   Prisoners in stocks

Source: Ahmad Tafrishi-Husayni, *Ruznameh-yi Akhbar-i Mashrutiyat va Inqilab-i Iran* (A Diary of Documents Concerning Constitutionalism and the Revolution of Iran), ed. Iraj Afshar (Tehran: Amir Kabir, 1351 [1972]), from the appendix of photographs following p. 302.

Figure A.24 Qasr prison, the first modern prison

Source: Amnesty International, *Iran: Briefing* (London: Amnesty International, 1987), p. 6.

Figure A.25 Heads of Turkmen chieftains stuffed with straw

Source: W. Morgan Schuster, *The Strangling of Persia* (New York: Century, 1912), p. 322. Reprinted by permission of Mage Publishers, New York.

Figure A.26   Execution of a royalist general by a
firing squad

Source: W. Morgan Schuster, *The Strangling of Persia* (New York:
Century, 1912), p. 126. Reprinted by permission of Mage Publishers,
New York.

Figure A.27 A public hanging during the Constitutional Revolution

Source: Ahmad Tafrishi-Husayni, *Ruznameh-yi Akhbar-i Mashrutiyat va Inqilab-i Iran* (A Diary of Documents Concerning Constitutionalism and the Revolution of Iran), ed. Iraj Afshar (Tehran: Amir Kabir, 1351 [1972]), from the appendix of photographs following p. 302.

Figure A.28 "Execution of *Mujahidin* in the jungle revolution"

Source: Suroosh Irfani, *Revolutionary Islam in Iran: Popular Liberation or Religious Dictatorship?* (London: Zed Press, 1983), collection of photographs following p. 150. Reprinted by permission of Zed Press, London.

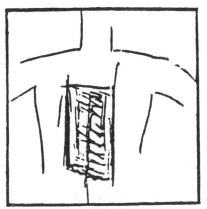

Figure A.29 Torture on the hot table: A sketch of Prisoner Ahmadzadeh's "toasted" back made by his lawyer

Source: Ali-Reza Nobari, ed. *Iran Erupts* (Stanford: Iran-America Documentation Group, 1978), p. 148.

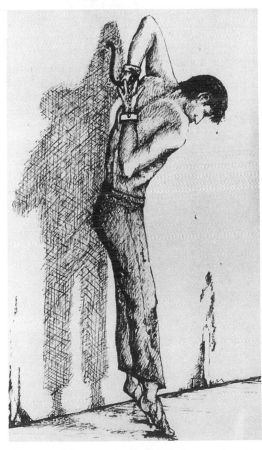

Figure A.31 Body of Suroor Aladpush after torture by SAVAK

Source: Reza Baraheni, "The SAVAK Documents," *The Nation*, 23 February 1980, 200. This photograph is reprinted from *The Nation* magazine/ The Nation Company, Inc., © 1980.

Figure A.30 Handcuffed with the weightcuff

Source: Amnesty International, *Iran: Violations of Human Rights, 1987–1990* (AI Index: MDE 13/21/90).

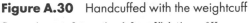

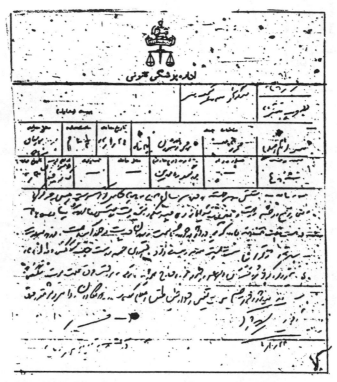

Figure A.32 Coroner's report from the file of Bahman Ruhi-Ahangaran

Source: Reza Baraheni, "The SAVAK Documents," *The Nation,* 23 February 1980, 201. This photograph is reprinted from *The Nation* magazine/The Nation Company, Inc., © 1980.

Ministry of Justice
Office of Medical Examiner

Place of exam.: Police hospital   Cause of death: fracture
of skull and brain damage

Time of exam.: 10:30 a.m.   M.E.: Dr. Qorbani
Date of exam.: 24/10/54   Interrogator:
(Dec. 4, 1975)   Colonel Azodi-Qajar

Specifications of the deceased: Name:
Bahman (Ali-Asqar) Roohi-Ahangaran
Age: about 27

Permit No. 5
Nature of accident: confrontation with the officers
Date of death: 23/10/54
Place of accident: ——. Place of death: ——
Reported by: Army Interrogation Office & Counter-
insurgency Committee

Autopsy Report: The body belongs to a man of about 27.
Preliminary examination did not show any sign of poison or
suffocation. The eye is bruised. There are abrasions of the
chest, belly, right hand and both legs. There are several
bruises on the right-hand side of the chest and both legs. In
autopsy of the head the scalp was opened; a vast bruise on
the right side of head and forehead was located. The skull
has a fracture of about 3 centimeters on the left from which
brain and blood are flowing out. Thus the cause of death is
fracture of the skull and brain damage, and the permit is
released according to the report of the Counterinsurgency
Committee and Army's Interrogation Office.
Dr. Qorbani   Colonel Azodi-Qajar

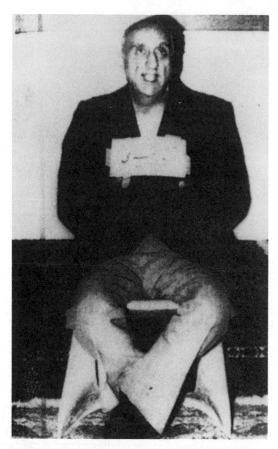

Figure A.33 General Nassiri, head of SAVAK

Source: "Guns, Death and Chaos," *Time*, 26 February 1979, p. 33. Reprinted by permission of UPI/The Bettmann Archive.

Figure A.34 Execution of homosexuals by a firing squad

Source: "Khomeini's Kingdom Qum," *Time*, 12 March 1979, p. 33. Reprinted by permission of AP/Wide World Photos.

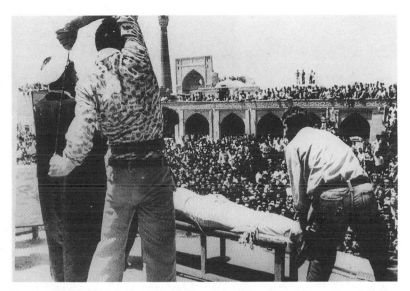

Figure A.35 Public flogging in the early days of the Islamic Republic

Source: Amnesty International, *Iran: Violations of Human Rights, 1987–1990* (AI Index: MDE 13/21/90).

Figure A.36 Public hangings in Tabriz on portable gibbets in the postrevolutionary period

Source: Amnesty International, *Iran: Violations of Human Rights, 1987–1990* (AI Index: MDE 13/21/90).

Figure A.37 A man about to be stoned to death

Source: Amnesty International, *Iran: Violations of Human Rights, 1987–1990* (AI Index: MDE 13/21/90).

Figure A.38 The workshop floor of Evin prison

Source: Amnesty International, *Iran: Briefing* (London: Amnesty International, 1987), p. 5. Reprinted by permission of Rex Features.

Figure A.39 Women prisoners eating in a communal cell, Evin prison

Source: Amnesty International, *Iran: Briefing* (London: Amnesty International, 1987), p. 5.
Reprinted by permission of Rex Features.

Figure A.40 The accused in a revolutionary court surrounded by pictures of their victims

Source: Amnesty International, *Iran: Briefing* (London: Amnesty International, 1987), p. 7.

Figure A.41 Women in *Behesht-i Zahra* (Cemetery of Martyrs)

Source: David Albert, ed., *Tell the American People: Perspectives on the Iranian Revolution* (Philadelphia: Movement for a New Society, 1980), p. 173.

Appendix B
A Chronology of Events in Modern Iranian History, 1790–1991

Qajar Dynasty

1790–1797 Agha Muhammad Khan reigns.
1796 Agha Muhammad Khan establishes the Qajar dynasty.
1797 Agha Muhammad Shah is assassinated.

1797–1834 Fath 'Ali Shah reigns.
1804–1813 The first Russo-Iranian war occurs. Iran is defeated.
1826–1828 The second Russo-Iranian war occurs. Iran is defeated again.
1833 'Abbas Mirza, the heir to the throne, dies.
1834 Muhammad Shah ascends to the throne with British support and Russian consent.

1834–1848 Muhammad Shah reigns.
1844 Sayyid 'Ali Muhammad proclaims himself Bab and founds Babism.

1848–1896 Nasser id-Din Shah reigns.
1848–1851 Babi revolts occur throughout Iran and are severely repressed.
1850 The Bab is executed at Tabriz.
1852 Nasser id-Din Shah narrowly avoids assassination.
1856–1857 The Anglo-Iranian war occurs. With the Peace of Paris (1857), Iran loses western Afghanistan.
1891 The Great Tobacco Rebellion against monopoly concessions occurs.
1896 Nasser id-Din Shah is assassinated.
1896 Muzzafar id-Din Shah ascends to the throne with the backing of the Cossack Brigade.

1896–1905 Muzzafar id-din Shah reigns.

Constitutional Revolution

1905 The Constitutional Revolution begins. The shah concedes a parliament and a constitution but dies shortly afterward. Muhammad 'Ali Shah is crowned.

1905 The shah moves to crush revolutionaries. Civil war follows.

1909 The Constitutionalists win. The shah flees to Russia.

1909 Ahmad Shah is installed on the throne with British and Russian support.

1909–1925 Ahmad Shah reigns.

1911–1918 Iranian territory is occupied by British, Russian, and Ottoman troops. Britain emerges as the main power broker. Iran almost becomes a British protectorate.

1921 In a coup, the Persian Cossack Brigade installs Sayyid Zia, a pro-British civilian, as prime minister. Reza Khan, the brigade commander, is named minister of war.

1924 Parliament declares a republic but then retracts the declaration.

1925 Ahmad Shah is deposed. Reza Khan founds the Pahlavi dynasty.

Pahlavi Dynasty

1925–1941 Reza Shah reigns.

1925–1934 Tribal wars occur.

1941–1946 The Allies occupy Iran, depose Reza Shah, and install Muhammad Reza as shah.

1941–1979 Muhammed Reza Shah reigns.

1941–1953 A constitutional monarchy is established.

1951 The oil crisis occurs. Premier Mossadeq gains power with the aid of the Tudeh party. Muhammad Reza Shah flees to Iraq. Iranian oil is nationalized.

1953 Muhammad Reza Shah is reinstalled in a coup assisted by the CIA.

1961–1963 The 'ulema lead public protests. Student groups turn to guerrilla activities.

1978–1979 The Islamic Revolution occurs. Muhammad Reza Shah is deposed.

Islamic Republic

1979 Ayatollah Khomayni founds the Islamic Republic.

1981 Civil war breaks out between the Revolutionary Guards and the *Mujahidin*.

1980–1988 War is waged between Iran and Iraq.

1989 Mass executions of political prisoners follow the war.
1989 Ayatollah Khomayni dies.
1991 The Gulf war is waged. Iran remains neutral.

For a more detailed description of these events, see Nikki Keddie, *The Roots of Revolution: An Interpretive History of Modern Iran* (New Haven: Yale University Press, 1981); and Ervand Abrahamian, *Iran Between Two Revolutions* (Princeton: Princeton University Press, 1982).

Appendix C
A Glossary of Farsi and Arabic Terms

akhund: a teacher, a master, a preacher

anderun: the segregated interior area of a traditional Persian home

ayatollah: literally, a sign of Allah; a title of veneration given to the highest theologians

bast: a place of sanctuary from the ill-will of others or the law, usually a religious shrine

bid'a: an innovation or novelty, a thing or mode of action the like of which has not existed or been practiced, dissent or independence of action going to the point of heresy although not of actual unbelief

birun: the reception area of a traditional Persian home

chaqukesh: a rogue, a bully, a petty criminal

darugha: a headman, a superintendent of a town or market, the elder of any guild, the head of local law officers and night-watchmen

diyeh: money given in recompense for murder or injury, blood money

farrash (or ferrash): one who spreads the carpets or cushions, the chamberlain in the palaces of kings and great men, an officer who superintends the pitching of tents, a footman

farrashbashi: see farrash

fetva: a judicial or religious sentence pronounced by learned men in the science of religion

firman: an injunction, an order to be obeyed by all, an imperial mandate

haakim-i shar': a judge trained in the Shari'a, a clerical judge

hakim: a physician, especially one trained in Galenic medicine

hudud: limits, extremities, a restrictive ordinance of divine law, punishments specifically prescribed by the Quran

hujjat ul-Islam: a person who guides others in the path of religion, a preacher, a scholar

kalantar: a Qajar law enforcement officer, often called a sheriff

lavaht: homosexuality

luti: a rascal, a bully, a jester, a sodomite, an impudent and forward fellow

luti-bazaar: literally, market of the lutis; rioting and pillaging

madrassa: a school, a seminary, a university, an academy, a college

maktab: a place or time of writing, a writing school

mashq: a drill, a model for imitation, a copy to write after, exercise, practice

maydan: an open field without buildings, an arena, a place for exercises or walking

meerghazab: literally, master of wrath; a royal executioner

mir asa: a nightwatchman

monafiq: a hypocrite, a term given to political prisoners in the Islamic Republic

mufsid fil-ard: from Sura 5:33 of the Quran, spreading mischief on the earth, corruption on earth, a term given to members of the Pahlavi regime but now extended to cover immorality in any form

mujtahid: a person who strives hard to acquire sound views, a person who has arrived at the highest degree of legal understanding, a title given to the highest ecclesiastical dignitaries

mullah: a learned man, a judge, a preacher

munavir ul-fekr: an enlightened person, a Western-educated individual

otaq-i tamshiyaat: literally, walking room; a room in which prisoners walk to get their blood circulating after torture

pasdar: a sentinel, a guard, a watchman

qanun: a law, a regulation, a rule

qisas: retribution, reproof, correction, the law of retaliation, revenge or homicide

rajm: lapidation, death by stoning

rowshanfekr: an enlightened person, a Western-educated individual

safa-yi batin: interior purity, transparency, harmony, purity of faith

salb: death by crucifixion

sham'i ajjin: inserting many burning candles into an individual's flesh

shar': literally, making a road straight; a law prescribed by the Muslim tradition of jurisprudence

shari'a: the path that the believer must tread, the totality of Allah's commandments, the laws of Islamic jurisprudence

t'aarof: recognizing or welcoming one another, etiquette, a manner of comportment with respect to various social occasions

t'azir: reproving, censuring, discretionary punishments prescribed by a judge

t'aziya: consoling, enjoining patience, mourning for the dead, a performance of the story of the life and martyrdom of Imam Husayn

toman: Iranian currency, 10 rials equal 1 toman

'ulema: learned men, scholar-theologians

umma: Quranic word for people or community, ethnic, linguistic, or religious bodies of people who are objects of the divine plan of salvation

'urf: being known, public, a just and lawful action, a benefit, a favor, generosity, customary law in general

zarurat: the doctrine of overriding necessity, one that excuses Muslims from performing religious requirements under extraordinary conditions

zena: adultery

zendeh beh gur: burying an individual alive

Notes

Chapter 1

1. Janice T. Gibson and Mika Haritos-Fatouros, "The Education of a Torturer," *Psychology Today* (November 1986):50–56; Milovan Djilas, *Of Prisons and Ideas*, trans. Michael Boro Petrovich (San Diego: Harcourt Brace Jovanovich, 1986), pp. 7–10; Hannah Arendt, *Eichmann in Jerusalem: A Report on the Banality of Evil*, rev. enlarged ed. (Harmondsworth, England: Penguin, 1979).

2. Edward Peters, *Torture* (Oxford: Basil Blackwell, 1985), pp. 120–140.

3. See Elaine Scarry, *The Body in Pain: The Making and Unmaking of the World* (Oxford: Oxford University Press, 1985), pp. 27–59; Jean Paul Sartre, "Introduction: A Victory," in Henri Alleg, *The Question*, trans. John Calder (New York: George Braziller, 1958), pp. 20–21.

4. Friedrich Nietzsche, *On the Genealogy of Morals and Ecce Homo*, trans. Walter Kaufmann and R.J. Hollingdale (New York: Vintage Books, 1969), pp. 76–79.

5. Ludwig Wittgenstein, *Philosophical Investigations*, 3rd ed., trans. G.E.M. Anscombe (Oxford: Basil Blackwell, 1976), p. 31e, Section 66.

6. Walter Benjamin, *Reflections*, trans. Edmund Jephcott (New York: Harcourt Brace Jovanovich, 1978), pp. 189–190.

7. Michel Foucault, *Discipline and Punish: The Birth of the Prison*, trans. Alan Sheridan (New York: Vintage Books, 1978), pp. 23–24.

8. Quentin Skinner, "Meaning and Understanding in the History of Ideas," in *Meaning and Context: Quentin Skinner and His Critics*, ed. James Tully (Cambridge: Polity Press, 1988), pp. 61–63. See also Quentin Skinner, "Motives, Intentions and the Interpretation of Texts," in Tully, *Meaning and Context*, pp. 74–75.

9. Charles Taylor, "Interpretation and the Sciences of Man," in *Interpretive Social Science: A Second Look*, ed. Paul Rabinow and William M. Sullivan (Berkeley and Los Angeles: University of California Press, 1987), pp. 35–36.

10. St. Augustine, *The City of God*, trans. Henry Bettenson (Harmondsworth, England: Penguin, 1987), pp. 593–594.

11. American "observer," cited in William H. Forbis, *The Fall of the Peacock Throne: The Story of Iran* (New York: Harper and Row, 1980), p. 132.

12. Karl Marx, *Capital*. Vol. 1, *A Critical Analysis of Capitalist Production*, trans. Samuel Moore and Edward Aveling (New York: International Publishers, 1979), pp. 765–766.

13. Peters, *Torture*, p. 3.

PART 1

1. 'Itizad as-Saltanih, *Fitnih-yi Bab* (Revolt of the Bab), ed. Abd ul-Husayn Nava'i (Tehran: M'asood S'uud, 1333 [1954]), p. 41.

2. Ibid., p. 42.

3. Mary L.W. Sheil, *Glimpses of Life and Manners in Persia* (London: John Murray, 1856), p. 276.

4. 'Itizad as-Saltanih, *Fitnih*, pp. 42–43.

5. *Tehran Gazette*, cited in Sheil, *Glimpses*, p. 280.

6. Sheil, *Glimpses*, p. 276.

7. Hassan Fasa'i, *The History of Persia Under Qajar Rule*, trans. Heribert Busse (New York: Columbia University Press, 1972), p. 304.

8. Sheil, *Glimpses*, p. 277.

9. *Tehran Gazette*, cited in Sheil, *Glimpses*, pp. 279–280.

10. Carla Serena, *Hommes et choses en Perse* (Paris: G. Charpentier, 1883), p. 35.

11. Sheil, *Glimpses*, pp. 279, 281.

12. Shokrollah Paknezhad, "The Defense of Shokrollah Paknezhad in the Third Normal Court of the Military Tribunal," cited in Reza Baraheni, *The Crowned Cannibals: Writings on Repression in Iran* (New York: Vintage Books, 1977), p. 214.

13. Baraheni, *The Crowned Cannibals*, p. 170.

14. Muhammad Reza Pahlavi, cited in Richard F. Nyrop, ed., *Iran: A Country Study*, Area Handbook Program (Washington, DC: U.S. Department of Army, 1978), p. 381.

15. Ibid.

16. Amnesty International, *Report on Torture* (London: Gerald Duckworth and Co., 1973), p. 7.

17. Michel Foucault, *Discipline and Punish: The Birth of the Prison*, trans. Alan Sheridan (New York: Vintage Books, 1978).

18. Ibid., pp. 220–221.

19. Edward Peters, *Torture* (Oxford: Basil Blackwell, 1985), p. 105.

20. Ibid., pp. 103–140. For an account of corporal punishments employed in prisons, see David Rothman, *Conscience and Convenience: The Asylum and Its Alternatives in Progressive America* (Boston: Little, Brown, 1980), pp. 17–40.

21. Apart from an aside in *Discipline and Punish* (p. 40), Foucault's most extensive discussion of modern torture occurred in his articles on the Islamic Revolution in Iran. See Michel Foucault, "À quoi rêvent les Iranienne?" *Le Nouvel Observateur*, 9 October 1978, p. 48; Michel Foucault, "Lettre ouverte à Mehdi Bazargan," *Le Nouvel Observateur*, 14 April 1979, p. 46; Michel Foucault, "Inutile de se soulever?" *Le Monde*, 11 May 1979, translated as "Is It Useless to Revolt?" *Philosophy and Social Criticism* 8, 1 (Spring 1981): 7, 8; and Michel Foucault, "L'esprit d'un monde sans esprit," in *Iran: La révolution au nom de Dieu*, ed. Claire Brière and Pierre Blanchet (Paris: Editions de Seuil, 1979), p. 232. See also Laurence Olivier and Sylvain Labbé, "Foucault et l'Iran: À propos du désir de révolution," *Canadian Journal of Political Science* 24, 2 (June 1991): 219–236.

22. Foucault, "L'esprit d'un monde sans esprit," p. 239.

23. Edward Said, *The Word, the Text, and the Critic* (Cambridge, MA: Harvard University Press, 1983), p. 222. See also Timothy Mitchell, *Colonising Egypt* (Cambridge: Cambridge University Press, 1988).

24. Amnesty International, *Report*, p. 25.

Chapter 2

1. Ervand Abrahamian, *Iran Between Two Revolutions* (Princeton: Princeton University Press, 1982), p. 46.

2. Homa Katouzian, *The Political Economy of Modern Iran: Despotism and Pseudomodernism, 1926–1979* (New York: New York University Press, 1981), p. 24.

3. For the classic statement, see Jamal ad-Din al-Afghani, "The Reign of Terror in Persia," *Contemporary Review* 61 (February 1892): 238–248. See also Ali Asghar Shamim, *Iran dar Dowreh-yi Saltanat-i Qajar* (Iran During the Period of Qajar Rule) (Tehran: Ibn Sina, 1342 [1963]), pp. 282–284; Mehdi Malikzadeh, *Tarikh-i Inqilab-i Mashrutiyyat-i Iran* (The History of the Constitutional Revolution of Iran), vol. 1, *Falsafeh-yi Peydayesh-i Inqilab-i Mashrutiyyat* (The Philosophical Causes of the Constitutional Revolution) (Tehran: Ibn Sina, 1327–1335 [1948–1956]), pp. 64–68; Mehdi Malekzadeh, *Zindigani-yi Malek al-Motakallemin* (The Life of Malek al-Motakallemin) (Tehran: 'Ilmi, 1325 [1946]), p. 83; Fereydun Adamiyat, *Amir Kabir va Iran* (Amir Kabir and Iran) (Tehran: Kharazmi, 1348 [1969]), p. 132; Sa'id Nafisi, *Tarikh-i Mu'asir-i Iran* (Short History of Iran) (Tehran: Furughi, 1345 [1966]), p. 59; Muhammad Nazim ul-Islam Kirmani, *Tarikh-i Bidari-yi Iraniyan* (The History of Iranian Enlightenment), 2d ed. (Tehran: Ibn Sina, 1352 [1954]), p. 66; Katouzian, *The Political Economy*, pp. 24–25 and Abrahamian, *Iran*, p. 68.

4. Citing the authority of al Magni, al Mukhtassar, Sharh al Zurkani, and Ibn Sharif en Nawawi, *Minhaj et Talibin*, in Amnesty International, *Law and Human Rights in the Islamic Republic of Iran* (London: Amnesty International, 1980), p. 89. For views other than the Shi'a Imamiyya traditions on punishment, see an excellent overview of the major schools of law in Hideaki Homma, *Structural Characteristics of Islamic Penal Law*, Institute of Middle East Studies–International University of Japan Working Paper Series (Institute of Middle Eastern Studies, 1986).

5. *Shara'i al-Islam* (Al-Mazhab al-Ja'afari), cited in Amnesty International *Law*, pp. 98, 81–82.

6. Ibid., p. 83.

7. Herbert J. Liebesnay, *The Law of the Near and Middle East* (Albany: State University of New York Press, 1975), p. 229.

8. George N. Curzon, *Persia and the Persian Question*, 2d ed. (New York: Barnes and Noble, 1966), vol. 1, p. 457.

9. *Tehran Gazette*, cited in Mary L.W. Sheil, *Glimpses of Life and Manners in Persia* (London: John Murray, 1856), p. 280. Cf. Uriel Heyd, *Studies in Old Ottoman Criminal Law*, ed. V.L. Menage (Oxford: Clarendon Press, 1973), p. 118.

10. Carla Serena, *Hommes et choses en Perse* (Paris: G. Charpentier, 1883), p. 133.

11. Hakim Muhammad, cited in Cyril Elgood, *Safavid Medical Practice or the Practice of Medicine, Surgery, and Gynaecology in Persia Between 1500 A.D. and 1750 A.D.* (London: Luzac, 1970), p. 183. For a particularly vivid account of this process, see James B. Fraser, *A Winter's Journey from Constantinople to Tehran, with Travels Thence to Various Parts of Persia* (London: Richard Bentley, 1840), vol. 2, p. 191.

12. Elgood, *Safavid Medical Practice*, p. 186.

13. Ibid., pp. 180–181.

14. Eugene Flandrin, *Voyage en Perse* (Paris: Gide et J. Baudry, 1851), vol. 2, p. 36. See also Robert Ker Porter, *Travels in Georgia, Persia, Armenia, Ancient Babylonia &c. &c. During the Years 1817, 1818, 1819, 1820* (London: Longman Hurst, Rees, Orme and Browne, 1821–1822), vol. 1, p. 453.

15. *The Dynasty of Kajars, with a Succinct Account of the History of Persia Previous to That Period*, trans. Harford Jones Brydges (London: John Bohn, 1825), p. 38. This view of the soul is consistent with the Galenic account of the spirit. See Elgood, *Safavid Medical Practice*, p. 14.

16. Sheil, *Glimpses*, p. 276.

17. Ibid.

18. For an account of *t'azir*, see Liebesnay, *The Law*, pp. 229–230.

19. 'Itizad as-Saltanih, *Fitnih-yi Bab* (Revolt of the Bab), ed. Abd ul-Husayn Nava'i (Tehran: M'asood S'uud, 1333 [1954]), p. 41. The most important torture interrogation available from this period is "The Interrogation of Mirza Reza Kirmani and Those Persons Related to Him" (1899). The full report is available in Ali Khan Qajar Zahir id-Duwlih, *Tarikh-i Bi-durugh dar Vaqayle-i Qatl-i Nassir id-Din Shah* (A True History of the Events Concerning the Death of Nasser id-Din Shah), ed. Ali Reza Khusravi (Tehran: Ukhuvat, 1336 [1957]), pp. 60–105. Portions of the report are published in English in E.G. Browne, *The Persian Revolution of 1905–1909*, 2d ed. (London: Frank Cass, 1966), pp. 63–92. This interrogation closely resembles old Ottoman torture proceedings. Cf. Heyd, *Studies*, pp. 106, 118, 119, 132, 149, 252–254.

20. Zahir id-Duwlih, *Tarikh*, p. 85; see also p. 60.

21. Ibid., pp. 65–67.

22. Ibid., p. 69.

23. Ibid., p. 85. Cf. Heyd, *Studies*, pp. 252–254.

24. Liebesnay, *The Law*, p. 230.

25. See M.C. Bateson, J.W. Clinton, J.B.M. Kassarjian, H. Safavi, and M. Soraya, "*Safa-yi Batin:* A Study of the Interrelation of a Set of Iranian Ideal Character Types," in *Psychological Dimensions of Near Eastern Studies*, ed. L. Carl Brown and Norman Itzkowitz, (Princeton: Darwin Press, 1977), pp. 257–273; William O. Beeman, "What Is (IRANIAN) National Character?: A Sociolinguistic Approach," *Iranian Studies* 9, 1 (Winter, 1976): 22–48; and a stimulating discussion on the subject in Dale F. Eickelman, *The Middle East: An Anthropological Approach* (Englewood Cliffs, NJ: Prentice-Hall, 1981), pp. 196–199.

26. Zahir id-Duwlih, *Tarikh*, p. 92.

27. See Mahmoud Ayoub, *Redemptive Suffering in Islam: A Study of the Devotional Aspects of "Ashura" in Twelver Shi'ism* (The Hague: Mouton, 1978), p. 26.

28. Akbar Hashemi-Rafsanjani, *Amir Kabir ya Qahriman-i Mubarizih ba Est'imar* (Amir Kabir or the Hero of the Struggle Against Colonialism) (Tehran: Farahani, 1346 [1971]), p. 440. See also 'Itizad as-Saltanih, *Fitnih*, pp. 42–43; Zahir id-Duwlih, *Tarikh*, p. 52; and Mirza Ghullam Hussayn Khan Afzal ul-Mulk, *Qajariyeh* (The Qajar Period) (Tehran: Islami, 1361 [1982]), vol. 6, p. 33.

29. Mirhusayn Yekrangan, *Sarnevesht-i Iran: Zindigani-yi Siyassi va Adabi-yi Sadr-i 'Azam-i Shahid Qa'im Maqam-i Farahani* (The Destiny of Iran: The Politi-

cal and Cultural History of the Martyred Sadr 'Azam Qa'im Maqam Farahani) (Tehran: 'Ilmi, 1334 [1955]), p. 24.

30. Browne, *The Persian Revolution*, p. 444.

31. Fraser, *A Winter's Journey*, p. 191.

32. Abbas Iqbal, "Hujjat ul-Islam Haj Sayyed Muhammad Baqer Shafti," *Yadigar* 5, 10 (1327)[1948]:41.

33. Sheil, *Glimpses*, p. 246. See also Liebesnay, *The Law*, p. 229.

34. John Malcolm, *The History of Persia from the Most Early Period to the Present Times* (London: John Murray, 1815), vol. 2, p. 454.

35. Hashemi-Rafsanjani, *Amir Kabir*, p. 440.

36. Francis B. Forbes-Leith, *Checkmate: Fighting Tradition in Central Persia* (New York: Robert M. McBride, 1927), p. 82.

37. Malcolm, *The History of Persia*, vol. 2, p. 455.

38. William O. Beeman, "Status, Style and Strategy in Iranian Interaction," *Anthropological Linguistics* 18 (October 1976):312. See also Beeman, "What Is (IRANIAN) National Character?"

39. Ervand Abrahamian, "Oriental Despotism: The Case of Qajar Iran," *IJMES* 10 (1979):25.

40. Malcolm, *The History of Persia*, vol. 2, p. 461.

41. See Abrahamian, *Iran*, pp. 26–33; and Hossein MirJafari, "The Haydari-N'imati Conflicts in Iran," *Iranian Studies*, 12, 3–4 (Summer-Autumn 1979):135–162.

42. Curzon, *Persia*, vol. 2, p. 457.

43. Robert Grant Watson, *A History of Persia from the Beginning of the Nineteenth Century to the Year 1858, with a Review of the Events That Led to the Establishment of the Kajar Dynasty* (London: Smith, Elder, 1866), pp. 409–410.

44. Muhammad Taqi Sipihr, *Nasikh at-Tavarikh* (Historical Notes) (Tehran: Islamiyeh, 1344 [1965]), vol. 4, p. 40.

45. Malcolm, *The History of Persia*, vol. 2, p. 463.

46. See Serena, *Hommes*, p. 118.

47. See Samuel G.H. Benjamin, *Persia and the Persians* (Boston: Ticknor, 1887), pp. 399, 405. The martyrdom of Nasser id-Din Shah was explicitly identified with that of Husayn. See Peter Chelkowsky, "Majlis-i Shahinshah-i Iran Nasir al-Din Shah," in *Qajar Iran: Political, Social and Cultural Change, 1800–1925*, ed. Edmund Bosworth and Carole Hillenbrand (Edinburgh: Edinburgh University Press, 1983), pp. 230–231.

48. Muhammad Fard-Saidi, "The Early Phases of Political Modernization in Iran: 1870–1925" (Ph.D. diss., University of Pennsylvania, 1974), p. 170.

49. Watson, *A History of Persia*, p. 356. See also Sheil, *Glimpses*, p. 280; and Hassan Fasa'i, *The History of Persia Under Qajar Rule*, trans. Heribert Busse (New York: Columbia University Press, 1972), p. 79.

50. See 'Itizad as-Saltanih, *Fitnih*, p. 43; Browne, *The Persian Revolution*, p. 408.

51. See Hashemi-Rafsanjani, *Amir Kabir*, pp. 432, 439–440; Yekrangan, *Sarnevesht-i Iran*, p. 25; and Browne, *The Persian Revolution*, p. 95.

52. See Willem Floor, "Change and Development in the Judicial System in Qajar Iran (1800–1825)" in Bosworth and Hillenbrand, *Qajar Iran*, pp. 114, 137.

53. See Porter, *Travels*, vol. 1, p. 453; Watson, *A History of Persia*, p. 136; Fasa′, *The History*, pp. 105, 240; Fraser, *A Winter's Journey*, pp. 189–191; Serena, *Hommes*, p. 134; Mahmud Himmat-Kirmani, *Tarikh-i Mofassal-i Kirman az 'Asr-i Hakhamaneshi ta Tulu-'i Silsileh-ye Pur-iftikhar-i Pahlavi* (A Complete History of Kiram from the Achaemenid Period to the Dawn of the Pahlavi Dynasty) (Tehran: Sherkat-i Sahami-yi Tab-'i Kitab, 1351 [1971]), p. 243; Percy M. Sykes, *A History of Persia*, 3rd ed. (London: Macmillan, 1951), vol. 2, p. 423. The Qajars were less fastidious than the Safavids (1503–1722), who used exoculation only to eliminate rivals to the throne. Blindness, "whether natural or deliberately inflicted," was "an absolute disqualification for the exercise of regal functions." E.G. Browne, *A Literary History of Persia* (Cambridge: Cambridge University Press, 1951), vol. 4, p. 98.

54. Floor, "Change," p. 141.

55. John Malcolm, *Sketches of Persia, from the Journals of a Traveller of the East* (London: John Murray, 1827), vol. 1, pp. 83–84.

56. Abrahamian, "Oriental Despotism," p. 10.

57. Ann K.S. Lambton, *Landlord and Peasant in Persia: A Study of Land Tenure and Land Revenue Administration* (London: Oxford University Press, 1953), p. 144.

58. Himmat-Kirmani, *Tarikh*, p. 147. See also Bastani Parizi, "Ba Dard-i Kashan Har Keh Dar Uftad" (He Who Deals with the Agony of Kashan), *Yaqma* (Plundering) 17 (1343): 502–505. The people of Kirman say the figure was, by tradition, 7.5 *man*, which may come to either 23 kilos of eyes in Tabrizi *man* or 45 kilos in shah *man*. The number of eyes taken thus varies from 7,000 to 20,000.

59. For further accounts of this concept, see Nikki Keddie, "The Roots of the Ulama's Power in Modern Iran," in *Scholars, Saints and Sufis: Muslim Religious Institutions in the Middle East since 1500*, ed. Nikki R. Keddie (Berkeley and Los Angeles: University of California Press, 1972), pp. 211–229; Ann K.S. Lambton, "Quis Custodiet Custodes? Some Reflections on the Persian Theory of Government," *Studia Islamica* 5 (1955):125–148 and 6 (1956):125–146; and Joseph Eliash, "Misconceptions Regarding the Juridical Status of the 'Ulama" *IJMES* 10 (1979):24.

60. Abrahamian, *Iran*, p. 49.

61. Kashif al-Ghita′, cited in Ann K.S. Lambton, "A Nineteenth Century View of the Jihad," *Studia Islamica* 32 (1970):189. See also Lambton, "Quis Custodiet Custodes?" pp. 137–148.

62. Norman Calder, "Accommodation and Revolution in Imami Shi'i Jurisprudence: Khumayni and the Classical Tradition," *Middle Eastern Studies* 18, 1 (January 1982):6.

63. Sheil, *Glimpses*, p. 169; and John G. Wishard, *Twenty Years in Persia* (New York: Flemming H. Revel, 1908), p. 274.

64. *The Dynasty of Kajars*, p. 38. See also P. Hardy, "Force and Violence in Indo-Persian Writing on History and Government in Medieval South Asia," in *Islamic Society and Culture: Essays in Honor of Aziz Ahmad*, ed. Milton Israel and N.K. Wagle (New Delhi: Monohar, 1983), pp. 171–172, 183.

65. See A. Reza Arasteh, "The Character, Organization and Social Role of the Lutis (Javanmardan) in Traditional Iranian Society of the Nineteenth Century," *Journal of the Economic and Social History of the Orient* 4 (1961):47–52; A. Reza Arasteh, "The Social Role of the Zurkhana (House of Strength) in Iranian Urban

Communities During the Nineteenth Century," *Der Islam* 37 (1961):256–259; Asghar Fathi, "The Role of the Rebels in the Constitutional Movement in Iran," *IJMES* 10 (1979):55–66; and Ann K.S. Lambton, *Islamic Society in Persia* (London: School of Oriental and African Studies, University of London, 1954).

66. *The Glory of the Shia World: Tale of a Pilgrimage*, trans. and ed. Percy M. Sykes (London: Macmillan, 1910), p. 211. Robbers, however, had some trepidation about killing holy men directly and preferred to bury them and let them die of hunger, thirst, or marauding animals. See C.J. Wills, *In the Land of the Lion and Sun (Modern Persia) Being Experiences of Life in Persia from 1866–1881* (London: Ward, Lock, 1891), p. 265.

67. Willem M. Floor, "The Lutis—A Social Phenomenon in Qajar Perisa," *Die Welt des Islams* 13 (1971):115.

68. Willem M. Floor, "The Office of Kalantar in Qajar Persia" *Journal of the Economic and Social History of the Orient* 14 (1971):263–264. See also Abrahamian, *Iran*, pp. 41–42.

69. Benjamin, *Persia*, p. 405.

70. William P. Cresson, *Persia: The Awakening East* (Philadelpha: Lippincott, 1908), p. 65.

71. Abrahamian, "Oriental Despotism," pp. 28–29.

72. David Fraser, *Persia and Turkey in Revolt* (Edinburgh: William Blackwood, 1910), pp. 56–57.

73. Hamid Algar, *Religion and State in Iran, 1785–1906: The Role of the Ulema in the Qajar Period* (Berkeley and Los Angeles: University of California Press, 1969), pp. 19, 109–110.

74. Alessandro Bausani, "The Qajar Period: An Epoch of Decadence?" in Bosworth and Hillenbrand, *Qajar Iran*, p. 257.

75. See Browne, *A Literary History of Persia*, vol. 4, p. 368; and Iqbal, "Hujjat ul-Islam," p. 41.

76. Floor, "Change," p. 114.

77. Calder, "Accommodation," pp. 3, 6.

78. Malcolm, *Sketches of Persia*, vol. 2, pp. 137–138.

Chapter 3

1. For accounts of the execution, see E.G. Browne, *The Persian Revolution of 1905 1909*, 2d ed. (London: Frank Cass, 1966), p. 40; Mirza Ghullam Hussayn Khan Afzal ul-Mulk, *Qajariyeh* (The Qajar Period) (Tehran: Islami, 1361 [1982]), vol. 6, pp. 32–33; and 'Ali Khan Qajar Zahir id-Dowleh, *Tarikh-i Bi-durugh dar Vaqay'e-i Qatl-i Nasser id-Din Shah* (A True History of the Events Concerning the Death of Nasser id-Din Shah), ed. Ali Reza Khusravi (Tehran: Ukhuvat, 1336 [1957]), pp. 50–52.

2. Browne, *The Persian Revolution*, p. 93. The only recorded case of public penal torture between 1896 and 1921 in which the government had a hand was the exhibition of the head of Mirza Kuchek Khan, the leader of the Jangali Movement, in 1921. Kuchek Khan had died in the snow, and the point of the exhibition was to prove he was dead. Politics, not a lively interest in tradition, necessitated this display. It is said that in the 1920s the secret police would place a cushion on the face of the condemned and sit on him until he was dead. Perkins reported a similar *public* execu-

tion from the mid-nineteenth century. Justin Perkins, *A Residence of Eight Years in Persia Among the Nestorian Christians* (Andover, MA: Allen, Morill and Wardwell, 1843), p. 455. Cf. Reza Baraheni, *The Crowned Cannibals: Writings on Repression in Iran* (New York: Vintage Books, 1977), p. 42.

3. George N. Curzon, *Persia and the Persian Question*, 2d ed. (London: Barnes and Noble, 1966), vol. 1, p. 457. See also Browne, *The Persian Revolution*, p. 93; C.J. Wills, *In the Land of the Lion and Sun (Modern Persia) Being Experiences of Life in Persia from 1866–1881* (London: Ward, Lock, 1891), pp. 205, 277; and Ervand Abrahamian, *Iran Between Two Revolutions* (Princeton: Princeton University Press, 1982), p. 57.

4. Mohammad Fard-Saidi, "The Early Phases of Political Modernization in Iran: 1870–1925" (Ph.D. diss., University of Pennsylvania, 1974), pp. 166–174; Robert Grant Watson, *A History of Persia* (London: Smith, Elder, 1866), pp. 352–353; and Abrahamian, *Iran*, pp. 37–49.

5. Fard-Saidi, "The Early Phases," p. 177.

6. Charles Issawi, ed., *The Economic History of Iran, 1800–1914* (Chicago: University of Chicago Press, 1971), pp. 14–19; Bizhan Jazani, *Capitalism and Revolution in Iran*, trans. Iran Committee (London: Zed Press, 1980), p. 6; Homa Katouzian, *The Political Economy of Modern Iran: Despotism and Pseudo-modernism, 1926–1979* (New York: New York University Press, 1981), pp. 45–47.

7. John H. Lorentz, "Modernization and Political Change in 19th Century Iran: The Role of Amir Kabir" (Ph.D. diss., Princeton University, 1974), Chap. 5.

8. Michel Foucault, *Discipline and Punish: The Birth of the Prison*, trans. Alan Sheridan (New York: Vintage Books, 1979), p. 137.

9. Lorentz, "Modernization," p. 197.

10. Ibid., p. 197.

11. Issa Khan Sadiq, *Modern Persia and Her Educational System* (New York: Bureau of Publications, Teachers College, Columbia University, 1931), p. 37.

12. Lorentz, "Modernization," p. 200.

13. Samuel G. Wilson, *Persian Life and Customs*, 2d ed. (Edinburgh: Oliphant Anderson and Ferrier, 1896), p. 152.

14. Cf. Thomas Kuhn, *The Structure of Scientific Revolutions*, 2d ed. (Chicago: University of Chicago Press, 1970), pp. 181–187. For an important elaboration of Kuhn's notion, see Herbert Dreyfus and Paul Rabinow, *Michel Foucault: Beyond Structuralism and Hermeneutics* (Chicago: University of Chicago Press, 1982), pp. 160–167.

15. Mary L.W. Sheil, *Glimpses of Life and Manners in Persia* (London: John Murray, 1856), p. 380.

16. William P. Cresson, *Persia: The Awakening East* (Philadelphia: Lippincott, 1908), p. 79.

17. A. Reza Arasteh, *Education and Social Awakening in Iran, 1850–1968* (Leiden: E.J. Brill, 1969), p. 88. See also Fard-Saidi, "The Early Phases," pp. 120–124, 134–137.

18. Sadiq, *Modern Persia*, p. 58.

19. Foucault, *Discipline*, pp. 135–169.

20. Firuz Kazemzadeh, "The Origin and Early Development of the Persian Cossack Brigade," *American Slavic and East European Review* 15 (October 1956):362.

21. Ibid., p. 354. See also Muriel Atkin, *Russia and Iran, 1780–1828* (Minneapolis: University of Minnesota Press, 1980), p. 111.

22. James J. Morier, *A Second Journey Through Persia, Armenia, and Asia Minor to Constantinople Between the Years 1810 and 1816* (London: Longman, Hurst, Rees, Orme and Brown 1818), p. 216. See also Cresson, *Persia*, p. 78.

23. Robert Ker Porter, *Travels in Georgia, Persia, Armenia, Ancient Babylonia, &c, &c, during the Years 1817, 1818, 1819, and 1820* (London: Longman, Hurst, Rees, Orme and Brown, 1821–1822), vol. 1, p. 227.

24. Amir Kabir, untitled correspondence with Nasser id-Din Shah, cited by Lorentz, "Modernization," p. 289.

25. Abraham V. Williams-Jackson, *Persia, Past and Present* (New York: Macmillan, 1909), p. 424. See also Abbas Iqbal, "Sabzeh Maydan va Majm'a-i Dar ul-Sanay'i" (Sabzeh Maydan and the House of Industries Complex), *Yadigar* 4, 9–10 (1326) [1947]:59–70.

26. Sadiq, *Modern Persia*, p. 109.

27. Perkins, *A Residence*, p. 437; Curzon, *Persia*, vol. 1, p. 492.

28. Perkins, *A Residence*, p.437.

29. Curzon, *Persia*, vol. 1, p. 492.

30. Ibid., p. 494.

31. Ibid., p. 495.

32. C. MacGregor, *Journey Through Khurasan*, cited in Curzon, *Persia*, vol. 1, p. 611.

33. Ibid., p. 495.

34. Nusratullah Bastan, "Khaterat-i az Ruzha-yi Tahsil dar Dar ul-Fonun" (Memories of School Days at the Dar ul-Fonun) in *Amir Kabir va Dar ul-Fonun* (Amir Kabir and the Dar ul-Fonun), ed. Qodratullah Rowshani Z'afaranlu (Tehran: Tehran University, 1354 [1957]), p. 8.

35. Cameron Afzal, "Interview with William McElwee Miller: Missionary to Iran, 1919–1962" (Manuscript, 1985), pp. 39–40.

36. Muhammad Husayn Adib, "Yadgarha'i az Dar ul-Fonun-i Qadim" (Memories of the Old Dar ul-Fonun), in *Amir Kabir va Dar ul-Fonun* (Amir Kabir and the Dar ul-Fonun), ed. Qodratullah Rowshani Z'afaranlu (Tehran: Tehran University, 1354 [1975]), p. 60.

37. Curzon, *Persia*, vol. 1, p. 495.

38. Adib, "Yadgarha," p. 61.

39. Curzon, *Persia*, vol. 1, p. 495.

40. Afzal, "Interview," p. 40.

41. Ibid.

42. Sadiq, *Modern Persia*, p. 102.

43. Bastan, "Khaterat," p. 6.

44. Lorentz, "Modernization," p. 20; see also pp. 195, 223.

45. Overseas Consultants, "Report on the Seven Year Development Plan for the Plan Organization of the Imperial Iranian Government," cited by Amin Banani, *The Modernization of Iran, 1921–1941* (Stanford, CA: Stanford University Press, 1961), pp. 110–111.

46. Foucault, *Discipline*, pp. 177–194.

47. For a complete list, see E.G. Browne, *The Press and Poetry of Modern Persia* (Cambridge: Cambridge University Press, 1914), pp. 157–159. See also Fereydun Adamiyat, *Amir Kabir va Iran* (Amir Kabir and Iran) (Tehran: Kharazmi Press, 1969), p. 374.

48. Lorentz, "Modernization," p. 226.

49. Dreyfus and Rabinow, *Michel Foucault*, p. 160.

50. Alinaghi Asrari, "Education and Economic Development in Iran," *International Education* 6, 1 (1976):16.

51. Rouhullah K. Ramazani, "Modernization and Social Research in Iran," *American Behavioral Scientist* 6 (1962):19.

52. Marvin Zonis, "Higher Education and Social Change: Problems and Prospects," in *Iran Faces the Seventies*, ed. Ehsan Yar-Shater (New York: Praeger, 1971), p. 231.

53. Ibid., p. 249.

54. Samuel P. Huntington, *Political Order in Changing Societies* (New Haven: Yale University Press, 1968), p. 24.

Chapter 4

1. Malkum Khan, *Majmu'e-yi Asar* (Collected Works), ed. Muhit Tabataba'i (Tehran: Danesh, 1329 [1948]), p. 10.

2. Ibid.

3. Ibid., p. 11.

4. Homa Katouzian, *The Political Economy of Iran: Despotism and Pseudo-modernism, 1926–1979* (New York: New York University Press, 1981), p. 45.

5. Jalal Al-e Ahmad, *Gharbzadegi* [Plagued by the West], (N.p.: Itihadiye-yi Anjuman-i Islami-yi Daneshjuyan-i Urupa va Anjuman-i Islami-yi Danishjuyan-i Amrika va Kanada, n.d.), p. 104. For an English translation, see Jalal Al-e Ahmad, *Plagued by the West (Gharbzadegi)*, trans. Paul Sprachman (Delmar, NY: Caravan Books, 1982), pp. 100–101. I cite both works, the Farsi text and then the Sprachman translation (with page numbers given in brackets).

6. John H. Lorentz, "Modernization and Political Change in 19th Century Iran: The Role of Amir Kabir" (Ph.D. diss., Princeton University, 1974), p. 79.

7. Ibid., p. 82; see also Muriel Atkin, *Russia and Iran, 1780–1828* (Minneapolis: University of Minnesota Press, 1980), pp. 102–104.

8. Ibid., p. 72.

9. Ibid.; see also pp. 107–111.

10. Russian officer, cited in George N. Curzon, *Persia and the Persian Question*, 2d ed. (London: Barnes and Noble, 1922), vol. 1, p. 607.

11. John Malcolm, *The History of Persia from the Most Early Period to the Present Times* (London: John Murray, 1815), vol. 2, pp. 297–298.

12. James Morier, *A Second Journey Through Persia, Armenia, and Asia Minor to Constantinople Between the Years 1810 and 1816* (London: Longman, Hurst, Rees, Orme and Browne, 1818), p. 211.

13. Lorentz, "Modernization," p. 83; see also Atkin, *Russia and Iran*, pp. 136–144.

14. Curzon, *Persia*, vol. 1, p. 580.

15. Henry Rawlinson, *England and Russia in the East* (New York: Praeger, 1970), p. 31.

16. Ibid., p. 31.

17. E.G. Browne, *The Persian Revolution of 1905–1909*, 2d ed. (London: Frank Cass, 1966), p. 40. The word *Tihran* has been changed to *Tehran* for the sake of clarity.

18. Firuz Kazemzadeh, "The Origin and Early Development of the Persian Cossack Brigade," *American Slavic and East European Review* 15 (October 1956):360.

19. Ibid., p. 361.

20. Ervand Abrahamian, *Iran Between Two Revolutions* (Princeton: Princeton University Press, 1982), p. 58.

21. Lorentz, "Modernization," p. 202.

22. Ann K.S. Lambton, "The Impact of the West on Persia," *International Affairs* 33 (January 1957):16.

23. Abrahamian, *Iran*, p. 50.

24. Ibid., p. 62.

25. Ibid., pp. 61–62.

26. Malik al-Motakallemin, untitled, cited in Abrahamian, *Iran*, p. 76.

27. It is all very interesting that certain notable exceptions, such as Afghani, existed, but one would not want to use exceptions to the run of the mill modernist work as Bayat-Phillip did. Mangol Bayat-Phillip, "Tradition and Change in Iranian Socio-Religious Thought," in *Continuity and Change in Modern Iran*, ed. Michael E. Bonine and Nikki R. Keddie (Albany: State University of New York Press, 1981), pp. 35–56. I disagree, therefore, with efforts to characterize enlightened thinkers as academic mystics. Such a claim simply ignores what most modernist scholars actually did—namely, write narrow technical manuals on European techniques. For a complete list of modernist works, see E.G. Browne, *The Press and Poetry of Modern Persia* (Cambridge: Cambridge University Press, 1914), pp. 157–165.

28. Malkum Khan, "God Has Blessed Iran," cited by Abrahamian, *Iran*, p. 68.

29. Ashraf, "Remonstrance of a Reactionary," in Browne, *The Press and Poetry*, p. 189, lines 6–10. See also "Muhammad 'Ali Mirza's Despair," in Browne, *The Press and Poetry*, pp. 242–246.

30. Abrahamian, *Iran*, p. 69.

31. Kazemzadeh, "The Origin," p. 363.

32. Browne, *The Persian Revolution*, pp. 321–322; see also pp. 329–330.

33. Issa Khan Sadiq, *Modern Persia and Her Educational System* (New York: Bureau of Publications, Teachers College, Columbia University, 1931), p. 24.

34. Malkum Khan, "A Letter from Qazvin," cited in Abrahamian, *Iran*, p. 69.

35. Abrahamian, *Iran*, p. 66. Some 'ulema recognized this by declaring "qanun" to be *bid'a*, or a "heretical innovation." Leading 'ulema backed the Constitutionalist forces because they anticipated the Constitutionalists could be more easily persuaded to enforce religious laws, not because they saw constitutional laws as legitimate. See Norman Calder, "Accommodation and Revolution in Imami Shi'i Jurisprudence: Khumayni and the Classical Tradition," *Middle Eastern Studies* 18, 1 (January 1982):7–8.

36. Browne, *The Press and Poetry*, p. 18. See also Hamid Algar, *Mirza Malkum Khan: A Study in the History of Iranian Modernism* (Berkeley and Los Angeles: University of California Press, 1973), pp. 28–29.

37. Abrahamian, *Iran*, p. 68. For a spirited defense of the Constitutionalist perspective as well as its tacit disciplinarian spirit, see Katouzian, *The Political Economy*, pp. 56–58.

38. John G. Wishard, *Twenty Years in Persia* (New York: Flemming H. Revel, 1908), p. 220. See also Cyril Elgood, *A Medical History of Persia and the Eastern Caliphate: The Development of Persian and Arabic Medical Sciences from the Earliest Times Until the Year A.D. 1932, Including the Mongol Domination and Western Influences* (Amsterdam: A.P.A.-Philo Press, 1979); Byron J. Good, "The Transformation of Health Care in Modern Iranian History," in Bonine and Keddie, *Continuity and Change*, pp. 57–80; Donald N. Wilber, *Iran: Past and Present*, 8th ed. (Princeton: Princeton University Press, 1976); A. Reza Arasteh, *Education and Social Awakening in Iran, 1850–1968* (Leiden: Brill, 1969); Denis Wright, *The English Amongst the Persians During the Qajar Period, 1787–1921* (London: Morrison and Gibb, 1977); League of Nations, Health Organisation, *Report on an Investigation into the Sanitary Conditions in Persia* (Geneva: 1925), C.H. 262; Sadiq, *Modern Persia*; Abrahamian, *Iran*, pp. 50–58; and Amin Banani, *The Modernization of Iran, 1921–1941* (Stanford, CA: Stanford University Press, 1961), pp. 62–67.

39. Good, *A Medical History*, p. 63.

40. John McNeill, Public Records Office, "Record of a Conversation Between Palmerston and McNeill, December 18, 1835," F0/60/38, cited by Wright, p. 124.

41. Wright, *The English*, p. 125.

42. Elgood, *A Medical History*, p. 523.

43. Ibid., p. 126.

44. Wright, *The English*, p. 126.

45. Elgood, *A Medical History*, p. 530.

46. Ibid., p. 524.

47. Ibid., p. 528. See also Willem M. Floor, "The Office of Kalantar in Qajar Persia," *Journal of the Economic and Social History of the Orient* 14 (1971):259.

48. Abbas Iqbal, "Abeleh Kubi" (Smallpox Inoculation), *Yadigar* 4, 3 (1326) [1947]:69.

49. Browne, *The Press and Poetry*, p. 94.

50. Mehdi Malekzadeh, *Tarikh-i Inqilab-i Mashrutiyat-i Iran* (History of the Constitutional Revolution in Iran), cited in Abrahamian, *Iran*, p. 75.

51. Sadiq, *Modern Persia*, p. 36. See also Abrahamian, *Iran*, pp. 75–76.

52. See Ann K.S. Lambton, "Secret Societies and the Persian Revolution of 1905," *St. Antony's Papers* 4 (1958):43–60; Abrahamian, *Iran*, pp. 69–101; Mehdi Malekzadeh, *Zindigani-ye Malek al-Motakallemin* (The Life of Malek al-Motakallemin) (Tehran: 'Ilmi, 1325 [1946]), pp. 91–93; William Green Miller, "Political Organizations in Iran: From Dowreh to Party," *Middle East Journal* 23, 2–3 (Spring-Summer 1969):156–167, 343–350; and James A. Bill, "The Plasticity of Informal Politics: The Case of Iran," *Middle East Journal* 27, 2 (Spring 1973):131–151.

53. Nikki Keddie, *Roots of Revolution: An Interpretive History of Modern Iran* (New Haven: Yale University Press, 1981), p. 67.

54. Wright, *The English*, p. 182.

55. Bahar of Mashad, "The Disordered Dream of Muhammad 'Ali Mirza on the First Night of His Arrival at Odessa in Russia," in Browne, *The Press and Poetry*, p. 220.

56. Bahar of Mashad, "Al-Hamdolellah!" in ibid., p. 118, line 13.

57. Ahmad Kasravi, "Why We Are Not Politicians," cited in Abrahamian, *Iran*, p. 126; see also p. 127.

58. "Religion and Nationality," cited in Abrahamian, *Iran*, p. 123.

59. A. Kazemi, "What Do We Want?" cited in Abrahamian, *Iran*, p. 124.

60. Abrahamian, *Iran*, p. 343.

61. Tabataba'i, *Parliamentary Proceedings*, 14th Majles, 11 September 1944, cited in Abrahamian, *Iran*, p. 340.

62. Muhammad Reza Pahlavi, speech of 2 March 1975, cited in Fred Halliday, *Iran: Dictatorship and Development* (Bungay, England: Richard Clay [The Chaucer Press], 1979), p. 47.

63. Arasteh, *Education*, p. 89.

64. Reza Baraheni, *The Crowned Cannibals: Writings on Repression in Iran* (New York: Vintage Books, 1977), p. 214.

65. Curzon, *Persia*, vol. 1, pp. 458–459. See also Carla Serena, *Hommes et choses en Perse* (Paris: G. Charpentier, 1883), pp. 130–131.

66. Curzon, *Persia*, vol. 1, p. 458. See also Hideaki Homma, *Structural Characteristics of Islamic Penal Law*, Institute of Middle East Studies–International University of Japan Working Paper Series (N.p.: Institute of Middle Eastern Studies, 1986), p. 31.

67. Curzon, *Persia*, vol. 1, pp. 458–459. See also Homma, *Structural Characteristics*, pp. 13, 17–19, 23.

68. League of Nations, *Report*, p. 51.

69. Abdu'l Majid, untitled, in Browne, *The Press and Poetry*, p. 306.

70. Herbert H. Vreeland, ed., *Iran*, Country Survey Series (New Haven: Human Relations Area Files, 1957), pp. 96–99. See also Negley King Teeters, *World Penal Systems: A Survey* (Philadelphia: Pennsylvania Prison Society, 1944), p. 135.

71. Halliday, *Iran*, p. 85.

72. Ann K.S. Lambton, *Islamic Society in Persia* (London: School of Oriental and African Studies, University of London, 1954), p. 14.

73. Charles Jeffries, *The Colonial Police* (London: Max Parish, 1952), p. 213.

74. Johann von Justi, *Éléments généraux de police*, cited by Jacques Donzelot, *The Policing of Families*, trans. Robert Hurley (New York: Pantheon Books, 1979), p. 7.

75. For an excellent series of articles on traditional police officers and Qajar era reforms, see Willem M. Floor, "The Office of Kalantar in Qajar Persia," *Journal of the Economic and Social History of the Orient* 14 (1971):153–168; Willem M. Floor, "The Marketpolice in Qajar Persia," *Die Welt des Islams* 13 (1971):212–229; and Willem M. Floor, "The Police in Qajar Persia," *Zeitschrift der Deutschen Morgenlandischen Gesellschaft* 123 (1973):293–315.

76. Kazemzadeh, "The Origin," p. 362. Nasr ed-Din has been changed to Nasser id-Din for the sake of clarity.

77. Tehran police officer, cited in Farhad Kazemi, *Poverty and Revolution in*

Iran: The Migrant Poor, Urban Marginality and Politics (New York: New York University Press, 1980), p. 124.

78. R. Reinhard Loeffler, "From Tribal Order to Bureaucracy: The Political Transformation of the Boir Ahmad," cited in Abrahamian, *Iran*, p. 439. See also Halliday, *Iran*, pp. 29–30.

79. Abrahamian, *Iran*, p. 439.

80. Eric J. Hooglund, *Land and Revolution in Iran, 1960–1980* (Austin: University of Texas Press, 1982), p. 115.

81. Michel Foucault, *The History of Sexuality: An Introduction*, trans. Robert Hurley (New York: Vintage Books, 1980), p. 138.

82. Howard J. Rotblat, "Social Organization and Development in an Iranian Provincial Bazaar," *Economic Development and Culture Change* 23 (1974–1975):293.

83. Ibid., p. 294.

84. Ibid., p. 303.

85. Lord George Curzon, *Documents on British Foreign Policy, 1919–1939*, cited by Wright, *The English*, p. 179.

86. "British Minister to Foreign Office," cited by Abrahamian, *Iran*, p. 117.

87. Edmund Ironside, from *The Personal Diaries of the Late Field Marshall the Lord Ironside*, cited in Wright, *The English*, p. 181.

88. M. Makki, *Tarikh-i Bist Saleh-yi Iran* (Twenty Year History of Iran), cited in Abrahamian, *Iran*, p. 131.

89. Al-e Ahmad, *Gharbzadegi*, p. 102 [p. 99].

Chapter 5

1. Charles S. Prigmore, *Social Work in Iran Since the White Revolution* (University: University of Alabama Press, 1976), chap. 7; Nasir id-Din Saheb oz-Zamani, *Kitab-i Ruh-i Bashar* (Book of the Human Psyche) vol. 3, *Ansu-yi Chihriha* (Behind the Masks) (Tehran: 'Ata'i, 1343 [1964]), p. 195; Muhammad Husayn Adib, "Yadgarha'i az Dar ul-Fonun-i Qadim" (Memories of the Old Dar ul-Fonun), in *Amir Kabir va Dar ul-Fonun* (Amir Kabir and the Dar ul-Fonun), ed. Ghodratullah Rowshani Z'afaranlu (Tehran: Tehran University, 1354 [1975]), pp. 58–59; and Donne Raffat, *The Prison Papers of Bozorg Alavi: A Literary Odyssey* (Syracuse, NY: Syracuse University Press, 1985), pp. 50–51, 53.

2. Sadiqi, cited in Nasir id-Din Saheb oz-Zamani, *Javani-yi Pur Ranj* (Agonized Youth) (Tehran: 'Ata'i, 1344 [1965]), p. 325.

3. Herbert H. Vreeland, ed., *Iran*, Country Survey Series (New Haven: Human Relations Area Files, 1957), pp. 98–99.

4. Ali Dashti, parliamentary deputy, cited in ibid., p. 97.

5. Prigmore, *Social Work*, pp. 98–99. See also Raffat, *The Prison Papers*, p. 49.

6. Saheb oz-Zamani, *Ansu-yi Chihriha*, p. 195.

7. Bozorg Alavi, cited in Raffat, *The Prison Papers*, p. 60; see also pp. 49–51, 67.

8. Ervand Abrahamian, *The Iranian Mojahedin* (New Haven: Yale University Press 1989), pp. 138, 139, 148, 164, 172, 175, 177; and Ervand Abrahamian, "Communism and Communalism in Iran: The Tudah and the Firqah-i Dimukrat," *International Journal of Middle East Studies* 1 (1970):299.

9. Georges Levasseur, "Report on the Legal System in Iran," in *Human Rights and the Legal System in Iran: Two Reports by William J. Butler, Esq. and Profes-*

sor Georges Levasseur (Geneva: International Commission of Jurists, 1976), pp. 68–69; Gerald T. McLaughlin and Thomas M. Quinn, "Drug Control in Iran: A Legal and Historical Analysis," *Iowa Law Review* 59 (February 1974):498, 507; M.R. Moharreri, "Out-Patient Treatment of Opium Addicts: Report on a Pilot Project in Shiraz," *Bulletin on Narcotics* 28 (July-September 1976):31.

10. McLaughlin and Quinn, "Drug Control," p. 498.

11. Prigmore, *Social Work*, p. 94.

12. McLaughlin and Quinn, "Drug Control," p. 488.

13. Ibid., p. 489.

14. Ibid., p. 497.

15. Ibid., pp. 470, 489. See also Gerald T. McLaughlin, "The Poppy Is Not an Ordinary Flower: A Survey of Drug Policy in Iran," *Fordham Law Review* 44 (March 1976):701–772; and "Towards a Solution of Regional Narcotics Problems: Recent Projects of U.N. Technical Assistance," *Bulletin on Narcotics* 20 (January-March 1968):41–49.

16. Levasseur, "Report," p. 69. See also Harvey H. Smith et al., *Area Handbook for Iran*, Area Handbook Program (Washington, DC: U.S. Government Printing Office, 1971), p. 568; and Richard F. Nyrop, ed., *Iran: A Country Study*, Area Handbook Program (Washington, DC: U.S. Department of the Army, 1978), p. 384.

17. Harold Irnberger, *SAVAK oder Der Folterfreund des Westens* (Reinbek bei Hamburg: Rowohlt Taschenbuch Verlag, 1977), pp. 24, 27, 29–31.

18. Nyrop, *Iran*, p. 371.

19. Hafez Iyman, *Def'a-i Jam'i-i dar Muqabel-i Jurm va Mujrem* (The Defense of Society Against Crime and the Criminal) (Tehran: Chehr, 1343 [1964]), p. 153.

20. Muhammad Reza Shah Pahlavi, *Mission for My Country* (New York: McGraw-Hill, 1960), p. 129.

21. "Towards a Solution," p. 42.

22. McLaughlin, "The Poppy," pp. 751–753.

23. McLaughlin and Quinn, "Drug Control," pp. 493, 507.

24. "Towards a Solution, p. 43; Moharreri, "Out-Patient Treatment of Opium Addicts," p. 33.

25. Prigmore, *Social Work*, p. 99; McLaughlin, "The Poppy," p. 748; McLaughlin and Quinn, "Drug Control," p. 508.

26. Levasseur, "Report," pp. 68–69.

27. McLaughlin and Quinn, "Drug Control," p. 503.

28. Nyrop, *Iran*, p. 384; Levasseur, "Report," p. 69.

29. Levasseur, "Report," p. 67.

30. William J. Butler, "Report on Human Rights in Iran," in *Human Rights*, p. 21.

31. Prigmore, *Social Work*, p. 98.

32. Ibid., p. 95.

33. Dr. Rezvan, SAVAK interrogator, cited in Reza Baraheni, *The Crowned Cannibals: Writings on Repression in Iran* (New York: Vintage Books, 1977), p. 147.

34. Vreeland, *Iran*, p. 276.

35. Saheb oz-Zamani, *Kitab-i Ruh-i Bashar* (Book of the Human Psyche), 3d ed. (Tehran: 'Ata'i, 1343 [1964]), pp. 94–95.

36. Helmut Richards, "Carter's Human Rights Policy and the Pahlavi Dictatorship," in *Iran Erupts*, ed. Ali-Reza Nobari (Stanford, CA: Iran-America Documentation Group, 1978), p. 92.

37. Levasseur, "Report," p. 51.

38. Dott. Giancarlo-Lannutti, observer for the Italian Committee for the Defense of Political Prisoners, cited in Butler, "Report on Human Rights," p. 9.

39. Levasseur, "Report," p. 52.

40. Dr. Parviz Sabeti, SAVAK official, cited in Baraheni, *The Crowned Cannibals*, p. 192.

41. As in Page duBois, *Torture and Truth* (New York: Routledge, 1991), pp. 152–153.

42. Carol Ackroyd et al., *The Technology of Political Control*, rev. 2d ed. (London: Pluto Press, 1980), pp. 277–278.

43. K.W. Bash, "Report on a Visit to Isfahan," cited in Saheb oz-Zamani, *Ansu-yi Chihriha*, pp. 366–367.

44. Baraheni, *The Crowned Cannibals*, p. 42.

45. Ibid., pp. 210–212. This is the only instrument that was reputedly constructed originally by the SS to facilitate interrogations and was introduced into Iran by Nazi advisers. The technique consisted of cuffing the hands behind the back, one arm over the shoulder and one not. This position puts pressure on the shoulderbones, especially the clavicle, slowly constraining and breaking it.

46. Bahman Nirumand, *Iran: The New Imperialism in Action*, trans. Leonard Mins (New York: Monthly Review Press, 1969), p. 164.

47. Baraheni, *The Crowned Cannibals*, p. 14.

48. Ibid.

49. Ibid., pp. 158–159. See also Reza Reza'i, "Letter," in Nobari, *Iran Erupts*, p. 154.

50. "Torture as Policy: The Network of Evil," *Time*, 16 August 1976, p. 32.

51. Baraheni, *The Crowned Cannibals*, p. 196.

52. *The Times*, 6 January 1969, cited in Butler, "Report on Human Rights," p. 11.

53. Baraheni, *The Crowned Cannibals*, pp. 149, 164–165.

54. Ibid., pp. 63–64. The main exception is when the death is attributed to internal struggles within guerrilla organizations. See Abrahamian, *The Iranian Mojahedin*, p. 163.

55. Jerrold D. Green, *Revolution in Iran: The Politics of Countermobilization* (New York: Praeger, 1982), p. 44.

56. Muhammad Reza Pahlavi, cited in Nyrop, *Iran*, p. 381.

57. See duBois, *Torture*, p. 153.

58. Baraheni, *The Crowned Cannibals*, p. 187.

59. Brig. Gen. Abdi, Army general prosecutor, cited in *Iran Almanac 1962* (Tehran: Echo of Iran, 1962), p. 56.

60. Abrahamian, *The Iranian Mojahedin*, pp. 109, 135, 151.

61. Baraheni, *The Crowned Cannibals*, p. 185. Fred Halliday, *Iran: Dictatorship and Development* (Bungay, England: Richard Clay [The Chaucer Press], 1979), p. 80.

62. Halliday, *Iran*, p. 81.

63. Ibid., pp. 81–82.

64. Albie Sachs, *The Jail Diaries of Albie Sachs*, cited in Ackroyd, *The Technology*, p. 239.

65. Baraheni, *The Crowned Cannibals*, pp. 175–176.

66. Ibid., p. 193.

67. Edward Peters, *Torture* (Oxford: Basil Blackwell, 1985), pp. 175–176.

68. Bozorg Alavi, cited in Raffat, *The Prison Papers*, p. 95.

69. Baraheni, *The Crowned Cannibals*, p. 198. See also SAVAK official, cited in "SAVAK: Like the CIA" *Time*, 19 February 1979, p. 32.

70. Butler, "Report on Human Rights," p. 7.

71. Halliday, *Iran*, p. 89.

72. SAVAK autopsy report, cited in Reza Baraheni, "The SAVAK Documents," *The Nation*, 23 February 1980, p. 199. See also Halliday, *Iran*, p. 88.

73. See Ervand Abrahamian, "The Crowd in Iranian Politics, 1905–1953," *Past and Present* 41 (December 1968):207; Farhad Kazemi, *Poverty and Revolution in Iran: The Migrant Poor, Urban Marginality and Politics* (New York: New York University Press, 1980), pp. 1–2; Nasrollah Saifpour Fatemi, *Oil Diplomacy: Powderkeg in Iran* (New York: Whittier Books, 1954), p. 216; and Misagh Parsa, *The Social Origins of the Iranian Revolution* (New Brunswick, NJ: Rutgers University Press, 1989), p. 234.

74. See Ervand Abrahamian, *Iran Between Two Revolutions* (Princeton: Princeton University Press, 1982), p. 322.

75. McLaughlin and Quinn, "Drug Control," p. 512.

76. Ervand Abrahamian, "The Guerrilla Movement in Iran, 1963–1977," *MERIP Reports* (March-April 1980):4.

77. Helmut Richards, "America's Shah; Shahanshah's Iran," *MERIP Reports* (September 1975):17.

78. McLaughlin, "The Poppy," p. 742; McLaughlin and Quinn, "Drug Control," pp. 505, 514.

79. William F. Hickman, *Ravaged and Reborn: The Iranian Army, 1982* (Washington, DC: Brookings Institition, 1982), pp. 2–3. See also Nyrop, *Iran*, p. 371; and Irnberger, *SAVAK*, pp. 24, 36–38.

80. See Franklin Mark Osanka, ed., *Modern Guerrilla Warfare: Fighting Communist Guerrilla Movements, 1941–1961* (New York: Free Press, 1962); Samuel P. Huntington, ed., *Changing Patterns of Military Politics* (New York: Free Press, 1962); John Pustay, *Counterinsurgency Warfare* (New York: Free Press, 1965); Charles W. Thayer, *Guerrilla* (London: Michael Joseph, 1964); Rogert Trinquier, *Modern Warfare: A French View of Counterinsurgency*, trans. Daniel Lee (New York: Praeger, 1964); and Russel F. Weigley, ed., *New Dimensions in Military History: An Anthology* (San Rafael, CA: Presidio Press, 1975), pp. 329–384.

81. U.S. Congress, Senate, Committee on Appropriations, "Foreign Assistance Appropriations, 1965," *Hearings*, 89th Cong., 2nd sess., 1964, pp. 72–73.

82. Michael T. Klare and Cynthia Arnson, *Supplying Repression* (Washington, DC: Institute of Policy Studies, 1977), pp. 17–40.

83. See Nyrop, *Iran*, pp. 361–374; Irnberger, *SAVAK*, pp. 24–25; Israel Shahak, *Israel's Global Role: Weapons for Repression* (Bell Mair, MA: Association of Arab-

American University Graduates, 1982); and Robert B. Reppa, Sr., *Israel and Iran: Bilateral Relationship and Effect on the Indian Ocean Basin* (New York: Praeger, 1974), pp. 96–98.

84. Seymour M. Hersh, "Ex-Analyst Says CIA Rejected Warnings on Shah," *New York Times*, 7 January 1978, p. A3. Other analysts have pointed to the CIA's experiments with hallucinogenic drugs, psychosurgery, sensory deprivation, and electroshock therapy. See John Marks, *The CIA and Mind Control: The Search for the Manchurian Candidate* (New York: McGraw-Hill, 1980); and James A.C. Brown, *Techniques of Persuasion: From Propaganda to Brainwashing* (Harmondsworth England: Penguin, 1969).

85. Even Chomsky and Herman cautioned against overemphasizing the U.S. origins of modern tortures and drew attention instead to the extensive moral and technical support for "the widespread adoption of torture as an administrative practice by client fascist states." See Noam Chomsky and Edward Herman, *The Political Economy of Human Rights*. Vol. 1, *The Washington Connection and Third World Fascism* (Montreal: Black Rose Books, 1979), p. 49.

86. Halliday, *Iran*, p. 84.

87. Alec Mellor, cited in Peters, *Torture*, p. 106.

PART 2

1. Hafez Iyman, *Def'a-i Jam'i-i dar Mughabel-i Jurm va Mujrem* (The Defense of Society Against Crime and the Criminal) (Tehran: Chehr, 1343 [1964]), p. dal.

2. Ibid.

Chapter 6

1. See, for example, Herbert H. Vreeland, ed., *Iran*, Country Study Series (New Haven: Human Relations Area Files, 1977), pp. 275–277.

2. Jerry Zarit, "Intimate Look at the Iranian Male," in *Sexuality and Eroticism Among Males in Moslem Socities*, ed. Arno Schmitt and Jehoeda Sofer (New York: Hayworth Press, 1992), p. 56.

3. Muhsin Shafa'i, *Khesaal-i Shafa'i* (Shafa'i's Praiseworthy Virtures). Vol. 4, *Khanevadeh va Asrar-i Khushbakhti-yi An* (The Family and the Secrets to Its Happiness) (Tehran: A'in-i No, 1341 [1962]), p. 116.

4. Nasir id-Din Saheb oz-Zamani, *Kitab-i Ruh-i Bashar* (Book of the Human Psyche). Vol. 3, *Ansu-yi Chihriha* (Behind the Masks) (Tehran: 'Ata'i, 1343 [1964]), p. 170.

5. Ibid.

6. Jamshid Behnam and Shahpour Rasekh, *Muqadameh bar Jam'i-i Shenassi-yi Iran* (Introduction to the Sociology of Iran), 3d ed. (Tehran: Khwarazmi, 1348 [1968]), pp. 435–436.

7. Nasir id-Din Saheb oz-Zamani, *Kitab-i Ruh-i Bashar* (Book of the Human Psyche), 3d ed. (Tehran: 'Ata'i, 1343 [1964]), p. 152.

8. Qudsiyeh Hejazi, *Barresi-yi Jara'im-i Zan dar Iran* (A Study of Female Criminality in Iran) (Tehran: Inteshar, 1341 [1963]), p. 173.

9. Nur al-Huda Manganeh, *Rah Amuz-i Khanevadeh* (Guide for the Family) (Tehran: Rangin, 1333 [1954]), p. 206; see also pp. 241–242.

10. Ibid., p. dal.

11. Ibid., p. 206.

12. Saheb oz-Zamani, *Ansu-yi Chihriha*, p. 246.

13. Mahmud Sana'i, "Tarh-i Jadid-i Barnameh-yi Madares" (The New Scheme of School Programs), cited in Nasir id-Din Saheb oz-Zamani, *Javani-yi Pur-ranj* (Agonized Youth) (Tehran: 'Ata'i, 1344 [1965]), p. 20.

14. Saheb oz-Zamani, *Ansu-yi Chihriha*, p. 245.

15. Shahpour Rasekh, "Muqadameh'i dar Bareh-yi Tahavul-i Tehran va Masa'el-i An" (An Introduction Concerning the Changes of Tehran and Its Problems), in *Sukhanraniha va Guzaresh-ha dar Nukhustin Seminar-i Barresi-yi Masa'el-i Shahr-i Tehran* (Speeches and Reports During the First Seminar for the Investigation of the Social Problems of the City of Tehran) (Tehran: Institute of Social Work and Research, Tehran University, 1343 [1964]), p. 239. See also Assadollah Shifteh, "Tafrihat-i Saalem dar Jahan-i Emrooz va Iran: Barressi-yi Niyazmandiha-yi Shahr-i Tehran be Tafrihat-i Saalem" (Healthy Social Activities in Today's World and Iran: An Investigation into the Needs of the Tehran Municipality for Healthy Social Activities), in *Sukhanraniha*, p. 405.

16. Overseas Consultants, "Report on the Seven-Year Development Plan for the Plan Organization of the Imperial Government of Iran," cited in A. Banani, *The Modernization of Iran, 1921–1941* (Stanford, CA: Stanford University Press, 1961), pp. 110–111. See also Ali-Muhammad Kardan, "Mokhtassari az Nabessamaniha dar Barkhi az Madares-i Tehran va 'Elal-i An" (A Summary of Delinquencies in Some of the Schools of Tehran and Their Causes), in *Sukhanraniha*, pp. 394–400.

17. Manganeh, *Rah Amuzi-i Khanevadeh*, p. 8.

18. Sana'i, cited in Saheb oz-Zamani, *Javani-yi Pur-ranj*, p. 20.

19. Gholam Husayn Sadiqi, untitled, cited in ibid., p. 19.

20. See Farah Azari, "Sexuality and Women's Oppression in Iran," in *Women of Iran: The Conflict with Fundamentalist Islam*, ed. Farah Azari (London: Ithaca Press, 1983), pp. 110, 122; and Jacquiline Rudolph Touba, "The Widowed in Iran" in *Widows*. Volume 1, *The Middle East, Asia and the Pacific*, ed. Helena Zananiecka Lopata (Durham, NC: Duke University Press, 1987), pp. 115–117.

21. John Gulick and Margaret E. Gulick, "The Domestic Social Environment of Women and Girls in Isfahan, Iran," in *Women in the Muslim World*, ed. Lois Beck and Nikki R. Keddie (Cambridge, MA: Harvard University Press, 1978), p. 513.

22. Ibid. See also Shafa'i, *Khesaal-i Shafa'i*, p. 135.

23. Beck and Keddie, *Women in the Muslim World*, p. 260.

24. Manganeh, *Rah Amuzi-i Khanevadeh*, p. 208.

25. Vreeland, *Iran*, p. 263. See also Shafa'i, *Khesaal-i Shafa'i*, p. 135.

26. Georges Levasseur, "Report on the Legal System in Iran," in *Human Rights and the Legal System in Iran: Two Reports by William J. Butler, Esq. and Professor Georges Levasseur* (Geneva: International Commission of Jurists, 1976), p. 56.

27. Azari, "Sexuality," p. 113.

28. K.W. Bash, "Foreword," in Nasir id-Din Saheb oz-Zamani, *Va Namidanand Chira* ... (And They Know Not Why ...) (Tehran: 'Ata'i, 1344 [1965]), p. 8.

29. See ibid., pp. 45–55. For a brief account of the trials of one group, sociologists, see Gholam Husayn Sadiqi, "'Avamel-i Peydayesh-i Nahanjariha va Bimariha-

yi Shahr-i Ma" (Factors Causing the Appearance of Improprieties and Diseases in Our City), in *Sukhanraniha*, pp. 323–324.

30. Bash, "Foreword," p. 10. For a history of this procedure, see Michel Foucault, *The History of Sexuality: An Introduction*, trans. Robert Hurley (New York: Vintage Books, 1980), pp. 57–70.

31. Saheb oz-Zamani, *Kitab-i Ruh-i Bashar*, p. 8.

32. Saheb oz-Zamani, *Javani-yi Pur-ranj*, p. 9.

33. Behnam and Rasekh, *Muqadameh*, pp. 173–174.

34. Hejazi, *Barresi-yi Jara'im Zan*, p. 172.

35. Behnam and Rasekh, *Muqadameh*, p. 179, see also p. 119.

36. See, for example, Saheb oz-Zamani, *Kitab-i Ruh-i Bashar*, p. 149.

37. Manganeh, *Rah Amuzi-i Khanevadeh*, p. 85.

38. Shafa'i, *Khesaal-i Shafa'i*, p. 116.

39. Manganeh, *Rah Amuzi-i Khanevadeh*, p. 104.

40. Shafa'i, *Khesaal-i Shafa'i*, pp. 155–169, 195; Manganeh, *Rah Amuzi-i Khanevadeh*, pp. 92–97, 153–155.

41. Shafa'i, *Khesaal-i Shafa'i*, p. 129.

42. Ibid., p. 171.

43. Ervand Abrahamain, *Iran Between Two Revolutions* (Princeton: Princeton University Press, 1982), p. 162.

44. Fred Halliday, *Iran: Dictatorship and Development* (Harmondsworth, England: Penguin, 1979), pp. 193, 202; William H. Bartsch, "The Industrial Labor Force of Iran: Problems of Recruitment, Training and Productivity," in *The Population of Iran: A Selection of Readings*, ed. Jamshid A. Momeni (Honolulu: East-West Population Institute, East-West Center, 1977), pp. 322–326.

45. Gerald T. McLaughlin and Thomas M. Quinn, "Drug Control in Iran: A Legal and Historical Analysis." *Iowa Law Review* 59 (February 1974):489. See also Charles S. Prigmore, *Social Work in Iran Since the White Revolution* (University: University of Alabama Press, 1976), p. 119.

46. Richard Moore, Khalil Asayesh, and Joel Montague, "Population and Family Planning in Iran," in Momeni, *The Population of Iran*, p. 285.

47. Julian Bharier, "A Note on the Population of Iran, 1900–1956," in ibid., p. 59.

48. Prigmore, *Social Work*, pp. 38–39.

49. Julian Bharier, "The Growth of Towns and Villages in Iran, 1900–1966," in Momeni, *The Population of Iran*, pp. 336–337.

50. See Hannah Arendt, *The Human Condition* (Chicago: University of Chicago Press, 1958), p. 68; and Gilles Deleuze, "Foreword: The Rise of the Social," in Jacques Donzelot, *The Policing of Families* (New York: Random House, 1979), pp. ix–xvii.

51. Cyril Elgood, *Safavid Medical Practice or the Practice of Medicine, Surgery and Gynaecology in Persia Between 1500 A.D. and 1750 A.D.* (London: Luzac, 1970), p. 219.

52. Eliz Sanasarian, *The Women's Rights Movement in Iran: Mutiny, Appeasement, and Repression from 1900 to Khomaini* (New York: Praeger, 1982), p. 46.

53. Ibid., pp. 70–71.

54. Byron J. Good, "The Transformation of Health Care in Modern Iranian History," in *Continuity and Change in Modern Iran*, ed. Michael E. Bonine and Nikki R. Keddie (Albany: State University of New York Press, 1981), pp. 68–69.

55. Muhammad Reza Pahlavi, cited in Sanasarian, *The Women's Rights Movement*, pp. 68–69.

56. Population Council, "Iran: Report on Population Growth and Family Planning," in Momeni, *The Population of Iran*, pp. 235–236; Prigmore, *Social Work*, p. 58.

57. Iran, Vezarat-i Behdari (Ministry of Health), Idai-yi Kul-i Behdasht (Central Health Office), *Guzaresh-i Saal 1341* (Annual Report 1962) (Tehran: n.p., 1962), p. 120.

58. Michael Fischer, "Persian Society: Transformation and Strain," in *Twentieth Century Iran*, ed. Husayn Amir-Sadeghi (London: Heinemann, 1978), p. 193.

59. Banani, *The Modernization of Iran*, p. 65.

60. Fischer, "Persian Society," p. 72; Abrahamian, *Iran*, pp. 446–447.

61. See Dorothy Pawluch, "New Directions in Pediatrics," *Social Science Forum* 1 (March 1983):2.

62. Vreeland, *Iran*, p. 243.

63. Abrahamian, *Iran*, pp. 446–447.

64. Banani, *The Modernization of Iran*, p. 65.

65. Good, *Safavid Medical Practice*, pp. 58, 75–76. See also Brian D. Clark, "Urban Planning: Perspectives and Problems," in *The Changing Middle Eastern City*, ed. Gerald H. Blake and Richard I. Lawless (London: Croom Helm, 1980), pp. 93, 408; Robert J. Haggerty, "The Boundaries of Health Care," in *Ways of Health: Holistic Approaches to Ancient and Contemporary Medicine*, ed. David S. Sobel (New York: Harcourt Brace Jovanovich, 1979), pp. 45–60; Edward H. Kass, "Infectious Diseases and Social Change," *Journal of Infectious Diseases* 123 (1971):110–114; and Thomas McKeown, *The Rise of Population* (New York: Academic Press, 1977).

66. Good, *Safavid Medical Practice*, pp. 64, 74.

67. Banani, *The Modernization of Iran*, p. 84.

68. Elgood, *Safavid Medical Practice*, p. 211.

69. Reza'i, "Afzayesh-i Bimariha-yi Ravani dar Shahr-i Ma" (The Increase of Psychological Diseases in Our City), in *Sukhanraniha*, p. 388; see also p. 322.

70. Saheb oz-Zamani, *Kitab-i Ruh-i Bashar*, p. 9. See also Prigmore, *Social Work*, pp. 125–126.

71. Saheb oz-Zamani, *Kitab-i Ruh-i Bashar*, p. 9.

72. Prigmore, *Social Work*, p. 82.

73. Police officer, cited in Saheb oz-Zamani, *Ansu-yi Chihriha*, pp. 235–236. See also Barry Rubin, *Paved with Good Intentions: The American Experience in Iran* (Harmondsworth, England: Penguin, 1981), p. 177.

74. Faqih, "Kuyha-yi Faqirneshin-i Junub-i Shahr" (The Alleys of the Squatter Settlements in the South of the City), in *Sukhanraniha*, p. 342.

75. See Saheb oz-Zamani, *Ansu-yi Chihriha*, pp. 223–227.

76. See Prigmore, *Social Work*, p. 58.

77. Michel Foucault, "Afterword: The Subject and Power," in Hubert L. Dreyfus and Paul Rabinow, *Michel Foucault: Beyond Structuralism and Hermeneutics* (Chicago: University of Chicago Press, 1982), p. 213.

78. Iraj 'Itisaam, "Maskan: Dar Guzashteh, Haal, va Ayandeh" (Housing: In the Past, Today, and the Future), in *Sukhanraniha*, pp. 248–249.

79. Ibid., p. 249.

80. Hushang Sayhun, "M'emari-yi Novin-i Ma" (Our New Architecture), in *Sukhanraniha*, p. 270.

81. Traditional housing was composed of a *birun* and an *anderun* area. The *birun* embraced the reception area for guests. The *anderun* was the area in which women were secluded. Entrance to the *anderun* was limited to male family members and doctors of both sexes. See Leonid Bogdanov, "The Home and Life in Persia," *Islamic Culture* 5 (1931):418.

82. Ibid., p. 421.

83. 'Itisaam, "Maskan," p. 249.

84. Ibid.

85. Sayhun, "M'emari-yi Novin-i Ma," p. 265.

86. Behnam and Rasekh, *Muqadameh*, p. 50.

87. Ahmad Ashraf, "Iran: Imperialism, Class and Modernization," cited in Farhad Kazemi, *Poverty and Revolution in Iran: The Migrant Poor, Urban Marginality and Politics* (New York: New York University Press, 1980), p. 110.

88. William H. Bartsch, "The Industrial Labor Force of Iran: Problems of Recruitment, Training and Productivity," in Momeni, *The Population of Iran*, p. 317.

89. Michael M.J. Fischer, *Iran: From Religious Dispute to Revolution* (Cambridge, MA: Harvard University Press, 1980), p. 97.

90. *Kar*, Khurdad 3, 1358 (1979), cited in Kazemi, *Poverty*, p. 116.

91. *Washington Post*, 14 January 1979, cited in ibid., p. 95.

Chapter 7

1. See Amin Banani, *The Modernization of Iran* (Stanford, CA: Stanford University Press, 1961), pp. 68–96; Ervand Abrahamian, *Iran Between Two Revolutions* (Princeton: Princeton University Press, 1982), pp. 140–141, 444–445; Shahrough Akhavi, *The Relationship Between Religion and the State in Iran Under the Pahlavi Dynasty* (Binghamton: State University of New York Press, 1980); Michael M.J. Fischer, *Iran: From Religious Dispute to Revolution* (Cambridge, MA: Harvard University Press, 1980), pp. 108–122; Nikki R. Keddie, ed., *Religion and Politics in Iran: Shi'ism from Quietism to Revolution* (New Haven: Yale University Press, 1981); and an illuminating discussion of the subject in Roy Mottahedeh, *The Mantle of the Prophet: Religion and Politics in Iran* (New York: Simon and Schuster, 1985), pp. 198–247.

2. Charles S. Prigmore, *Social Work in Iran Since the White Revolution* (University: University of Alabama Press, 1976), p. 120.

3. Azar Tabari, "The Enigma of the Veiled Iranian Woman," *MERIP Reports* (February 1982):23.

4. Resurgence Party, *The Philosophy of Iran's Revolution*, cited in Abrahamian, *Iran*, pp. 441–442.

5. Fred Halliday, *Iran: Dictatorship and Development* (Harmondsworth, England: Penguin, 1979), p. 205.

6. Ibid.

7. Ibid.

8. Ibid., p. 206.

9. Labor Minister Moini, cited in Halliday, *Iran*, p. 206.

10. Ahmad Ashraf, "Bazaar and Mosque in Iran's Islamic Revolution," *MERIP Reports* (March-April 1983):18.

11. Mehdi Tayyeb, former official of the Hujjatiyeh, cited in Douglas Martin, "The Persecution of the Baha'is of Iran, 1844–1984," *Bahai Studies* 12–13 (1984):32.

12. Ibid.

13. Ashraf, "Bazaar," p. 18.

14. Martin, "The Persecution of the Baha'is," p. 32.

15. Mehdi Tayyeb, cited in ibid. See also Nikola B. Schahgaldian, *The Clerical Establishment in Iran*, Rand Publication Series (Santa Monica, CA: Rand Corporation, June 1989), pp. 61–62.

16. Martin, "The Persecution of the Baha'is," p. 34.

17. Afsaneh Najmabadi, "Iran's Turn to Islam: From Modernism to a Moral Order," *Middle East Journal* 41, 2 (Spring 1987):62.

18. See Ashraf, "Bazaar," p. 18; and Martin, "The Persecution of the Baha'is," pp. 32–36.

19. *Ettela'at*, cited in Martin, "The Persecution of the Baha'is," p. 61.

20. Ibid., p. 36.

21. Slogan cited in Ervand Abrahamian, *The Iranian Mojahedin* (New Haven: Yale University Press, 1989), p. 213.

22. Emad Ferdows, "The Reconstruction Crusade and Class Conflict in Iran," *MERIP Reports* 13, 3 (March-April 1983):11. See also Fred Halliday, "The First Year of the Islamic Republic," *MERIP Reports* (June 1980):4; Ramy Nima, *The Wrath of Allah: Islamic Revolution and Reaction in Iran* (London: Pluto Press, 1983), pp. 136–137; Cheryl Bernard and Zalmay Khalilzad, *"The Government of God"—Iran's Islamic Republic* (New York: Columbia University Press, 1984), pp. 123–124; Eric Rouleau, "The War and the Struggle for the State," *MERIP Reports* (July-August 1981):5–6; and Suroosh Irfani, *Revolutionary Islam in Iran: Popular Liberation or Religious Dictatorship?* (London: Zed Press, 1983), pp. 183–207.

23. See Said Amir Arjomand, *The Turban for the Crown: The Islamic Revolution in Iran* (New York: Oxford University Press, 1988), pp. 157–159.

24. Schahgaldian, *The Clerical Establishment*, p. 64.

25. Abrahamian, *Iran*, p. 474.

26. Ayatollah Khomayni, *Kashif ul-Asrar*, cited in Edward Mortimer, *Faith and Power: The Politics of Islam* (London: Faber and Faber, 1982), p. 324.

27. Ibid., p. 325.

28. Muhammad Taqi Falsafi, *Kudak az Nazar-i Verasat va Tarbiyat* (The Child from the Perspective of Heredity and Training) (Tehran: Hey'at-i Nashr-i Ma'arif-i Islami, 1341 [1962]), pp. 22–25.

29. Muhsin Shafa'i, *Khessal-i Shafa'i* (Shafa'i's Praiseworthy Virtures). Vol. 4, *Khanevadeh va Asrar-i Khushbakhti-yi An* (The Family and the Secrets to Its Happiness) (Tehran: A'in-i No, 1341 [1962]), p. 49.

30. Fischer, *Iran*, p. 96.

31. Prigmore, *Social Work*, p. 110.

32. Gerald T. McLaughlin and Thomas M. Quinn, "Drug Control in Iran: A Legal and Historical Analysis." *Iowa Law Review* 59 (February 1974):487–491.

33. Schahgaldian, *The Clerical Establishment*, p. 62.

34. Ahmad Khomayni, cited in Abrahamian, *Iran*, p. 474.

35. Najmabadi, "Iran's Turn," p. 210.

36. Abrahamian, *Iran*, p. 433.

37. Sharif Arani, "From the Shah's Dictatorship to Khomeini's Demagogic Theocracy," *Dissent* 27 (Winter 1980):9–26.

38. Abrahamian, *Iran*, p. 533. Sepehr Zabih, *Iran Since the Revolution* (London: Croom Helm, 1982), p. 70; and Fred Halliday, "Year Three of the Islamic Revolution," *MERIP Reports* (March-April, 1982):4.

39. Ayatollah Morteza Motahheri, "Objectives of the Islamic Revolution," in *Tell the American People: Perspectives on the Iranian Revolution*, ed. David H. Albert, 2d ed. rev. and enl. (Philadelphia: Movement for a New Society, 1980), p. 201.

40. Ayatollah Rafsanjani, cited in Najmabadi, "Iran's Turn," p. 216.

41. Ayatollah Khomayni, cited in Amnesty International, *Law and Human Rights in the Islamic Republic of Iran* (London: Amnesty International, 1980), p. 84.

42. International Solidarity Front for the Defense of the Iranian People's Democratic Rights (ISF-Iran), *The Crimes of Khomeini's Regime*, 2d ed. (Geneva: ISF-Iran, 1982), p. 25.

43. Abrahamian, *The Iranian Mojahedin*, pp. 143–144.

44. A. Mas'oud, "The War Against Profiteers," cited in Abrahamian, *Iran*, p. 498.

45. Jerrold D. Green, *Revolution in Iran: The Politics of Countermobilization* (New York: Praeger, 1982), p. 105.

46. Ibid., p. 123.

47. Ibid., p. 161.

48. Prime Minister Shahpour Bakhtiar, cited in Barry Rubin, *Paved with Good Intentions: The American Experience and Iran* (Harmondsworth, England: Penguin, 1981), p. 239.

49. Amnesty International, *Law*, p. 18.

50. Ibid., p. 85.

51. Ayatollah Khomayni, cited in Amnesty International, *Law*, p. 29.

52. Ibid., p. 42.

53. Amnesty International, *Law*, pp. 41, 42.

54. Ibid., p. 90.

55. Premier Muhammed 'Ali Raja'i, cited in Assef Bayat, "Workers' Control after the Revolution," *MERIP Reports* (March-April 1983):23.

56. Ayatollah Khomayni, cited in Abrahamian, *The Iranian Mojahedin*, p. 210.

57. ISF-Iran, *The Crimes*, p. 68.

58. Ibid., p. 15.

59. Elaine Sciolino, "Iran's Durable Revolution," *Foreign Affairs* 61, 4–5 (Spring 1983):901.

60. ISF-Iran, *The Crimes*, p. 55.

61. Amnesty International, "Ill-Treatment of Prisoners in Iran" (Manuscript, 9 December 1982), p. 2.

62. Ibid., p. 11.

63. Ibid.

64. Ayatollah Beheshti, cited in Sciolino, "Iran's Durable Revolution," p. 898.

65. Social studies textbook, cited in Golnar Mehran, "Socialization of School-children in the Islamic Republic of Iran," *Iranian Studies* 22, 1 (Winter 1989):39.

66. Ibid., pp. 39–40.

67. For a complete list, see Arjomand, *The Turban*, pp. 163–173; and Dilip Hiro, *Iran Under the Ayatollahs* (London: Routledge and Kegan Paul, 1985), pp. 251–263.

68. Shahrzad Azad, "Workers' and Peasants' Councils in Iran," *Monthly Review* 32, 5 (October 1980):21.

69. Chris Goodey, "Workers' Councils in Iranian Factories," *MERIP Reports* (June 1980):6–7.

70. Ibid., p. 8.

71. Assef Bayat, "Labor and Democracy in Post-Revolutionary Iran," in *Post-Revolutionary Iran*, ed. Hooshang Amirahmedi and Manoucher Parvin (Boulder: Westview, 1988), p. 47.

72. Ibid., p. 48.

73. Azad, "Workers and Peasants' Councils," p. 21.

74. Assef Bayat, "Workers' Control After the Revolution," *MERIP Reports* (March-April 1983):23.

75. Amnesty International, *Law*, p. 20.

76. Sciolino, "Iran's Durable Revolution," p. 900.

77. Emad Ferdows, "The Reconstruction Crusade and Class Conflict in Iran," *MERIP Reports* (March-April 1983):12.

78. Nima, *The Wrath*, p. 89.

79. Fred Halliday, "The First Year," p. 4.

80. Fred Halliday, "Year IV of the Islamic Republic," *MERIP Reports* (March April 1983):4.

81. Akbar Aghajanian, "Post-Revolutionary Demographic Trends in Iran," in Amirahmadi and Parvin, *Post-Revolutionary Iran*, p. 164.

82. Schahgaldian, *The Clerical Establishment*, p. 154.

83. "Religion and Nationality," cited in Abrahamian, *Iran*, p. 123.

84. Bernard and Khalilzad, *"The Government of God,"* p. 116.

85. Ayatollah Khomayni, cited in ISF-Iran, *The Crimes*, p. iv.

Chapter 8

1. See Amnesty International, *Law and Human Rights in the Islamic Republic of Iran* (London: Amnesty International, 1980; Amnesty International, "Ill-Treatment of Prisoners in Iran" (Manuscript, 9 December 1982); Amnesty International, *Iran: Briefing* (London: Amnesty International, 1987); Amnesty International, *Iran: Violations of Human Rights* (London: Amnesty International Publications, 1987); Amnesty International, *Iran: Violations of Human Rights, 1987–1990* (New York: Amnesty International U.S.A., 1991).

2. Amnesty International, *Iran: Violations*, pp. 17, 81, 88, 91–92; Amnesty International, *Iran: Violations, 1990*, p. 46.

3. Amnesty International, *Iran: Violations*, p. 87.

4. Ibid., p. 88.

5. Ibid., p. 22.

6. Amnesty International, *Iran: Briefing*, p. 8.

7. Amnesty International, *Iran: Violations*, p. 74.

8. Cigarette burns (Amnesty International, *Iran: Violations*, pp. 20, 22; Amnesty International, *Iran: Violations, 1990*, p. 46); battery (Amnesty International, *Iran: Violations*, pp. 9, 18, 93); sexual assault (Amnesty International, *Iran: Briefing*, p. 10; Amnesty International, *Iran: Violations*, pp. 19, 72); mock executions (Amnesty International, *Iran: Briefing*, p. 10; Amnesty International *Iran: Violations, 1990*, pp. 44, 45); flogging (Amnesty International, *Iran: Violations, 1990*, p. 44).

9. Amnesty International, *Iran: Briefing*, p. 9; Amnesty International, *Iran: Violations*, pp. 19, 78, 87; Amnesty International, *Iran: Violations, 1990*, p. 44.

10. Amnesty International, *Iran: Violations*, pp. 16, 74, 92; Amnesty International, *Iran: Violations, 1990*, pp. 46, 48.

11. Amnesty International, *Iran: Violations*, p. 82.

12. Amnesty International, "Ill-Treatment," p. 7.

13. Ibid., p. 8.

14. International Solidarity Front for the Defense of the Iranian People's Democratic Rights (ISF-Iran), *The Crimes of Khomeini's Regime*, 2d ed. (Geneva: ISF-Iran, 1982), p. 13; see also p. 14.

15. Amnesty International, *Iran: Violations*, pp. 20, 83; Amnesty International, *Iran: Violations, 1990*, p. 47.

16. Amnesty International, *Iran: Violations*, p. 87.

17. Ibid., pp. 31–32. See also Suroosh Irfani, *Revolutionary Islam in Iran: Popular Liberation or Religious Dictatorship?* (London: Zed Press, 1983), p. 264.

18. Ibid., p. 19.

19. Ibid., pp. 265–266. Cf. Douglas Martin, "The Persecution of the Baha'is of Iran, 1844–1984," *Bahai Studies* 12–13 (1984):54. There has not been an independent confirmation of this charge by Amnesty International. However, there are reports of such procedures from organizations that have little in common: the Mujahidin Organization and the Baha'i ministries. Consequently, even though evidence does not constitute conclusive proof, there seems to be a high probability that extracting blood from the condemned did occasionally occur.

20. Amnesty International, "Ill-Treatment," p. 2; see also p. 10; Amnesty International, *Iran: Violations, 1990*, pp. 14–15; Amnesty International, *Iran: Violations*, p. 20; and ISF-Iran, *The Crimes*, p. 17.

21. Amnesty International, *Iran: Violations*, p. 77.

22. Ibid., p. 75.

23. Ibid., p. 92.

24. Ibid., p. 80.

25. Ibid., pp. 81, 91.

26. Ibid., p. 81.

27. Ibid., p. 75.

28. Confess (Amnesty International, *Iran: Violations, 1990*, pp. 44, 48, 39); recant (Amnesty International, *Iran: Violations, 1990*, pp. 18, 21); condemn (Amnesty International, *Iran: Violations, 1990*, p. 37); renounce (Amnesty International, *Iran: Briefing*, p. 9).

29. Amnesty International, *Iran: Violations*, pp. 79, 88, 92–93.

30. Cynthia Brown Dwyer, "Women Imprisoned in the Kingdom of the Mullahs," in *Women and Revolution in Iran*, ed. Guity Nashat (Boulder: Westview, 1983), p. 271.

31. Ibid., p. 266.

32. Richard Dowden, "In the Terror of Tehran," *New York Review of Books*, 2 February 1984, p. 8.

33. Ibid.

34. Amnesty International, *Iran: Violations*, p. 21.

35. Shaul Bakhash, "The Revolution Against Itself," *New York Review of Books*, 18 November 1982, p. 20.

36. Martin, "The Persecution of the Baha'is," p. 68.

37. Amnesty International, *Iran: Violations*, p. 15.

38. Martin, "The Persecution of the Baha'is," pp. 68, 65; Dwyer, "Women Imprisoned," pp. 270, 271, 275; Amnesty International, "Ill-Treatment," p. 5; ISF-Iran, *The Crimes*, p. 182; and Robin Woodsworth Carlsen, *The Imam and His Islamic Revolution: A Journey into Heaven and Hell* (Victoria, BC: Snow Man Press, 1982), p. 157.

39. Amnesty International, *Iran: Violations, 1990*, p. 16.

40. Ibid., pp. 14–18.

41. Amnesty International, *Iran: Violations*, pp. 20–21, 72, 86; Amnesty International, *Iran: Violations, 1990*, p. 15.

42. Amnesty International, *Iran: Violations*, pp. 83, 84; Amnesty International, *Iran: Briefing*, p. 2.

43. Amnesty International, *Iran: Violations, 1990*, p. 17.

44. Amnesty International, "Ill-Treatment," p. 8.

45. Amnesty International, *Iran: Violations, 1990*, p. 15.

46. Amnesty International, *Iran: Violations*, p. 86.

47. Tehran bus driver, cited by ISF-Iran, *The Crimes*, p. 16.

48. Carlsen, *The Imam*, pp. 147–148.

49. Prison chant at Evin prison, cited in Dowden, "In the Terror," p. 8.

50. Amnesty International, *Iran: Violations, 1990*, p. 17.

51. Amnesty International, *Iran: Violations*, p. 91.

52. Ibid., pp. 21, 89.

53. Dowden, "In the Terror," p. 8.

54. Amnesty International, *Iran: Violations*, p. 77.

55. Ibid., p. 71.

56. Dwyer, "Women Imprisoned," p. 271.

57. Amnesty International, "Ill-Treatment," p. 6.

58. Amnesty International, *Iran: Violations*, p. 71.

59. Ibid., p. 80.

60. Ibid., pp. 81–82.

61. ISF-Iran, *The Crimes*, p. 18.

62. Amnesty International, *Iran: Violations*, p. 22; see Amnesty International, *Iran: Violations, 1990*, p. 47.

63. Amnesty International, *Iran: Violations*, p. 71.

64. Hujjat ul-Islam Lajevardi, cited by ISF-Iran, *The Crimes*, p. 32.

65. Ervand Abrahamian, *The Iranian Mojahedin* (New Haven: Yale University Press, 1989), pp. 225–226.

66. Amnesty International, *Iran: Briefing*, p. 12; Amnesty International, *Iran: Violations*, p. 58.

67. Amnesty International, *Iran: Violations, 1990*, pp. 6, 10.

68. Amnesty International, *Iran: Violations*, p. 44; Amnesty International, *Iran: Violations, 1990*, p. 10.

69. Amnesty International, *Iran: Violations, 1990*, pp. 6, 9, 10–11, 35.

70. Abrahamian, *The Iranian Mojahedin*, p. 220.

71. ISF-Iran, *The Crimes*, p. 20.

72. Amnesty International, *Iran: Violations, 1990*, p. 10.

73. Ibid., p. 57.

74. Amnesty International, *Iran: Violations*, p. 47.

75. Amnesty International, *Torture in the Eighties* (London: Amnesty International Publications, 1984), p. 229.

76. Amnesty International, *Iran: Violations, 1990*, p. 47.

77. Ibid., p. 53.

78. Amnesty International, *Iran: Briefing*, p. 11.

79. Amnesty International, *Iran: Violations*, p. 47.

80. Amnesty International, *Iran: Violations, 1990*, p. 53. See also Amnesty International, *Iran: Violations*, p. 47.

81. Cyril Elgood, *Safavid Medical Practice or the Practice of Medicine, Surgery, and Gynaecology in Persia Between 1500 A.D. and 1750 A.D.* (London: Luzac, 1970), p. 183.

82. Amnesty International, *Iran: Briefing*, p. 11; Amnesty International, *Iran: Violations, 1990*, p. 52.

83. Amnesty International, *Iran: Violations, 1990*, p. 52.

84. Amnesty International, *Iran: Violations*, pp. 59–60.

85. Amnesty International, *Iran: Violations, 1990*, p. 4.

86. For a complete list of punishments prescribed by the Revolutionary Tribunals in the early revolutionary period, see Amnesty International, *Law*, pp. 136–188.

87. Amnesty International, *Iran: Violations*, p. 62.

88. See John H. Langbein, *Torture and the Law of Proof: Europe and England in the Ancien Regime* (Chicago: University of Chicago Press, 1977).

89. Ayatollah Khomayni, *Tahrir al-Wasila*, cited in Said Amir Arjomand, *The Turban for the Crown: The Islamic Revolution in Iran* (New York: Oxford University Press, 1988), p. 187.

90. Amnesty International, *Iran: Violations*, p. 79; see also pp. 89, 93. Amnesty International, *Iran: Violations, 1990*, p. 26.

91. Shaul Bakhash, "The Politics of Land, Law and Social Justice in Iran," *Middle East Journal* 43, 2 (Spring 1989):196.

92. Ibid.

93. Minister of justice, cited in Amnesty International, *Law*, p. 40.

94. Ayatollah Khomayni, cited in ibid., p. 42.

95. Revolutionary judge, cited in ibid., p. 63.

96. Ayatollah Qoddusi, cited in Shaul Bakhash, *The Reign of the Ayatollahs: Iran and the Islamic Revolution* (New York: Basic Books, 1984), p. 102.

97. See Arjomand, *The Turban*, p. 167; and Amnesty International, *Law*, p. 56.

98. Ayatollah Khomayni, cited in Amnesty International, *Law*, p. 47.

99. Amnesty International, *Iran: Violations, 1990*, pp. 55, 57.

100. Amnesty International, *Iran: Briefing*, p. 7.

101. Ibid., p. 6.

102. Ibid., p. 2.

103. Ayatollah Khalkhali, "All the People Who Are Opposed to Our Revolution Must Die," *MERIP Reports* (March-April 1982):31.

104. Amnesty International, *Iran: Violations, 1990*, pp. 6–9, 28.

105. Hujjat ul-Islam Karrubi, cited in ibid., p. 9.

106. Bakhash, "The Politics of Land," p. 198.

107. *Resaleh-ye Novin*, cited in Arjomand, *The Turban*, p. 188.

108. Amnesty International, *Iran: Violations*, p. 89.

109. Amnesty International, *Iran: Violations*, p. 19.

110. Ibid., p. 12.

111. Ibid. See also Amnesty International, *Law*, p. 52.

112. Amnesty International, *Iran: Violations*. See also Amnesty International, *Iran: Violations, 1990*, p. 31.

113. Amnesty International, *Iran: Violations*, p. 79; see also pp. 24–25. Amnesty International, *Iran: Briefing*, p. 7.

114. Amnesty International, *Iran: Violations, 1990*, p. 45.

115. Amnesty International, *Iran: Violations*, pp. 10, 46.

116. Ibid., pp. 45–46, 71, 73, 79, 92; Amnesty International, *Iran: Violations, 1990*, p. 17.

117. Amnesty International, *Torture*, p. 23.

118. Ibid.

119. Elaine Sciolino, "Iran's Durable Revolution," *Foreign Affairs* 61, 4–5 (Spring 1983):900.

120. Sepehr Zabih, *Iran Since the Revolution* (London: Croom Helm, 1982), p. 79.

121. Cheryl Bernard and Zalmay Khalilzad, *"The Government of God"—Iran's Islamic Republic* (New York: Columbia University Press, 1984), p. 122.

122. Ayatollah Tabataba'i Qomi, cited in Amnesty International, *Law*, p. 54.

123. Report of the Torture Probe Commission, cited in Amnesty International, *Torture*, p. 230. Cf. Nikki Keddie, *Roots of Revolution: An Interpretive History of Modern Iran* (New Haven: Yale University Press, 1981), p. 261.

124. Bakhash, *The Reign of the Ayatollahs*, p. 149.

125. Dwyer, "Women Imprisoned," pp. 271, 275, 276, 279.

126. Prison guard at Evin Prison, cited in ibid., p. 281.

127. Keddie, *Roots*, pp. 261–262; Dwyer, "Women Imprisoned," p. 284; and Ramy Nima, *The Wrath of Allah: Islamic Revolution and Reaction in Iran* (London: Pluto Press, 1983), p. 98.

128. Sciolino, "Iran's Durable Revolution," p. 900.

129. Abol-Hassan Bani-Sadr, "I Defeated the Ideology of the Regime," *MERIP Reports* (March-April 1982):6.

PART 3

1. Samuel Huntington, *Political Order in Changing Societies* (New Haven: Yale University Press, 1968), p. 144.

2. John Malcolm, *Sketches of Persia, from the Journals of a Traveller of the East* (London: John Murray, 1827), vol. 2, p. 138.

Chapter 9

1. For an exposition of the distinction between *batin* and *zahir*, see M.C. Bateson, J.W. Clinton, J.B.M. Kassarjian, H. Safavi, and M. Soraya, "Safa-yi Batin: A Study of the Interrelation of a Set of Iranian Ideal Character Types," in *Psychological Dimensions of Near Eastern Studies*, ed. L. Carl Brown and Norman Itzkowitz (Princeton: Darwin Press, 1977), pp. 257–273; and Mary Catherine Bateson, " 'This Figure of Tinsel': A Study of Themes of Hypocrisy and Pessimism in Iranian Culture," *Daedalus* 108, 3 (Summer 1979):125–134.

2. Samuel Huntington, *Political Order in Changing Societies* (New Haven: Yale University Press, 1968), p. 29. See also Leonard Binder, *Iran: Political Development in a Changing Society* (Berkeley and Los Angeles: University of California Press, 1962), pp. 127–144; Andrew F. Westwood, "Politics of Distrust in Iran," *Annals of the American Academy of Political and Social Sciences* 358 (March 1965):123–135; James Alban Bill, *The Politics of Iran: Groups, Classes and Modernization* (Columbus: Charles E. Merrill, 1972); Ali Banuazizi, "Iranian 'National Character': A Critique of Some Western Perspectives," in Brown and Itzkowitz, *Psychological Dimensions*, pp. 210–239; Robert Graham, *Iran: The Illusion of Power* (London: Croom Helm, 1978), pp. 194–198; and Marvin Zonis, *The Political Elite of Iran* (Princeton: Princeton University Press, 1971), pp. 198–208.

3. See Ervand Abrahamian, *Iran Between Two Revolutions* (Princeton: Princeton University Press, 1982), p. 167; see also pp. 4–6, 171–172.

4. See William O. Beeman, "What Is (IRANIAN) National Character?: A Sociolinguistic Approach," *Iranian Studies* 9, 1 (Winter 1976):22–48; William O. Beeman, "Status, Style and Strategy in Iranian Interaction," *Anthropological Linguistics* 18 (October 1976): 305–322; and Dale F. Eickelman, *The Middle East: An Anthropological Approach* (Englewood Cliffs, NJ: Prentice-Hall, 1981), pp. 196–199.

5. Nikki R. Keddie, *Roots of Revolution: An Interpretive History of Modern Iran* (New Haven: Yale University Press, 1981), p. 67.

6. Harney provided the most extensive inventory and evaluation of the tactics that characterized the Islamic Revolution. Desmond Harney, "Some Explanations for the Iranian Revolution," *Asian Affairs* 11, 2 (June 1980):137.

7. See James J. Reid, *Tribalism and Society in Islamic Iran, 1500–1629* (Malibu, CA: Undena Publications, 1983), pp. 135–138, 141–153; Laurence Lockhart, *The Fall of the Safavid Dynasty and the Afghan Occupation of Persia* (Cambridge: Cambridge University Press, 1958); John R. Perry, *Karim Khan Zand: A History of Iran, 1747–1779* (Chicago: University of Chicago Press, 1979); and Keddie, *Roots*.

8. Abrahamian, *Iran*, pp. 26–32, 36–37. See Marshall G.S. Hodgson, *The Venture of Islam: Conscience and History in a World Civilization*. Vol. 2, *The Gunpowder Empires and Modern Times* (Chicago: University of Chicago Press, 1974), pp. 154–155.

9. Political violence is only partially correlated with economic factors. See Farhad Kazemi, "Economic Indices of Political Violence in Iran: 1946–1968," *Iranian Studies* 8, 1–2 (Winter-Spring 1975):82; Manoucher Parvin, "Economic Determinants of Political Unrest," *Journal of Conflict Resolution* 17, 2 (June 1973):271–296; and Nasser Momayezi, "Economic Correlates of Political Violence: The Case of Iran," *Middle East Journal* 40, 1 (Winter 1986):68–81.

10. See Fred Halliday, "Theses on the Iranian Revolution," *Race and Class* 21 (Summer 1979):84–85, 88; Fred Halliday, *Iran: Dictatorship and Development* (Bungay, England: Richard Clay [The Chaucer Press], 1979), pp. 296–298; and Shahrzad Azad, "Workers' and Peasants' Councils in Iran," *Monthly Review* 32, 5 (October 1980):19.

11. See Nikki R. Keddie, "Iran: Change in Islam; Islam and Change," *International Journal of Middle East Studies* 11 (1980):529–530; Richard W. Cottam, *Nationalism in Iran*, rev. 2d ed. (Pittsburgh: University of Pittsburgh Press, 1979), p. 352; and John D. Stempel, *Inside the Iranian Revolution* (Bloomington: Indiana University Press, 1981), p. 41. Xenophobia is a common theme in American writers. See Graham, *Iran*, pp. 192–194; and Zonis, *The Political Elite*, pp. 300–311.

12. See, for example, Harney, "Some Explanations," p. 138; and Stempel, *Inside the Iranian Revolution*, pp. 41–42.

13. Jalal Al-e Ahmad, *Gharbzadegi* (Plagued by the West) (N.p: 'Itihadiye-yi Anjuman-i Islami-yi Daneshjuyan-i Urupa va Anjuman-i Islami-yi Danishjuyan-i Amrika va Kanada, n.d.). For an English translation, see Jalal Al-e Ahmad, *Plagued by the West (Gharbzadegi)*, trans. Paul Sprachman, ed. Ehsan Yarshater (Delmar, NY: Caravan Books, 1982). The English translation includes passages that are missing in the Farsi text in my possession and appears to be based on a more complete Farsi edition. Consequently, I cite both works, the Farsi text first and then the Sprachman translation (with page numbers cited in brackets).

14. Malkum Khan, *Majmu'e-yi Asar* (Collected Works), ed. Muhit Tabataba'i (Tehran: Danesh, 1329 [1948]), p. 10.

15. Al-e Ahmad, *Gharbzadegi*, p. 5 [p.3]

16. Ibid., p. 102 [p. 99].

17. Ibid., p. 7 [p. 4].

18. Ibid., pp. 102–103 [p. 99].

19. Ibid., p. 103 [pp. 99–100].

20. Ibid., p. 61 [p. 56].

21. Ibid., p. 65 [p. 59].

22. Ibid., p. 21 (incomplete) [p. 19].

23. Ibid., p. 31 [p. 32].

24. Sprachman, *Plagued*, p. 9.

25. Al-e Ahmad, *Gharbzadegi*, pp. 5–6 [p. 3].

26. Sprachman, *Plagued*, p. 8.

27. Al-e Ahmad, *Gharbzadegi*, p. 21 [p. 19].

28. Ibid., p. 104 [pp. 100–101].

29. Ibid., p. 21 [p. 19].

30. Ibid., p. 5 [p. 3].

31. Ibid., p. 71 [p. 67].

32. Ibid., pp. 73–74 [p. 69].

33. Ibid., p. 72 [p. 68].

34. Ibid., p. 71 [p. 67].

35. Ibid., p. 71 [p. 67].

36. Ibid., p. 72 (incomplete) [p. 68].

37. Ibid., p 75 [p. 70].

38. Sprachman, *Plagued*, pp. 9–10.

39. Al-e Ahmad, *Gharbzadegi*, p. 92 (incomplete) [p. 84].

40. For a brief history of modernist literature, see Michael C. Hillman, "The Modernist Trend in Persian Literature and Its Social Impact," *Iranian Studies* 15, 1–4 (1982):7–28.

41. Ahmad Karimi-Hakkak, "Protest and Perish: A History of the Writers Association of Iran," *Iranian Studies* 18, 2–4 (Spring-Autumn 1985):205.

42. Gholam Husayn Saedi, "Mah-i Asal" [Honeymoon], in *Iranian Drama: An Anthology*, ed. M.R. Ghanoonparvar and J. Green (Costa Mesa, CA: Mazda Publishers, 1989), pp. 63–132.

43. Reza Baraheni, *The Crowned Cannibals: Writings on Repression in Iran* (New York: Vintage Books, 1977), p. 60. See also Michael C. Hillman, "Reza Baraheni: A Case Study of Politics and the Writer in Iran, 1953–1977," *Literature East and West* 20, 1–4 (January-December 1976):309–310.

44. Ibid., p. 61.

45. Ibid., p. 84.

Chapter 10

1. See Max Weber, *The Sociology of Religion*, trans. Ephraim Fischoff (Boston: Beacon Press, 1964), pp. 30, 24, 216, 235. In this work, Weber not only distinguished among economic, political, and ethical rationalization but also pointed out how they can conflict. These observations would seem to suggest that Weber's analysis of rationalization ought not to be taken as a conflict between rationality and irrationality, but as the interrelation and conflict between different activity-related rationalities.

2. Ibid., pp. 30, 224.

3. Here I follow Norbert Elias's analysis of court rationality. See Norbert Elias, *The Court Society*, trans. Edmund Jephcott (New York: Pantheon Books, 1983), pp. 78–116.

4. For an interesting contrast between different forms of self-fashioning, see Peter Brown, "Late Antiquity and Islam: Parallels and Contrasts," in *Moral Conduct and Authority*, ed. Barbara Metcalf (Berkeley and Los Angeles: University of California Press, 1984), pp. 23–37.

5. Charles Issawi, ed., *The Economic History of Iran, 1800–1914* (Chicago: University of Chicago Press, 1971).

6. Ervand Abrahamian, *Iran Between Two Revolutions* (Princeton: Princeton University Press, 1982), p. 149.

7. For a forceful example, see Afsaneh Najmabadi, "Iran's Turn to Islam: From Modernism to a Moral Order," *Middle East Journal* 41, 2 (Spring 1987):202–217.

8. Ibid., p. 215.

9. Resurgence Party, *The Philosophy of Iran's Revolution,* cited in Abrahamian, *Iran,* pp. 441–442.

10. Aleksandr I. Solzhenitsyn, *The Gulag Archipelago, 1918–1956: An Experiment in Literary Investigation,* trans. Thomas P. Whitney (New York: Harper and Row, 1974), p. 460.

11. SAVAK official, cited in Fred Halliday, *Iran: Dictatorship and Development* (Bungay, England: Richard Clay [The Chaucer Press], 1979), p. 80.

12. See ibid.

13. Ibid. The enigma of SAVAK concerns not only its size but also its efficiency. Graham emphasized the inefficiency of SAVAK. See Robert Graham, *Iran: The Illusion of Power* (London: Croom Helm, 1978), pp. 144–146. Other argue that SAVAK's inefficiency has been exaggerated by opposition forces. Cottam prudently summarized the argument in this way: "How efficient was SAVAK? There is really no way of knowing." Richard W. Cottam, *Nationalism in Iran,* rev. 2d ed. (Pittsburgh: University of Pittsburgh Press, 1979), p. 326.

14. Social studies textbook, cited in Golnar Mehran, "Socialization of Schoolchildren in the Islamic Republic of Iran," *Iranian Studies* 22, 1 (Winter 1989):39–40.

15. Halliday, *Iran,* p. 41.

16. Ibid., p. 40.

17. Ibid., pp. 49–50. Although the extent of civil violence has been substantial when compared with regimes such as Brazil, there is no evidence to suggest that Iran bears any similarity to such extreme cases as Cambodia and Uganda. For a criticism of postrevolutionary accounts, see Barry Rubin, *Paved with Good Intentions: The American Experience in Iran* (Harmondsworth, England: Penguin, 1981), pp. 176–177.

18. Halliday, *Iran,* p. 50. See also Rubin, *Paved,* p. 178.

19. Halliday, *Iran,* p. 50.

20. Abrahamian, *Iran,* p. 149.

21. Ibid., p. 164.

22. Anthony Giddens, *A Contemporary Critique of Historical Materialism.* Vol. 2, *The Nation-State and Violence* (Cambridge: Polity Press, 1985), pp. 2, 19, 46–47, 184. See also Joel S. Migdal, *Strong Societies and Weak States: State-Society Relations and State Capabilities in the Third World* (Princeton: Princeton University Press, 1988).

23. Communist states inherited this disciplinary ethic from Leninism. Lenin's heritage includes, among other things, an emphasis on party discipline (*What Is to Be Done?* [1902], *One Step Forward, Two Steps Back* [1904]) and a role for a disciplined bureaucratic structure to suppress the old ruling class and distribute economic resources in the transition to communism (*The State and Revolution* [1917]). See Samuel Huntington, *Political Order in Changing Societies* (New Haven: Yale University Press, 1968), pp. 334–343; Sheldon Wolin, *Politics and Vision: Continuity and Innovation in Western Political Thought* (Boston: Little, Brown, 1960), pp. 421–429; and Anthony J. Polan, *Lenin and the End of Politics* (Berkeley and Los Angeles: University of California Press, 1984).

24. Halliday, *Iran,* p. 42.

25. William F. Hickman, *Ravaged and Reborn: The Iranian Army, 1982* (Washington, DC: Brookings Institution, 1982), pp. 2–3.

26. See William Green Miller, "The Political Organizations in Iran: From Dowreh to Party," *Middle East Journal* 23, 2–3 (Spring-Summer 1969):156–167, 343–350; James A. Bill, *The Politics of Iran: Groups, Classes, and Modernization* (Columbus: Merrill, 1972); and James A. Bill, "The Plasticity of Informal Politics: The Case of Iran," *Middle East Journal* 27, 2 (Spring 1973):131–151.

Chapter 11

An earlier version of this chapter was published in Martha K. Huggins, ed., *Vigilantism and the State in Modern Latin America: Essays in Extralegal Violence* (New York: Praeger, 1991), pp. 127–144, an imprint of Greenwood Publishing Group, Inc., Westport, CT.

1. See, for example, Henry Charles Lea, *Superstition and Force* (New York: Haskell, 1971) and William E.H. Lecky, *History of the Rise and Influence of the Spirit of Rationalism in Europe*, rev. ed. (New York: Appleton, 1872). For some contemporary examples of this view, see Peter Spierenberg, *The Spectacle of Suffering: Executions and the Evolution of Repression: From a Preindustrial Metropolis to the European Experience* (Cambridge: Cambridge University Press, 1984); and Myra C. Glenn, *Campaigns Against Corporal Punishment: Prisoners, Sailors, Women, and Children in Antebellum America* (Albany: State University of New York Press, 1984).

2. The point of reference for Americans was the "third degree" treatment of prisoners by American police; for the British, the paramilitary tactics of the Royal Irish Constabulary. An excellent account of European police practice can be found in Edward Peters, *Torture* (Oxford: Basil Blackwell, 1985), pp. 103–114. For the use of these tactics in torture in India and the Philippines, see Edmund Cox, *Police and Crime in India* (London: Hazell, Watson, and Viney, n.d.), pp. 170, 180–183; William Thaddeus Sexton, *Soldiers in the Sun: An Adventure in Imperialism* (Freeport, NY: Libraries Press, 1939), pp. 238–242; Daniel B. Schirmer, *Republic or Empire: American Resistance to the Philippine War* (Cambridge, MA: Schenkman, 1972), pp. 225–240; and Richard E. Welch, Jr., *Response to Imperialism: The United States and the Philippine-American War, 1899–1902* (Chapel Hill: University of North Carolina Press, 1979), pp. 133–149.

3. Hannah Arendt, *The Origins of Totalitarianism*, new ed. (New York: Harcourt, Brace and World, 1966), pp. 443–446.

4. Henri Alleg, *The Question*, trans. John Calder (New York: George Braziller, 1958); George Orwell, *Nineteen Eighty Four* (Harmondsworth, England: Penguin Books, 1954); and Arthur Koestler, *Arrival and Departure* (London: Hutchinson, 1966), pp. 104–113.

5. Max Weber, *From Max Weber: Essays in Sociology*, trans. and ed. Hans H. Gerth and C. Wright Mills (New York: Oxford University Press, 1958), p. 226.

6. Hannah Arendt, *On Violence* (New York: Harcourt, Brace and World, 1969), p. 46.

7. Hannah Arendt, *Eichmann in Jerusalem: A Report on the Banality of Evil* (Harmondsworth, England: Penguin, 1965), pp. 135–150.

8. For some recent examples, see Anthony J. Polan, *Lenin and the End of Politics* (Berkeley: University of California Press, 1984); Peters, *Torture;* Michael Ignatieff, "Torture's Dead Simplicity," *New Statesman,* 20 September 1985, pp. 24–26; and Richard Rubinstein, "The Bureaucratization of Torture," *Journal of Social Philosophy* 13 (1982):31–51.

9. See Frantz Fanon, *The Wretched of the Earth* (New York: Grove Press, 1968), pp. 283–288. Michel Foucault characterized this exercise of power as "pastoral power" as opposed to the more familiar way in which persons are trained through "disciplinary power." See Michel Foucault, "Omnes et Singulatim: Towards a Criticism of Political Reason," in *The Tanner Lectures on Human Values,* ed. Sterling McMurrin (Salt Lake City: University of Utah Press, 1981), pp. 225–254.

10. I adopt and adapt these distinctions from Jurgen Habermas's work, particularly *The Theory of Communicative Action.* Vol. 1, *Reason and the Rationalization of Society,* Volume 2, *Lifeworld and System: A Critique of Functionalist Reason,* trans. Thomas McCarthy (Boston: Beacon Press, 1981, 1987).

11. See John H. Langbein, *Torture and the Law of Proof: Europe and England in the Ancien Regime* (Chicago: University of Chicago Press, 1976). See also Gavan McCormack, "Crime, Confession, and Control in Contemporary Japan," and Igarashi Futaba, "Forced to Confess," both in *Democracy in Contemporary Japan,* ed. Gavan McCormack and Yoshio Sugimoto (Armonk, NY: Sharpe, 1986).

12. Amnesty International, *Briefing, Guatemala* (London: Amnesty International Publications, December 1976), pp. 5–6, 11–16.

13. See Franklin Mark Osanka, ed., *Modern Guerrilla Warfare: Fighting Communist Guerrilla Movements, 1941–1961* (New York: Free Press, 1962), pp. 175–212.

14. See Futaba, "Forced to Confess"; and Hylah M. Jacques, "Spain: Systematic Torture in a Democratic State," *Monthly Review* 37 (November 1985):57–62.

15. For the full argument, see James David Barber, "Rationalizing Torture: The Dance of the Intellectual Apologists," *Washington Monthly* 17 (December 1985):17–18.

16. See Marjorie Agosin, "Notes on the Poetics of the Acevedo Movement Against Torture," *Human Rights Quarterly* 10 (1988):339–443; and Amnesty International, *Torture in the Eighties* (London: Amnesty International, 1984), pp. 71–72.

17. Max Weber, *The Protestant Ethic and the Spirit of Capitalism,* trans. Talcott Parsons (New York: Scribner's, 1958), pp. 97, 128, 197; see also p. 167.

18. Seymour Martin Lipset, "Some Social Requisites of Democracy: Economic Development and Political Legitimacy," *American Political Science Review* 53 (March 1959):91.

19. Mancur Olson, "Rapid Growth as a Destabilizing Force," *Journal of Economic History* 23 (1983):529–552; Samuel P. Huntington, *Political Order in Changing Societies* (New Haven: Yale University Press, 1968); and Lucian W. Pye, *Aspects of Political Development* (Boston: Little, Brown, 1966).

20. See Pye, *Aspects,* p. 127; and Samuel Huntington, "Civil Violence and the Process of Development," *Adelphi Papers* 83 (December 1971):6.

21. Huntington, *Political Order in Changing Societies,* p. 23.

22. Ibid., p. 24.

23. Lucian Pye, "The Roots of Insurgency and the Commencement of Rebellions," in *Internal War*, ed. H. Eckstein (New York: Free Press, 1964), pp. 157–179; and Samuel Huntington, "Guerrilla Warfare in Theory and Policy," in Osanka, *Modern Guerrilla Warfare*, pp. xv–xxii. See also Barber, "Rationalizing Torture," pp. 12–13.

24. Huntington, "Civil Violence," p. 15.

25. See Miles Wolpin, *Militarization, Internal Repression and Social Welfare in the Third World* (London: Croom Helm, 1986).

26. See Alfred Stepan, "The New Professionalism of Internal Warfare and Military Role Expansion," in *Armies and Politics in Latin America*, ed. Abraham F. Lowenthal (New York: Holmes and Meier, 1976), pp. 244–260.

27. David Pion-Berlin, "Political Repression and Economic Doctrines: The Case of Argentina," *Comparative Political Studies* 16, 1 (April 1983):37–66; Barry Rubin, *Paved with Good Intentions: The American Experience in Iran* (Harmondsworth, England: Penguin Books, 1981), pp. 177–178; and Fred Halliday, *Iran: Dictatorship and Development* (Harmondsworth, England: Penguin Books, 1979), p. 50.

28. In the case of South Africa, this point is made cogently in Diana E.H. Russell, *Rebellion, Revolution and Armed Force* (New York: Academic Press, 1974). For a more general criticism along the same lines, see Charles Tilly, "Does Modernization Breed Revolution?" *Comparative Politics* 5, 3 (April 1973):425–448.

29. Pye, "The Roots of Insurgency," pp. 159, 170, 178–179. See also Barber, "Rationalizing Torture," pp. 13–14. Huntington distinguished between Western revolutions (in which the state has lost popular consensus) and Eastern revolutions (in which the state possesses some measure of popular consensus). But Huntington's examples of the latter sort of state (Chiang Kai-shek's China or South Vietnam) could be understood better as highly repressive military regimes led by determined minorities.

30. Noam Chomsky and Edward S. Herman, *The Political Economy of Human Rights.* Volume 1, *The Washington Connection and Third World Fascism* (Montreal: Black Rose Books, 1979); and Edward S. Herman, *The Real Terror Network* (Boston: South End Press, 1982). See also Michael Stohl and George A. Lopez, eds., *The State as Terrorist* (Westport, CT: Greenwood Press, 1984); and Amnesty International, *Report on Torture* (London: Gerald Duckworth, 1973), pp. 18, 27.

31. I adapt this phrase from Sheldon Wolin's discussion of Niccolò Machiavelli and of the role of violence in politics. See Sheldon Wolin, *Politics and Vision: Continuity and Innovation in Western Political Thought* (Boston: Little, Brown, 1960), pp. 220–224.

32. Herman, *The Real Terror Network*, p. 113.

33. Ibid., pp. 112–113.

34. David Hawk, "Tuol Sleng Extermination Centre," *Index on Censorship* 15, 1 (January 1986):25–31.

35. Amnesty International, *Torture*, p. 66.

36. Chomsky and Herman, *The Washington Connection*, p. 8.

37. See Wolpin, *Politics and Vision;* Lars Schoultz, *Human Rights and United States Policy Towards Latin America* (Princeton: Princeton University Press, 1981); Michael Klare and Cynthia Arnson, *Supplying Repression* (Washington, DC: Institute for Policy Studies, 1977); Carol Ackroyd et al., *The Technology of Political*

Control (Wolfboro, NH: Longwood, 1980); Suzanne Franks and Ivor Gaber, "The UK's Torture Trade Has Quietly Resumed," *New Statesman* 108, 4 (21 September 1984):4; and Amnesty International, *Torture*.

38. Herman, *The Real Terror Network*, pp. 3, 84.

39. Hawk, "Tuol Sleng," p. 27.

40. Ibid.

41. Amnesty International, *Torture*, p. 68.

42. Karl Marx, *Capital: A Critique of Political Economy* (Harmondsworth, England: Penguin, 1976), vol. 1, pp. 344–352.

43. See Georg Rusche and Otto Kirchheimer, *Punishment and Social Structure* (New York: Columbia University Press, 1939).

44. Halliday, *Iran*, pp. 193–197; 202–206. See also William H. Bartsch, "The Industrial Labor Force of Iran: Problems of Recruitment, Training, and Productivity," in *The Population of Iran: A Selection of Readings*, ed. Jamshid Momeni (Honolulu: East-West Center, 1977), pp. 322–326.

45. See Pion-Berlin, "Political Repression."

46. See Thomas R. Forstenzer, *French Provincial Police and the Fall of the Second Republic: Social Fear and Counterrevolution* (Princeton: Princeton University Press, 1981); Jean Gottman, "Bugeaud, Gallieni, Lyautey: The Development of French Colonial Warfare," in *Makers of Modern Strategy: Military Thought from Machiavelli to Hitler*, ed. Edward Mead Earle (New York: Atheneum, 1966), pp. 234–256; Anthony Thrall Sullivan, *Thomas-Robert Bugeaud, France, and Algeria, 1784–1849: Politics, Power and the Good Society* (Hamden, CT: Archon Books, 1983); and Melvin Richter, "Tocqueville in Algeria," *Review of Politics* 25, 3 (July 1963):362–398.

47. Friedrich Nietzsche, *On the Genealogy of Morals and Ecce Homo*, trans. Walter Kaufmann and R.J. Hollingdale (New York: Vintage Books, 1969), pp. 57–96.

48. Weber, *From Max Weber*, pp. 194–198; see also, pp. 97, 108, 128, 167, 178, 180, 179, 267.

49. See Rusche and Kirchheimer, *Punishment*.

50. Michael Ignatieff, *A Just Measure of Pain: The Penitentiary in the Industrial Revolution, 1750–1850* (New York: Pantheon Books, 1978), p. 215.

51. David J. Rothman, *The Discovery of the Asylum: Social Order and Disorder in the New Republic* (Boston: Little, Brown, 1971); and David J. Rothman, *Conscience and Convenience: The Asylum and Its Alternatives* (Boston: Little, Brown, 1977).

52. See Langbein, *Torture*.

53. Gerhard Oestreich, *Neostoicism and the Early Modern State*, ed. Brigitta Oestreich and Helmut G. Koenigsberger, trans. David McLintock (Cambridge: Cambridge University Press, 1982).

54. Marc Raeff, *The Well-Ordered Police State: Social and Institutional Change Through Law in the Germanies and Russia, 1600–1800* (New Haven: Yale University Press, 1983).

55. Michel Foucault, *Discipline and Punish: The Birth of the Prison*, trans. Alan Sheridan (New York: Vintage Books, 1979), p. 221.

56. Michel Foucault, *Power/Knowledge: Selected Interviews and Other Writings*,

1972–1977, ed. Colin Gordon; trans. Colin Gordon, Leo Marshall, John Mepham, and Kate Soper (New York: Pantheon Books, 1980), pp. 135, 137, 139.

57. Michel Foucault, *The History of Sexuality: An Introduction,* trans. Robert Hurley (New York: Vintage Books, 1980), p. 149.

58. Michel Foucault, "Why Study Power: The Question of the Subject," in Hubert L. Dreyfus and Paul Rabinow, *Michel Foucault: Beyond Structuralism and Hermeneutics* (Chicago: University of Chicago Press, 1982), p. 210.

59. Jurgen Habermas emphasized this connection in "The French Economics," *New German Critique* 33 (Fall 1984): 79–102; and in "The Genealogical Writing of History: On Some Aporias in Foucault's Theory of Power," *Canadian Journal of Political and Social Theory,* 10, 1–2 (1986):1–9. See also Gregory Ostrander, "Knowledge and Experience in the Work of Michel Foucault" (Ph.D. diss., McGill University, 1985).

60. Michel Foucault, "L'esprit d'un monde sans esprit," in *Iran: La révolution au nom de Dieu,* ed. Claire Brière and Pierre Blanchet (Paris: Editions de Seuil, 1979), p. 233.

61. Foucault, *Discipline,* p. 40.

62. Foucault broke with Bataille here. Bataille maintained that we cannot see the general economy of waste because the dynamics of capitalism and socialism have marginalized moments of waste to such a degree that they are manifested only occasionally in daily life.

63. See Sullivan, *Thomas-Robert Bugeaud;* Richter, "Tocqueville"; and Gottman, "Bugeaud, Galliei, Lyautey," pp. 234–256.

64. Amnesty International, *Report on Torture,* p. 25.

65. Ibid.

66. John Stuart Mill, *On Liberty,* ed. Gertrude Himmelfarb (Harmondsworth, England: Penguin Books, 1978), p. 82.

67. See Eric Stover and Elena O. Nightingale, *The Breaking of Bodies and Minds: Torture, Psychiatric Abuse, and the Health Professions* (New York: Freeman, 1985); and Richard H. Goldstein and Patrick Breslin, "Technicians of Torture: How Physicians Became Agents of State Terror," *The Sciences* (March-April 1986):14–19.

68. See Peters, *Torture,* pp. 174–176, and Kevin Krajick, "Healing Broken Minds," *Psychology Today* (November 1986):66–69.

69. Theorists justifying torture draw on a variety of penal philosophies. Here I am concerned especially with the utilitarian justifications of torture. See Michael Levin, "The Case for Torture," *Newsweek,* 7 June 1982, p. 13; and the more cautious and thorough arguments in Gary E. Jones, "On the Permissibility of Torture," *Journal of Medical Ethics* 6 (March 1980):11–13. For retributivist justifications, see Edward G. Rozycki, "Pain and Anguish: The Need for Corporal Punishments," *Proceedings of the Philosophical Education Society of Australasia* 34 (1978):380–392; Graeme Newman, *Just and Painful: A Case for the Corporal Punishment of the Criminal* (London: Macmillan, 1983); Ernest Van den Haag, "Refuting Reiman and Nathanson," *Philosophy and Public Affairs* 14, 2 (Spring 1985):171. One of the earliest defenses of torture in the utilitarian vein was provided in Roger Trinquier, *Modern Warfare: A French View of Counterinsurgency* (New York: Praeger, 1964).

70. Rubinstein, "The Bureaucratization," pp. 37–38.

71. See Forstenzer, *French Provincial Police.*

72. Peters, *Torture*, pp. 40–73.

73. Weber, *The Protestant Ethic*, p. 181.

74. See Barber, "Rationalizing Torture," pp. 12–13; Agosin, "Notes," p. 339; Peters, *Torture*, pp. 6–7; Michael Taussig, "Terror as Usual," (Paper delivered at the conference Talking Terrorism: Ideologies and Paradigms in a Postmodern World, Stanford University, Palo Alto, California, February 4–6, 1988); and idem, "Culture of Terror—Space of Death. Roger Casement's Putumayo Report and the Explanation of Torture," *Contemporary Studies in Society and History* 26 (1984):466–497.

Selected Bibliography

IRAN, 1800–1896

Primary Sources

Al-Afghani, Jamal ad-Din. "The Reign of Terror in Persia." *Contemporary Review* 61 (February 1892):238–248.

Benjamin, Samuel G.W. *Persia and the Persians*. Boston: Ticknor, 1887.

Bradley-Birt, Francis B. *Persia: Through Persia from the Gulf to the Caspian*. Boston: Millet, 1910.

Cresson, William P. *Persia: The Awakening East*. Philadelphia: Lippincott, 1908.

Curzon, George N. *Persia and the Persian Question*. 2 vols. 2d ed. New York: Barnes and Noble, 1966.

The Dynasty of Kajars, with a Succinct Account of the History of Persia Previous to That Period. Translated by Harford Jones Brydges. London: John Bohn, 1833.

Fasai, Hasan. *The History of Persia Under Qajar Rule*. Translated by Heribert Busse. New York: Columbia University Press, 1972.

Flandrin, Eugene. *Voyage en Perse*. 2 vols. Paris: Gide et J. Baudry, 1851.

Fraser, James B. *Narrative of a Journey into Khurasan in the Years 1821 and 1822. Including Some Account of the Countries Northeast of Persia with Remarks upon the National Character, Government and Resources of That Kingdom*. London: Longman, Hurst, Rees, Orme, Browne and Green, 1825.

_____. *A Winter's Journey from Constantinople to Tehran, with Travels Thence to Various Parts of Persia*. London: Richard Bentley, 1840.

'Itizad as-Saltaneh. *Fitnih-yi Bab* (Revolt of the Bab). Edited by Abdul-Husayn Nava'i. Tehran: M'asood S'uud, 1333 [1954].

Malcolm, John. *The History of Persia from the Most Early Period to the Present Times*. 2 vols. London: John Murray, 1815.

_____. *Sketches of Persia, from the Journals of a Traveller of the East*. 2 vols. London: John Murray, 1827.

Malkum Khan. *Majmu'e-yi Asar* (Collected Works). Edited by Muhit Tabataba'i. Tehran: Danesh, 1327 [1948].

Morier, James J. *A Second Journey Through Persia, Armenia, and Asia Minor to Constantinople Between the Years 1810 and 1816. With a Journal of the Voyage by the Brazils and Bombay to the Persian Gulf; Together with an Account of the Proceedings of His Majesty's Embassy Under Sir Gore Ouseley*. London: Longman, Hurst, Rees, Orme and Browne, 1818.

Mostowfi, Abdullah. *Sharh-i Zendegani-yi Man ya Tarikh-i Ijtima'i va Idari-yi Dowreh-yi Qajariyeh* (The Story of My Life or the Social and Political History of the Qajar Period). 2 vols. Tehran: 'Ilmi, 1324 [1945].

Perkins, Justin. *A Residence of Eight Years in Persia Among the Nestorian Christians*. Andover, MA: Allen, Morrill and Wardwell, 1843.

Porter, Robert Ker. *Travels in Georgia, Persia, Armenia, Ancient Babylonia, &c. &c. During the Years 1817, 1818, 1819, and 1820*. 2 vols. London: Longman, Hurst, Rees, Orme and Browne, 1821–1822.

Rawlinson, Henry. *England and Russia in the East: A Series of Papers on the Political and Geographical Condition of Central Asia*. New York: Praeger, 1970.

Serena, Carla. *Hommes et choses en Perse*. Paris: G. Charpentier, 1883.

Sheil, Mary L.W. *Glimpses of Life and Manners in Persia*. London: John Murray, 1856.

Sipihr, Muhammad Taqi. *Nasikh at-Tavarikh* (Historical Notes). 4 vols. Tehran: Islamiyeh, 1344 [1965].

Upton, Emory. *The Armies of Asia and Europe. Embracing Official Reports on the Armies of Japan, China, India, Persia, Italy, Austria, Germany, France and England Accompanied by Letters Descriptive of a Journey from Japan to the Caucasus*. New York: Appleton, 1878.

Watson, Robert Grant. *A History of Persia from the Beginning of the Nineteenth Century to the Year 1858. With a Review of the Principal Events That Led to the Establishment of the Kajar Dynasty*. London: Smith, Elder, 1866.

Wills, C.J. *In the Land of the Lion and Sun (Modern Persia) Being Experiences of Life in Persia from 1866–1881*. London: Ward, Lock, 1891.

Wilson, Samuel G. *Persian Life and Customs. With Scenes and Incidents of Residence and Travel in the Land of the Lion and the Sun. With Map and Illustrations*. 2d ed. Edinburgh: Oliphant, Anderson and Ferrier, 1896.

Z'afaranlu, Qodratullah Rowshani, ed. *Amir Kabir va Dar ul-Fonun* (Amir Kabir and the Dar ul-Fonun). Tehran: Tehran University, 1354 [1975].

Zahir id-Dowleh, 'Ali Khan Qajar. *Tarikh-i Bi-durugh dar Vaqay'e-i Qatl-i Nasser id-Din Shah* (A True History of the Events Concerning the Death of Nasser id-Din Shah). Edited by Ali Reza Khusravi. Tehran: Ukhuvat, 1336 [1957].

Secondary Sources: Books

Adamiyat, Fereydun. *Amir Kabir va Iran* (Amir Kabir and Iran). Tehran: Kharazmi, 1348 [1969].

Afzal ul-Mulk, Mirza Ghullam Hussayn Khan. *Qajariyeh* (The Qajar Period). 8 vols. Tehran: Islami, 1361 [1982].

Algar Hamid. *Mirza Malkum Khan: A Study in the History of Iranian Modernism*. Berkeley and Los Angeles: University of California Press, 1973.

————. *Religion and State in Iran, 1785–1906: The Role of the Ulema in the Qajar Period*. Berkeley and Los Angeles: University of California Press, 1969.

Arasteh, A. Reza. *Education and Social Awakening in Iran, 1850–1968*. Rev. 2d ed. Leiden: E.J. Brill, 1969.

Atkin, Muriel. *Russia and Iran, 1780–1828*. Minneapolis: University of Minnesota Press, 1980.

Ayoub, Mahmoud. *Redemptive Suffering in Islam: A Study of the Devotional Aspects of 'Ashura' in Twelver Shi'ism*. The Hague: Mouton, 1978.

Bakhash, Shaul. *Iran: Monarchy, Bureaucracy, and Reform Under the Qajars, 1858–1896.* St. Anthony's Middle East Monographs No. 8. London: Ithaca Press, 1978.

Bayat, Mangol. *Mysticism and Dissent: Socio-Religious Thought in Qajar Iran.* Syracuse, NY: Syracuse University Press, 1982.

Bosworth, Edmund, and Carole Hillenbrand, eds. *Qajar Iran: Political, Social and Cultural Change, 1800–1925.* Edinburgh: Edinburgh University Press, 1983.

Brown, L. Carl, and Norman Itzkowitz. *Psychological Dimensions of Near Eastern Studies.* Princeton: Darwin Press, 1977.

Crime and Punishment Under Hanbali Law. Translated by George M. Baroody. Cairo: American University of Cairo, 1961.

Eickelman, Dale. *The Middle East: An Anthropological Approach.* Englewood Cliffs, NJ: Prentice-Hall, 1981.

Elgood, Cyril. *A Medical History of Persia and the Eastern Caliphate: The Development of Persian and Arabic Medical Sciences from the Earliest Times Until the Year A.D. 1932. Including the Mongol Domination and Western Influences Based on Original and Contemporary Sources with Additions and Corrections from the Author's Copy.* Amsterdam: APA-Philo Press, 1979.

———. *Medicine in Persia.* New York: Paul B. Hoeber, 1934.

———. *Safavid Medical Practice or the Practice of Medicine, Surgery and Gynaecology in Persia Between 1500 A.D. and 1750 A.D.* London: Luzac, 1970.

Garthwaite, Gene R. *Khans and Shahs: A Documentary Analysis of the Bakhtiyari in Iran.* Cambridge: Cambridge University Press, 1983.

Hashemi-Rafsanjani, Akbar. *Amir Kabir ya Qahriman-i Mubarizeh ba Est'emar* (Amir Kabir or the Hero of the Struggle Against Colonialism). Tehran: Farahani, 1346 [1967].

Himmat-Kirmani, Mahmud. *Tarikh-i Mofassal-i Kirman az 'Asr-i Hakhamaneshi ta Tulu-'i Silsileh-yi Puriftikhar i Pahlavi* (Complete History of Kirman from the Achaeminid Period to Dawn of the Pahlavi Dynasty). Tehran: Shirkat-i Sahami-yi Tab-'i Kitab, 1351 [1971].

Hodgson, Marshall G.S. *The Venture of Islam: Conscience and History in a World Civilization.* 3 vols. Chicago: University of Chicago Press, 1974.

Homma, Hideaki. *Structural Characteristics of Islamic Penal Law.* Institute of Middle East Studies–International University of Japan Working Paper Series. N.p.: Institute of Middle Eastern Studies, 1986.

Iranshahr. 2 vols. Tehran: Tehran University Press, 1342 [1963].

Israel, Milton, and N.K. Wagle, eds. *Islamic Society and Culture: Essays in Honor of Aziz Ahmad.* New Delhi: Manohar, 1983.

Issawi, Charles, ed. *The Economic History of Iran, 1800–1914.* Chicago: University of Chicago Press, 1971.

Keddie, Nikki R. *Iran: Religion, Politics, and Society: Collected Essays.* London: Frank Cass, 1980.

———. *Religion and Revolution in Iran: The Tobacco Protest of 1891–1892.* London: Frank Cass, 1966.

_____. *Sayyid Jamal ad-Din "Al-Afghani": A Political Biography.* Berkeley and Los Angeles: University of California Press, 1972.

Keddie, Nikki R., ed. *Scholars, Saints, and Sufis: Muslim Religious Institutions in the Middle East Since 1500.* Berkeley and Los Angeles: University of California Press, 1972.

Khalili, Mahyar. *Tarikh-i Shikanjeh: Tarikh-i Kushtar va Azar dar Iran* (The History of Torture: The History of Killing and Assault in Iran). Tehran: Nashr-i Gustarah, 1359 [1980].

Kirmani, Muhammad Nazim ul-Islam. *Tarikh-i Bidari-yi Iraniyan* (The History of Iranian Enlightenment). 2d ed. Tehran: Ibn Sina, 1352 [1954].

Lambton, Ann K.S. *Islamic Society in Persia.* London: School of Oriental and African Studies, University of London, 1954.

_____. *Landlord and Peasant in Persia: A Study of Land Tenure and Land Revenue Administration.* London: Oxford University Press, 1953.

Lockhart, Lawrence. *The Fall of the Safavid Dynasty and the Afghan Occupation of Persia.* Cambridge: Cambridge University Press, 1958.

Lorentz, John H. "Modernization and Political Change in Nineteenth Century Iran: The Role of Amir Kabir." Ph.D. diss., Princeton University, 1974.

Malikzadeh, Mehdi. *Tarikh-i Inqilab-i Mashrutiyyat-i Iran* (The History of the Constitutional Revolution of Iran). Vol. 1, *Falsafeh-yi Peydayesh-i Inqilab-i Mashrutiyyat* (The Philosophical Causes of the Constitutional Revolution). Tehran: Ibn Sina, 1327 [1948].

_____. *Zindigani-yi Malek al-Motakallemin* (The Life of Malek al-Motakallemin). Tehran: 'Ilmi, 1325 [1946].

Metcalf, Barbara Daly, ed. *Moral Conduct and Authority.* Berkeley and Los Angeles: University of California Press, 1984.

Nafisi, Sa'id. *Tarikh-i Mu'asir-i Iran* (Short History of Iran). Tehran: Furughi, 1345 [1966].

Nashat, Guity. *The Origins of Modern Reform in Iran, 1870–1880.* Urbana: University of Illinois Press, 1982.

Perry, John R. *Karim Khan Zand: A History of Iran, 1747–1779.* Chicago: University of Chicago Press, 1979.

Qa'im Maqami, Jahangir. *Tarikh-i Tahavullaat-i Siyasi-yi Nezam-i Iran as Aghaz-i Qarn-i Yazdah-i Hejri ta Saal-i 1301 Hejri-yi Shamsi* (The History of Political Reform of the Iranian Military from the Beginning of the 11th Century A.H. Until the Year 1301 A.H.). Tehran: 'Ilmi, 1326 [1947].

Reid, James J. *Tribalism and Society in Islamic Iran, 1500–1629.* Malibu, CA: Undena Publications, 1983.

Safi, Ghasem. *Historical Photographs of Iran: Dignitaries, Spectacles, Architecture and Social Environment.* 2d ed. Tehran: Tehran University Press, 1370 [1991].

Shamim, Ali Asghar. *Iran dar Dowreh-yi Saltanat-i Qajar* (Iran During the Period of Qajar Rule). Tehran: Ibn-i Sina, 1342 [1963].

Waterfield, Robin E. *Christians in Persia: Assyrians, Armenians, Roman Catholics, and Protestants.* London: George, Allen and Unwin, 1973.

Yekrangan, Mirhusayn. *Sarnivesht-i Iran: Zindigani-yi Siyassi va Adabi-yi Sadr-i 'Azam-i Shahid Qa'im Maqam Farahani* (The Destiny of Iran: The Political and Cultural Life of the Martyred Sadr 'Azam Qa'im Maqam Farahani). Tehran: 'Ilmi, 1334 [1955].

Secondary Sources: Articles

Abrahamian, Ervand. "Oriental Despotism: The Case of Qajar Iran." *International Journal of Middle East Studies* 5 (1974):3–31.

Arasteh, A. Reza. "The Character, Organization and Social Role of the Lutis (Javanmardan) in Traditional Iranian Society of Nineteenth Century." *Journal of the Economic and Social History of the Orient* 4 (1961):47–52.

_____. "The Social Role of the Zurkhana (House of Strength) in Iranian Urban Communities During the Nineteenth Century." *Der Islam* 37 (1961):256–259.

Floor, Willem M. "The Lutis—A Social Phenomenon in Qajar Persia." *Die Welt des Islams* 13 (1971):103–120.

_____. "The Marketpolice in Qajar Persia." *Die Welt des Islams* 13 (1971):212–229.

_____. "The Office of Kalantar in Qajar Persia." *Journal of the Economic and Social History of the Orient* 14 (1971):153–168.

_____. "The Police in Qajar Persia." *Zeitschrift der Deutschen Morgenlandischen Gesellschaft* 123 (1973):293–315.

Helfgott, Leonard M. "Tribalism as a Socioeconomic Formation in Iranian History." *Iranian Studies* 10, 12 (Winter-Spring 1977):36–61.

_____. "Tribe and Uymaq in Iran: A Reply." *Iranian Studies* 16, 1–2 (Winter-Spring 1983):73–78.

Iqbal, Abbas. "Abeleh Kubi" (Smallpox Inoculation). *Yadigar* (Remembrances) 4, 3 (1326) [1947]:68–72.

_____. "Hujjat ul-Islam Haj Seyyed Muhammad Baqer Shafti." *Yadigar* 5, 10 (1327) [1948]:28–42.

_____. "'Itizad as-Saltaneh va Zuhur-i Babiyeh" ('Itizad as-Saltaneh and the Emergence of Babism). *Yadigar* 2, 1 (1324) [1945]:54–66.

_____. "Sabzeh Maydan va Majm'a-i Dar ul-Sanay'i" (Sabzeh Maydan and the House of Industries Complex). *Yadigar* 4, 9–10 (1326) [1947]:59–70.

Kazemzadeh, Firuz. "The Origin and Early Development of the Persian Cossack Brigade." *American Slavic and East European Review* 15 (October 1956):351–363.

Lambton, Ann K.S. "A Nineteenth Century View of Jihad." *Studia Islamica* 32 (1970):181–192.

_____. "Quis Custodiet Custodes: Some Reflections on the Persian Theory of Government." *Studia Islamica* 5 (1955):125–148; 6 (1956):125–146.

_____. "A Reconsideration of the Position of the Marja'-i Taqlid and the Religious Institutions." *Studia Islamica* 20 (1964):114–135.

McChesney, R.D. "Comments on 'The Qajar Uymaq in the Safavid Period, 1500–1722.'" *Iranian Studies* 14, 1–2 (Winter-Spring 1981):87–105.

MirJafari, Hossein. "The Heydari-N'imati Conflicts in Iran." *Iranian Studies* 12, 3–4 (Summer-Autumn 1979):135–162.

Momen, Moojan. "The Social Basis of the Babi Upheavals in Iran (1848–1851): A Preliminary Analysis." *International Journal of Middle East Studies* 15 (1983):157–183.

Parizi, Bastani. "Ba Dard-i Kashan Har Keh Dar Uftad" (He Who Deals with the Agony of Kashan). *Yaqma* (Plundering) 17 (1343):364–371, 465–509.

Reid, James J. "Comments on 'Tribalism as a Socioeconomic Formation.'" *Iranian Studies* 12, 3–4 (Summer-Autumn 1979):175–198.

_____. "The Qajar Uymaq in the Safavid Period, 1500–1722." *Iranian Studies* 11 (1978):117–143.

_____. "Studying Clans in Iranian History: A Response." *Iranian Studies* 17, 1 (Winter 1984):85–92.

IRAN, 1896–1987

Primary Sources: Books

Afzal, Cameron. "An Interview with William McElwee Miller: Missionary to Iran, 1919–1962." Manuscript, 1985.

Al-e Ahmad, Jalal. *Gharbzadegi* (Plagued by the West). N.p.: 'Itihadiy-yi Anjuman-i Islami-yi Daneshjuyan-i Urupa va Anjuman-i Islami-yi Danishjuyan-i Amrika va Kanada, n.d.

_____. *Plagued by the West (Gharbzadegi)*. Translated by Paul Sprachman. Delmar, NY: Caravan Books, 1982.

Amnesty International. *Amnesty International Report 1980*. London: Amnesty International Publications, 1980.

_____. *Amnesty International Report 1982*. London: Amnesty International Publications, 1982.

_____. *Amnesty International Report 1983*. London: Amnesty International Publications, 1983.

_____. *Amnesty International Report 1984*. London: Amnesty International Publications, 1984.

_____. *Amnesty International Report 1986*. London: Amnesty International Publications, 1986.

_____. *Amnesty International Report 1987*. London: Amnesty International Publications, 1987.

_____. *Amnesty International Report 1988*. London: Amnesty International Publications, 1988.

_____. *Iran: Briefing*. London: Amnesty International, 1987.

_____. *Iran: Violations of Human Rights*. London: Amnesty International Publications, 1987.

_____. *Iran: Violations of Human Rights, 1987–1990*. New York: Amnesty International U.S.A., 1991.

_____. *Law and Human Rights in the Islamic Republic of Iran*. London: Amnesty International, 1980.

_____. *Report on Torture*. London: Gerald Duckworth, 1973.

Arfa, Hassan. *Under Five Shahs*. Edinburgh: John Murray, 1964.

Bakhtiari, H. *Az Shahr-i Tehran Cheh Midanim?* (What Do We Know About the City of Tehran?). Tehran: Sa'eb, 1345 [1966].

Balfour, James M. *Recent Happenings in Persia*. Edinburgh: William Blackwood, 1922.

Baraheni, Reza. *The Crowned Cannibals: Writings on Repression in Iran*. New York: Vintage Books, 1977.

Behnam, Jamshid, and Shahpour Rasekh. *Muqadameh bar Jam'i-i Shenassi-yi Iran* (Introduction to the Sociology of Iran). 3d ed. Tehran: Kharazmi, 1348 [1969].

Browne, E.G. *A Literary History of Persia.* 4 vols. Cambridge: Cambridge University Press, 1951.

———. *The Persian Revolution of 1905–1909.* 2d ed. London: Frank Cass, 1966.

———. *The Press and Poetry of Modern Persia.* Cambridge: Cambridge University Press, 1914.

Butler, William J., and Georges Levasseur. *Human Rights and the Legal System in Iran: Two Reports by William J. Butler, Esq. and Professor Georges Levasseur.* Geneva: International Commission of Jurists, 1976.

Carlsen, Robin Woodsworth. *The Imam and His Islamic Republic: A Journey into Heaven and Hell.* Victoria, BC: Snow Man Press, 1982.

Central Treaty Organization. *CENTO Seminar on Public Health and Medical Problems Involved in Narcotics Drug Addiction.* Ankara: Central Treaty Organization, 1972.

———. *The 1974 CENTO Seminar on the Epidemiology of Non-Medical Drug Use.* Ankara: Central Treaty Organization, 1974.

Committee for the Defence of Political Prisoners in Iran. *The Iranian Bulletins.* London: Index on Censorship, 1979.

Falsafi, Muhammad Taqi. *Kudak az Nazar-i Verasat va Tarbiyat* (The Child from the Perspective of Heredity and Cultivation). 2 vols. Tehran: Hey'at-i Nashr-i Ma'arif-i Islami, 1341 [1962].

Forbes-Leith, Francis A.C. *Checkmate: Fighting Tradition in Central Asia.* New York: Robert M. McBride, 1927.

Fraser, David. *Persia and Turkey in Revolt.* Edinburgh: William Blackwood, 1910.

Ghanoonparvar, Mohammad R., and John Green, eds. *Iranian Drama: An Anthology.* Costa Mesa, CA: Mazda Publishers, 1989.

The Glory of the Shia World: Tale of a Pilgrimage. Translated and edited by Percy M. Sykes. London: Macmillan, 1910.

Hejazi, Muhammad. *Mihan-i Ma* (Our Nation). Tehran: Vezarat-i Farhang, 1338 [1959].

Hejazi, Qudsiyeh. *Barresi-yi Jara'im-i Zan dar Iran* (A Study of Female Criminality in Iran). Tehran: Sherkat-i Sahami-yi Inteshar, 1341 [1963].

Iran, Vezarat-i Behdari, Idari-yi Kul-i Behdasht. *Guzaresh-i Saal 1341* (Annual Report 1962). Tehran: n.p., 1962.

Iran Almanac 1962. Tehran: Echo of Iran, 1962.

Iran Almanac 1964–1965. Tehran: Echo of Iran, 1965.

Iran Almanac 1967. Tehran: Echo of Iran, 1967.

Irani, T. *Usul-i 'Ilm-i Ruh: Psychology-yi 'Umumi* (The Principles of the Science of the Psyche: General Psychology). Tehran: Matb'a-i Sirus, 1311 [1932].

Irani, Taqi. *Akharin Def'a-i Doktor Taqi Irani dar Dadgah-i Jena'i-ye Tehran* (The Final Defense of Doctor Taqi Irani in the Tehran Criminal Court). N.p.: Tudeh Party of Iran, 1353 [1974].

Irnberger, Harold. *SAVAK oder Der Folterfreund des Westens.* Reinbek bei Hamburg: Rowohlt Taschenbuch Verlag, 1977.

International Solidarity Front for the Defense of the Iranian People's Democratic Rights (ISF-Iran). *The Crimes of Khomeini's Regime.* 2d ed. Geneva: ISF-Iran, 1982.

Iyman, Hafez. *Defa'i Jam'i-i dar Muqabel-i Jurm va Mujrem* (The Defense of Society Against Crime and the Criminal). Tehran: Chehr, 1343 [1964].

Jazani, Bizhan. *Capitalism and Revolution in Iran.* Translated by the Iran Committee. London: Zed Press, 1980.

League of Nations. *Commission of Enquiry into the Production of Opium in Persia.* Geneva: 1927, XI.A.8.

_____. *Commission of Enquiry into the Production of Opium in Persia.* Geneva: 1927, XI.A.16.

_____. Health Organisation. *Report on an Investigation into the Sanitary Conditions in Persia.* Geneva: 1925, C.H.262.

Manganeh, Nur ul-Huda. *Rah Amuz-i Khanevadeh* (Guide for the Family). Tehran: Rangin, 1333 [1954].

Millspaugh, Arthur C. *Americans in Persia.* Washington, DC: The Brookings Institution, 1946.

Nirumand, Bahman. *Iran: The New Imperialism in Action.* Translated by Leonard Mins. New York: Monthly Review Press, 1969.

Nobari, Ali-Reza, ed. *Iran Erupts.* Stanford, CA: Iran-America Documentation Group, 1978.

Pahlavi, Muhammad Reza. *Mission for My Country.* New York: McGraw-Hill, 1960.

Raffat, Donne. *The Prison Papers of Bozorg Alavi: A Literary Odyssey.* Syracuse, NY: Syracuse University Press, 1985.

Sadiq, Issa Khan. *Modern Persia and Her Educational System.* New York: Bureau of Publications, Teachers College, Columbia University, 1931.

_____. *Tarikh-i Farhang-i Iran az Aghaz ta Zaman-i Hazer* (The History of Education in Iran [Persia] from the Earliest Times to the Present Day). 2d ed. Tehran: Tehran University Press, 1338 [1959].

Saheb oz-Zamani, Nasir id-Din. *Javani-yi Pur-ranj* (Agonized Youth). Tehran: 'Ata'i, 1344 [1965].

_____. *Kitab-i Ruh-i Bashar* (Book of the Human Psyche). 3d ed. Tehran: 'Ata'i, 1343 [1964].

_____. *Kitab-i Ruh-i Bashar* (Book of the Human Psyche). Vol. 3, *Ansu-yi Chihriha* (Behind the Masks). Tehran: 'Ata'i, 1343 [1964].

_____. *Va Namidanand Chira ...* (And They Know Not Why ...). Tehran: 'Ata'i, 1344 [1965].

Schuster, W. Morgan. *The Strangling of Persia.* New York: Century, 1912.

Shafa'i, Muhsin. *Khesaal-i Shafa'i* (Shafa'i's Praiseworthy Virtues). Vol. 4, *Khanevadeh va Asrar-i Khushbakhti-yi An* (The Family and the Secrets to Its Happiness). Tehran: A'in No, 1341 [1962].

Sukhanraniha va Guzarishha dar Nukhustin Seminar-i Barressi-yi Masa'el-i Shahr-i Tehran (Speeches and Reports During the First Seminar for the Investigation of the Social Problems of the City of Tehran). Tehran: Institute of Social Work, 1343 [1964].

Sykes, Ella C. *Persia and Its People.* New York: Macmillan, 1910.

Sykes, Percy. *A History of Persia.* 2 vols. 3d ed. London: Macmillan, 1951.

Taleghani, Ayatullah Sayyid Mahmud. *Society and Economics in Islam: Writings and Declarations of Ayatullah Sayyid Mahmud Taleghani.* Translated by R. Campbell. Contemporary Islamic Thought, Persian Series, No. 4. Berkeley: Mizan Press, 1982.

Williams-Jackson, A.V. *Persia, Past and Present.* New York: Macmillan, 1909.

Wilson, Arnold. *Southwest Persia: A Political Officer's Diary, 1907–1914.* London: Oxford University Press, 1941.

Wishard, John G. *Twenty Years in Persia.* New York: Flemming H. Revel, 1908.

Primary Sources: Articles

Amnesty International, "Ill-Treatment of Prisoners in Iran." Manuscript, 9 December 1982.

_____. "Torture in Iran, 1971–1976." Manuscript, January 1979.

Ashraf, Ahmad. "Bazaar and Mosque in Iran's Islamic Revolution." *MERIP Reports* (March-April 1983):16–18.

Bani-Sadr, Abol-Hassan. "I Defeated the Ideology of the Regime." *MERIP Reports* (March-April 1982):5–8.

Baraheni, Reza. "The Savak Documents." *The Nation,* 23 February 1980, pp. 198–202.

Dowden, Richard. "In the Terror of Tehran." *New York Review of Books,* 2 February 1984, pp. 8–12.

International Committee of the Red Cross. "Treatment of Prisoners-of-War in the Iran-Iraq Conflict." *MERIP Reports* 14, 6–7 (July-September 1984):38–39.

Khalkhali, Sadegh. "All the People Who Are Opposed to Our Revolution Must Die." *MERIP Reports* (March-April 1982):30–31.

Lawyers Committee for Human Rights. "Little Discernible Progress in Respect for Human Rights in Iran Despite Eight Years of International Scrutiny." *Middle East,* 12 November 1992, pp. 1–6.

"SAVAK: Like the CIA." *Time,* 19 February 1979, p. 32.

"Towards a Solution of Regional Narcotics Problems: Recent Projects of U.N. Technical Assistance." *Bulletin on Narcotics* 20 (January-March 1968):41–49.

Secondary Sources: Books

Abrahamian, Ervand. *Iran Between Two Revolutions.* Princeton: Princeton University Press, 1982.

_____. *The Iranian Mujahidin.* New Haven: Yale University Press, 1989.

Akhavi, Shahrough. *The Relationship Between Religion and the State in Iran Under the Pahlavi Dynasty.* Binghamton: State University of New York Press, 1980.

Albert, David H., ed. *Tell the American People: Perspectives on the Iranian Revolution.* Rev. 2d ed. Philadelphia: Movement for a New Society, 1980.

Amir-Ahmadi, Hooshang, and Manoucher Parvin, eds. *Post-Revolutionary Iran.* Boulder: Westview Press, 1988.

Amir-Sadeghi, Husayn, ed. *Twentieth-Century Iran.* London: Heinemann, 1978.

Arasteh, A. Reza. *Faces of Persian Youth: A Sociological Study.* Leiden: Brill, 1970.

Arjomand, Said Amir. *The Turban for the Crown: The Islamic Revolution in Iran.* New York: Oxford University Press, 1988.

Azari, Farah, ed. *Women of Iran: The Conflict with Fundamentalist Islam.* London: Ithaca Press, 1983.

Bakhash, Shaul. *The Reign of the Ayatollahs: Iran and the Islamic Revolution.* New York: Basic Books, 1984.

Banani, Amin. *The Modernization of Iran, 1921–1941.* Stanford: Stanford University Press, 1961.

Bashiriyeh, Hossein. *The State and Revolution in Iran, 1962–1982.* London: Croom Helm, 1984.

Beck, Lois, and Nikki Keddie, eds. *Women in the Muslim World.* Cambridge, MA: Harvard University Press, 1978.

Bernard, Cheryl, and Zalmay Khalilzad. *"The Government of God"—Iran's Islamic Republic.* New York: Columbia University Press, 1984.

Bill, James A. *The Politics of Iran: Groups, Classes, and Modernization.* Columbus: Merrill, 1972.

Binder, Leonard M. *Iran: Political Development in a Changing Society.* Berkeley and Los Angeles: University of California Press, 1962.

Blake, Gerald H., and Richard I. Lawless, eds. *The Changing Middle Eastern City.* London: Croom Helm, 1980.

Bonine, Michael E., and Nikki R. Keddie, eds. *Continuity and Change in Modern Iran.* Albany: State University of New York, 1981.

Braswell, George Wilbur, Jr. "A Mosaic of Mullahs and Mosques: Religion and Politics in Iranian Shi'ah Islam." Ph.D. diss., University of North Carolina, 1975.

Cottam, Richard W. *Nationalism in Iran.* Rev. 2d ed. Pittsburgh: University of Pittsburgh Press, 1979.

Dwyer, Daisy Hilse. *Law and Islam in the Middle East.* New York: Bergin and Garvey, 1990.

English, Paul Ward. *City and Village in Iran: Settlement in the Kirman Basin.* Madison: University of Wisconsin Press, 1966.

Fard-Saidi, Mohammad. "The Early Phases of Political Modernization in Iran: 1870–1925." Ph.D. diss., University of Pennsylvania, 1974.

Fischer, Michael M.J. *Iran: From Religious Dispute to Revolution.* Cambridge, MA: Harvard University Press, 1980.

Forbis, William H. *The Fall of the Peacock Throne: The Story of Iran.* New York: Harper and Row, 1980.

Graham, Robert. *Iran: The Illusion of Power.* London: Croom Helm, 1978.

Green, Jerrold D. *Revolution in Iran: The Politics of Countermobilization.* New York: Praeger, 1982.

Haas, William S. *Iran.* New York: Columbia University Press, 1946.

Halliday, Fred. *Iran: Dictatorship and Development.* Bungay, England: Richard Clay (The Chaucer Press), 1979.

Hickman, William F. *Ravaged and Reborn: The Iranian Army, 1982.* Washington, DC: Brookings Institution, 1982.

Hiro, Dilip. *Iran Under the Ayatollahs.* London: Routledge and Kegan Paul, 1985.

Hooglund, Eric J. *Land and Revolution in Iran, 1960–1980.* Austin: University of Texas Press, 1982.

Irfani, Suroosh. *Revolutionary Islam in Iran: Popular Liberation or Religious Dictatorship?* London: Zed Books, 1983.

Katouzian, Homa. *The Political Economy of Modern Iran: Despotism and Pseudomodernism, 1926–1979.* New York: New York University Press, 1981.

Kazemi, Farhad. *Poverty and Revolution in Iran: The Migrant Poor, Urban Marginality and Politics.* New York: New York University Press, 1980.

Keddie, Nikki R. *Roots of Revolution: An Interpretive History of Modern Iran.* With a Section by Yann Richard. New Haven: Yale University Press, 1981.

Keddie, Nikki R., ed. *Religion and Politics in Iran: Shi'ism from Quietism to Revolution.* New Haven: Yale University Press, 1983.

Lambton, Ann K.S. *The Persian Land Reform: 1962–1966.* Oxford: Clarendon Press, 1969.

Lopata, Helena Zananiecka, ed. *Widows.* Volume 1, *The Middle East, Asia and the Pacific.* Durham, NC: Duke University Press, 1987.

Momeni, Jamshid A., ed. *The Population of Iran: A Selection of Readings.* Honolulu: East-West Population Institute, East-West Center, 1977.

Mottahedeh, Roy. *The Mantle of the Prophet: Religion and Politics in Iran.* New York: Simon and Schuster, 1985.

Nash, Geoffrey. *Iran's Secret Pogrom.* Suffolk: Neville Spearman, 1982.

Nashat, Guity, ed. *Women and Revolution in Iran.* Boulder: Westview Press, 1983.

Nima, Ramy. *The Wrath of Allah: Islamic Revolution and Reaction in Iran.* London: Pluto Press, 1983.

Nyrop, Richard F., ed. *Iran: A Country Study.* Area Handbook Program. Washington, DC: U.S. Department of the Army, 1978.

Oberling, Pierre. *The Qashqa'i Nomads of Fars.* The Hague: Mouton, 1974.

Overseas Liaison Committee. *An Analysis of U.S.-Iranian Co-operation in Higher Education.* Washington, DC: American Council on Education, 1976.

Parsa, Misagh. *The Social Origins of the Iranian Revolution.* New Brunswick, NJ: Rutgers University Press, 1989.

Prigmore, Charles S. *Social Work in Iran Since the White Revolution.* University: University of Alabama Press, 1976.

Roosevelt, Kermit. *Countercoup: The Struggle for the Control of Iran.* New York: McGraw-Hill, 1979.

Rubin, Barry. *Paved with Good Intentions: The American Experience and Iran.* Harmondsworth, England: Penguin, 1981.

Sanasarian, Eliz. *The Women's Rights Movement in Iran: Mutiny, Appeasement, and Repression from 1900 to Khomaini.* New York: Praeger, 1982.

Schahgaldian, Nikola B. *The Clerical Establishment in Iran.* Santa Monica, CA: Rand Corporation, June 1989.

Schmitt, Arno, and Jehoeda Sofer, eds. *Sexuality and Eroticism Among Males in Moslem Societies.* New York: Hayworth Press, 1992.

Smith, Harvey H., William W. Cover, John B. Folan, Michael L. Meissenburg, Julius Szentadorjany, and Suzanne Teleki. *Area Handbook for Iran.* Area Handbook Program. Washington, DC: U.S. Government Printing Office, 1971.

Stempel, John D. *Inside the Iranian Revolution.* Bloomington: Indiana University Press, 1981.

Tabari, Azar, and Nahid Yeganeh, eds. *In the Shadow of Islam: The Women's Movement in Iran.* London: Zed Press, 1982.

Tafrishi-Husayni, Ahmad. *Ruznameh-yi Akhbar-i Mashrutiyyat va Inqilab-i Iran* (Diary of Documents Concerning Constitutionalism and the Revolution of Iran). Edited by Iraj Afshar. Tehran: Amir Kabir, 1351 [1972].

Tapper, Richard, ed. *The Conflict of Tribe and State in Iran and Afghanistan.* London: Croom Helm, 1983.

Vreeland, Herbert H., ed. *Iran.* Country Survey Series. New Haven: Human Relations Area Files, 1957.

Wright, Denis. *The English Amongst the Persians During the Qajar Period, 1787–1921.* London: Morrison and Gibb, 1977.

Yar-Shater, Ehsan, ed. *Iran Faces the Seventies.* New York: Praeger, 1971.

Yodfat, Aryeh Y. *The Soviet Union and Revolutionary Iran.* London: Croom Helm, 1984.

Zabih, Sepehr. *Iran Since the Revolution.* London: Croom Helm, 1982.

_____. *The Left in Contemporary Iran: Ideology, Organisation, and the Soviet Connection.* London: Croom Helm, 1986.

Zonis, Marvin. *The Political Elite of Iran.* Princeton: Princeton University Press, 1971.

Secondary Sources: Articles

Abrahamian, Ervand. "The Causes of the Constitutional Revolution in Iran." *International Journal of Middle East Studies* 10 (1979):381–414.

_____. "Communism and Communalism in Iran: The Tudah and the Firqah-i Dimukrat." *International Journal of Middle East Studies* 1 (1970):191–316.

_____. "The Crowd in Iranian Politics, 1905–1953." *Past and Present* 41 (December 1968):184–210.

_____. "The Crowd in the Persian Revolution, 1905–1911." *Iranian Studies* 2, 4 (Autumn 1969):128–150.

_____. "The Guerrilla Movement in Iran, 1963–1977." *MERIP Reports* (March-April 1980):3–15.

Antoun, Richard T. "The Gentry of a Traditional Peasant Community Undergoing Rapid Technological Change: An Iranian Case Study." *Iranian Studies* 9, 1 (Winter 1976):2–21.

Asrari, Alinaghi. "Educational and Economic Development in Iran." *International Education* 6, 1 (1976):15–21.

Azad, Shahrzad. "Workers' and Peasants' Councils in Iran." *Monthly Review* 32, 5 (October 1980):14–30.

Bakhash, Shaul. "The Politics of Land, Law and Social Justice in Iran." *Middle East Journal* 43, 2 (Spring 1989):186–201.

_____. "The Revolution Against Itself." *New York Review of Books*, 18 November 1982, pp. 19–26.

Bateson, Mary Catherine. "'This Figure of Tinsel': A Study of Themes of Hypocrisy and Pessimism in Iranian Culture." *Daedalus* 108, 3 (Summer 1979):125–134.

Bayat, Assef. "Workers' Control After the Revolution." *MERIP Reports* (March-April 1983):19–23, 33–34.

Beeman, William O. "Status, Style and Strategy in Iranian Interaction." *Anthropological Linguistics* 18 (October 1976):305–322.

_____. "What Is (IRANIAN) National Character? A Sociolinguistic Approach." *Iranian Studies* 9, 1 (Winter 1976):22–48.

Bill, James A. "The Plasticity of Informal Politics: The Case of Iran." *Middle East Journal* 27, 2 (Spring 1973):131–151.

_____. "Power and Religion in Revolutionary Iran." *Middle East Journal* 36, 1 (Winter 1982):22–47.

_____. "The Social and Economic Foundations of Power in Contemporary Iran." *Middle East Journal* 17, 4 (Autumn 1963):400–413.

Bogdanov, Leonid. "The Home and Life in Persia." *Islamic Culture* (1931):407–421; (1932):290–306, 468–485.

Calder, Norman. "Accommodation and Revolution in Imami Shi'i Jurisprudence: Khumayni and the Classical Tradition." *Middle Eastern Studies* 18, 1 (January 1982):3–20.

Eliash, Joseph. "The Ithna-Ashari Juristic Theory of Political and Legal Authority." *Studia Islamica* 29 (1969):17–30.

_____. "Misconceptions Regarding the Juridical Status of the Iranian 'Ulama'." International Journal of Middle East Studies 10 (1979):9–25.

Fathi, Asghar. "The Role of the 'Rebels' in the Constitutional Movement in Iran." *International Journal of Middle East Studies* 10 (1979):55–66.

Ferdows, Amir H. "Khomaini and Fadayan's Society and Politics." *International Journal of Middle East Studies* 15 (1983):241–257.

Ferdows, Emad. "The Reconstruction Crusade and Class Conflict in Iran." *MERIP Reports* (March-April 1983):11–15.

Friedl, Erika. "Division of Labor in an Iranian Village." *MERIP Reports* (March-April 1981):12–18.

Goodey, Chris. "Workers' Councils in Iranian Factories." *MERIP Reports* (June 1980):5–9.

Habib, Mohammad. "The Administration of Justice in Modern Persia." *Islamic Culture* 7 (1933):234–248, 410–416, 573–582.

Halliday, Fred. "The First Year of the Islamic Republic." *MERIP Reports* (June 1980):3–5.

_____. "Theses on the Iranian Revolution." *Race and Class* 21 (Summer 1979):81–90.

_____. "Year IV of the Islamic Republic." *MERIP Reports* (March-April 1983):3–8.

_____. "Year Three of the Iranian Revolution." *MERIP Reports* (March-April 1982):3–5.

Harney, Desmond. "Some Explanations for the Iranian Revolution." *Asian Affairs* 11, 2 (June 1980):134–143.

Hersh, Seymour M. "Ex-Analyst Says CIA Rejected Warning on Shah," *New York Times*, 7 January 1979, p. 3.

Hillman, Michael C. "The Modernist Trend in Persian Literature and Its Social Impact." *Iranian Studies* 15, 1–4 (1982):7–28.

_____. "Reza Baraheni: A Case Study of Politics and the Writer in Iran, 1953–1977." *Literature East and West* 20, 1–4 (January-December 1976):301–313.

Hooglund, Eric. "Rural Iran and the Clerics." *MERIP Reports* (March-April 1982):23–26.

Jandaghi, Ali. "The Present Situation in Iran." *Monthly Review* (November 1973):34–47.

Karimi-Hakkak, Ahmad. "Protest and Perish: A History of the Writers Association of Iran." *Iranian Studies* 18, 2–4 (Spring-Autumn 1985):189–229.

Kazemi, Farhad."Economic Indices of Political Violence in Iran: 1946–1968." *Iranian Studies* 8, 1–2 (Winter-Spring 1975):70–86.

Kazemi, Farhad, and Ervand Abrahamian."The Nonrevolutionary Peasantry of Modern Iran." *Iranian Studies* 11 (1978):259–304.

Keddie, Nikki R. "Material Culture and Geography: Toward a Holistic Comparative History of the Middle East." *Comparative Studies in Society and History* 26 (1984):709–735.

————. "The Origins of the Religious-Radical Alliance in Iran." *Past and Present* 7 (July 1966):70–80.

Lambton, Ann K.S. "The Impact of the West on Persia." *International Affairs* 33 (January 1957):12–25.

————. "The Secret Societies and the Persian Revolution of 1905." *St. Antony's Papers* 4 (1958):43–60.

Martin, Douglas. "The Persecution of the Bahais of Iran, 1844–1984." *Bahai Studies* 12–13 (1984).

McLaughlin, Gerald T., and Thomas M. Quinn,"Drug Control in Iran: A Legal and Historical Analysis." *Iowa Law Review* 59 (February 1974):469–524.

McLaughlin, Gerald T. "The Poppy Is Not an Ordinary Flower: A Survey of Drug Policy in Iran." *Fordham Law Review* 44 (March 1976):701–772.

Mehran, Golnar. "The Socialization of Schoolchildren in the Islamic Republic of Iran." *Iranian Studies* 22, 1 (Winter 1989):35–50.

Miller, William Green. "The Political Organizations in Iran: From Dowreh to Party." *Middle East Journal* 23, 2–3 (Spring-Summer 1969):156–167, 343–350.

Millward, William G. "The Social Psychology of Anti-Iranology." *Iranian Studies* 8, 1–2 (Winter-Spring 1975):48–69.

Moharreri, M. R. "Out-patient Treatment of Opium Addicts: Report of a Pilot Project in Shiraz." *Bulletin on Narcotics* 28 (July-September 1976):31–39.

Momayezi, Nasser. "Economic Correlates of Political Violence: The Case of Iran." *Middle East Journal* 40, 1 (Winter 1986):68–81.

Najmabadi, Afsaneh. "Iran's Turn to Islam: From Modernism to Moral Order." *Middle East Journal* 41, 2 (Spring 1987):202–217.

Parvin, M. "Economic Determinants of Political Unrest." *Journal of Conflict Resolution* 17, 2 (June 1973):271–296.

Ramazani, Rouhullah K. "Modernization and Social Research in Iran." *American Behavioral Scientist* 5 (1962):17–20.

"Report from an Iranian Village." *MERIP Reports* (March-April 1982):26–29.

Richards, Helmut. "America's Shah; Shahanshah's Iran." *MERIP Reports* (September 1975):3–20.

Rotblat, Howard J. "Social Organization and Development in an Iranian Provincial Bazaar." *Economic Development and Culture Change* 23 (January 1975):293–305.

Rouleau, Eric. "The War and the Struggle for the State." *MERIP Reports* (July-August 1981):3–8.

Sciolino, Elaine. "Iran's Durable Revolution." *Foreign Affairs* 61, 4–5 (Spring 1983):893–920.

Tabari, Azar. "The Enigma of the Veiled Iranian Woman." *MERIP Reports* (February 1982):22–27.

Vali, Abbas, and Sami Zubaida. "Factionalism and Political Discourse in the Islamic Republic of Iran: The Case of the Hujjatiyeh." *Economy and Society* 14, 2 (May 1985):139–173.

Veille, Paule. "Birth and Death in Islamic Society." *Diogenes* 57 (1969):101–127.

Westwood, Andrew F. "Politics of Distrust in Iran." *Annals of the American Academy of Political and Social Sciences* 358 (March 1965):123–135.

Young, T. Cuyler. "The Problem of Westernization in Modern Iran." *Middle East Journal* 2, 1 (January 1948):47–59.

POLITICAL THEORY

Arendt, Hannah. *Eichmann in Jerusalem: A Report on the Banality of Evil.* Harmondsworth, England: Penguin, 1979.

_____. *The Human Condition.* Chicago: University of Chicago Press, 1958.

_____. *On Violence.* New York: Harcourt, Brace and World, 1969.

_____. *The Origins of Totalitarianism.* New York: Harcourt, Brace, 1951.

St. Augustine. *The City of God.* Translated by Henry Bettenson. Harmondsworth, England: Penguin, 1987.

Beccaria, Cesare. *On Crimes and Punishments.* Translated by Henry Paolucci. Indianapolis: Bobbs-Merrill, 1963.

Benjamin, Walter. *Reflections.* Translated by Edmund Jephcott. New York: Harcourt Brace Jovanovich, 1978.

Clausewitz, Carl von. *On War.* Edited by Anatol Rapoport. London: Cox and Wyman, 1974.

Donzelot, Jacques. *The Policing of Families.* Translated by Robert Hurley. New York: Pantheon Books, 1979.

Dreyfus, Hubert L., and Paul Rabinow. *Michel Foucault: Beyond Structuralism and Hermeneutics.* Chicago: University of Chicago Press, 1982.

DuBois, Page. *Torture and Truth.* New York: Routledge, 1991.

Dunn, John. *Rethinking Modern Political Theory.* Cambridge: Cambridge University Press, 1985.

_____. *Western Political Theory in the Face of the Future.* Cambridge: Cambridge University Press, 1979.

Eckstein, Harry. "Case Study and Theory in Political Science." In *Handbook of Political Science.* Vol. 7, *Strategies of Inquiry.* Edited by Fred I. Greenstein and Nelson W. Polsby. Reading, MA: Addison-Wesley, 1975, pp. 79–137.

Elias, Norbert. *The Civilizing Process.* 2 vols. Translated by Edmund Jephcott. New York: Pantheon Books, 1982.

————. *The Court Society.* Translated by Edmund Jephcott. New York: Pantheon Books, 1983.

Escobar, Arturo. "Discourse and Power in Development: Michel Foucault and the Relevance of His Work to the Third World." *Alternatives* 10 (Winter 1984-1985):377–400.

Fanon, Frantz. *A Dying Colonialism.* Translated by Hakkon Chevalier. New York: Grove Press, 1967.

————. *The Wretched of the Earth.* Translated by Constance Farrington. New York: Grove Press, 1979.

Fay, Brian. *Critical Social Science: Liberation and Its Limits.* Ithaca, NY: Cornell University Press, 1987.

Foucault, Michel. "À quoi rêvent les Iranienne?" *Le Nouvel Observateur*, 9 October 1978, p. 48.

————. *Discipline and Punish: The Birth of the Prison.* Translated by Alan Sheridan. New York: Vintage Books, 1979.

————. "L'esprit d'un monde sans esprit." In *Iran: La révolution au nom de Dieu.* Edited by Claire Brière and Pierre Blanchet. Paris: Editions de Seuil, 1979, pp. 225–241.

————. *The Foucault Reader.* Edited by Paul Rabinow. New York: Pantheon Books, 1984.

————. *The History of Sexuality: An Introduction.* Translated by Robert Hurley. New York: Vintage Books, 1980.

————. "How We Behave." *Vanity Fair* 46 (November 1983):61–69.

————. "Is It Really Important to Think? An Interview with Michel Foucault." *Philosophy and Social Criticism* 9 (1982):30–42.

————. "Is It Useless to Revolt?" *Philosophy and Social Criticism* 8 (1982):5–9.

————. *Language, Counter-Memory, Practice: Selected Essays and Interviews.* Edited by Donald F. Bouchard. Translated by Donald F. Bouchard and Sherry Simon. Ithaca, NY: Cornell University Press, 1977.

————. "Lettre ouverte à Mehdi Bazargan." *Le Nouvel Observateur*, 14 April 1979, p. 46.

————. *The Order of Things: An Archaeology of the Human Sciences.* New York: Vintage Books, 1973.

————. "Orders of Discourse." Translated by Rupert Swyer. *Social Scientist* 10 (April 1976):1–24.

————. *Power/Knowledge: Selected Interviews and Other Writings, 1972–1977.* Edited by Colin Gordon. Translated by Colin Gordon, Leo Marshall, John Mepham, and Kate Soper. New York: Pantheon Books, 1980.

————. "Structuralism and Post-Structuralism: An Interview with Michel Foucault." *Telos* 55 (Spring 1983):195–211.

————. *The Use of Pleasure.* New York: Random House, 1984.

Giddens, Anthony. *A Contemporary Critique of Historical Materialism.* Volume 2, *The Nation-State and Violence.* Cambridge: Polity Press, 1985.

Gordon, Colin. "Question, Ethos, Event: Foucault on Kant and the Enlightenment." *Economy and Society* 15, 1 (February 1986):71–87.

Hanna, Thomas. *Bodies in Revolt: A Primer in Somatic Thinking.* New York: Dell, 1970.

Hegel, Georg W.F. *Hegel's Philosophy of Right*. Translated by T.M. Knox. Oxford: Clarendon Press, 1978.

Heidegger, Martin. *Basic Writings*. Edited by David Farrell Krell. New York: Harper and Row, 1977.

Hirschman, Albert O. *The Passions and the Interests: Political Arguments for Capitalism Before Its Triumph*. Princeton: Princeton University Press, 1977.

Honderich, Ted. *Punishment: The Supposed Justifications*. Rev. ed. Harmondsworth, England: Peregrine Books, 1976.

Horkheimer, Max, and Theodor W. Adorno. *The Dialectic of Enlightenment*. Translated by John Cumming. New York: Seabury Press, 1972.

Huizinga, Johan. *Homo Ludens: A Study of the Play Element in Culture*. Boston: Beacon Press, 1967.

Kafka, Franz. *The Penal Colony: Stories and Short Pieces*. Translated by Willa and Edwin Muir. New York: Schocken Books, 1969.

Kant, Immanuel. *Kant's Political Writings*. Edited by Hans Reiss. Translated by Hugh B. Nisbet. Cambridge: Cambridge University Press, 1980.

Kuhn, Thomas S. *The Structure of Scientific Revolutions*. Enlarged 2d ed. Chicago: University of Chicago Press, 1970.

Levin, Michael. "The Case for Torture." *Newsweek*, 7 June 1982, p. 3.

Lukes, Stephen. *Power: A Radical View*. London: Macmillan, 1980.

Machiavelli, Niccolo. *The Prince*. Translated and edited by Robert M. Adam. New York: Norton, 1977.

MacIntyre, Alasdair. *After Virtue: A Study in Moral Theory*. South Bend: University of Notre Dame Press, 1981.

_____. *Against the Self-Images of the Age*. Notre Dame, IN: University of Notre Dame Press, 1979.

Marx, Karl. *Capital*. Vol. 1, *A Critical Analysis of Capitalist Production*. Edited by Frederick Engels. Translated by Samuel Moore and Edward Aveling. New York: International Publishers, 1979.

McPherson, C.B. *The Political Theory of Possessive Individualism: Hobbes to Locke*. Oxford: Oxford University Press, 1962.

Nietzsche, Friedrich. *On the Genealogy of Morals and Ecce Homo*. Edited by Walter Kaufmann. Translated by Walter Kaufmann and R.J. Hollingdale. New York: Vintage Books, 1969.

_____. *Twilight of the Idols and the Anti-Christ*. Translated by R.J. Hollingdale. Harmondsworth, England: Penguin, 1979.

_____. *The Will to Power*. Edited by Walter Kaufmann. Translated by Walter Kaufmann and R.J. Hollingdale. New York: Random House, 1968.

Oestreich, Gerhard. *Neostoicism and the Early Modern State*. Edited by Brigitta Oestreich and Helmut G. Koenigsberger. Translated by David McLintock. Cambridge: Cambridge University Press, 1982.

Olivier, Laurence, and Sylvain Labbé. "Foucault et l'Iran: À propos du désir de révolution." *Canadian Journal of Political Science* 24, 2 (June 1991):219–236.

Ostrander, Gregory. "Knowledge and Experience in the Work of Michel Foucault." Ph.D. diss., McGill University, 1985.

Paz, Octavio. *The Other Mexico: Critique of the Pyramid*. Translated by Lysander Kemp. New York: Grove Press, 1972.

Polan, Anthony J. *Lenin and the End of Politics.* Berkeley and Los Angeles: University of California Press, 1984.

Rajchman, John. "Ethics After Foucault." *Social Text* 13–14 (Winter-Spring 1986):165–183.

Rousseau, Jean-Jacques. *The Social Contract and the Discourse on the Origin of Inequality.* Edited by Lester G. Crocker. New York: Pocket Books, 1967.

Rule, James B. *Theories of Civil Violence.* Berkeley and Los Angeles: University of California Press, 1988.

Said, Edward. *Covering Islam.* New York: Pantheon Books,1981.

———. *Orientalism.* New York: Pantheon Books, 1978.

———. *The Word, The Text, and the Critic.* Cambridge, MA: Harvard University Press, 1983.

Scarry, Elaine. *The Body in Pain: The Making and Unmaking of the World.* Oxford: Oxford University Press, 1985.

Skinner, B.F. *Beyond Freedom and Dignity.* New York: Bantam/Vintage Books, 1972.

Skinner, Quentin. *The Foundations of Modern Political Thought.* 2 vols. Cambridge: Cambridge University Press, 1978.

Taylor, Charles. "Foucault on Freedom and Truth." *Political Theory* 12 (May 1984):152–183.

———. "Interpretation and the Sciences of Man." In *Interpretive Social Science: A Second Look.* Edited by Paul Rabinow and William M. Sullivan. Berkeley and Los Angeles: University of California Press, 1988, pp. 35–36.

Tuck, Richard. *Natural Rights Theories: Their Origin and Development.* Cambridge: Cambridge University Press, 1979.

Tully, James, ed. *Meaning and Context: Quentin Skinner and His Critics.* Cambridge: Polity Press, 1988.

Turner, Bryan S. *The Body and Society: Explorations in Social Theory.* Oxford: Basil Blackwell, 1984.

Weber, Max. *From Max Weber: Essays in Sociology.* Translated and edited by Hans H. Gerth and C. Wright Mills. New York: Oxford University Press, 1979.

———. *The Protestant Ethic and the Spirit of Capitalism.* Translated by Talcott Parsons. New York: Charles Scribner's, 1958.

———. *The Sociology of Religion.* Translated by Ephraim Fischoff. Boston: Beacon Press, 1964.

Wittgenstein, Ludwig. *The Blue and Brown Books.* 2d ed. New York: Harper and Row, 1965.

———. *Philosophical Investigations.* Translated by G.E.M. Anscombe. 3d ed. Oxford: Basil Blackwell, 1976.

———. *Zettel.* Edited by G.E.M. Anscombe and G.H. von Wright. Translated by G.E.M. Anscombe. Berkeley and Los Angeles: University of California Press, 1975.

OTHER WORKS CONSULTED

Ackroyd, Carol, Karen Margolis, Jonathan Rosenhead, and Tim Schallic. *The Technology of Political Control.* Rev. 2d ed. London: Pluto Press, 1980.

Alavi, Hamza, and Teodor Shanin. *Introduction to the Sociology of "Developing" Societies.* London: Macmillan, 1982.

Alleg, Henri. *The Question.* Translated by John Calder. New York: George Braziller, 1958.

Amnesty International. *Political Imprisonment in South Africa.* London: Amnesty International Publications, 1978.

_____. *Report on Allegations of Torture in Brazil.* 3d ed. London: Amnesty International Publications, 1976.

_____. *Report on Torture.* London: Gerald Duckworth, 1973.

_____. *Torture in the Eighties.* London: Amnesty International Publications, 1984.

Asad, Talal. "Notes on Body Pain and Truth in Medieval Christian Ritual." *Economy and Society* 12, 3 (1983):287–327.

Bayley, David H. *The Police and Political Development in India.* Princeton: Princeton University Press, 1969.

Brown, James A.C. *Techniques of Persuasion: From Propaganda to Brainwashing.* Harmondsworth, England: Penguin, 1969.

Chomsky, Noam, and Edward S. Herman. *The Political Economy of Human Rights.* Vol. 1, *The Washington Connection and Third World Fascism.* Montreal: Black Rose Books, 1979.

Colligan, Douglas. "The New Science of Torture." *Science Digest* (July 1976):44–49.

Cox, Edmund. *Police and Crime in India.* London: Hazell, Watson and Viney, n.d.

Djilas, Milovan. *Of Prisons and Ideas.* Translated by Michael Boro Petrovich. San Diego: Harcourt Brace Jovanovich, 1986.

Earle, Edward Mead. *Makers of Modern Strategy: Military Thought from Machiavelli to Hitler.* New York: Atheneum, 1966.

Fagen, Richard R., ed. *Capitalism and the State in U.S.–Latin American Relations.* Stanford: Stanford University Press, 1979.

Farrell, Thomas D. "The Founding of the North-West Frontier Militias." *Asian Affairs* 61 (June 1972):165–178.

General Accounting Office. *Stopping U.S. Assistance to Foreign Police and Prisons.* Washington, DC: General Accounting Office, 1976.

Germans Against Hitler, July 20, 1944. 3d ed. Translated by Allan and Lieseotte Yahraes. Bonn: Press and Information Office of the Federal German Government, 1960.

Gibson, Janice T., and Mika Haritos-Fatouros. "The Education of a Torturer." *Psychology Today* (November 1986):50–56.

Glenn, Myra C. *Campaigns Against Corporal Punishment: Prisoners, Sailors, Women and Children in Antebellum America.* Albany: State University of New York Press, 1984.

Goldstein, Richard H., and Patrick Breslin. "Technicians of Torture: How Physicians Became Agents of State Terror." *The Sciences* (March-April 1986):14–19.

Gordon, Thomas. *Journey into Madness: Medical Torture and the Mind Controllers.* London: Bantam, 1988.

Gupta, Anandswarup. *The Police in British India, 1861–1947.* New Delhi: Concept Publishing, 1979.

Herman, Edward S. *The Real Terror Network.* Boston: South End Press, 1982.

Heyd, Uriel. *Studies in Old Ottoman Criminal Law*. Edited by V.L. Menage. Oxford: Clarendon Press, 1973.

Higgot, Richard A. *Political Development Theory: The Contemporary Debate*. New York: St. Martin's Press, 1983.

Hoffman, Peter. *The History of the German Resistance, 1933–1945*. Translated by Richard Barry. Cambridge, MA: MIT Press, 1977.

Huggins, Martha, ed. *Vigilantism and the State in Modern Latin America: Essays in Extralegal Violence*. New York: Praeger, 1991.

Huntington, Samuel P. "Civil Violence and the Process of Development." *Adelphi Papers* 82–83 (December 1971):1–15.

———. *Political Order in Changing Societies*. New Haven: Yale University Press, 1968.

Huntington, Samuel P., ed. *Changing Patterns of Military Politics*. New York: Free Press, 1962.

Ignatieff, Michael. *A Just Measure of Pain: The Penitentiary in the Industrial Revolution, 1750–1850*. New York: Pantheon Books, 1978.

———. "State, Civil Society, and Total Institutions: A Critique of Recent Social Histories of Punishment." *Crime and Justice: A Review of Research* 6 (September 1981):153–192.

———. "The Truth About Torture." *New Republic*, 9 December 1985, pp. 24–31.

Jeffries, Charles. *The Colonial Police*. London: Max Parish, 1952.

Kierkvliet, Benedict J. *The Huk Rebellion*. Berkeley and Los Angeles: University of California Press, 1977.

Klare, Michael T., and Cynthia Arnson. *Supplying Repression*. Washington, DC: Institute for Policy Studies, 1981.

Krausnick, Helmut, Hans Buchheim, Martin Broszat, and Hans-Adolf Jacobsen. *Anatomy of the SS State*. Translated by Richard Barry, Marian Jackson, and Dorothy Long. London: Collins, 1968.

Langbein, John H. *Torture and the Law of Proof: Europe and England in the Ancien Regime*. Chicago: University of Chicago Press, 1977.

LeMay, Godfried H.L. *British Supremacy in South Africa, 1899–1907*. Oxford: Clarendon Press, 1965.

Liebesnay, Herbert J. *The Law of the Near and Middle East*. Albany: State University of New York Press, 1975.

Lipset, Seymour Martin. "Some Social Requisites of Democracy: Economic Development and Political Legitimacy." *American Political Science Review* 53 (March 1979):69–105.

Lowenthal, Abraham F., ed. *Armies and Politics in Latin America*. New York: Holmes and Meier, 1976.

Maran, Rita. *Torture: The Role of Ideology in the French-Algerian War*. New York: Praeger, 1989.

Marks, John. *The CIA and Mind Control: The Search for the Manchurian Candidate*. New York: McGraw-Hill, 1980.

McKeown, Thomas. *The Rise of Population*. New York: Academic Press, 1977.

Melzack, Ronald, and Patrick Wall. *The Challenge of Pain*. Rev. ed. Harmondsworth, England: Penguin, 1984.

Migdal, Joel. *Strong Societies and Weak States: State-Society Relations and State Capabilities in the Third World.* Princeton: Princeton University Press, 1988.

Mitchell, Timothy. *Colonising Egypt.* Cambridge: Cambridge University Press, 1988.

Muller, Ingo. *Hitler's Justice: The Courts of the Third Reich.* Translated by D.L. Schneider. Cambridge, MA: Harvard University Press, 1991.

Nyiszli, Miklos. *Auschwitz: A Doctor's Eye-witness Account.* Translated by Tibere Kremer and Richard Seaver. London: Granada Publishing, 1982.

Osanka, Franklin Mark, ed. *Modern Guerrilla Warfare: Fighting Communist Guerilla Movements, 1941–1961.* New York: Free Press, 1962.

Peters, Edward. *Torture.* New York: Basil Blackwell, 1985.

Pion-Berlin, David. "Theories of Political Repression in Latin America: Conventional Wisdom and an Alternative." *PS* 19, 1 (Winter 1986):49–54.

Podrabinek, Alezander. *Punitive Medicine.* Translated by Alexander Lehrman. Ann Arbor, MI: Karoma Publishers, 1980.

Pustay, John. *Counterinsurgency Warfare.* New York: Free Press, 1965.

Pye, Lucian W. *Aspects of Political Development.* Boston: Little, Brown, 1966.

Raeff, Marc. *The Well-Ordered Police State: Social and Institutional Change Through Law in the Germanics and Russia, 1600–1800.* New Haven: Yale University Press, 1983.

Richler, Melvin. "Tocqueville on Algeria." *Review of Politics.* 25, 3 (July 1963):362–398.

Rothman, David J. *Conscience and Convenience: The Asylum and Its Alternatives in Progressive America.* Boston: Little, Brown, 1980.

————. *The Discovery of the Asylum: Social Order and Disorder in the New Republic.* Boston: Little, Brown, 1971.

Rusche, Georg, and Otto Kirchheimer. *Punishment and Social Structure.* New York: Columbia University Press, 1939.

Schoultz, Lars. *Human Rights and United States Policy Towards Latin America.* Princeton: Princeton University Press, 1981.

Shahak, Israel. *Israel's Global Role: Weapons for Repression.* Bell Mair, MA: Association of Arab-American Graduates, 1982.

Solzhenitsyn, Aleksandr I. *The Gulag Archipelago, 1918–1956: An Experiment in Literary Investigation.* 3 vols. Translated by Thomas P. Whitney. New York: Harper and Row, 1974.

Spierenburg, Pieter. *The Spectacle of Suffering: Executions and the Evolution of Repression; from a Preindustrial Metropolis to the European Experience.* Cambridge: Cambridge University Press, 1984.

Stainbrook, Edward. "The Use of Electricity in Psychiatric Treatment During the Nineteenth Century." *Bulletin of the History of Medicine* 22, 3 (May-June 1948):156–177.

Stohl, Michael, and George A. Lopez, eds. *The State as Terrorist.* Westport, CT: Greenwood Press, 1984.

Sullivan, Anthony Thrall. *Thomas-Robert Bugeaud, France and Algeria: Politics, Power and the Good Society, 1784–1849.* Hamden, CT: Archon Books, 1983.

Taussig, Michael. "Culture of Terror—Space of Death. Roger Casement's Putumayo Report and the Explanation of Torture." *Contemporary Studies in Society and History* 26 (1984):466–497.

Teeters, Negley King. *World Penal Systems: A Survey.* Philadelphia: Pennsylvania Prison Society, 1944.

Thayer, Charles W. *Guerrilla.* London: Michael Joseph, 1964.

Timmerman, Jacobo. *Prisoner Without a Name, Cell Without a Number.* New York: Vintage Books, 1982.

Tipps, Dean C. "Modernization Theory and the Comparative Study of Societies: A Critical Perspective." *Comparative Studies in Society and History* 15 (1973):199–227.

"Torture as Policy: The Network of Evil." *Time,* 16 August 1976, pp. 31–33.

Trinquier, Roger. *Modern Warfare: A French View of Counterinsurgency.* Translated by Daniel Lee. New York: Praeger, 1964.

U.S. Congress, Senate, Committee on Appropriations. "Foreign Assistance Appropriations, 1965." Hearings. 89th Cong., 2d sess. 1964.

Weisser, Michael R. *Crime and Punishment in Early Modern Europe.* Atlantic Highlands, NJ: Humanities Press, 1979.

Ziadeh, Farhat J., and R. Bayly Winder. *An Introduction to Modern Arabic.* Princeton: Princeton University Press, 1957.

About the Book and Author

What does the practice of torture presuppose about human beings and human society? How does one explain a society in which institutional torture persists despite massive changes in government and class structure? What, indeed, are the social foundations of modern torture? In *Torture and Modernity*, Darius M. Rejali investigates torture in Iran in order to understand and critically reconsider the politics and psychology of modern torture. In a world in which one out of every three governments uses torture, Rejali points to a common past, one shared by Iranians and non-Iranians alike, that supports this practice.

"My aim," Rejali writes, "is to use the study of torture, and of punishment more generally, to unearth deep and important assumptions about society, history, politics and the 'good life' that I believe underpin the life of a torturer."

Exploring the four principle explanations of modern torture—those offered by human rights activists, modernization theorists, state terrorist theorists such as Noam Chomsky, and poststructuralists, especially Michel Foucault—Dr. Rejali asks, "Do the accounts of political violence that we have developed over the past century have any real ... explanatory or even moral significance in ... [today's] world, or are they just consolations in the face of events we cannot fully understand?" His answers lead him to reconsider how Middle Eastern and European history are written and move him to question cherished assumptions about state formation, modernization, and postmodernism.

Torture and Modernity is a deeply unsettling book—it contains not only graphic verbal passages but also an extensive photographic essay—yet it is intended to serve as a guide to rethinking current attitudes and reshaping political policies. How people are punished necessarily invokes conceptions of what human beings are and what they might become. A work such as this offers an understanding of what it means to "become modern," and it is only when this notion of modernity is made manifest and analyzed that one can firmly grasp the prospects for a world without torture.

Darius M. Rejali teaches political philosophy and comparative politics at Reed College. He was raised in Iran and has since lived in the United States, Canada, and England.

Index